# HANDBOOK
# FOR LITURGICAL STUDIES

# III

# The Eucharist

THE PONTIFICAL LITURGICAL INSTITUTE

# HANDBOOK
# FOR LITURGICAL STUDIES
VOLUME III

# The Eucharist

## ANSCAR J. CHUPUNGCO, O.S.B.

EDITOR

## A PUEBLO BOOK

The Liturgical Press   Collegeville Minnesota

A Pueblo Book published by The Liturgical Press

Design by Frank Kacmarcik, Obl.S.B.

Library of Congress Cataloging-in-Publication Data

Handbook for liturgical studies / Anscar J. Chupungco, editor.
    p.   cm.
   "A Pueblo book."
   Includes bibliographical references and index.
   Contents: v. 1. Introduction to the liturgy.
   ISBN 0-8146-6161-0 (vol. I)
   ISBN 0-8146-6162-9 (vol. II)
   ISBN 0-8146-6163-7 (vol. III)
   1. Liturgics—Study and teaching.   2. Catholic Church—Liturgy--Study and teaching.   I. Chupungco, Anscar J.
BV176.H234   1997
264—dc21

                             97-20141
                               CIP

# Contents

    * translated by Madeleine Beaumont
   ** translated by Matthew J. O'Connell
  *** translated by Edward Hagman, O.F.M.Cap.
 **** translated by Lisa Twomey

# Introduction

"At the Last Supper, on the night when he was betrayed, our Savior instituted the eucharistic sacrifice of his body and blood. He did this in order to perpetuate the sacrifice of the cross throughout the centuries until he should come again and in this way to entrust to his beloved Bride, the Church, a memorial of his death and resurrection: a sacrament of love, a sign of unity, a bond of charity, a paschal banquet 'in which Christ is eaten, the heart is filled with grace, and a pledge of future glory given to us'" (*SC* 47).

This conciliar teaching on the meaning and purpose of the eucharistic celebration deserves a continuing reflection. In fact much, though never enough, has been published on it after the council. This volume aims not only to contribute to the ongoing reflection but also to offer to teachers and students of liturgy a handbook for studying the subject according to a system which is based on historical development, theology and doctrine, liturgical texts and traditions in both East and West, and pastoral considerations.

The volume opens with a lexicon in which basic eucharistic terms like *missa, collecta, praefatio, canon,* and *offertorium* are explained. These terms, which are recurrent in this volume, are still much in use today. They need to be defined as preliminary notions, even if they are treated at greater length at the appropriate places.

The volume is organized in several sections. The first section deals with the shape of the eucharistic celebration during the first four centuries. The time frame refers to the centuries before the eucharistic celebrations developed particular characteristics in East and West for doctrinal and cultural reasons. One may say that during this period the Churches seemed to have enjoyed a certain ritual affinity because of mutual influences and the practice of borrowing from each other, especially in the East. Nonetheless, variations already existed especially in the area of early Eucharistic Prayers, thus confirming the tradition of local liturgies.

The second section focuses on the East. Different eucharistic orders, particularly of the Byzantine liturgy, are described with reference to their genesis. The elements present in the anaphoras of the three great Eastern traditions are described, but a more detailed analysis is given to the Byzantine anaphoras of John Chrysostom and Basil the Great because of their wide use.

The third section directs attention to the historical development and shape of the Eucharist in Rome and the non-Roman West. The Roman history stretches from as early as the second century to the Franco-Germanic era which left significant marks on the Roman Eucharist. As one should expect, special treatment is given to the various elements of the Order of Mass of Paul VI, namely, the sacramentary, lectionary, homily, and musical elements. This section concludes with a detailed description of the different eucharistic orders in the non-Roman West, such as the African, Ambrosian, Gallican, Hispanic, and Celtic in order to have a broader vision of how the Eucharist was celebrated in the West outside the Roman tradition.

The fourth section is devoted to the eucharistic liturgies outside Mass. This includes questions both theological and liturgical regarding communion outside Mass and other eucharistic practices such as processions and expositions. The section includes also a description of the liturgy of the presanctified as it is kept today in Eastern Churches. A treatment of the liturgy of viaticum, which may also be celebrated within Mass, concludes this section.

The fifth section deals with particular questions, often of great pastoral and liturgical interest, such as concelebration, the mode and frequency of receiving Communion, and the Sunday assemblies in the absence of a priest. These are treated from historical and pastoral perspectives and in the light of the conciliar and postconciliar reform.

The last section is a fitting conclusion to the study of the eucharistic liturgy. After studying the manifold reality of the Eucharist which runs the gamut of history, doctrinal underpinnings, and ritual concerns the reader is led to reflect theologically on the Eucharist as a celebration. Methodological principles and directives are stated as premises for the reflection. On the other hand, the areas on which reflection is made include the New Testament sources, the meaning of eucharistic Communion, the Eucharistic Prayer (especially as anamnesis, epiclesis, and sacrifice), the issue of offering and gifts, and the eucharistic ministries.

Anscar J. Chupungco, O.S.B.
Editor

# Abbreviations

| | |
|---|---|
| *A* | *Ambrosius.* Milan, 1925–. |
| *AA* | Vatican II, decree *Apostolicam actuositatem* (Decree on the Apostolate of the Lay People). *AAS* 58 (1966) 837–864; Abbott, 489–521; Flannery, 766–798. |
| *AAS* | *Acta Apostolicae Sedis.* Rome, 1909–. |
| *AB* | *Analecta Bollandiana.* Brussels, 1882–. |
| Abbott | Walter M. Abbott, S.J., ed. *The Documents of Vatican II.* New York, 1966. |
| ACC | Alcuin Club Collections. London, 1899–. |
| ACW | Ancient Christian Writers. New York, 1946–. |
| A.Dmitr | A. Dmitrievskij, *Opisanie liturgiceskich rukopisej hransjascihsja v bibliotekach pravoslavnago Vostoka,* I–II. Kiev, 1895, 1902. |
| *AG* | Vatican II, decree *Ad gentes* (Decree on the Church's Missionary Activity). *AAS* 58 (1966) 947–990; Abbott, 584–630; Flannery, 813–856. |
| AGreg | Analecta Gregoriana. Rome, 1930–. |
| AL | Analecta liturgica. Rome (see SA). |
| *ALW* | *Archiv für Liturgiewissenschaft.* Regensburg, 1950–. |
| Anàmnesis | *Anàmnesis: Introduzione storico-teologica alla liturgia.* Edited by the professors at the Pontificio Istituto Liturgico S. Anselmo, Rome, under the direction of S. Marsili and others. Casale Monferrato, 1974ff. Vol. 1, *La liturgia: Momento nella storia della salvezza.* Turin, 1974. Vol. 2, *La liturgia: Panorama storico generale.* Casale, 1978. Vol. 3/1, *La liturgia: I sacramenti. Teologia e storia della celebrazione.* 1986. Vol. 3/2: *La liturgia eucaristica: Teologia e storia della celebrazione.* Casale Monferrato, 1983. Vol. 5, *Liturgia delle ore.* 1990. Vol. 6, *L'anno liturgico: Storia, teologia e celebrazione.* Genoa, 1988. Vol. 7, *I sacramentali e le benedizioni.* 1989. |
| *ASE* | *Annali di storia dell'esegesi.* Bologna. |
| AST | Analecta sacra Tarraconensia. Barcelona, 1925–. |
| BA | Bibliothèque Augustinienne. Oeuvres de S. Augustin. Paris, 1949–. |

| | |
|---|---|
| *BAR* | S. Parenti and E. Velkovska, *L'eucologio Barberini gr. 336* (BELS 80). Rome, 1995. |
| BEL | Bibliotheca Ephemerides liturgicae. Rome, 1932–. |
| BELS | Bibliotheca Ephemerides liturgicae Subsidia. Rome, 1975–. |
| Bugnini | A. Bugnini, *The Reform of the Liturgy: 1948–1975*. Collegeville, Minn., 1990. |
| *ButLitEc* | *Bulletin de littérature ecclésiastique*. Toulouse, 1899–1936. |
| *CAO* | *Corpus antiphonalium officii*. Rome, 1963–1979. |
| CBL | Collectanea biblica Latina. Rome. |
| CCL | Corpus Christianorum. Series Latina. Turnhout, 1954–. |
| CCCM | Corpus Christianorum Continuatio Mediaevalis. Turnhout, 1971–. |
| *CL* | *Communautés et liturgies*. Ottignies, Belgium. |
| *CLLA* | *Codices liturgici Latini antiquiores*. Freiburg/Schweiz. 1968. |
| *Conc* | *Concilium*. Edinburgh. |
| *CPG* | *Clavis Patrum Graecorum*. Turnhout, 1974–. |
| CSEL | Corpus scriptorum ecclesiasticorum Latinorum. Vienna, 1886. |
| CSIC | Consejo superior de investigaciones científicas. Madrid, 1940–1941. |
| *DACL* | *Dictionnaire d'archeologie chrétinne et liturgie*. Paris, 1907–1953. |
| *DB* | *Rituale Romanum, De benedictionibus* (Kaczynski). Vatican City, 1984. |
| *DMP* | *Directorium de Missis cum pueris (Directory for Masses with Children)*. Vatican City, 1973. *EDIL 1*, ##3115–3169, pp. 968–980; *DOL* 276. |
| *DOL* | International Commission on English in the Liturgy, *Documents on the Liturgy 1963–1979: Conciliar, Papal and Curial Texts*. Collegeville, Minn., 1982. |
| *DPAC* | *Dizionario patristico e di antichità cristiane*. 3 vols. Casale Monferrato, 1983–1988. |
| DS | H. Denzinger and A. Schönmetzer, *Enchiridion symbolorum*. 32nd ed. Freiburg, 1963. |
| *DSp* | *Dictionnaire de spiritualité ascétique et mystique*. Paris, 1932–. |
| *DSPB* | *Dizionario di spiritualità biblico-patristica*. Turin, 1993. |
| *DV* | Vatican II, dogmatic constitution *Dei verbum* (Dogmatic Constitution on Divine Revelation). *AAS* 58 (1966) 817–835; Abbott, 111–128; Flannery, 750–765. |
| *EDIL 1* | *Enchiridion documentorum instaurationis liturgicae 1* (1963–1973). Ed. R. Kaczynski. Turin, 1976. |

| | |
|---|---|
| *JThS* | *Journal of Theological Studies.* London, 1900–1905; Oxford, 1906–1949; n.s., Oxford, 1950–. |
| Jungmann | J. A. Jungmann, *Missarum sollemnia.* 2 vols. Casale Monferrato, 1963. English translation: *The Mass of the Roman Rite: Its Origins and Development.* Trans. F. Brunner. Christian Classics. Westminster, Md., 1986. Originally published New York, 1951–1955. |
| *KB* | *Katechetische Blätter.* Munich, 1875–. |
| *Lat* | *Lateranum.* Rome, 1919–. |
| *LeV* | *Lumière et vie.* Lyons, 1951–. |
| LG | Vatican II, dogmatic constitution *Lumen gentium* (Dogmatic Constitution on the Church). *AAS* 57 (1965) 5–71; Abbott, 14–96; Flannery, 350–423. |
| *Lit* | *Liturgia.* Rome, n.s., 1967ff. |
| LJ | *Liturgisches Jahrbuch.* Münster, 1951–. |
| LL | A. Nocent, "I libri liturgici." *Anàmnesis* 2: *La liturgia: Panorama storico generale.* |
| LO | Lex Orandi. Paris, 1944–. |
| LQF | Liturgie- (until 1957: geschichtliche) wissenschaftliche Quellen und Forschungen. Münster, 1909–1940; 1957–. |
| *LThK* | *Lexikon für Theologie und Kirche.* Freiburg, 1957–1965. |
| *LV* | *Lumen vitae.* Brussels, 1946–. |
| *MD* | *La Maison-Dieu.* Paris, 1945–. |
| MA1981 | *Missale Ambrosianum.* Iuxta ritum sanctae Ecclesiae Mediolanensis. Ex decreto Sacrosancti Oecumenici Concilii Vaticani II instauratum. Milan, 1981; new ed. 1990. |
| Mansi | J. D. Mansi, *Sacrorum conciliorum nova et amplissima collectio.* 31 vols. Florence–Venice, 1757–1798; reprinted and continued by L. Petit and J. B. Martin, 53 vols. in 60. Paris, 1889–1927; reprinted Graz, 1960–. |
| MEL | Monumenta Ecclesiae liturgica. Paris, 1890–1912. |
| *MelScRel* | *Mélanges de science religieuse.* Lille, 1944–. |
| MGH | Monumenta Germaniae historica. Berlin, 1826. |
| MHS | Monumenta Hispaniae sacra. Madrid, 1946–. |
| ML | C. Vogel, *Medieval Liturgy: An Introduction to the Sources.* Washington, 1986. |
| MR1570 | *Missale Romanum* ex decreto Sacrosancti Concilii Tridentini restitutum Pii V Pont. Max. iussu editum (various editions; here Missale Romanum ex decreto Sacrosancti Concilii Tridentini restitutum Summorum Pontificum cura recognitum. Editio XIX iuxta typicam. Turin–Rome, 1961). |

| | |
|---|---|
| *MR1975* | *Missale Romanum* ex decreto Sacrosancti Oecumenici Concilii Vaticani II instauratum auctoritate Pauli Pp. VI promulgatum. Editio typica. Vatican City, 1970; 2nd editio typica, 1975. English text: *The Sacramentary*. Trans. International Committee on English in the Liturgy. Collegeville, Minn., 1973, 1985. |
| *MS* | *Medieval Studies*. Toronto–London, 1938–. |
| *MuS* | *Musicam sacram*. EDIL 1, ##733–801, pp. 275–291; DOL 508. |
| NBA | Nuova biblioteca Agostiniana. Rome. |
| *NDL* | *Nuovo dizionario di liturgia*. Rome, 1984. |
| *NHL* | *Neues Handbuch der Literaturwissenschaft*. Frankfurt-am-Main. |
| *Not* | *Notitiae*. Vatican City, 1965–. |
| *NRT* | *Nouvelle revue théologique*. Louvain, 1869–. |
| *OB* | *Rituale Romanum, Ordo benedictionum*. Vatican City, 1984. |
| *OBP* | *Rituale Romanum, Ordo baptismi parvulorum*. Vatican City, 1969, 1973. |
| OCA | Orientalia christiana analecta. Rome, 1935–. |
| *OChr* | *Oriens Christianus*. |
| *OCM* | *Rituale Romanum, Ordo celebrandi matrimonium*. Vatican City, 1969. |
| *OCP* | *Orientalia christiana periodica*. Rome, 1935–. |
| ODEA | Pontificale Romanum, *Ordo dedicationis ecclesiae et altaris*. Vatican City, 1977. |
| *OE* | Vatican II, decree *Orientalium Ecclesiarum* (Decree on the Catholic Eastern Churches). *AAS* 57 (1965) 76–89; Abbott, 373–386; Flannery, 441–451. |
| Oe | Rituale Romanum, Ordo exsequiarum. Vatican City, 1969. |
| OICA | Rituale Romanum, *Ordo initiationis christianae adultorum*. Vatican City, 1972; rev. ed. 1974. |
| *OLM* | *Ordo lectionum Missae*. Editio typica, Vatican City, 1969. 2nd editio typica, Vatican City, 1981. EDIL 2, ##4057–4181, pp. 337–370; English text: *Lectionary for Mass*. Collegeville, Minn., 1970, 1981, 1998. |
| OM | Order of Mass (*Ordo Missae*). Vatican City, 1969. |
| *OP* | *Rituale Romanum, Ordo paenitentiae*. Vatican City, 1974. |
| *OPR* | *Rituale Romanum, Ordo professionis religiosae*. Vatican City, 1970; rev. ed. 1975. |
| *OS* | *L'Orient syrien*. |
| *OUI* | *Rituale Romanum, Ordo unctionis infirmorum*. Vatican City, 1972. |
| *PDOC* | *Petit dictionnaire de l'Orient chrétien*. |

| | |
|---|---|
| PG | J. P. Migne, Patrologia cursus completus: Series Graeca. Paris, 1857–1866. |
| *Ph* | *Phase: Revista de pastoral liturgica.* Barcelona, 1961–. |
| PL | J. P. Migne, Patrologia cursus completus: Series Latina. Paris, 1844–1855. |
| *PO* | Vatican II, *Presbyterorum ordinis* (Decree on the Ministry and Life of Priests). *AAS* 58 (1966) 990–1024; Abbott, 532–576; Flannery, 863–902. |
| *POC* | *Proche-Orient chrétien.* |
| *PRG* | *Pontificale Romano-Germanicum.* |
| *QL* | *Questions liturgiques.* Louvain, 1911–. |
| *RAC* | *Reallexikon für Antike und Christentum.* Stuttgart, 1950–. |
| *RB* | *Revue biblique.* Paris, 1892–. |
| *RBén* | *Revue bénédictine.* Maredsous, 1884–. |
| *RCT* | *Revista catalana de teología.* Barcelona, 1976–. |
| RED | Rerum ecclesiasticarum documenta. Rome, 1954. |
| *RET* | *Revista Española de teología.* Madrid, 1940–. |
| *Rev Lit et Monastique* | *Revue de liturgie e monastique.* Maredsous, 1911–1940. |
| *RG* | *Revue grégorienne.* Paris, 1911–. |
| *RHE* | *Revue d'histoire ecclésiastique.* Louvain, 1900–. |
| Righetti | *Manuale di storia liturgica.* Vol. 1 (2nd ed., 1950); vol. 2 (2nd ed., 1955); vol. 3 (1949); vol. 4 (1953). Milan. |
| *RL* | *Rivista liturgica.* Praglia-Finalpia, 1914–. |
| *RPL* | *Rivista di pastorale liturgica.* Brescia, 1963. |
| *RSPT* | *Revue des sciences philosophiques et théologiques.* Paris, 1907–. |
| *RSR* | *Recherches de science religieuse.* Paris, 1910–. |
| SA | Studia Anselmiana. Rome, 1933–. |
| *SAEMO* | *Sancti Ambrosii Episcopi Mediolanensis Opera.* |
| *SC* | Vatican II, constitution *Sacrosanctum concilium* (Constitution on the Sacred Liturgy). *AAS* 56 (1964) 97–138; Abbott, 137–178; Flannery, 1–36. |
| *ScC* | *Scuola cattolica.* Milan, 1873–. |
| SCA | Studies in Christian Antiquity. Washington, 1941–. |
| SCh | Sources chrétiennes. Paris, 1941–. |
| *SE* | *Sacris erudiri.* Steenbruge, 1948–. |
| SF | Spicilegium Friburgense. Freiburg, 1957. |
| SFS | Spicilegii Friburgensis Subsidia. |
| *SL* | *Studia liturgica.* Rotterdam, 1962. |
| ST | Studi e testi. Vatican City, 1900–. |
| *StudPad* | *Studia patavina.* Padua, 1954. |
| *ThRv* | *Theologische Revue.* Münster, 1902–. |

| | |
|---|---|
| *ThS* | *Theological Studies.* Woodstock, 1940–. |
| *TQ* | *Theologische Quartalschrift.* Tübingen, 1819–. |
| *TRE* | *Theologische Realenzyklopädie.* Berlin, 1947–. |
| *TS* | *Typologie des sources du moyen âge occidental.* |
| *TTZ* | *Trierer theologische Zeitschrift.* Trier, 1945–. |
| *TU* | Texte und Untersuchungen zur Geschichte der altchristlichen Literatur. Berlin, 1882–. |
| *TuA* | Texte und Arbeite. Beuron, 1917–. |
| *UR* | Vatican II, decree *Unitatis redintegratio* (Decree on Ecumenism). *AAS* 57 (1965) 90–112; Abbott, 341–366; Flannery, 452–470. |
| *VC* | *Vigiliae Christianae.* Amsterdam, 1947–. |
| *Ve* | *Sacramentarium Veronense.* |
| *ViSpi* | *Vie spirituelle.* Paris, 1947–. |
| WUNT | Wissenschaftliche Untersuchungen zum Neuen Testament. Tübingen, 1950. |
| *Wor* | *Worship.* Collegeville, Minn., 1951–. Formerly *Orate Fratres,* 1926–1951. |
| *ZAW* | *Zeitschrift für Alttestamentliche Wissenschaft.* Berlin, 1881–. |
| *ZKTh* | *Zeitschrift für katholische Theologie.* Vienna and Innsbruck, 1877–. |
| *ZRG RA* | *Zeitschrift der Savigny-Stiftung für Rechtsgeschichte (Romantische Abteilung).* Weimar. |

Marcel Metzger

# 1

# A Eucharistic Lexicon

The vocabulary of Christian institutions has been fashioned by custom. This was the case for the Latin liturgy, as Battifol observed, "In many instances, the liturgy has appropriated terms used in common parlance, terms whose meaning becomes fixed without regard for their etymology."[1] The adoption of books of Roman origin entailed the ratification of their liturgical vocabulary. This remained unchanged through the successive generations of books. After the Council of Trent, liturgical fixity having set in, this vocabulary was imposed *ne varietur* ["without any variation allowed"; "immutable"] through the successive reeditions of the standard books and the manuals giving directions for their use.

Now and then commentators have attempted to promote a better understanding of these terms. They interpreted certain of these terms in new ways, with a mystical or allegorical sense, and they developed spiritual and moral considerations, often with an array of etymological arguments. These efforts did not cause any evolution in practice, because those terms had become codified. Evolution became possible only after Vatican II which allowed innovations, especially with regard to translations into vernacular languages.

*MISSA*
The liturgical books of Roman origin designate the eucharistic celebration and the formularies intended for it by the word *missa* in the singular or *missae* in the plural. In the *Hadrianum* Gregorian Sacramentary, this word appears in the very first title: *Qualiter missa romana*

---

[1] P. Battifol, *Leçons sur la messe*, Paris 1923, 121.

1

*celebratur.* It is found again in the *Ordines romani,* particularly the *Ordo* I, which presents the expression *missarum solemnia* (par. 105) ("solemnities of the Mass"). When the contents of the lectionaries, sacramentary, and antiphonal were combined into one single book for the eucharistic celebration, the name given to this new book was derived from *missa;* the book was called *missale.* The term *missa* remained entrenched in the Latin ecclesiastical vocabulary until Vatican II.

However, before custom gave it an exclusively eucharistic meaning, the word *missa* was also used to designate other liturgical institutions. The most eloquent document in this regard is the *Pilgrimage of Etheria*[2] in which the word *missa* occurs over seventy times. Most often, it means the dismissal of the faithful at the end of the celebrations, *cum missa ecclesiae facta fuerit,* ("when the dismissal of the assembly has taken place" (25, 10; see also 27, 6). Sometimes, it designates a service, *missa vigiliarum* ("the office of vigils") (38, 2; see also 39, 1 and 43, 3). In 27, 8, the word is explicitly applied to the eucharistic celebration, *missa autem, quae fit sabbato ad Anastase, ante solem fit, hoc est oblatio* ("as to the assembly that takes place at the church of the Resurrection on Saturday, before sunrise, it is the [eucharistic] offering").

The earliest attestation of the eucharistic meaning of *missa* is found in a letter of Ambrose of Milan in 386.[3] During a Sunday assembly, someone came to warn the bishop about certain incidents; despite this, he celebrated the Eucharist, *Ego tamen mansi in munere, missam facere coepi. Dum offero. . . .*[4] ("As for me, I remained in my office [of celebrant] I began the Eucharist. While I am offering. . . .")

But in the writings of the Fathers and the acts of the councils, the word *missa* designates also other liturgical institutions, prayers,[5] elements of the penance service,[6] readings or lessons at the office.[7] The meaning of dismissal is still well attested in the *Statuta Ecclesiae anti-*

[2] P. Maraval, *Égérie, Journal de voyage,* SCh 296, Paris 1982.

[3] *Epistola 20, 4, PL* 16, col. 995.

[4] See R. Johnanny, *L'eucharistie, centre de l'histoire du salut,* Paris, 83–4; A. Jungmann, *Missarum solemnia,* t. I, Wien, Freiburg, Basel, 1962, 231.

[5] *Concile de Milève* 402, *Collect. Hispana* c. 12, CCL 149, 365.

[6] Concile de Carthage 390, c. 3, CCL 149, 14.

[7] See M. Férotin, *Le Liber mozarabicus sacramentorum . . . ,* Paris 1912, reprinted Rome 1995, 755.

*qua*, in chapter 16, *Ut episcopus nullum prohibeat ingredi ecclesiam et audire verbum Dei . . . usque ad missam catechumenorum*[8] ("That the bishop should not forbid anyone to enter the church and hear the word of God until the dismissal of the catechumens").

But in the course of the centuries, it became customary to use the word *missa* exclusively in its eucharistic sense, and to utterly forget all its other previous meanings, except in the phrase *Ite, missa est*.

## ITE, MISSA EST

From the seventh to the ninth centuries, the commentators have acknowledged the eminently practical meaning of this call to the people. Thus Florus of Lyons,[9] following Isidore of Seville, *Missa ergo nihil aliud intelligitur quam dimissio, id est absolutio, quam celebratis omnibus tunc diaconus adesse pronuntiat cum populus a solemni observatione dimittitur. . . . Missa ergo catechumenorum fiebat ante actionem sacramentorum; missa fidelium fit post confectionem et participationem.* ("The word *missa* therefore has to be understood as nothing else than the dismissal, that is the dissolution [of the assembly] which, at the completion of all parts of the celebration, the deacon pronounces as the people is dismissed from the solemn rites just observed. . . . The dismissal of the catechumens therefore took place before the sacramental action, whereas the dismissal of the faithful is done after the confection [of the sacrament] and the participation in it"). Still more concretely, in the twelfth century, Honorius of Autun explains,[10] *Ite missa est licentia abeundi* ("*Ite missa est* is the permission to leave" or "The meeting is adjourned"). On the contrary, Amalarius (d. ca. 850) and his successors developed the spiritual sense,[11] *Quid est namque Ite missa est frater mi, nisi: Ite in pace in domos vestras?* ("What is *Ite missa est*, my brother, if not, Go home in peace?")

More recently, some persons have attempted to sublimate the quite practical meaning of *Ite, missa est* by giving to *missa* the meaning of mission. But this hypothesis is without foundation and the liturgical reform of Vatican II has rendered it useless, since it has allowed episcopal conferences to propose other formulas of dismissal.

[8] *CCL* 148, 169.
[9] *Exp. missae* 92, *PL* 119, col. 72.
[10] *Gemma animae*, I, III, *PL* 172, col. 581.
[11] *Ecl.* 32, éd. J.-M. Hanssens, *ST* 140, 263–4.

Speaking of the Roman Eucharistic Prayer in his *Letter to Decentius* (par. 2), in 416, Pope Innocent uses the expression *Prex (antequam precem sacerdos faciat)* ("The prayer before the priest offers the prayer"). Pope Vigilius[12] uses the same language *(canonicae precis textum)* ("the text of the canonical prayer"), and so does Pope Gregory,[13] when speaking of the place of the *Pater noster, mox post precem* ("Pater noster, immediately after the prayer"). Pope Vigilius adds the adjective *canonica* ("canonical"), and the *Liber Pontificalis* employs the corresponding substantive, in its notice on Pope Gregory,[14] *in praedicatione canonis* (in the proclamation of the Canon).

In the Gelasian Sacramentary (Vat. Regin. 216), the Eucharistic Prayer is introduced with these words, *Incipit canon actionis* ("here begins the canon of the [eucharistic] action") (III. XVII, no. 1242). The text is continuous, without a break, from the *Sursum corda* to the *Per ipsum*. Besides, the word *Actio* appears in the formularies of the Temporal which contain the variable parts of the canon, *Infra actionem* ("within the action"), *Communicantes . . .* (nos. 21 and foll.) ("Being in fellowship . . .").

To designate the first part of the Eucharistic Prayer between the initial dialogue and the *Sanctus*, both the collection called "Leonine" and the Gelasian have *Vere digum*, or simply *VD*, in the formularies, and *Preces* in the titles. In the Gelasian, *Praefatio* appears only once (no. 924). But in the Hadrianum Gregorian, this title precedes every one of the nineteen *Vere dignum*, and the *Missale Romanum* will make it the standard term to call this variable part of the Roman Eucharistic Prayer.

To sum up, the earliest Roman usage was to name the Eucharistic Prayer *Prex*. By being qualified with the adjective *canonica* (the Rule of the Prayer), it became the norm. This is the vocabulary that custom subsequently imposed everywhere; *canon actionis, canon*. But at the same time, custom caused a break between the first part, by naming it *Praefatio* and the whole, so that the word *canon* came to designate the Eucharistic Prayer minus the *Praefatio*, a fact which the Missals contributed to reinforce by emphasizing the *Te igitur*.

---

[12] Letter to the Bishop of Braga in 538, *PL* 69, col. 18.

[13] *Ep.* IX, 12, *PL* 77, col. 956.

[14] *Liber Pontificalis*, Duchesne, t. I, p. 109 et 312.

## OFFERTORIUM

By the word *offertorium*, the *Ordo Romanus* I designates the rite of the bringing and reception of the gifts. The *ordo missae* of the Hadrianum Gregorian Sacramentary mentions it in paragraph 2: *postmodum legitur evangelium, deinde offertorium et oblationem super oblatam* ("after the reading of the gospel, come the offertory and the oration over the gifts"). The word *offertorium* itself obviously suggests the act of bringing gifts (the verb *offerre*, and the related words, *oblationes, oblatas* (*OR* I, 74). This vocabulary is also found in the Gelasian Sacramentary (*Vat. Reg.* 316, no. 368, *Post haec offert plebs* ("Afterwards, the people bring the gifts").

However, this same term *offertorium* designates a piece of linen with which one holds the chalice (*OR* I, 84): *calicem . . . involutis ansis cum offerturio* ("the chalice . . . with its handles enveloped in the *offertorium*") and also the chant that accompanies the procession with the gifts, short for the longer expression *antiphona ad offertorium* ("offertory antiphon").

## COLLECTA

The noun *collecta* is the translation of the Greek "σύναξις," meaning "assembly." In the *OR* XXI which describes the Major Litany, the word applies to the beginning of the celebration, characterized by an initial gathering in a church, from which the procession will depart on its way to another church where the *statio* takes place: *Collecta in basilica beati Illius; statio in basilica sancti Illius. . . . Die nuntiata, colligit se omnis clerus vel omnis populus in ecclesia supraindicata.* ("The gathering takes place in the basilica of such and such a blessed person; the *statio* takes place in the church of such an such a saint. . . . On the appointed day, all the clergy and the people gather in the church named above"). The Gregorian Sacramentary has codified this practice by recording in succession the collect recited in the church where the gathering takes place and that recited in the *statio* church; *Oratio collecta ad Sanctum Hadrianum* (Hadrianum, no. 123); *Oratio ad collectam* (Paduense 103) ("The oration at the place of gathering"); and *Collecta ad sanctam Anastasiam* (Hadrianum, no. 153) ("Oration for the gathering at Saint Anastasia's"); *Oratio ad collectam* (Paduense 127).

In both the Gregorian and Gelasian sacramentaries, the first *oratio* of the Mass formularies is written without any title, following the heading of the formulary, for example, *Item ad missa* (Hadrianum, no. 124); *Ad missas* (Paduense 104). In the *Missale romanum*, this prayer is called *Oratio*. By contrast, a Romano-Frankish *ordo*, which describes the eucharistic celebration, the *OR V*, calls it *collecta; Deinde dicit; Oremus. Sequitur oratio prima, quam collectam dicunt . . .* (par. 25), ("Afterwards he says, let us pray. Then follows the first oration which is called collect") but the *OR VI, 25* only has *primam orationem* ("the first oration.")

B. Capelle has tried to explain this designation *collecta* as resulting from a contamination due to Gallican traditions which had made *collecta* the technical term to name the oration. This explanation has met with a mixed reception.

## SECRET
In the Gregorian Sacramentary, the second oration of the Mass formulary is entitled *Oratio super oblata*. But in the Gelasian Sacramentary, it is called *Secreta*, a name that will subsequently prevail in the *Missale Romanum*. In the ritual described by the *OR I* (par. 87), there is no place for such an oration. By contrast, the Romano-Frankish *OR V*, which derives from the *OR I* mentions it, specifying that it is recited in a low voice; *dicta oratione super oblationes secreta et episcopo alta voce incipiente; Per omnia. . . .* (par. 58) (after the oration over the gifts has been said secretly, the bishop intones aloud *Per omnia. . .*). In later times, the explanations, commentaries, and lectures on the Mass will usually interpret the term *secreta* as the result of the custom of reciting that oration in a low voice.

## THE GREETINGS
To the greetings *Dominus vobiscum* and *Pax vobis*, the assembly replies *Et cum spiritu tuo* ("And with your spirit"). These locutions come from the Bible. The greeting of the angel to Mary in Luke 1:28, contains the formula *Dominus tecum* without any verb, which is frequent in the Old Testament, in particular in passages where the faithful were being entrusted with a mission by God (Gen 26:24; 28:15; 39:2, 3, 21, 23; Exod 3:12; Deut 20:1; Judg 6:12-14; Isa 41:10; 53:5; 7:14). It corresponds to Jesus's promise in Matthew 28:20 (*vobiscum sum* "I am with you"). Similarly, in the greeting *Pax vobis*, one recognizes the salutation of the Risen One in John 20:19, 21, 26; Luke 24:26. It is also a biblical formula (see Judg 6:23; 19:20; 4 Kgs 4:23-26; Dan 10:19).

The response *Et cum spiritu tuo* corresponds to the salutations of Paul's letters (Gal 6:18; Phil 4:23; 2 Tim 4:22; Phlm 25). In biblical anthropology, the term πνεῦμα designates the most personal part of the human being. The Church Fathers have at times interpreted it in a theological sense, as a reference to priestly ordination:[15] "It is not the soul that they mean by these words *Et cum spiritu tuo*. But it is the grace of the Holy Spirit through which those who are entrusted to his care believe that he entered the ranks of the priesthood. . . ."

For the response *Et cum spiritu tuo*, A. Jungmann[16] has proposed a restrictive interpretation by translating in a pedestrian manner by "And with you too." But this explanation is not acceptable. However, a difficulty remains because of the conflict with modern anthropology. The solution is a pastoral one; it resides in a deepening of the biblical culture of the believers who should thus become more familiar with the biblical vocabulary.

The new liturgical books promulgated by the episcopal conferences since Vatican II have incorporated the recent changes in the liturgical vocabulary, introduced by theologians. Words better rooted in the Bible have superseded the word *missa*. Nevertheless, to promote the evolution of vocabulary is a perilous undertaking, because authoritative decrees rarely overcome customs. It happens that a word suddenly is invested with a new meaning which will grow richer within a tradition, in spite of the deficiency of its etymology. This is the case of the word *missa*, which will not disappear anytime soon, because it has been used for several centuries throughout the Catholic literature. But this vocabulary is in our day delivered to a society which misuses religious terms without the least scruple. Thus in France, journalists have appropriated for themselves the word Mass to designate any political manifestation; they do not hesitate to headline their reports thus: "The High Mass of football, of such and such a political party, and so on." And this poses pastoral problems.

---

[15] Théodore of Mopsuestia, *Hom. cat.* XV, 37–8, T-D, 519–21; see J. Lécuyer, *Le sacrement de l'ordination*, Paris 1983, 106.

[16] A. Jungmann, *Missarum solemnia*, t. I, 466.

## Bibliography

Blaise, A., and H. Chirat. "Missa." *Dictionnaire latin-français des auteurs chrétiens,* 535. Turnhout, 1954.

Botte, B., and C. Mohrmann. *L'ordinaire de la messe,* 145–9. Paris and Louvain, 1953.

Capelle, B. "Collecta." *RBén* 42 (1930) 197–204. Reprinted in *Travaux liturgiques* 2:192–9. Louvain, 1962.

Chavasse, A. "La *Prex,* à Rome, dans les anciens livres liturgiques." *EO* (1993/2) 231–5.

Jungmann, J. *The Mass of the Roman Rite: Its Origins and Development.* Trans. F. Brunner. Christian Classics. Westminster, Md., 1986. Reprint 1992. Originally published in New York, 1951–1955.

Enrico Mazza

2

# The Eucharist in the First Four Centuries*

INTRODUCTION

*1. The State of Studies of the Eucharist*
In the miscellany published in honor of Arthur Hubert Couratin, Geoffrey J. Cuming provided a critical review of the more important studies published on the eucharistic liturgy from the work of Gregory Dix[1] to 1977.[2] He described the subjects of the various studies, their method, and the perspective adopted by the several authors. About fifteen years later, in a miscellany in honor of Balthasar Fischer, Albert Gerhards published an essay which surveyed the results reached by eucharistic studies that investigated the early liturgical sources.[3] Finally, let me mention that studies and researches on the East Syrian anaphoras were discussed by A. Gelston on occasion of

---

* A more detailed commentary on the Eucharist is found in chapters 1–7 of the author's *Celebration of the Eucharist: The Origin of the Rite and the Development of Its Interpretation* (Collegeville: The Liturgical Press, 1999).

[1] G. Dix, *The Shape of the Liturgy* (London, 1945).

[2] G. J. Cuming, "The Early Eucharistic Liturgies in Recent Research," in *The Sacrifice of Praise. Studies on the Themes of Thanksgiving and Redemption in the Central Prayers of the Eucharistic and Baptismal Liturgies. In Honour of A. H. Couratin* (BELS, 19; Rome, 1981) 65–69. To this may be added some other contributions of Cuming: "Four Very Early Anaphoras," *Wor* 58 (1984) 168–72; "The Shape of the Anaphora," *Studia Patristica XX* (Kalamazoo-Louvain, 1989) 333–45; *The Liturgy of St. Mark* (OCA 234; Rome, 1990) (published posthumously by Bryan D. Spinks).

[3] A. Gerhards, "Entstehung und Entwicklung des eucharistischen Hochgebets im Spiegel der neueren Forschung. Der Beitrag der Liturgiewissenschaft zur liturgischen Erneuerung," in *Gratias Agamus. Studien zum eucharistischen Hochgebet. Für Balthasar Fischer,* ed. A. Heinz and H. Rennings (Freiburg-Basel-Vienna: Herder, 1992) 75–96.

the critical edition of the Anaphora of Addai and Mari.[4] Also to be mentioned are the critical essays of Thomas J. Talley.[5]

## 2. Method

The problem of the origin of the Eucharistic Prayer was posed back in the seventeenth century, but without result, since it was not possible to go beyond a general assertion of its apostolic origin. Beginning in the second quarter of the present century, certain factors radically transformed studies of the origin and development of the Eucharistic Prayer, so that they bore ever richer fruit. Thus there came into being a true and specific method of work that has four main components, which I shall describe briefly. 1) Comparison of the earliest Christian liturgies with the rites of the Jewish liturgy; this systematic study arose among Jewish scholars because the archaic Christian liturgies, being related to the Jewish liturgy, served in the scientific study of the latter.[6] Later, this methodology was taken over by Christian scholars in the studies of Dix, Ligier, Bouyer, and others, and is now commonly used.[7]

2) Thanks to Gregory Dix, researchers have shifted their interest from a conjectural reconstruction of the "original account" (Urtext) of the Last Supper to a description of the actions of Jesus that is based on practices at the Jewish ritual meal. This means a consideration of the entire celebration in its complexity: not only of what Jesus said, but also of what he himself did and, above all, what he told others to do. The focus of research on the "actions at the Last Supper," rather than on a

[4] A. Gelston, The Eucharistic Prayer of Addai and Mari (Oxford, 1992). See also B. D. Spinks, Worship: Prayers from the East (Washington, D.C., 1993); P. Yousif, L'Eucharistie chez saint Ephrem de Nisibe (OCA 224; Rome, 1984); idem, A Classified Bibliography (Rome, 1990).

[5] T. J. Talley, "De la 'berakah' à l'eucharistie. Une question à réexaminer," MD no. 125 (1976) 11–39; idem, "The Eucharistic Prayer: Tradition and Development," in Liturgy Reshaped (London, 1982) 48–54; idem, "The Literary Structure of the Eucharistic Prayer," Wor 58 (1984) 404–20; idem, Worship. Reforming Tradition (Washington, D.C., 1990); idem, "Structures des anaphores anciennes et modernes," MD no. 191 (1992) 15–43.

[6] See, e.g., L. Finkelstein, "The Birkat ha-mazon," Jewish Quarterly Review, N.S. 19 (1928–1929) 211–62; F. Gavin, "Rabbinic Parallels in Early Church Orders," in Contributions to the Scientific Study of Jewish Liturgy (New York, 1970) 305–17; E. Werner, "The Doxology in Synagogue and Church," ibid., 318–70; I. Elbogen, Der jüdische Gottesdienst in seiner geschichtlichen Entwicklung (Hildesheim, 1962).

[7] See E. Mazza, L'anaphora eucaristica. Studi sulle origini (Rome, 1992) 7–17.

reconstruction of the words spoken,[8] is the method that has yielded the most fruit, especially through comparison with Jewish usages.

3) Not only are anaphoral texts compared with the Jewish sources; they are also, and above all, compared among themselves, both in order to determine the original form of the text and in order to draw a kind of map or genealogical tree that shows the development of the texts and their influences on one another. In this context I must mention the names of Engberding, Botte, Lanne, and others.[9]

4) The application of the historico-critical method, instead of a predominantly theological method, has made it possible to achieve unexpected results; in fact, this method, which has already been used to good effect in biblical studies, makes it possible to demonstrate detailed relationships between anaphoral texts seemingly remote from each other. The historico-critical method should show whence a text derives and what other texts it generates.[10] It should also explain the textual content of a Eucharistic Prayer, that is, whether it looks upon the celebration as an act of obedience to Christ's command, "Do this in remembrance of me."

This method is simply a particular application of a well-known general principle: the interpretation of sources, including the theological interpretation, comes after the historico-critical study of these sources. It seems right that theology should profit from the strict historical method as applied to the liturgy, just as in the recent past it profited from its application to biblical studies.

THE JEWISH SETTING OF THE CHRISTIAN EUCHARIST
In shedding light on the Christian Eucharist the Old Testament can be used in several ways that are reducible to two different methods: the typological method and the historical method. The typological method

---

[8] Cuming, "The Early Eucharistic Liturgies," 65.

[9] For the works of these authors and for other studies space does not allow me to cite, see my *L'anafora eucaristica*, 7–17, 363–87.

[10] According to Jungmann, for example, the eucharist in the *Didache* cannot be regarded as a sacrament because it lacks the formula of consecration; this is a theological approach to a historical problem, namely, whether the *Didache* has a place in the historical genesis of the Eucharist that originated at the Last Supper. See J. A. Jungmann, *The Early Liturgy to the Time of Gregory the Great*, trans. F. A. Brunner (Notre Dame: University of Notre Dame Press, 1959) 35–6. For the various opinions on the eucharist of the *Didache* see J. Ayán Calvo (ed.), *Didaché, Doctrina apostolorum. Epístola del Pseudo-Bernabé* (Fuentes patrísticas 3; Madrid, 1992) 41–58.

shows how the old law is a prefiguration of the new and therefore how it is fulfilled in the realities of the new covenant. In this perspective, the eucharistic celebration, too, will be seen as a fulfillment of such Old Testament types as Melchizedek, the manna, and the various kinds of sacrifice. This method is especially suited to shedding light on the salvific value of the Eucharist.[11] The historical method, on the other hand, brings to light relationships between the New Testament liturgy and the Old Testament rites, as it tries to show how the Christian liturgy derives from the Jewish liturgy: in what forms and ritual structures, by what avenues and with what transformations.

First, we will have to see what the origin was of the Jewish ritual meal, then bring out the connection between the liturgy of the Jewish meal and the liturgy of the Lord's Supper. Study of the Jewish ritual meal and its origins leads us to the area of Jewish sacrifices, and therefore we must look first of all at these.

## 1. The Jewish Ritual Meal and Sacrifice

In the time when ritual slaughter of animals was practiced, every meal was a religious event and in some way connected with sacrifice. It was the Deuteronomic reform that introduced the practice of the nonreligious slaughter of animals; the result was a clear differentiation between sacrifice with its sacred meal and the "secular" meal, taken solely for nourishment.[12] This reform gave rise to the special liturgy of the Jewish ritual meal, which was traced back to the divine command given in Deut 8:10: "You shall eat your fill and bless the Lord your God for the good land that he has given you." It is not the prayer that sanctifies the meal; on the contrary, the meal itself, being the expression of the divine gift of the land, has its own sacral character that calls for the presence of prayer. It is God who is blessed, and not the meal. Since every meal, as such, stems from God's gift, it follows that all meals should be celebrated with prayer. The purpose

[11] E. Mazza, "L'interpretazione del culto nella chiesa antica," in *Celebrare il mistero di Cristo. Manuale di Liturgia* 1 (Rome, 1993) 229–79.

[12] It is incorrect to speak, in connection with Israel, of either a "sacred meal" or a "secular meal." In Israel, meals were neither sacred nor secular but religious; this fact requires us to move beyond the category of the sacred and speak directly of a relationship with God. For this interpretation of the concepts of the sacred and the profane see J.-P. Audet, "Le sacré et le profan. Leur situation en christianisme," *NRT* 79 (1957) 33–61.

of the prayer is not to turn a secular meal into a sacred meal; the prayer is an acknowledgment of God's gift.[13]

## 2. The Basic Prayer of the Jewish Meal

The rabbis were very clear on the connection between a meal and the prayer of thanksgiving with which it ended, and they asked what the source was of the obligation to recite such a prayer. They found their answer in Deut 8:10, which came to them as a divine command establishing the Jewish "meal." This divine institution gave rise to the theology and juridical obligation of the prayer said at the end of meals. This prayer was the *Birkat ha-Mazon*.[14] Whenever there is a meal, provided it consists in something more than a medium-size olive, the *Birkat ha-Mazon* is said.

It is extremely difficult to establish the exact original tenor of this prayer, since there never existed a single, normative text which everyone had to follow. According to the rules governing Jewish prayer, every kind of prayer had to follow a pattern, but within the pattern the one praying was free to formulate his or her own prayer, thus creating an improvised text. For this reason it is very difficult to find detailed testimonies regarding the *Birkat ha-Mazon*. A further difficulty is that there were specific prohibitions against putting the prayer in writing.[15]

---

[13] In explaining the origin of the sacrificial character of the Christian Eucharist authors have often had recourse to the sacrificial character of the prayer of thanksgiving that accompanied the Old Testament rites and now accompanies the Christian eucharistic celebration. See, e.g., the writings of H. Cazelles: "L'anaphore et l'Ancien Testament," in *Eucharisties d'Orient et d'Occident,* ed. B. Botte et al., 1 (Lex orandi 46; Paris, 1970) 11–22; "Eucharistie, bénédiction et sacrifice dans l'Ancien Testament," *MD* no. 123 (1975) 7–28. For an original development of this kind of interpretation see C. Giraudo, *La struttura letteraria della preghiera eucaristica. Saggio sulla genesi letteraria di una forma. Toda veterotestamentaria, Beraka giudaica, Anafora cristiana* (Analecta biblica 92; Rome, 1981).

[14] This prayer is also used at the Passover meal, during the ritual of the third cup, which stands out as very important. It was also used in the rite of communion sacrifices, as can be seen from the account of Abraham's death in the *Book of Jubilees* 22, 1–10. Here again it must have played an important role, since it is cited rather extensively as one of the most important moments in the events surrounding Abraham's death as told in this Old Testament apocryphal work.

[15] This prohibition would have been one of the rabbinical norms and an element in the rabbinical theology of the prayer. But there is not, of course, always a correspondence of practice to rule. On the subject see J. Heinemann, *Prayer in the Talmud. Forms and Patterns* (Studia judaica 9; Berlin-New York, 1977).

Scholars have made an effort to reconstruct, from the few texts that have come down to us, a text that would serve as a general pattern for the *Birkat ha-Mazon*. Here is the text proposed by Finkelstein.[16]

a) Blessed are you, Lord, our God, king of the universe, who feed the whole world in goodness, kindness, and mercy. Blessed are you, Lord, who feed the universe.

b) We thank you, Lord, our God, who have given us as an inheritance a desirable land, that we might eat of its fruits and nourish ourselves on its goodness. Blessed are you, Lord, our God, for the land and the food.

c) Have mercy, Lord, our God, on Israel your people and on Jerusalem your city and on Zion the dwelling place of your glory and on your altar and sanctuary. Blessed are you, Lord, who build Jerusalem.

We must bear in mind that this pattern is a reconstruction by Finkelstein, who proposes it as a kind of basic model. This text never existed as such and therefore can be used only with great caution. Unfortunately, many make use of the pattern without dealing with actually existing texts, though these are much more interesting because of the parallels they show with the later Christian development of the prayer. One text, among other, is especially important: the *Birkat ha-Mazon* in the *Book of Jubilees* (22, 6–9), which was written around 100 B.C.:

⁶"And he [Abraham] ate and drank and blessed God Most High who created heaven and earth and who made all the fat of the earth and gave it to the sons of man so that they might eat and drink and bless their Creator. ⁷ 'And now I thank you, my God, because you have let me see this day. Behold, I am one hundred and seventy-five years old, and fulfilled in days. And all of my days were peaceful for me. ⁸ The sword of the enemy did not triumph over me in anything which you gave to me or my sons all of the days of my life until this day. ⁹ O my God, may your mercy and peace be upon your servant and upon the seed of his sons so that they might become an elect people for you and an inheritance from all the nations

---

[16] Finkelstein, "The Birkat ha-Mazon." [I have not had access to this publication and have had to backtranslate the text from the author's Italian version. — Tr.]

of the earth from henceforth and for all the days of the generations of the earth forever.'"[17]

The *Birkat ha-Mazon* tells of the meaning the meal has in Judaism. The land was given to the Jewish people by Yahweh as a pledge of the covenant. In the rite for the contracting or renewal of the covenant, the eating of the produce of the country is therefore, in itself, an acceptance of the covenant. At the end of the meal, these themes are voiced again in the *Birkat ha-Mazon;* we may therefore conclude that in every meal the devout Jew celebrates and remembers the gift of the land that is a pledge of the covenant.[18]

## THE ORIGIN OF THE CHRISTIAN EUCHARIST

### 1. The Last Supper

The Christian Eucharist has its origin in the Last Supper: Jesus took bread, blessed God, broke the bread, and gave it to his disciples, telling them to take it and eat of it, because it was his body. In the same way, after they had eaten, he took the cup, gave thanks, and gave it to his disciples, telling them all to take it and drink of it, because it was the cup of the covenant in his blood. At the end he said: "Do this in remembrance of me." With this action he established a model so that we might do the same, that is, do what he himself had done. To celebrate the Eucharist, then, is to obey Christ's command and do what he himself did.

The bread and the wine, which are the elements of this ritual meal, are given their meaning by the two prayers that accompany them: the blessing over the bread, the thanksgiving over the cup.

These prayers that Jesus uttered at the supper are the origin and model of the Church's Eucharistic Prayer, or anaphora. These two

---

[17] *Book of Jubilees,* trans. O. S. Wintermute, in *The Old Testament Pseudepigrapha,* ed. J. H. Charlesworth (2 vols.; New York: Doubleday, 1983, 1985) 2, 97. On the Jewish literary genre of the *berakah* ("blessing") see J.-P. Audet, "Literary Forms and Content of a Normal *Eucharistia* in the First Century," in K. Aland and F. L. Cross (eds.), *Studia Evangelica* (TU 18; Berlin, 1959) 643–62; idem, "Esquisse du genre littéraire de la 'Bénédiction' juive et de l'"Eucharistie' chrétienne," *RB* 65 (1958) 371–99; Talley,, "De la 'berakah' . . . ," "The Literary Structure . . . ," and "Structures . . . " (all in note 5, above).

[18] The divine blessing that comes down from heaven is matched by an ascending response from the heart of the devout Jew. It is in this way that God saves his people: by placing on their lips a response in the form of a blessing.

thanksgiving texts were the starting point of a very complex textual development that leads us to the anaphoral texts which we find today in the Missal of the Roman Church.

Since the Mass is an act of *obedience* to the command of Christ and an *imitation*[19] of his supper in the upper room, it follows that the Eucharistic Prayer determines the very nature of the Church's Eucharist.

As the Eucharistic Prayer is an imitation of the thanksgiving offered by Jesus in the upper room, so the elements making up the meal, the bread and wine, will be like the bread and wine of Jesus in the upper room; to use the technical term, they will be a *likeness*[20] of the bread and wine of the upper room and therefore of the body and blood of Christ.

## 2. Conformity to the Last Supper

The Eucharist of the Church is quite different from the rite at the Last Supper; the Last Supper was also a meal in the full sense of the word, with the participants taking food as at any other meal. Yet in the Mass, from the second century on, there was no longer any connection with a supper, and the eucharistic rite was separated from any meal proper. Furthermore, at the supper of Jesus, there were two separate and distinct prayers of thanksgiving, one for the bread and one for the cup, whereas in the Mass there is only one, the Eucharistic Prayer or anaphora, which embraces both the bread and the cup, since the rite of the bread has been completely fused with the rite of the cup.

In light of this difference, it is clear that the very early Church reinterpreted the "this" in the command, "Do this in remembrance of me." The rite at the Last Supper was reinterpreted by the apostolic Church so as to bring out which elements of the Last Supper were normative and which were not, or, in other words, which elements

---

[19] Such terms as "imitation," "likeness," "figure," "image," "form," and "act of obedience" are to be understood not in their present-day sense but according to their acceptation in the Fathers. If we had to translate this understanding into today's language, we would have to use the term "sacrament," and it would be an excellent translation. On the meaning and use of this terminology see my essay "L'interpretazione del culto nella chiesa antica."

[20] Jesus said of the bread and wine which he gave to his disciples in the upper room that they were his body and his blood; we rightly say the same of the bread and wine on our altars: we say that they are the *sacrament* of his body and blood.

16

were essential if the ritual supper of the Church were to be a faithful and effective carrying out of the command "Do 'this' in remembrance of me." This reinterpretation of the Last Supper had already been completed when the New Testament was written. For, in fact, the Supper is not reported with all its ritual details, as in a chronicle, but in a liturgical perspective, that is, as "the model" which Jesus left to the Church that it might do the same.

Because the Church's celebration is an act of obedience to Christ's command, it must include all the actions that are part of the rite which Jesus gave as a *model* and which the New Testament describes. These, then, are the parts judged to be constitutive of the Church's rite: (1) he took bread, (2) gave thanks, (3) broke the bread, (4) gave it, (5) while saying . . . ; (6) he took the cup, (7) gave thanks, (8) gave it, (9) while saying. . . .

The Eucharist of the Church is "conformed" to the rite carried out by Jesus in the Upper Room, and it is such because it consists of the series of actions listed. In the language of the Fathers, the rite performed by Jesus at the Last Supper was a *traditio mysteriorum* ("handing on of the mysteries") and therefore a *typos* ("model") of the celebration. The Eucharist would therefore be called an antitype (ἀντίτυπος), a mystery, and, using a word more familiar to us, a sacrament.

### 3. The Accounts of the Last Supper

The New Testament contains four reports of the Last Supper. These belong to two different traditions which are independent of each other.[21]

As we are well aware, the story of the Last Supper was told by the various traditions in accordance with the kerygma (κήρυγμα) of the

---

[21] On the one hand, we have the tradition of Mark and Matthew, and, on the other, that of Luke and Paul. To these may be added a third tradition that is attested by a sentence in the gospel of John which reports only the words of Jesus over the bread: "The bread that I will give for the life of the world is my flesh" (John 6:51c). From a literary point of view, the text of Paul is the oldest, composed probably in the spring of A.D. 54 (see J. Jeremias, *The Eucharistic Words of Jesus*, trans. N. Perrin [London: SCM, 1966] 138), but the Pauline tradition must have taken shape even earlier, since Paul refers to "what I also handed on to you" (1 Cor 11:23), alluding probably to the fall of 49, at the beginning of his missionary activity in Corinth.

various Churches and with their liturgical forms. The form of the narrative served not only the needs of the kerygma but also its liturgical use.[22]

If we are to learn which narrative best corresponds to the events of the Last Supper, we must follow a route other than that of purely linguistic considerations; to arguments of a linguistic and literary kind we must add liturgical arguments, with special attention to the rites that made up the Last Supper.[23] We must study the customary Jewish ritual meal and decide which of the New Testament data are most compatible with that usage. It is on the basis of such arguments as these that Luke's account becomes quite uniquely important in sketching the history of the Eucharist in its first moments. Following Heinz Schürmann,[24] I maintain that the text in Luke should be regarded as the redaction that best mirrors the events of the Last Supper. Luke's is a heavily grecized text, but that does not prevent our regarding it as a very early text.

### 4. The Ritual Structure of the Last Supper

Luke describes the rite in a way that brings out the ritual structure of the Last Supper. The Last Supper has three parts: the introductory rite, the supper in the normal sense of the word, and the concluding rite. The introduction is made up of two elements: the rite of the cup and the rite of the bread, each accompanied by explanatory words.[25] The ritual of the cup comes first and is accompanied by an eschatological discourse:

"When the hour came, he took his place at the table, and the apostles with him. He said to them, 'I have eagerly desired to eat this Passover with you before I suffer; for I tell you, I will not eat it until it is fulfilled in the kingdom of God.' Then he took a cup, and after giving

---

[22] The construction of the account of the Last Supper also serves to account for the development of the Christian liturgy.

[23] Mazza, L'anafora eucaristica.

[24] H. Schürmann, Der Einsetzungsbericht Lk 22, 19-20 (Münster, 1955).

[25] In the German-speaking world the term Deutewort ("word of explanation") became the common name for the words accompanying the cup and the bread, since the purpose of these words is to explain the nature and function of the bread and wine of the Last Supper. From a literary point of view, the words do indeed have an explanatory function and nothing more. From the viewpoint of western theology they have a further function, which is to "consecrate."

thanks he said: 'Take this and divide it among yourselves; for I tell you that from now on I will not drink of the fruit of the wine until the kingdom of God comes'" (Luke 22:14-18).

This is followed by the ritual of the bread, which is accompanied both by explanatory words and by the command to repeat the rite in memory of Christ: "Then he took a loaf of bread, and when he had given thanks, he broke it and gave it to them, saying: 'This is my body, which is given for you. Do this in remembrance of me'" (22:19).

The eschatological words over the cup establish the significance both of the Passover meal and of the rite of the cup. The "fruit of the vine" will not be drunk again nor will the Passover be eaten again until the kingdom of God comes in its fullness. The present time with its impending darkness is thus already set in the light of the future, so that the image of the kingdom of God is made part of the Last Supper.[26] In the words of Jesus, this meal, which is, theologically, a Passover meal, takes on the value of a "type" and becomes a model for that future meal, that is, the eschatological banquet in the coming kingdom. By this is meant that there will be no further stages between the Last Supper and the coming of the reign of God. This fact is important for a correct understanding of the sacraments. The words over the bread, which is broken as it is at the beginning of any meal, establish a clear connection of identity between the bread and the body of Christ: the bread which Jesus gives his disciples to eat is his body.

After the introductory rite comes the supper in the ordinary, every-day sense of the word. At its end, in keeping with the Jewish custom that I have already explained, the prayer of thanksgiving, the *Birkat ha-Mazon*, is said by Christ while he holds the cup that ends the rite. Luke does not explicitly say that the final cup was accompanied by a prayer of thanksgiving; the fact is inferred from the adverb ὡσαύτως ("in the same way") which v. 20 puts in an appositive position in relation to the cup: "the cup *in the same way*." The point of the adverb is that the actions previously done are done again for the cup. The cup is accompanied by explanatory words that say: "This cup that is poured out for you is the new covenant in my blood" (Luke 22:20). Here the account of the Last Supper ends without a command of

---

[26] K. H. Rengstorf, *Il vangelo secondo Luca* (Nuovo Testamento 3; Brescia, 1980) 410.

19

repetition, although this was indeed given earlier, at the end of the words over the bread.

This fact, together with the brusque way in which v. 20 is introduced ("in the same way"), without any reference to the prayer of thanksgiving, suggests that v. 20 is an addition which Luke introduced later on as being an important element in one of his sources. In this interpretation, the earliest stage of the narrative in the Antiochene tradition (Luke, Paul) would have contained only vv. 17-19.[27]

We may therefore conclude that according to Luke, the liturgy celebrated by Jesus at the Last Supper had the following structure: the rite of the cup, the rite of the bread, the supper, the final rite of the cup. Each of the three rites was accompanied by its prayer of thanksgiving.

## FROM THE JEWISH LITURGY TO THE CHRISTIAN EUCHARIST

### 1. The Rite of the Jewish Festive Meal

After seeing the structure of the Last Supper, we must ask whether there existed a Jewish rite with a structure analogous to that which Luke describes. There was: the Jewish festive meal. This had three stages: it began with the rite of the *Qiddush* ("sanctification"), which introduced the celebration of the feast; when this rite was finished, the meal proper began; at the end of the meal came the concluding rite: the rite of the cup, which was accompanied by the prayer of thanksgiving, the *Birkat ha-Mazon*.

The *Qiddush* in turn had three parts. It opened with the rite of the cup, which began with the story in Genesis 1:31b–2:1-3. After this reading there was a short blessing: "Blessed are you, Lord, our God, king of the universe, who creates[28] the fruit[29] of the vine."[30] To this was added a second blessing for the sanctification of the sabbath or other feastday in the liturgical calendar. The rite of the cup was fol-

---

[27] Jeremias, *The Eucharistic Words of Jesus*, 138.

[28] The shift from the second to third person singular is due to the history of these blessings, which originally contained only what is now the second part and lacked the first part (i.e., "Blessed are you, Lord").

[29] "Fruit of the vine" is an expression Luke uses in 22:17 in referring to the first cup at the Last Supper.

[30] Text in A. Hänggi and I Pahl (eds.), *Prex eucharistica. Textus e variis liturgiis antiquioribus selecti* (SF 12; Fribourg, 1968) 6.

lowed by the rite of the bread. The father of the family took the bread and, elevating it a little, recited the following blessing: "Blessed are you, Lord, our God, king of the universe, who produce bread from the earth."[31] After the blessing, the father of the family broke the bread and distributed it for the meal, which followed directly.

After the meal, at which time *Zemirot* or ritual hymns were sung, the *Birkat ha-Mazon* was recited, the thanksgiving that was to be said at the end of every meal and that on feastdays was one with the rite of the cup. Rabbis had a serious obligation to recite this prayer, an obligation based on the divine command in Deut 8:10.

### 2. *The Rite in* Didache *9–10*

From this description of the rites accompanying a Jewish festive meal and consisting of the *Qiddush* at its beginning and the *Birkat ha-Mazon* at its end, we can see that the sequence of ritual elements is the same as that found in the ritual supper described by Luke. But Luke is not the only instance.

From the very early Church we have a document, the *Didache*,[32] which describes the eucharistic celebration and is almost certainly of Antiochene origin. The description is of a celebration that has the same structure as the one I have just been describing and parallels both Luke and the Jewish festive meal. This Eucharist begins with the rite of the cup, accompanied by a short blessing[33]; it is followed by the rite of the bread broken, which is likewise accompanied by a blessing[34] and to which is added an expansion (known technically as an "embolism") in the form of a prayer for unity.[35] After this rite there is the meal, which is followed by a Christian *Birkat ha-Mazon*.[36] This further rite begins with the rubric: "After eating your fill, give thanks in this fashion"[37]; the rubric is based on Deut 8:10 and

---

[31] Ibid., 7. For a commentary see L. A. Hoffman, "Rabbinic *Berakhah* and Jewish Spirituality," in *Asking and Thanking*, ed. C. Duquoc and C. Florestan (*Concilium*, 1990, no. 3; London and Philadelphia, 1990) 18–30.

[32] W. Rordorf and A. Tuilier (eds.), *La doctrine des douze apôtres (Didaché)* (SCh 248; Paris, 1976).

[33] *Didache* 9, 2.

[34] Ibid., 9, 3.

[35] Ibid., 9, 4.

[36] Ibid., 10.

[37] Ibid., 10, 1.

indicates the point at which the prayer of thanksgiving is to be said: "after having supped." We should note that the rubric in *Didache* 10, 1, says the same thing as Luke: "In the same way, after having supped, he took the cup" (Luke 22:20).

A. EUCHARISTIC THEMES IN THE *DIDACHE*

In this document themes of thanksgiving are found in three successive "eucharists"[38]: two in chapter 9 and one in chapter 10, which is the Christian *Birkat ha-Mazon* and is the most important of the three. There are, however, only two prayers of petition, the first in chapter 10 and the second in chapter 9, the latter being taken from the former.

At the beginning of the meal, in the thanksgiving over the cup, thanks is offered for the vine of David, and in the Eucharist over the bread thanks is given for life and knowledge. After the meal, the thanksgiving reads: "We give you thanks for your holy name which you have made to dwell in our hearts, and for the faith, knowledge, and immortality which you have manifested to us through Jesus, your servant." The themes of life and knowledge are very close to those of faith, knowledge, and immortality, but I must briefly explain the other two: the dwelling of God in the hearts of the faithful and the vine of David.

B. THE VINE OF DAVID

The devout Jew says a blessing over the cup for the "fruit of the vine."[39] *Didache* 9, 2, makes its own the theme of the vine but changes the point of reference: the vine becomes the "vine of David" and is an object of revelation by Jesus. We cannot accept that the "vine of David" signifies Christ, since in this context the revealer is distinguished clearly from what he reveals. W. Rordorf has shown that in Judaism there was an important "current of ideas that represented the Davidic kingdom in the form of a vine."[40] From this it follows that the

---

[38] Two before the meal and one after it.

[39] "Blessed are you, Lord, God of the universe, who creates the fruit of the vine" (Blessing over the cup in the rite of the *Qiddush* at the beginning of the meal).

[40] It is worth recalling here that the vine was one of the most widespread symbols in Jewish art, from coins (see P. Romanoff, *Jewish Symbols on Ancient Jewish Coins* [Philadelphia, 1944] 23ff.) to mosaic paintings (see E. R. Goodenough, *Jewish Symbols in the Greco-Roman Period* [New York, 1964] 79ff.). In Herod's temple, which was destroyed in 70, there was a huge golden vine hanging over the entrance gate. According to Flavius Josephus' description of it, the clusters of grapes

great work of God for which thanks is given in *Didache* 9, 2, is the kingdom of David or, in other words, the economy of salvation that was carried out in the history of Israel.[41] In this same strophe of the *Didache* (9, 2), Jesus, like David, is also called "servant" (παῖς).[42] Jesus is the eschatological prophet who is the reality prefigured by David and his work for the people. In this perspective, Christianity is still a development and unfolding of Judaism, within which it remains.

## C. The Dwelling of God in Hearts

The object of the thanksgiving is the "holy Name" of God which he has "made to dwell in our hearts." This statement is very archaic in tone. In order correctly to interpret the phrase, we must hark back to Old Testament cultic usage. The place where God makes his name to dwell becomes a temple and place of worship: here people celebrate the liturgy before God who is present. Deuteronomistic theology teaches that the temple of God is the place in which he has made his name dwell (Deut 12:11) in order that it may be invoked. In this theology "name" stands for "God," but is not fully identical with him. The "name" is, in fact, a kind of hypostasis that is in every way like God but is not completely identical with him.[43] We may say that the

---

were as large as a man and, according to the Mishnah, it took three hundred priests to carry it. In Judaism the symbol of the vine expresses the whole messianic expectation of the people. See W. Rordorf, "La vigne et le vin dans la tradition juive et chrétienne," in his *Liturgie, foi et vie des premiers chrétiens. Etudes patristiques* (Théologie historique 53; Paris, 1989) 493–508.

[41] In my opinion, Rordorf's interpretation is better grounded than that which J. Jeremias takes over from R. Eisler: "'for the holy vine of David your servant,' that is, the vine of which David speaks (Ps 80:9ff.)." See J. Jeremias, "Pais Theou," *TDNT* 9:700.

[42] When Jesus is given the title *pais*, he is as it were set alongside David as a protagonist in God's saving work. The reign of David is seen as a fulfillment of the divine promise of the gift of the land, which is the Old Testament theme par excellence. David is the man *blessed* by God, "and the Lord gave victory to David wherever he went" (2 Sam 8:14). We should note especially that David's conquest is crowned by the capture of Jerusalem, which will be known as the city of David; thus David and the entire house of Israel form but a single people around their God. Once all this is applied to Christ, it acquires a new meaning and a greater scope, which, however, are neither different from nor opposed to the Israelite economy of salvation.

[43] T. N. D. Mettinger, *The Dethronement of Sabaoth. Studies in the Shem and Kabod Theologies* (Coniectanea biblica. Old Testament Series 18; Lund, 1982) 130.

role of the "name" is located between God and human beings; it is, however, something more than a mere intermediary, since the "name," as such, belongs to the realm of the divine. In the Deuteronomistic theology of the name, the sanctuary, the place where sacrifices are offered, becomes a house of prayer (1 Kgs 8:29ff.).

All this information is to be applied to *Didache* 10, 2: here, too, God's name dwells, but the place of dwelling is the heart. It follows that the hearts of believers are the place of God's presence, which is mediated by his Name that dwells there, and that in this place a liturgy consisting of prayer is celebrated.

This theme will subsequently be developed by Paul, who replaces the theology of the Name with a theology of the Spirit: "Because you are sons, God has sent the Spirit of his Son into our hearts, crying, 'Abba! Father!'"[44] *Didache* 10, 2, then, is saying that the newness Christ has brought consists in the revelation of a new place of worship and a new liturgy: the temple is no longer a building, but the hearts of the faithful, and the new liturgy consists, therefore, in the invocation of God. In conclusion: Through Jesus, God the Father reveals the nature of Israel and the temple, thereby performing a saving action that has, as its fruit, knowledge, faith, life, and immortality.

## D. THE PRAYER OF PETITION

The third strophe of the *Birkat ha-Mazon* contains a petition; in *Didache* 10, the third strophe likewise consists of a petition: "Remember your Church, Lord, and free it from every evil and make it perfect in your love. And gather it from the four winds as a holy Church, in your kingdom which you have prepared for it. For yours is the kingdom and the glory for ever and ever" (10, 5).

The content of this text does not correspond to that of the third strophe of the *Birkat ha-Mazon:* the *Didache* speaks of the Church and the kingdom of God, while the *Birkat ha-Mazon* speaks of Israel, Jerusalem, the temple which is God's dwelling, the dynasty of David, and the rebuilding of Jerusalem. It is easy to say that there is a theological correspondence between the two texts, since the Church is the new Israel and therefore that the theology of the Church is heir to the theology of the first Israel. This may be true from a theological point

---

[44] Gal 4:6f. See also the development in Rom 8:15.

of view, but it does not relieve us from the obligation to look for a Jewish source that is close enough to explain *Didache* 10, 5. In addition to this methodological argument, I must point out that the passage in the *Didache* is based on the idea of a "gathering" of the Church in the kingdom of God, and this idea is not expressed at all in the texts of the *Birkat ha-Mazon*.[45]

From the connection between the earliest form of the *Amidah* and Sirach 36:11-14 (RSV numbering), it follows that this prayer was composed during the period between Sirach and the *Book of Jubilees*.[46] In Sirach 36:10-14, verse 10 speaks of the gathering of the tribes; v. 11 asks for mercy on the people of Israel, whom God calls his first-born; v. 12 asks for mercy on Jerusalem, the dwelling place of God, and v. 14 asks that the glory of God may once again fill his temple. The *Birkat ha-Mazon* contains the themes of vv. 12-14, while *Didache* 10, 5, has only the gathering theme of v. 11.

By way of conclusion, it must be said that *Didache* 10, 5, has moved away from the *Birkat ha-Mazon* and has drawn on other Jewish prayers, such as the tenth blessing of the *Amidah,* or on the *Ahabhah Rabbah,* the second of the blessings before the *Shema'*. We do not know whether at the time of the *Didache* these texts already had their long form; we do know, however, that the source of this long form of the sentence about gathering was Sirach 36:11, the passage which, in its immediately following verses, was the source of the third strophe of the *Birkat ha-Mazon*. Consequently, the petition in *Didache* 10, 5, does not go back to the *Birkat ha-Mazon*, but goes back (directly or by way of the other Jewish prayers mentioned) to Sirach 36:11ff. and takes its theme of gathering from there. Sirach 36:11ff. is also the source of the third strophe of the *Birkat ha-Mazon* for the themes other than that of gathering.

---

[45] Even J. W. Riggs, who goes very carefully into the sources of *Didache* 9–10, points to the third strophe of the *Birkat ha-Mazon* as the source of *Didache* 10, 5, whereas he had shortly before pointed to the *Amidah* as source of *Didache* 9, 4, because of the theme of gathering from the four winds. See J. W. Riggs, "From Gracious Table to Sacramental Elements. The Traditions-History of *Didache* 9 and 10," *The Second Century* 4 (1984) 92–93, 94, 97.

[46] L. Finkelstein, "The Development of the Amidah," *Jewish Quarterly Review,* N.S. 16 (1925–1926) 1–43, 137–70; idem, "The Birkat ha-Mazon," ibid., 19 (1928–1929) 220.

In Judaism the gathering of the scattered was already a typical theme in prayer of petition to God, because it was one intrinsically connected with the covenant that was the object of the blessing.[47]

The third strophe, then, of the Christian *Birkat ha-Mazon*, namely, *Didache* 10, asks for the gathering of the Church into the kingdom of God. This gathering is already a part of salvation, and for this reason the Church thus gathered is called holy. This is the end toward which this petition is moving from its opening words: "Remember your Church, Lord, and free it from every evil and make it perfect[48] in your love." The gathering into the kingdom of God is the response to this petition.

### 3. The Rite in 1 Corinthians 10:16-17

The eucharistic rite in the Church of Corinth was similar to those we have seen thus far. In his First Letter to the Corinthians Paul offers us two descriptions of the Eucharist. In the first (10:16-17) we have the eucharistic rite of the Church, while in the second (11:23-25) we have the rite of the supper eaten by Jesus in the upper room, that is, an account of the institution of the Eucharist. The differences between the two texts make clear how rapidly, and in what way, the liturgical tradition developed between the rite of the Last Supper and the rite in Paul's Church. The latter had a eucharistic rite made up of two parts: a) the rite of the cup, with its blessing; and b) the rite of the bread broken, with which the theme of unity was connected.

In the *Didache*, too, there is a close connection between the rite of the bread and the theme of unity. In both Paul and the *Didache,* this connection is expressed in an embolism that has a key word as its focus.[49] The Eucharist in Corinth corresponds to that in *Didache* 9: rite of the cup, rite of the bread, embolism on unity.[50] In 1 Cor 10:16-17,

---

[47] This perspective may also be seen in much later writers, such as Rav Saadja Gaon; see L. A. Hoffman, *The Canonisation of the Synagogue Service* (Studies in Judaism and Christianity in Antiquity 4; Notre Dame-London, 1979) 45.

[48] τελειῶσαι means a complete dedication to the ways of God. See A. Võõbus, *Liturgical Traditions in the Didache* (Papers of the Estonian Theological Society in Exile 15; Stockholm, 1968) 127.

[49] In *Didache* 9, 4, the key word is "this [= bread that is broken]," whereas in 1 Cor 10:17 it is "bread."

[50] Observe that 1 Cor 10:1-4 shows a knowledge of *Didache* 10:3. See my *L'anafora eucaristica,* chapter 3.

however, there is a difference in comparison with both Luke and the *Didache*, because the meal proper has been eliminated. If there was no meal there could be no thanksgiving after the meal. There is, however, a reference to the *Birkat ha-Mazon* at the point where the eucharistic cup is called "cup of blessing," a phrase that is appropriate for the cup over which the *Birkat ha-Mazon* was recited at the end of a meal.[51]

According to the *Didache* the one bread is a *model* of the Church's unity, but the model is only an image; according to Paul, however, the *model* belongs in the realm of sacramentality, so that those who share in the one bread are one body; thus the bread broken, insofar as it is one, becomes a *type* of the Church's unity. The sacramental conception of the Eucharist and its efficacy is already fully formulated in Paul.

There is an important difference between Paul's conception of the Eucharist and that of the *Didache*, not only because two different ideas of sacramental efficacy are at work but also because there are two different ecclesiologies. That is why in the *Didache* it is the Church that must be made one, while in Paul it is the assembly itself, which he also describes with a simple "we," the many (1 Cor 10:17).[52] If, through and because of the one bread, Christians are in communion with the person of Christ, which is evidently one, it follows that they are also one among themselves.

Such a shift in ecclesiology has a direct connection with the conception of eschatology, which as a result also changes: the focus changes from the last times as the fulfillment of the reign of God, to the Church in its historical form as this manifests itself in the assembly. The consequence of this is immediately clear: the fruit of the Eucharist will be not so much the eschatological unity of the Church in the kingdom of God, as it is in *Didache* 9–10, but each community's unity in history. Unity becomes not an eschatological gift awaited from God in the last times, but a historical commitment which each Church must carry out in order to be in harmony with the Eucharist which it celebrates or, in other and better terms, in

---

[51] In Paul this cup is the one that precedes the rite of the bread and therefore does not belong to the rite at the end of the meal.

[52] This echoes the words of institution of the eucharistic meal: "for you and for many."

order to correspond to the type handed on by Jesus at the Last Supper. In passing from the *Didache* to Paul, the theological theme of unity moves from the dimension of eschatological gift to the dimension of historical commitment; it does not, however, cease to be a divine gift, since its accomplishment comes not from the social and political activity of human beings but from the one bread of the eucharistic celebration.

*4. The Development of the Structure of the Eucharist*
The evolution just described brought to term the tendency already discernible in Luke's account: everything concerning the Eucharist and placed in the rite at the end of the Supper had to be shifted to the rite at the beginning of the meal. This tendency is found in all the texts thus far examined and can be better perceived from the following synoptic outline:

| Jewish Rite | Luke | *Didache* | 1 Cor 10:16-17 |
|---|---|---|---|
| *Before supper* | *Before supper* | *Before supper* | *Before supper* |
| Rite of cup with blessing | Rite of cup with thanksgiving | Rite of cup with thanksgiving | Rite of cup with blessing |
| Rite of bread with blessing | Rite of bread with thanksgiving | Rite of bread with thanksgiving. Embolism | Rite of bread (with blessing) Embolism |
| *After supper* | *After supper* | *After supper* | *After supper* |
| Rite of cup with thanksgiving | Rite of cup with thanksgiving | ——— | ——— |
| | | Thanksgiving | ——— |

The development of the eucharistic liturgy was guided by the clear intention of combining the rite of the cup, which is a communion[53] in the blood of Christ, with the rite of the bread, which is a communion in the body of Christ. Both rites were to be placed before the meal.

---

[53] Today, people would say "sacrament," but I prefer "communion" because it is the word used by Paul in 1 Cor 10:16 as a technical term for sacramentality.

This development becomes even clearer if we place the New Testament accounts of the Last Supper side by side:

| Luke (long text) | 1 Cor 11:23-25 | Mark-Matthew | Luke (short text) |
|---|---|---|---|
| *Before supper* | *Before supper* | *Before supper* | *Before supper* |
| Rite of cup with thanksgiving | | | |
| Rite of bread with thanksgiving | Rite of bread with thanksgiving | Rite of bread with blessing | Rite of bread with thanksgiving |
| | | Rite of cup with thanksgiving | Rite of cup (with thanksgiving) |
| *After supper* | *After supper* | | |
| Rite of cup (with thanksgiving) | Rite of cup with thanksgiving | | |

Due to the elimination of the meal, the rite of the cup is placed immediately after the rite of the bread. As a result of this juxtaposition, the sequence that would prevail and become normal was bread-cup and no longer cup-bread.[54] This juxtaposition of the two rites, which were no longer separated by the meal, would become a union, so that the two prayers of thanksgiving (one over the bread and one over the cup) were merged into a single text that would hold for both the bread and the wine, these being henceforth regarded *per modum unius,* or as a single whole.

It was in this way that the Eucharistic Prayer came into existence as a single text down to the present time.

---

[54] The sequence cup-bread in texts stemming from the *Didache* was very carefully corrected and changed, as can be seen in the case of the so-called "Mystical Eucharist" of the *Apostolic Constitutions* (see my *L'anafora eucaristica,* chapters 2 and 6).

## 5. Conclusion

In the New Testament tradition of the Last Supper, the points calling for major attention are two: a) the sequence of rites that make up the Last Supper; and b) the use of the terms "bless" (εὐλογεῖν) and "give thanks" (εὐχαριστεῖν).

a) In the Lukan and Pauline tradition, to which the *Didache* also belongs, the Last Supper is composed of three elements that are the direct model of the Church's eucharistic celebration: (1) the rite of the cup, which opens the meal and is accompanied by its blessing; (2) the rite of the bread that is broken, which is accompanied by its usual blessing; in the *Didache* and Paul there is also an embolism in the form of a prayer for the assembly and for the unity of the Church; (3) after the Supper, there is the customary recitation of the *Birkat ha-Mazon*, which normally accompanies the last cup.

b) In Mark and Matthew, in accordance with Jewish custom, the prayer over the bread is a "blessing" (εὐλογία) and the prayer over the cup is a "thanksgiving" (εὐχαριστία), while in Luke, the *Didache*, and Paul (1 Cor 11:23-26), the prayer over the bread, like that over the cup, is a "thanksgiving" (εὐχαριστία). This difference between the two traditions is explained by the tendency, proper to the Antiochene tradition, to transfer all the elements found at the end of the Supper and incorporate them into the rite that begins it. For this reason Luke describes as a "thanksgiving," and not a "blessing," both the prayer accompanying the first cup (22:17) at the beginning of the meal and the prayer accompanying the bread (which also comes before the meal proper). On the other hand, when he comes to the cup that concludes the Supper and ought to be accompanied by its own "thanksgiving," he does not go into detail but is content with a very generic description, "in the same way" (ὡσαύτως).

In Paul, too, there is a shifting of the material in the direction of the rite that begins the Supper; in fact, both the Supper and, consequently, the rite after the Supper have completely disappeared. The cup, which the explanatory words identify as the blood of Christ, has been shifted from after the Supper to its beginning and is in the position occupied by the first cup that begins the introductory rite (*Qiddush*), becoming identical with this and replacing it. The *Birkat ha-Mazon* has undergone an analogous displacement, moving from after the Supper to its beginning and thereby replacing the short blessing over the cup that would have occurred at this point in the rite. As a result, the cup that begins the rite is described as "a communion in the blood of Christ" and is called "the cup of blessing" (1 Cor 10:16) — two descriptions that, as such, were proper to the cup that ended the meal, along with the *Birkat ha-Mazon*.

The same tendency is already evident in *Didache* 10. The cup that should have accompanied this Christian *Birkat ha-Mazon* has already disappeared and been identified with the cup that begins the meal rite in *Didache* 9. Here another change can be seen: the third strophe of *Didache* 10, a prayer of petition for the assembly of the Church, is duplicated and, in a slightly shorter form, becomes part of *Didache* 9. As a result, *Didache* 9 acquires a tripartite structure: (1) thanksgiving over the cup, (2) thanksgiving over the bread, (3) prayer for the assembly and for unity. This tripartite structure will remain a distinctive trait of the earliest anaphoras.

PRIMITIVE ANAPHORAS:
FROM THE *DIDACHE* TO THE MYSTICAL EUCHARIST
The Last Supper as reported by Luke is very closely connected with the Jewish rite for a festive meal. Starting with this basic relationship, I have tried to show the origin of the other descriptions of the Last Supper, which show a different structure from that of Luke. The same explanation applies to some other eucharistic celebrations such as the Eucharist of the Antiochene tradition that is attested in *Didache* 9–10, from which was derived the Eucharist of the Pauline community as described in 1 Cor 10:16-17.

Our task now is to see what subsequent developments took place, the starting point of which was the well documented Antiochene nucleus of which I spoke above. The first development is represented by the eucharistic liturgy [55] in Book VII of the *Apostolic Constitutions,* a work composed in Antioch in 380, using previous materials. This celebration depends directly on *Didache* 9–10, by way of an intermediate redaction that has not come down to us. When we set the two texts side by side, we immediately become aware of the great fidelity with which the Mystical Eucharist follows *Didache* 9–10: *Apostolic Constitutions* VII, 25, depends on *Didache* 9, while VII, 26, depends on *Didache* 10.

[55] For convenience, this liturgy is called the "Mystical Eucharist" ("sacramental thanksgiving") in accordance with the title given it in the manuscript tradition. The title is, in fact, a later addition and does not belong in the original redaction of the text.

The paralleling of the texts also shows the changes that were introduced having to do with both the structure and the text. In the celebration of the Eucharist in the *Didache,* the main element consists in the rite of Chapter 10, that is, in the Christianized *Birkat ha-Mazon* that is recited after the meal. The first change is the elimination of the meal that intervened between the rite in *Didache* 9 and that of *Didache* 10. As a result, the text of *Apostolic Constitutions* VII, 26, ceases to be a Christianized *Birkat ha-Mazon*[56] and becomes the thanksgiving after Communion.[57]

This change marks the end of the journey by which the rites at the end of the Supper were transferred to a different position, at the beginning of the meal, and were joined to the rites which opened the meal and with which they were henceforth identified.[58] As a matter of fact, the principal text in the *Apostolic Constitutions* is not VII, 26, but VII, 25, which derives from *Didache* 9, that is, from the rite preceding the ritual meal.

In the Mystical Eucharist this text has already become a Eucharistic Prayer, more or less as we understand the term today, although it has such markedly archaic traits and shows such obvious traces of the liturgy from which it derives and which still link it quite closely to Judaism, that I hesitate to describe the text as an anaphora; for this reason it may be called a "paleoanaphora" or "primitive anaphora."[59]

---

[56] The relationship of the text to the *Birkat ha-Mazon* is unrecognizable, although its origin can be traced to *Didache* 10, which derives directly from that Jewish prayer.

[57] This fact makes understandable the importance of the thanksgiving after Communion, which has its remote origin in the Last Supper and is therefore not to be understood as a devotional text, comparable to the thanksgiving after Communion as found in medieval devotionalism.

[58] Thus ends the shift from the Jewish rites after the meal to those for the beginning of the meal. This was truly a radical change of position, since in the beginning the rites for the end of the meal were more important than those for the meal's start. At the end of the development, however, the rites for the beginning of the meal clearly had the upper hand. The prayer that came into being as heir of the *Birkat ha-Mazon* henceforth lost its importance, since it was now simply a thanksgiving after Communion. The result was the severing of the link between the *Birkat ha-Mazon* and the developing Christian Eucharist.

[59] I give this name to all those texts that occupy an intermediate position between the Jewish liturgy and the later anaphoras, which were now structured in a clearly theological way, and which clearly distinguish the great liturgical families

Because of these changes that move the rites of the end of the meal into those of its beginning, the most important prayer is no longer the thanksgiving at the end of the meal (the *Birkat ha-Mazon*), but the prayer that precedes it and has its origin in practices that gradually gave rise to the Jewish rite of the *Qiddush*.

The shift I have been describing has further complicated the problem of the structure of these prayers of thanksgiving. In fact, the problem is created by the coming together and superposition of two very similar types of texts, inasmuch as both series have a tripartite structure. The first type depends on the *Birkat ha-Mazon*, and its three strophes are the classical strophes of the Christian *Birkat ha-Mazon*; the second type depends on rites which preceded the meal and which, once Christianized (as in *Didache* 9), are likewise tripartite.

The likeness should not deceive us, since the two series of texts differ from each other both in their origin and in their function. On the one hand, there are the three strophes of the *Birkat ha-Mazon*[60] and, on the other, the three of the rite that began the meal.[61] However, when the two tripartite structures are superimposed, it is no longer possible to decide whether a paleoanaphora or anaphora having a tripartite structure originated in the rites following the meal or in the rites preceding it.

After reproducing *Didache* 9,[62] the compiler of the Mystical Eucharist adds a lengthy narrative development[63] that is something more than simply a personal insertion of the compiler; it is to be seen as a confession of faith in the true and proper sense (although limited to the area of christology), one which previously had a life of its own

---

and have come down to our time almost unchanged. The paleoanaphoral texts go back to the end of the second century and the beginning of the third, while the major anaphoras had their golden age from the middle of the fourth century on.

[60] (1) Opening thanksgiving for the works God has done and for the gift of food, (2) thanksgiving for the present moment, (3) petition. For this structure see the *Birkat ha-Mazon* in the *Book of Jubilees* 22, 6–8 (Charlesworth 2, 97).

[61] (1) Thanksgiving over the cup, (2) thanksgiving over the bread, (3) petition.

[62] "We give you thanks, our Father, for the life which you have made known to us through Jesus your servant *(pais)*."

[63] "Through whom you have made all things and provide for all things and whom you have sent to become a human being for our salvation, and whom you permitted to suffer and die, and whom you raised up, willed to glorify, and made to sit at your right hand, and through whom you have promised us the resurrection from the dead" (VII, 25, 2–3; SCh 336:52f.).

and which the compiler introduces at this point and links to the rest of the text by means of one of his preferential themes: Christ as mediator. He has simply inserted at this point in the thanksgiving some elements from the profession of faith of his Church, which we can find already cited in Book VI of the *Apostolic Constitutions*.[64]

Another change can be found in the second strophe of the thanksgiving. This strophe, which is derived from *Didache* 9, 2, and specifically from the thanksgiving over the cup, is changed by the compiler into a thanksgiving for the precious blood and the precious body, at the end of which comes the account of institution.[65] Note, furthermore, that in this paleoanaphora the awareness of the sacramentality of the Eucharist is fully developed, to the point that it is explicitly formulated and brought into the text by use of the technical expression "antitype," which, however, cannot be translated simply as "sacrament" because its meaning is more complex. It will be worth our while if I explain briefly the use of this term.

We have seen how the eucharistic celebration came into being: at the Last Supper Jesus *handed on the mysteries*, since by the words "Do this in remembrance of me," he passed on the model, the *type*, of the Church's Eucharist. The latter is therefore an act of obedience to Christ's command and an imitation of the type. It follows that the nature of the Eucharist must be defined in relationship to its type and that the term "antitype" is therefore especially suited to expressing this conception of the Eucharist. In Paul, in the Pastoral Letters, and in the Letter of Peter, the word "type" occurs six times with the meaning of a model that shapes the obedience of faith.[66]

"Antitype" is not found in Philo and is attested for the first time in the Letter to the Hebrews (9:24). The term was coined precisely as part of the language of worship: on the basis of Exod 25:40, Hebrews 8:5 conceives of earthly worship as a "copy" of a heavenly "model"; this earthly "copy" is called an "antitype" (Heb 9:5) in relation to the celestial prototype which is described as "the true reality."

During the patristic period, a horizontal typology appears alongside the vertical typology: the actions by which Christ *hands on the mysteries* are called the type, while the rite of the Church, *corresponding* as it does

---

[64] *Constitutiones Apostolicae* VI, 11, 1–10 ; VII, 41, 3–8.
[65] Ibid., VII, 25, 4.
[66] L. Goppelt, "Typos," *TDNT* 8:250.

to that type, is called an antitype. The relationship between type and antitype was rethought by the Fathers with the help of Platonic categories.[67] The antitype is regarded as participating ontologically in the type; the result is that the type cannot be thought of as remaining external to the antitype, as though the former were a purely external ritual model. Inasmuch as the type is a model that distinguishes, defines, and shapes, it lives on and is present within, and pervades, the antitype. What is true of the type is also true of the antitype, even if only by participation; consequently, there is a real identity of type and antitype.

That is how the Pauline definition of the Eucharist as *the Lord's Supper* (1 Cor 11:20) must be understood; the words by themselves designate the Last Supper, while for Paul they must also designate every correct eucharistic liturgy, that is, every Eucharist that corresponds to its model.

DEVELOPMENTS OF THE EUCHARISTIC LITURGY
The texts I have just examined represent a kind of initial nucleus out of which the later anaphoras developed. All of the latter display some kind of relationship — some texts more, others less — with the texts I have been considering; the relationships pertain both to the structure and to the thematic contents. Let us now look at the main families of anaphoras.

*1. The Alexandrian Liturgy*
From the Church of Alexandria comes a very interesting paleo-anaphora that attests to the archaic character of the Egyptian Eucharist; it is the paleoanaphora in Strasbourg Papyrus Gr. 254. This text is important not only because of the archaic character of its structure and because it is the earliest testimony to the Eucharist of this Church, but above all because it enables us to understand the development of the three paleoanaphoral strophes that gave rise to later texts with their more complex theological structure.

The first strophe of the Alexandrian paleoanaphora gives thanks for creation, singling out the light[68] and leaving aside the theme of

[67] For further information on the typological conception of worship, see my "L'interpretazione del culto nella chiesa antica."
[68] The theme is supported by two citations from the Bible: "I am the Lord, and there is no other. I form light and create darkness, I make weal and create woe; I the Lord do all these things" (Isa 45:6-7). "O Lord, how manifest are your works!

redemption. At the close of the strophe, the theme of light is developed along messianic lines, with thanksgiving for Christ, who is the true light of God.

This strophe is linked to the Jewish liturgy of morning prayer and in particular with the *Yotser*, the first of the three blessings of the *Shema'*.

a) In this prayer,[69] on the basis of a citation from Ps 103:24,[70] God is praised for the work of creation; the prayer then turns to a contemplation of the light, with support from a citation of Isa 45:7. In the Jewish tradition this theme of light was interpreted along messianic lines, a development attested in the Academies both of Sura and of Pumbedita. The interpretation was thus widespread until Rav Saadja Gaon (928–942 A.D.) censured the messianic interpretation of the light in the *Yotser*, claiming that the light in question is simply the natural light of creation when the sun rises in the morning.[71] This is a specifically sapiential theme.

b) The first strophe of the Alexandrian paleoanaphora[72] has for its subject the work of creation,[73] which was accomplished through Christ; on the basis of the passage in Ps 103:24, Christ is identified with the divine Wisdom that presided over the work of creation. Furthermore, at the end of the strophe Jesus is given the titles "true light" and "Savior."

---

In wisdom you have made them all; the earth is full of your creatures. Yonder is the sea, great and wide, creeping things innumerable are there, living things both small and great" (Ps 103[104]:24-25.

[69] The *Yotser* praises God who creates the light and the entire universe (Isa 45:7) in wisdom (Ps 103:24); see the text in Hänggi-Pahl, 36–8.

[70] "O Lord, how manifold are your works! In wisdom have you made them all; the earth is full of your creatures."

[71] L. A. Hoffman, *The Canonisation of the Synagogue Service* (Studies in Judaism and Christianity in Antiquity 4; Notre Dame, 1979) 25ff. For the entire question see my *L'anaphora eucaristica*, 213ff.

[72] Here is the text of the first strophe of thanksgiving: "To praise, night and day . . . you who made the heaven and all that is in it; you who made man according to your image and likeness, and in your wisdom created all things in your true light, your Son, the Lord, our Savior Jesus Christ" (Hänggi-Pahl, 116–7).

[73] The text is based on Neh 9:6: "You are the Lord, you alone; you have made heaven, the heaven of heavens, with all their host, the earth and all that is on it, the seas and all that are in them. To all of them you give life, and the host of heaven worships you." Later developments of this anaphora will continue to draw on this prayer in the book of Nehemiah.

c) In conclusion, when we compare the Alexandrian paleoanaphora with the *Yotser,* we may say that there is a correspondence between the two texts, even though they differ in literary formulation and in breadth. The strophe and the *Yotser* are in fact identical in content, namely, (i) in the themes of thanksgiving (for creation and light); (ii) in the two controlling biblical citations; (iii) in the messianic interpretation of the theme of light; and (iv) in the sapiential perspective.

This comparison of the two texts enables us to conclude, then, that there is link between the Jewish blessing in the *Yotser* and the Alexandrian Eucharist. Once this fact is established, we need to ask how this influence was possible, since the Christian Eucharist was connected with the celebration of the Jewish ritual meal and not with Jewish morning prayer. We may hypothesize that the Jewish liturgy of the monastic community of the Therapeutae,[74] which is at the origin of Alexandrian Christianity, was the cradle of the Alexandrian Eucharist. I must refer, even if only in summary fashion, to two rites of this community: the ritual meal and morning prayer.

The meal[75] of the Therapeutae ended without the recitation of the *Birkat ha-Mazon,* the Jewish prayer after meals, because it concluded with the singing of a hymn that in turn began a vigil which finished at dawn the next day when the monks recited morning prayer. Here is how this morning liturgy is described in Philo's *The Contemplative Life:* "They stand with their faces and whole body turned to the

---

[74] J. Riaud, "Les Thérapeutes d'Alexandrie dans la tradition et dans la recherche jusqu'aux découvertes de Qumran," in *Aufstieg und Niedergang der Römische Welt,* Part II: *Principat,* vol. 20/2: *Religion (Hellenistisches Judentum in römischer Zeit, ausgenommen Philon und Josephus)* (Berlin-New York, 1987) 1189–1295; idem, "Thérapeutes," *DSp* 15, cols. 562–70; V. Nikiprowetzky, "Les Suppliants chez Philon d'Alexandrie," *Revue des études juives* 122 (1963) 241–78.

[75] The meal began with a commentary on a passage of the Bible, which was interpreted according to the allegorical method; those present listened with interest and involvement. After the homily, the speaker "rises and sings a hymn composed in honor of the Deity, either a new one of his own composition, or an old one by poets of an earlier age." After him, the others also sing in their proper order; finally the meal begins (*De vita contemplativa,* 75–81; ET: Philo of Alexandria, *The Contemplative Life, The Giants, and Selections,* trans. D. Winston [The Classics of Western Spirituality; New York, 1981] 54–6; citation from 55). The prayer before the meal asks that God may find the meal pleasing to him and that it be according to his will. See also Philo, *De plantatione,* 161–62.

east, and when they behold the rising sun, with hands stretched heavenward they pray for a joyous day, truth, and acuity of thought."[76] Both the meal and the morning and evening prayers were linked to the sacrifices that were offered, morning and evening, in the Jerusalem temple; the typological method ensured that the prayers of the Therapeutae were a participation in the nature of the temple sacrifices.[77] For the Therapeutae, then, their morning prayers *corresponded ontologically* to the sacrifices in the temple. In order to understand this point fully, we must bear in mind that in Israel the morning and evening sacrifices were a perpetual sacrifice or, in other words, worship par excellence. In fact, according to the *Midrash*, the sacrifice of Isaac was the origin of the later institution of perpetual sacrifice that was offered morning and evening in the temple, and every time this perpetual sacrifice was offered, God remembered the sacrifice of Isaac.[78]

This explains why, in the eyes of the Therapeutae, morning prayers were a primary element in their system of worship. In fact, since these prayers corresponded typologically to the perpetual sacrifice, they did, in fact, for all intents and purposes, have a sacrificial character, since *typological correspondence* implied *ontological correspondence*.

As a matter of fact, the life of Christian monks in the Scete desert displayed many elements quite similar to those found in Philo's description of the Therapeutae.[79] For our argument here it is important to emphasize one particular usage of the monks of the Scete desert: as late as the fourth century they were accustomed to celebrate a vigil, on Saturday evening, which lasted through the night and ended on the following morning at the time of morning prayer. As a

---

[76] *De vita contemplativa*, 89 (ET: 57).

[77] Those who presided at the meal were called *ephemereuti*, a term signifying not merely presidency but also the priestly office of those who are ministering that day (Riaud, "Thérapeutes," *DSp* 15:567). Many elements in the meal could be paralleled in the temple ceremony. The very name "Therapeutae" had a priestly meaning and was connected with the sacrificial role of the priest (Nikoprowetzky, "Les Suppliants," 256).

[78] K. Hruby, "La fête de Rosh ha-Shanah," in *Mémorial Mgr. Gabriel Khouri-Sarkis (1898–1968)* (Louvain, 1969) 62 (= *OS* 13 [1968] 47–71.)

[79] A. Guillaumont, "Philon et les origines du monachisme," in *Philon d'Alexandrie* (Colloque de Lyon, 11–5 septembre 1966; Paris, 1967) 361–73.

conclusion of the vigil the Sunday Eucharist was celebrated, this at the time of morning prayer.[80]

On Sunday morning, then, the eucharistic rite took place at the time of morning prayer, and we know that, in the thinking of the Therapeutae, morning prayer was the principal prayer of the day and was regarded as worship and a sacrifice. I maintain that for that reason the Alexandrian Eucharist was adapted to that particular hour and took over certain themes and characteristics proper to morning prayer in the Jewish tradition, as I have described it. The themes of light, creation, and the Messiah, as well as the cultic and sacrificial character of morning prayer, passed from the *Yotser* into the prayers of the Christian Eucharist.

The second strophe of the Alexandrian Eucharist likewise has links with Judaism and contains the following elements: (a) the sacrificial character of the prayer of thanksgiving; (b) the cultic character of the eucharistic celebration; (c) the use of Malachi 1:11 as an account of the institution of the sacrifice and worship that are brought to fulfillment in the Eucharist.[81]

In the Alexandrian paleoanaphora the citation from Mal 1:11 serves as an account of institution: this is possible precisely because the Eucharist is conceived as being a sacrifice.

Mal 1:11 foretells that in the last times all human beings will celebrate a perfect sacrifice that is accepted by God: "For from the rising of the sun to its setting my name is great among the nations, and in every place incense is offered to my name, and a pure offering; for my name is great among the nations, says the Lord of hosts." On the basis of this formulation of the account of institution the Eucharist becomes the fulfillment of Old Testament prophecy, that is, it is the perfect sacrifice.[82]

---

[80] See W. Hauser (general ed.), *The Monasteries of the Wadi 'n Natrûn*, Part II: H. G. E. White, *The History of the Monasteries of Nitria and Scetis* (Metropolitan Museum of Art, Egyptian Expedition; New York, 1932) 207–12. For a picture of the eucharistic celebration in Egypt see U. Zanetti, *Les lectionnaires coptes annuels: Basse-Egypte* (Publications de l'Institut Orientaliste de Louvain 3; Louvain-la-Neuve, 1985) 14–21, 133–39, 157–61, 166–75.

[81] As conceived according to the Alexandrian anaphora, the eucharistic celebration is worship paid to God, but this cultic character comes solely from the sacrificial character of the prayer of thanksgiving, which was the original nucleus.

[82] It should not surprise us that the account of institution should take the form of a citation from the Old Testament instead of the account of the Last Supper. We

The entire procedure which I have been describing is based on the typological method, and it was thanks to this method that the Alexandrian Church was able to think of the Eucharist as a *perfect sacrifice* and, therefore, as a *cultic actualization* of the ancient economy.

In order to appreciate the importance of the passage in Mal 1:11, we should bear in mind that the text is also echoed in the Letter to the Hebrews: "Through him, then, let us continually *offer* up a *sacrifice of praise* to God, that is, the fruit of lips that *acknowledge his name*" (13:15). In addition, Malachi 1:11 is the key text in the eucharistic theology of the first three centuries.

The third strophe, or petition, of the Alexandrian paleoanaphora is already rather developed in Strasbourg Papyrus Gr. 254 and will be developed still more extensively in later texts. The fundamental theme is *unity*, and it is a theme shared by all the texts that had their origin in the *Didache;* it is difficult, however, to say whether there is a connection between the latter and Strasbourg Papyrus Gr. 254. The theme had already undergone an interesting development that shows up also in the Roman Canon: it generated the theme of peace, in which God is asked to grant the gift of peace to the Church. The development was due to the special fortunes of the Church of Alexandria, which underwent a violent persecution, a persecution so important in its life that dates were given in years from the great persecution.

After the themes of unity and peace come the intercessions for the various orders making up the Church: the bishop with the entire clergy and various ministers, the king, the living and the dead. The intercession for the living is especially interesting because it immediately becomes an intercession for the offerers and is then transformed into a *commendatio sacrificii*, that is, God is asked to accept the offering of the faithful and find it pleasing.[83] This is a theme characteristic of

---

should bear in mind that the eucharistic use of this text (Mal 1:11) goes back to the *Didache* 14, and that at so early a time the Old Testament was still the scriptures from which citations were to be taken. Therefore the account of institution, which by definition is a citation from the Bible, had to come from the Old Testament. The use of Mal 1:11 to describe the Eucharist was characteristic of the Church from its beginnings to the first quarter of the third century, or from the *Didache* to Irenaeus, Justin, Tertullian, and Origen.

[83] Unfortunately, the text of the Strasbourg Papyrus was heavily damaged, so that only the beginning and end of the third strophe are legible. The entire part which I have called the *commendatio sacrificii* is lacking, as is the mention of the

sacrificial worship, but completely absent from the Jewish ritual meal; the blessings proper to the liturgy of a meal know nothing of any prayer for offering something to God or of any prayer that he would find the offering pleasing and acceptable.

There is, however, one interesting exception, and it occurs among the Therapeutae, who ask God that the meal may be pleasing to him and in accordance with his will.[84] In addition, in the prayer for the acceptance of the sacrifice, the Alexandrian anaphora speaks of how God was pleased with, and accepted, the sacrifices of Abel and Abraham, which are therefore viewed as the model of authentic worship that is acceptable to God. This view is also characteristic of the Therapeutae, who regarded Abel, Abraham, Henoch, and Moses as the true Therapeutae, that is, worshipers of God, the greatest of them having been Abraham. Thus the third strophe of the Alexandrian paleoanaphora likewise shows a precise and specific connection with Jewish liturgical practices.

In conclusion: none of these similarities between the Alexandrian liturgy and the Jewish liturgy is probative when taken by itself, but when all are taken together, they cannot be ignored. This is especially true since the elements of the Alexandrian paleoanaphora are not related to the elements in any of the other families of anaphoras.

The Alexandrian liturgy is very important in the history of the anaphora, because, as we shall see, it has links with the structure both of Antiochene anaphora and of the Roman Canon, which was the special text of the Roman Church from the patristic age down to the liturgical reform of the Second Vatican Council.

## 2. The Antiochene Anaphora and Its Structure

### A. DESCRIPTION OF THE ORIGIN OF THE STRUCTURE (ANAPHORA OF HIPPOLYTUS)

The Antiochene anaphora is the one best known because of its structure, and also because the recent liturgical reform in the Roman

---

heavenly altar, which is an integral part of it. As a result, we cannot be sure whether this section was part of the Alexandrian anaphora at the time of the Strasbourg Papyrus or was added later. However, because of the large space occupied by the now lost text and because of a few words that are still partially legible, we may think that the *commendatio sacrificii* and the mention of the heavenly altar were already present in the Alexandrian anaphora.

[84] *De vita contemplativa*, 66 (ET: 52–53). See also *De plantatione*, 161–62.

Church chose the structures of the Antiochene texts as a source of new anaphoras. When I say "Antiochene texts," I am referring, for example, to the anaphora in the document known as the *Apostolic Tradition* of Hippolytus, the Anaphora of Basil in its two redactions (the Alexandrian and the Byzantine), and the Anaphora of James the Brother of the Lord. These anaphoras are valuable for the harmony and unity of their content, which is developed in a homogeneous way, often on a trinitarian pattern, from the beginning of the thanksgiving to the final doxology.

The Antiochene structure has the following structure: (1) thanksgiving, (2) *Sanctus,* (3) *Post Sanctus,* (4) account of institution, (5) anamnesis, (6) offering, (7) epiclesis, (8) intercessions, (9) doxology, (10) Amen of the people.

This structure is obviously quite different from that of paleoanaphoras, which, as we have seen, were divided into three strophes. The question arises whether it is still possible to see this archaic tripartite structure in the Antiochene texts. The answer requires that we first investigate two other matters: (1) the entry into the anaphora of the account of the Last Supper; and (2) the origin of the anamnesis-offering block, which is characterized by the paired words *mindful-we offer.*

1) The Eucharistic Prayer of the *Apostolic Tradition,* which is attributed to Hippolytus,[85] shows how the account of institution found a place in the anaphora. The thanksgiving of this text came into being when expressions and themes characteristic of the Passover celebration[86] became part of a paleoanaphora. It was for this reason that in the text of Hippolytus the preface acquired, for the first time, a narrative character: the development of the history of salvation is described, in a Christocentric fashion, from creation to the passion,

---

[85] This text has three parts: two thanksgivings and a petition. This particular structure can be related to the development of the Christian *Birkat ha-Mazon.* The second thanksgiving has links to some texts belonging within the development of the *Birkat ha-Mazon;* this is true also of the epiclesis, which all the commentators evidently find to be a difficult and troublesome text. I offer the hypothesis that the difficulties in the epiclesis are due to the different strata that make it up. As for the development of the anaphora, I think that the theme of gathering and unity (in the epiclesis) signal a more or less direct connection with texts originating in the Christian *Birkat ha-Mazon.*

[86] See my *L'anafora eucaristica,* ch. 4, 111–94.

resurrection, and descent of Jesus into the world of the dead. In telling the history of salvation, the thanksgiving section of this anaphora draws its material from texts or, better, from the literary genre of Paschal Homilies; the anaphora here consists of a selection, as it were, of the key phrases used in the Paschal Homilies to describe salvation in its historical development.

Because of this connection with the paschal texts great emphasis is laid on the death of Christ, to which redemption is attributed, consistently with the concept of "pasch" as passion or suffering. Because of this close connection with paschal themes[87] that were still alive and seemed suitable for giving privileged expression to the faith of the Church, I think it possible to say that the second half of the second century was the most likely period for the composition of the first part of the anaphora of Hippolytus.[88] The account of the Last Supper entered the Eucharistic Prayer, which in this case was the anaphora of Hippolytus, along with the narrative material from the paschal liturgy. In Hippolytus, the *account of institution* is part of the preface and is the culminating point, the key point, in the narrative of salvation, that is, in the thanksgiving.[89]

The significance of this fact, namely, the introduction of the account of the Last Supper at the end of the first strophe of the thanksgiving, is very clear: the Eucharist was instituted in order to give believers the fullness of that entire course of Old Testament history that was fulfilled in Christ and in his Passover, which was, typologically, the fulfillment of the ancient Passover. Without the Eucharist there would be no access to the fulfillment of the ancient Passover.

---

[87] I am referring to the themes of pasch = suffering.

[88] At this point it will be helpful to recall a notice in the *Liber Pontificalis* that attributes to Alexander I (105?–115?) the introduction of the *Passio Domini* into the *Praedicatio sacerdotum*, a phrase signifying the Canon of the Mass; see L. Duchesne (ed.), *Le Liber Pontificalis* I (Bibliothèque des écoles françaises d'Athènes et de Rome; Paris, 1981) 217. The notice in the *Liber Pontificalis* may be accurate, but the attribution to Alexander I is really difficult; the notice becomes more credible if placed after the pontificate of Anicetus (155?–166?).

[89] In conclusion, we must acknowledge that with the anaphora of Hippolytus the evolution of the text is complete; add a few details, and we have our modern texts. In Hippolytus the thanksgiving becomes a narrative and has for its subject the history of salvation with all its stages, culminating in the death of Christ, his resurrection, and his descent among the dead.

Thanks is also given for the Last Supper because it was through it that the prefigurations reached their fulfillment for us.[90]

After showing, on the basis of the texts and a careful synoptic comparison of the anaphora of Hippolytus with the Paschal Homilies, how and why the account of the Last Supper became part of the anaphora. I must still determine whether all this has any connection with the Alexandrian paleoanaphora. As a matter of fact, the insertion of the account could not have been made directly into the anaphora of Hippolytus, because the latter can be read as having two different and irreconcilable structures.[91]

Given the first structure, the text is in the line of development of the Christian *Birkat ha-Mazon*. There is a first strophe of thanksgiving, which runs from the initial thanksgiving to the end of the offering; this is followed by a second that gives thanks for the present moment[92] and has parallels both in the second thanksgiving of the *Birkat ha-Mazon* in the *Book of Jubilees* (ca. A.D. 100) and in the second thanksgiving of the prayer in the *Martyrdom of Polycarp*.[93] The other structure has ties with the Alexandrian anaphora: the first strophe runs to the end of the account of institution, and the second consists of the anamnesis-offering.

2) The anamnesis-offering section of the Antiochene anaphora has its remote explanation in the Alexandrian paleoanaphora and has this, more specifically, at the beginning of the second strophe: "Giving thanks, we offer (εὐχαριστοῦντες προσφέρομεν) the spiritual sacrifice, this bloodless worship."[94] The received text of the Anaphora of St. Mark develops the text by eliminating the word "sacrifice" and connecting "spiritual" with "worship": "Giving thanks, we offer (εὐχαριστοῦντες προσφέρομεν) this spiritual and bloodless worship."[95] The same sentence occurs in the Greek Anaphora of St. John Chrysostom[96]: here the present participle μεμνήμενοι, which is the subject of the verb

[90] See the *Homily of Pseudo-Hippolytus*, no. 92.

[91] This is another reason why the text of this anaphora is so complex and difficult.

[92] "Thanking you for considering us worthy to stand before you and minister to you."

[93] See my *L'anafora eucaristica*, 170–7.

[94] "Εὐχαριστοῦντες προσφέρομεν τὴν θυσίαν τὴν λογικήν, ἀναίμακτον λατρείάν ταύτην" (Strasbourg Papyrus Gr, 254; Hänggi-Pahl, 102).

[95] "Εὐχαριστοῦντες προσφέρομεν τὴν λογικὴν καὶ ἀναίμακτον λατρείαν ταύτην" (Hänggi-Pahl, 102).

[96] Ibid., 226.

προσφέρομεν, has for its object τὰ σὰ ἐκ τῶν σῶν ("what is yours from what is yours"). Immediately afterwards the theme is repeated in this form: "We offer you this spiritual and bloodless worship."[97] This part of the Antiochene anaphora is similar to the Roman Canon: *Unde et memores . . . offerimus de tuis donis ac datis, hostiam puram, hostiam sanctam, hostiam immaculatam* ("Mindful, therefore . . . we offer you, from among the gifts you have given us, a pure victim, a holy victim, a spotless victim").[98]

All these texts display a surprising sameness that transcends the traditional subdivision into liturgical families. I think that the Rev. Dr. Geoffrey J. Cuming likewise saw a certain connection between these texts, since he says: "At a minimum, the words *memores . . . offerimus* recall the εὐχαριστοῦντες προσφέρομεν of the Anaphora of St. Mark."[99]

The verbs, which in participial form are the subjects of the verb "offer," may differ, but this is the only difference[100] within a substantial identity of sentences: in the one case, the participle is εὐχαριστοῦντες, in the other, μεμνήμενοι, which corresponds to the *memores* of the Roman Canon. It is possible, however, to explain this difference and thus to provide confirmation that the texts cited belong to a single homogeneous block because they have a single origin.

In the Alexandrian paleoanaphora the present participle εὐχαριστοῦντες comes at the beginning of the second strophe[101] and has for its function to describe the cultic value of the immediately preceding

[97] "Τὴν λογικὴν ταύτην καὶ ἀναίμακτον λατρείαν." This phrase occurs at the beginning of the epiclesis and is repeated immediately afterward, at the beginning of the intercessions, but without the word ἀναίμακτον. On the sacrificial character of the beginning of the intercessions see E. Lanne, "L'intercession pour l'Eglise dans la Prière Eucharistique," in *L'Eglise dans la liturgie* (Rome, 1980) 183–208.

[98] *Canon missae romanae*. Pars prior: *Traditio textus*, ed. L. Eizenhöfer (Collectanea Anselmiana. Rerum ecclesiasticarum documenta. Series minor. Subsidia studiorum 1; Rome, 1954) 34.

[99] G. J. Cuming, "The Shape of the Anaphora," *Studia patristica XX* (Kalamazoo-Louvain, 1989) 333–45.

[100] The difference is in fact only an apparent one, as we shall see when I explain the origin.

[101] The second strophe of the Alexandrian paleoanaphora expresses a theology of worship: the action just completed is a sacrifice (θυσία) and an act of worship (λατρεία).

action, that is, the action performed in the first strophe: the giving of thanks.

If this present participle is connected with the action just performed and is meant to express the content of the immediately preceding text, then, understandably, it must change, depending on the action expressed in the immediately preceding strophe. Therefore, when there is question of a strophe of thanksgiving, we will have εὐχαριστοῦντες; where there is question of remembering the "command" of Christ ("do this in remembrance of me"), we will have μεμνήμενοι in Greek texts and *memores* in the Roman Canon. But this is not the whole picture, since in the non-Roman western rites there are other kinds of anamnesis that focus not on "memory" (as contained in Christ's command) but on the word "do" or, more accurately, on the idea underlying this word, namely, obedience to the command of Christ. Here are some examples: "Haec facimus, haec celebramus tua, Domine, praecepta *servantes*" ("This we do, this we celebrate, Lord, as we *keep* your command").[102] There is a comparable text in the *Missale Gothicum:* "Haec igitur praecepta *servantes* sacrosancta munera nostrae salutis offerimus" ("*Keeping* this command, we offer the holy gifts of our salvation").[103]

In the light of these examples, we understand why when the Alexandrian liturgy took over from Antioch the second part of the anaphora[104] containing the anamnetic formula, it began it with the present participle καταγγέλλοντες (*proclaiming* the death, we offer) because of the particular Alexandrian formulation of the "command," which was modelled on 1 Cor 11:26: "Whenever you eat of this bread and drink of this cup, you *proclaim* the *death* of the Lord until he comes."

In conclusion, I may say that the present participle of which I have been speaking has its referent in the immediately preceding text, and that this reference is primarily of the literary order, since the present participle, which is the subject of "offer," simply cites the action described in the immediately preceding sentence.

We have here a fact that is very important for explaining the genesis of the anamnesis: the term "mindful" (or: "remembering") is a lit-

---

[102] *Feria V in authentica* (Hänggi-Pahl, 453).

[103] Ibid., 492.

[104] This part includes the account of institution, the mandate, the anamnesis with the offering, the epiclesis (the "second" epiclesis), and the doxology.

erary datum that is to be seen as simply that and not given a surplus of value by transferring its scope and role to the theological level.[105]

3) In the history of the epiclesis, the one in the so-called *Apostolic Tradition* (attributed to Hippolytus) occupies first place, not only chronologically but also morphologically, since it is the simplest form of the phenomenon.[106] For this reason, it must be said that an investigation of the sources of the anaphora of Hippolytus is indispensable for the entire history of the eucharistic anaphora.

The epiclesis in the Anaphora of Hippolytus is in two parts[107]: the first is concerned with the descent of the Spirit "on the offering of the holy Church,"[108] while the second asks for the gift of unity and prays that all who share in the holy mysteries may be filled with the Spirit so as to strengthen their faith in the truth.[109] These, then, are the elements of the epiclesis: (1) sending of the Spirit on the *oblatio* (offering) of the Church, (2) the theme of unity, (3) participation in the holy gifts, (4) fullness of the Holy Spirit, and (5) ultimate purpose: "to strengthen (our) faith in the truth, so that we may praise and glorify you."[110]

---

[105] What I mean is that the explanation of the present participle *memores* should remain a literary explanation and not become a theological explanation. That is, one may not use *memores* as a starting point for extracting an anamnetic conception of the Eucharist or, as one might say today, a theology of the Eucharist as memorial. If we wanted, we could construct other conceptions of the Eucharist (beside the anamnetic conception) on the basis of the other present participles that are the subject of the verb "offer," such as "giving thanks," "proclaiming," "confessing" (ὁμολογοῦντες), "awaiting (ἀπεκδεχόμενοι) his coming," "observing the command," and so on.

[106] B. Botte, "Les plus anciens collections canoniques," *OS* 5 (1960) 344.

[107] This two-part division is a classical structure and typical of the Antiochene epiclesis, with the first part referring to the holy gifts, and the second to the fruitfulness of the reception of the Eucharist.

[108] *Et petimus ut mittas Spiritum tuum sanctum in oblationem sanctae ecclesiae* ("And we ask you to send your holy Spirit on the offering of the holy Church").

[109] *In unum congregans, des omnibus qui percipiunt sanctis in repletionem Spiritus sancti, ad confirmationem fidei in virtute* ("Gathering them into unity, grant that all who participate in the holies may be filled with the Holy Spirit for the strengthening of their faith in the truth").

[110] The words *ut te laudemus et glorificemus* ("that we may praise and glorify you") serve as a bridge to the doxology and introduce it; for this reason they are part either of the epiclesis or of the doxology. I prefer to keep them with the epiclesis, since the epiclesis usually gives the purpose of its prayer.

The remote origin of the theme of unity is in Paul; it is a baptismal theme in which the action of the Spirit is connected with the building up of the Church, the latter being described as a single body.[111] To understand how the pneumatological epiclesis in the Anaphora of Hippolytus came to be, we must keep in mind that the theme of the Holy Spirit is found in both parts of the epiclesis, but in two different ways, since there is no continuity between the two parts and since, in addition, they show differing conceptions of the relation between Eucharist and Spirit. Let us look at these two points in succession.

The first part of the epiclesis says: "And we ask you to send your Holy Spirit on the offering of your Church." The request ends here; it is an end in itself and is not further developed by explaining the purpose of the petition. The purposes of the epiclesis are formulated rather in the second part of our text, but without any dependence on the first part, as though the latter did not exist. In fact, the second part of the epiclesis begins without any relation to the first and with a petition that is unconnected with what has preceded and that can exist independently of the descent of the Spirit on the offering.

This is a very important point: for if the second part is independent of the first part, if it is complete in itself and able to exist without the first part, whereas the first part is not equally autonomous, since it demands to be completed by a statement of the purpose of the coming of the Spirit, then I think it can be concluded that the two parts belong to two different redactional stages and that the first part was added to the second part when the latter was already in the form in which we know it today.

In the first part of the epiclesis the theme of the Holy Spirit is primary and stands at the center of the discourse; in the second part, however, the theme of the Spirit is only one of the points made in the petition, and it does not have a central role, a role it ought to have if this second part were a development and continuation of the first. The text of the second part reads: "Gathering [them] into one, grant *(des)* to all those who will partake of the holies [i.e., holy mysteries] that they may be filled *(in repletionem)* with the Holy Spirit, for the strengthening of [their] faith in the truth, so that we may praise and glorify you. . . ."

[111] "For in the one Spirit we were all baptized into one body — Jews or Greeks, slaves or free — and we were all made to drink of one Spirit" (1 Cor 12:13).

Conclusion: this comparison of the two parts shows that there is no connection between the prayer for the descent of the Spirit on the offerings and the prayer that God would give the Spirit to those who communicate, so that the gift of the Spirit may confirm their faith in the truth. The second part, then, is independent of the first, while the first shows that it belongs to a different order of ideas and therefore to a different stratum of the text of the anaphora.[112]

Just as the account of institution was completed by the anamnesis and offering, so the epiclesis was completed by the addition of the opening sentence: "And we ask you to send your Holy Spirit on the offering of the Holy Church."

The epiclesis of the Anaphora of Hippolytus became the model for the Antiochene epiclesis, which began with that in the Anaphora of Basil and developed into the form that is familiar to us and would become the model for almost all later texts.

## B. FINAL SYNTHESIS

Some elements in the structure of the Antiochene anaphora can be explained in light of the structure of the Alexandrian paleoanaphora (for example, the account of the Last Supper, and the anamnesis-offering), while others can be explained in light of the Christian development of the *Birkat ha-Mazon* tradition.

Let me sum up briefly:

1) If the account of institution is added to the end of the first strophe of the Alexandrian paleoanaphora, we have precisely the structure of the anaphora of Hippolytus: (i) thanksgiving, at the end of which comes the account of institution; (ii) anamnesis; (iii) offering. The structure is identical even though there is a difference in the choice of the verb (in the present participle) on which the anamnesis is based,[113] for this difference is irrelevant from the viewpoint of the succession of strophes and, therefore, from the viewpoint of the structure of the texts.

---

[112] I observe, finally, that all the anaphoras dependent on Hippolytus reworked the text, thus showing that even they had some trouble in interpreting it; this group includes the *Testamentum Domini*, which becomes intelligible and recovers its comprehensibility only through the backtranslation from Syriac into Greek which B. Botte produced with such critical skill; see his "l'Esprit-Saint et l'Eglise dans la *Tradition apostolique* de Saint Hippolyte," *Didaskalia* 2 (1972) 246.

[113] The paleoanaphora has εὐχαριστοῦντες (giving thanks), while Hippolytus has *memores*.

2) The historical development of the account of institution, from its Jewish origin down to the account of the Last Supper in the Antiochene anaphora, may be summarized in this way: the *Birkat ha-Mazon* has, as its account of institution, the citation of Deuteronomy 8:10, while *Didache* 10, which is a thanksgiving derived from the *Birkat ha-Mazon*, retains this citation but adds an embolism showing that the Christian ritual food (the spiritual food and drink) is irreducible to that of the Jewish ritual meal. The Mystical Eucharist, which is derived from the *Didache*, moves the account of institution from the thanksgiving after the meal to the thanksgiving before the meal, with the thanksgiving after the meal becoming simply a thanksgiving after Communion.

In the Mystical Eucharist the connection with the *Birkat ha-Mazon* is henceforth unrecognizable; consequently, there is no longer any trace of the citation from Deut 8:10. In this document, the account of institution, which has been moved from the thanksgiving after Communion to the earlier thanksgiving, is based on 1 Cor 11:16; as a result, the express referent of the account of institution is the Last Supper. In the Alexandrian paleoanaphora, on the other hand, the account of institution consists of Mal 1:11 (a prophetic announcement of the pure sacrifice which God accepts), and this citation is placed at the end of the second strophe. Deut 8:10, the account of institution used in the *Birkat ha-Mazon,* is likewise placed at the end of the second strophe both in this Jewish prayer and in *Didache* 10, which, as we saw, is the Christian *Birkat ha-Mazon.* Even in the Mystical Eucharist, the account of institution (consisting of 1 Cor 11:26) is placed at the end of the second strophe.

From all these paleoanaphoral texts we can conclude that the ordinary place of the account of institution was at the end of the thanksgiving, before the petitions began (third strophe). In the Anaphora of Hippolytus, on the other hand, the account of institution has a different place, being at the end of the first strophe of thanksgiving.[114] This

---

[114] In the Anaphora of Hippolytus the second strophe of thanksgiving is very short: "Thanking you for counting us worthy to stand before you and minister to you." This text is in the tradition of the *Birkat ha-Mazon,* as is clear when we look at the second strophe of Abraham's *Birkat ha-Mazon* in the *Book of Jubilees* 22, 7: "And now I thank you, my God, because you have let me see this day" (Charlesworth 2:97). The second strophe in the prayer of the martyred Polycarp, which is like a copy of a paleoanaphora, likewise attests to the same model of

is another reason why the Anaphora of Hippolytus cannot be classified as a paleoanaphora, but is to be regarded as the first anaphora in the strict sense of the term. The different placement of the account of institution, as well as the appearance of the anamnesis, are to be explained solely by the introduction of paschal themes into the first strophe of thanksgiving; among these themes is the account of the Last Supper. Thus there is something completely new, and it is due to the "paschalization" of the anaphora.

## 3. The Alexandrian Anaphora of St. Mark

Strasbourg Papyrus Gr. 254 with its paleoanaphoral characteristics was not bypassed and was not relegated to the bin of outdated texts; on the contrary, it continued to exist as the first part of the anaphora that goes under the name of St. Mark. To the end of the original paleoanaphora was added the entire collection of new anaphoral parts that had been developed in the meantime. The *Sanctus* was added, but in a still archaic form, inasmuch as it ends not with the *Benedictus*,[115] but with a short formula of invocation which turns on the word "full" and asks God to fill with his glory or blessing the liturgy being celebrated. Theologians have been accustomed to describe this text as an epiclesis,[116] but in fact it is simply an embolism in the *Sanctus* and lacks the characteristics proper to an epiclesis.[117]

After the *Sanctus* a whole block of texts was added: the account of institution in the form of an account of the Last Supper, the anamnesis-offering, and the epiclesis (commonly known as the "second epiclesis"). All these texts were imported, for they came from Antiochene anaphoras, which had developed them in the middle of the fourth century and given them the form they have today. The Antiochene

---

thanksgiving: "I bless thee for granting me [literally making me worthy of] this day and hour, that I may be numbered amongst the martyrs" (*Martyrdom of Polycarp* 14, 2, trans Maxwell Staniforth, *Early Christian Writings. The Apostolic Fathers* [Baltimore, 1968] 160).

[115] The *Sanctus* without a *Benedictus* is attested as late as the beginning of the fourth century.

[116] The epiclesis is called "antecedent" in virtue of its position in relation to the account of institution; it is called "consecratory" by reason of its supposed function in the eucharistic celebration.

[117] An exception is found in a rather late fragment: the *Dêr Balyzeh Papyrus*, which displays properly epicletic traits.

structure thus influenced the Alexandrian anaphora and served as a decisive norm. This was true not only of the second part of the Anaphora of St. Mark but also of other texts, the most interesting being the anaphora attributed to Serapion.

## 3. The Roman Canon

The Eucharistic Prayer of the Roman Church — the Roman Canon — is attested for the first time in the fourth century, in the *De sacramentis* of Ambrose, bishop of Milan. It is that form of it that we must use in looking for the origins of the Roman Canon.

When we compare this text directly with the other anaphoras of antiquity, we can only feel an exasperating sense of helplessness, for the Roman Canon shows no kinship with any of the structures of the other liturgical families. It is a text different from every other and is not reducible to any of the structures known to us today. At the beginning of the present century, A. Gastoué pointed out some textual links to the Alexandrian anaphora,[118] and in fact there are some prayers in the central part of the Roman Canon that are to some extent similar and to some extent identical with a particular section of the Alexandrian anaphora: the *commendatio* or "(re)commendation" of the offerers and the sacrifice, which is located at the center of the intercessions, that is, at the center of the third strophe, if I may continue to use the paleoanaphoral structure as a model. Despite this, however, and despite the later works of Botte[119] and Jungmann,[120] no one has ever succeeded in taking the relationship any further.

There was in fact an insurmountable obstacle that did not allow any further comparison with the Alexandrian anaphora; that obstacle was the fact of structure. Because of their different structures, the two texts could not be compared and were irreducible to a common origin. As a result, any kinship the texts presented seemed irrelevant and of no importance for the larger question of the origin of the Roman anaphora.

---

[118] A. Gastoué, "Alexandrie, Liturgie," *DACL* (Paris, 1907–1953) 1, cols. 1189–1193. See also A. Baumstarck, "Das 'Problem' des römischen Kanons: eine Retractatio auf geistesgeschichtlichem Hintergrund," *EphLit* 53 (1939) 204–43.

[119] B. Botte, *Le canon de la messe romaine. Edition critique* (Textes et études liturgiques 2; Louvain 1935); B. Botte and Ch. Mohrmann, *L'ordinaire de la messe* (Etudes liturgiques 2; Paris-Louvain, 1953).

[120] J. A. Jungmann, *The Mass of the Roman Rite: Its Origins and Development (Missarum Solemnia)*, trans. F. A. Brunner (2 vols.; St. Louis, 1951, 1955).

The similarity of the texts, despite the difference in anaphoral structure, is certainly a problem. To resolve it, we must ask whether the present structure of the two Eucharistic Prayers is original. If it is not, then we must uncover their primitive stage and then try once again to compare them. The present state of the Alexandrian anaphora, that is, the *textus receptus* of the Anaphora of St. Mark, is not the original state; we know in fact that it was originally made up of two parts: (a) the opening part came from the Alexandrian paleoanaphora, the substance of which is well represented by Strasbourg Papyrus Gr. 254; (b) the following part, from the account of institution to the epiclesis (inclusive), came from the Antiochene anaphora. Therefore, to bring the Alexandrian anaphora back to its archaic state means eliminating the entire second part and retaining only the part that corresponds to Strasbourg Papyrus Gr. 254.

An analogous operation must be performed on the Roman Canon. We know in fact that the *Sanctus* was added after Ambrose, and we know that the two prayers *Supra quae* and *Supplices* are not two separate texts in Ambrose's redaction, but a single prayer. We know, further, that today the *Supra quae* precedes the *Supplices*, whereas in Ambrose the text corresponding to the *Supplices* comes first, and then that corresponding to the *Supra quae*. The structure of the text cited by Ambrose corresponds exactly to that of the Anaphora of St. Mark; in the latter, too, the prayer corresponding to the *Supplices* precedes the prayer corresponding to the *Supra quae*, and here again these two prayers are a single text.

From this it is clear that the Roman Canon, too, has had a history involving an evolution, developments, and reworkings. The first step, then, consists in uncovering the earliest formulations of the Roman Canon. The second step will then be to work on this text so as to carry it to the same level of archaism as the Alexandrian anaphora. Otherwise, the two texts will be at different stages of development and cannot usefully be compared.

Such is the method to be used. After having thus worked out the two texts to be compared, we can set the Roman text and the Alexandrian paleoanaphora side by side. If we write the texts out in two parallel columns, we see that there is a complete correspondence between the Roman Eucharistic Prayer and the Alexandrian paleoanaphora. This correspondence holds both for the structure and for the sequence of the various anaphoral themes: a) the text has three strophes: the first is a thanksgiving, the second is the offering of the sacrifice (the subject of the verb "offer" is a present participle), and the third is the intercession with its *commendatio* of both the sacrifice and the offerers; b) throughout the anaphora and independently of the function proper to each of the three strophes, there are various themes of thanksgiving and intercession; the sequence of these themes is the same in both texts, with one exception: the position of the memento of the dead is different in the Alexandrian text than in the Roman Canon.[121]

We may therefore conclude that the Alexandrian paleoanaphora was the origin of the text and structure of the Roman Eucharistic Prayer, even before giving rise to the connection between the account of institution and the anamnesis in the Antiochene anaphora. The influence of the Alexandrian Eucharistic Prayer on the Roman Eucharist can be dated to the first half of the third century at the latest.

Finally, we must ask why the two texts developed into two such different structures. Everything depended on the point in the prayer at which the block consisting of the account of institution, anamnesis, and offering was placed, once this block had been given its definitive formulation in the Antiochene anaphora. The Roman liturgy took over this block as formulated in the Antiochene liturgy and placed it at a particular, carefully studied point in the Roman paleoanaphora, namely, in the middle of the *commendatio* of the offerers and the sacrifice, between the prayer *Fac nobis hanc oblationem* and the prayer *Et petimus et precamur*.[122] When, on the other hand, the Alexandrian liturgy took over this same section of the Antiochene liturgy, it did not insert it at a carefully studied point of the anaphora but simply added it on at the tail-end,[123] after the third strophe of the paleoanaphora, without concern for the logic of this step.

---

[121] This difference can be explained by the Antiochene influence to be seen in the Roman formulary of the memento of the dead. Once this difference is explained, the rest of the Alexandrian Eucharistic Prayer corresponds to the Roman text.

[122] These are the words with which the prayer *Quam oblationem* and the prayer *Supplices* (which is one prayer with the *Supra quae*), respectively, begin in Ambrose's text.

[123] I.-H. Dalmais claims that this is a general trait of the Coptic liturgical style: the Romans and the Syrians constructed "an ordered discourse" (this being the meaning of *sedro*), while the Copts were satisfied with "juxtaposing rites,

If we want confirmation of this explanation, we need only take the section consisting of the account of institution, anamnesis, and offering, and transpose it to the end of the Canon, after the intercessions; we will see that we have an anaphora very similar to the Anaphora of St. Mark. Conversely for the Alexandrian anaphora: if we take that same section and place it within the third strophe, at the center of the *commendatio* of the offerers and the sacrifice, we will have an exact replica of the Roman Canon.

### 4. *The Syrian Anaphoras*

The Syrian liturgy may be either Antiochene (West Syrian) or Chaldean (East Syrian). Furthermore, in the West Syrian area a distinction must be made between anaphoras in Greek and anaphoras in Syriac. We have only a few points of reference: one of them is the connection between the Anaphora of John Chrysostom and the Anaphora of the Twelve Apostles. Recent studies have shown that at least some parts of the anaphora attributed to John Chrysostom were composed by him, but certainly not starting from scratch; he started with an existing text that was completely like, perhaps even identical with, the Syriac Anaphora of the Twelve Apostles, and to it he attached his own material, which enriched the anaphora theologically.

### A. THE WEST SYRIAN ANAPHORA

Since all anaphoras have an origin, it is worthwhile for us to inquire into the origin of the pair of anaphoras just mentioned: the Anaphora of the Twelve Apostles and the Anaphora of St. John Chrysostom. It is possible that the Anaphora of the Twelve Apostles and, by way of it, the Anaphora of Chrysostom derived from a common Syrian source that can explain the rise and development of the structure of the anaphoras of this liturgical family. The argument has three steps.

1) In this pair of anaphoras the *Post-Sanctus* is very interesting; it is identical in both texts[124] and clearly subdivided into two parts: the

---

acclamations, and prayers." See his essay, "La liturgie alexandrine et ses relations avec les autres liturgies," in *Liturgie de l'église particulière et liturgie de l'église universelle*, ed. A. M. Triacca and A. Pistoia (BELS 7; Rome, 1976) 120.

[124] "Together with these powers, O kind and merciful Lord, we too cry out and say: You are holy and completely holy, as is your only-begotten Son and your Holy Spirit. You are holy and completely holy, and your glory is magnificent, you who so loved your world that you gave your only begotten Son in order that

first repeats the theme of the *Sanctus,* while the second, which consists of a citation of John 13:1, introduces the account of institution. The citation is, then, a transitional and purely redactional bit of text that serves to link the *Sanctus* to the account of institution. The text of the *Post-Sanctus* consists wholly of a citation of what has gone before and an introduction to what follows; it is a text that lacks a theme of its own and is explainable solely by its function. This supposes that the *Sanctus* and the account of the Last Supper are older than the *Post-Sanctus,* which now connects them, and that the *Post-Sanctus* was composed at a second stage, when the *Sanctus* and the account of institution had been set side by side and there was need of connecting them. This means, in turn, that one of the two texts was already part of the anaphora, while the other was introduced later. Which of the two was part of the original structure of the anaphora, and which was added later?

2) For an answer we must fall back on some patristic homilies on the mysteries that show the *Sanctus* to be already part of the structure of the Syrian anaphora when the account of institution had not yet been introduced. In some mystagogies from the end of the fourth century the commentary on the Eucharist is done in two stages, giving rise to two different homilies. This is the case, for example, with Cyril of Jerusalem, who comments on the account of the Last Supper in his fourth mystagogical homily, while in the fifth he comments on the anaphora, which includes the *Sanctus* but not the account of institution. Something similar is to be seen in the mystagogical homilies of Theodore of Mopsuestia.

Given this fact, we ask ourselves whether this subdivision does not imply that the anaphora did not yet contain the account of the Last Supper.[125] If we look only at the homilies of Cyril, the data are not sufficient for resolving the problem, but if we also take into account

---

everyone who believes in him may not perish but have everlasting life" (Hänggi-Pahl, 224: Anaphora of John Chrysostom, and 266: Anaphora of the Twelve Apostles).

[125] See, e.g., E. J. Cutrone, "The Liturgical Setting of the Institution Narrative in the Early East Syrian Tradition," in *Time and Community. In Honor of Thomas Julian Talley* (NPM Studies in Church Music and Liturgy; Washington, D.C., 1990) 105–14. The most recent writer to deal with this problem is S. Verhelst, "L'histoire de la liturgie melkite de saint Jacques. Interprétations anciennes et nouvelles," *POC* 43 (1993) 229–72.

Theodore's homilies on the mysteries, we can reach a positive result, since he says there that the account of institution was introduced only recently, whereas he treats the *Sanctus* as an early and traditional part. The structure of the anaphora in the old liturgical book cited by Theodore is the following: (a) opening dialogue, (b) praise of God (at the end of which should come the offering of the praise itself), (c) *Sanctus*, (d) epicletic invocation, and (e) intercession for the living and the dead. This description shows clearly that there was no account of institution and nothing that would make us think of its existence.

The account of institution found a place in this type of anaphora when the *Sanctus* was already present and when the *Post-Sanctus* already existed as a trinitarian embolism. To this would be added the citation of John 13:1 as a transition to the account of the Last Supper.

Given this state of affairs, we can try to remove the account of institution from the Anaphoras of the Twelve Apostles and of Chrysostom and see what the resultant structure is. The result is the following structure: (a) opening dialogue, (b) praise of God (at the end of which is the offering of the praise), (c) *Sanctus* with embolism, (d) epicletic invocation, and (e) intercession for the living and the dead. This anaphoral structure is the same as that seen in the *Ordo* cited by Theodore, with the addition of some developments found also in the anaphora of Theodore's Church, such as the trinitariam embolism of the *Post-Sanctus*. It is a rather strange structure that has no parallel in any of the other paleoanaphoras I have been studying. Nonetheless, it is a paleoanaphoral structure that was at the basis of the important Syrian family of anaphoras.

In this anaphora, praise of God is thought of as imaging the form of the heavenly liturgy, which is described on the lines of Isa 6:1-3: the choirs of angels singing the hymn of praise that proclaims the divine name. In this way it is saying that the earthly liturgy possesses cultic value because it participates in the heavenly worship. The introduction to the *Sanctus*, with its description of the angelic choirs, is a very important part of the anaphora because it describes the heavenly assembly and liturgy to which the Church on earth unites itself. The Eucharist is thus conceived as a participation in the angelic liturgy, from which it derives its value as worship.[126] It is for this reason

---

[126] It is important to recall that the Cherubim and Seraphim have also been given a christological and pneumatological interpretation; see E. Lanne,

that the *Sanctus* is the central point of these anaphoras and the high point of the celebration.

## B. The East Syrian Anaphora

The Anaphora of the Apostles Addai and Mari,[127] which belongs to the East Syrian or Chaldean Church, has a peculiarity that has made it famous: it lacks the account of institution in the form of an account of the Last Supper.

The question arises of why this anaphora lacks the account of institution: did it never have it, or did it lose it as a result of the liturgical reform by Isho'yab III in the seventh century? We know for certain that the oldest manuscript of this anaphora, the text from Mar Esa'ya,[128] does not have the account of institution, and we can therefore state that the manuscript tradition suggests the absence of this part of the anaphora.

In this Eucharistic Prayer there is the following sequence of parts: (1) praise, confession, adoration, and exaltation of the Name of the Father and of the Son and of the Holy Spirit; (2) introduction to the *Sanctus,* and the *Sanctus* itself; (3) *Post-Sanctus* (with trinitarian development and *apologiae*), recited quietly as a "private" prayer; (4) resumption of the theme of the *Sanctus,* but with a transitional phrase, centered on the word "powers" or "armies,"[129] that begins a great thanksgiving addressed to the Son; this becomes a real confession of faith, since it tells of Christ's saving actions; (5) a concluding doxology in which praise, worship, gratitude, and adoration are "offered" to God[130]; (6) within the intercessions there is the offering of the body and blood of the Lord; (7) mention of the institution: "as you taught us"; (8) followed by the intercessions; 9) the tradition of the myster-

---

"Cherubim et Seraphim. Essai d'interprétation du chapitre X de la *Démonstration* de saint Irénée," *RSR* 43 (1955) 524–35.

[127] There is a critical edition of the text in A. Gelston, *The Eucharistic Prayer of Addai and Mari* (Oxford, 1992). See also B. D. Spinks, *Worship: Prayers from the East* (Washington, D.C., 1993).

[128] W. F. Macomber, "The Oldest Known Text of the Anaphora of the Apostles Addai and Mari," *OCP* 32 (1966) 335–71.

[129] "And together with these heavenly powers we, too, Lord, your weak, frail, and infirm servants, give you thanks" (Hänggi-Pahl, 377).

[130] On the different verbs for "offering" in these texts see B. D. Spinks, "Eucharistic Offering in East Syrian Anaphoras," *OCP* 50 (1984) 347–71.

ies; (10) a pneumatological epiclesis; and (11) a doxology. This structure is confirmed both by a sixth-century anaphora[131] and by Anaphora III of St. Peter the Apostle,[132] which is a text paralleling the Anaphora of the Apostles Addai and Mari and is derived from the same source.[133]

## C. JEWISH ORIGIN OF THE THIS FAMILY OF ANAPHORAS

In order to convey an idea of the structure of the Syrian anaphora I have suggested as its remote source the *Ordo* that is cited at the beginning of the mystagogical homilies of Theodore of Mopsuestia. There are, however, differences of structure between the West Syrian and East Syrian families. My view is that the differences are due to the different development of the two families of texts out of the same source and especially to the different points at which the pneumatological epiclesis was inserted: before the intercessions at Antioch, and after the intercessions in eastern Syria. Moreover, the difference becomes clearer due to the different points at which the account of institution was inserted: after the *Sanctus* at Antioch, and after the tradition of the mysteries, within the intercessions, in eastern Syria.

Is it possible to go back even further? In other words, is it possible to establish a Jewish source of the *Ordo* that Theodore uses? It is difficult to give an answer, because the *Ordo* is little more than an outline and a list of themes. Perhaps, however, some good result might be reached by applying to the *Ordo* the results of studies of the Anaphora of Addai and Mari.[134]

---

[131] British Museum, Add. 14669; see R. H. Connolly, "Sixth-Century Fragments of an East Syrian Anaphora," *OChr* 12–4 (1925) 99–128.

[132] Hänggi-Pahl, 410.

[133] The only difference to be emphasized is the presence of the account of institution, which is placed after the tradition of the mysteries and completed by the citation of John 6:51, followed by 11:26 and 10:10: "and we remember your body and blood, which we offer to you on your holy altar, as you, our hope, taught us in your holy gospel and told us: 'I am the living bread that has come down from heaven' in order that 'in me' mortals 'might have life'" (Hänggi-Pahl, 412).

[134] See, e.g., B. D. Spinks, *The Sanctus in the Eucharistic Prayer* (Cambridge-New York, 1991) 60; see also Gelston, *The Eucharistic Prayer of Addai and Mari*, 70.

## Bibliography

Audet, J.-P. "Literary Forms and Contents of a Normal *Eucharistia* in the First Century." In *Studia Evangelica*, ed. K. Aland and F. L. Cross, 643–62. TU 73 (5th series, vol. 18). Berlin, 1959.

Botte, B., B. Borinskoy, R. Bornet, eds. *Eucharistie d'Orient et d'Occident*. Paris, 1970.

Cuming, G. "The Early Eucharistic Liturgies in Recent Research." In *The Sacrifice of Praise*, 65–9. Rome, 1981.

____. "Four Very Early Anaphoras." *Wor* 58 (1984) 168–72.

Dix, G. *The Shape of the Liturgy*. London, 1964.

Hänggi, A., and I. Pahl. *Prex eucharistica: Textus e variis liturgiis antiquioribus selecti*. SF 12. Fribourg, 1968.

Jeremias, J. *The Eucharistic Words of Jesus*. Trans. N. Perrin. Philadelphia, 1990.

Marsili, S. "L'eucaristia nella fede della Chiesa primitiva." *Anàmnesis* 3/2:19–32.

____. "La celebrazione dell'eucaristia nella teologia dei Padri." *Anàmnesis* 3/2:33–58.

Mazza, E. *L'anafora eucaristica: Studi sulle origini*. Rome, 1992.

____. *The Origins of the Eucharistic Prayer*. Trans. R. Lane. Collegeville, Minn., 1995.

Talley, T. "De la 'berakah' à l'eucharistie: Une question à réexaminer." *MD* 125 (1976) 11–39.

____. *Worship: Reforming Tradition*. Washington, 1990.

Stefano Parenti

# 3

# The Eucharistic Liturgy in the East:
# The Various Orders of Celebration

*1. The Course of a Process: Methodological Vestiges*
The fourth century and the Constantinian Peace of 313 can be taken
as the symbolic latest point *(terminus ante quem)* for the birth and development of the eucharistic rites *(ordines)* of the Christian East. It
was a period that already showed a clear development by comparison with, for example, the description of the Eucharist in the *First
Apology* of Justin Martyr, that is, Gregory Dix's "first stratum."[1] The
fact that the Church lived its life within the juridico-administrative
structures of the empire led naturally to the creation of its own cen-
tralized structures which, by centripetal force, drew local liturgical
traditions into their orbit. It is now a definitively established fact that
the liturgical diversity between East and West was not due to the
fragmentation of a single ancient apostolic tradition, but was the result precisely of bringing together and unifying numerous local traditions around an important regional center.

Unification was followed by a period of development in which characteristic traits became well established, turning each tradition into a
readily identifiable entity; this process ended in the modern era with
the fixing of each eucharistic tradition in liturgical books. It was during
that lengthy period of time that the eucharistic rites developed their
Armenian, Byzantine, East and West Syrian, and Alexandrian forms.

According to the structural analysis proposed by Robert Taft, there
were three "soft points" in the celebration: (1) before the biblical

---

[1] G. Dix, *The Shape of the Liturgy* (London, 1945²) 33.

readings, (2) between the Liturgy of the Word and the anaphora, and (3) at the Communion. In the preceding phase of development these moments passed in silence, but now they were filled with a set of rites (a second stratum) for the entrance, the preanaphoral part, and the Communion, each set having its own verbal accompaniment. Each of the three had basically the same structure: a procession accompanied by singing and ending with a prayer. This structure is easily verifiable in the post-Vatican II Roman rite.

The process of development was, however, marked in both East and West by regressive features that affected even elements of the first stratum; for example, the shortening of the biblical readings, the atrophy or elimination of the psalmody, the decline in the prayer of the faithful, the suppression or clericalization of the sign of peace, and the recitation of the celebrant's prayers, including the anaphora, in a low voice.

The gradual loss of a clear understanding of the structure of the liturgical action led to compositions in the genre seen in the medieval liturgical commentaries. The eucharistic celebration which is a *re-presentation* to the Father of the redemptive economy of Christ, this being rendered actual by the action of the Holy Spirit, becomes, in the literary genre of the liturgical commentaries, a *representation* of the life of Christ for the sake of the faithful.

The textual history of the various eucharistic *ordines,* from the first witnesses to each tradition down to the *editio princeps,* also regularly records the various recensions, thus making it possible to identify local traditions within the same liturgical family.

*2. Soft Points in the Eucharist of the Christian East*
Consistently with what has been said, it was natural that the Oriental eucharistic rites differed from the Roman eucharistic rite chiefly in the verbal accompaniment of the soft points in the original structure. I shall now review some of the more characteristic aspects of the Oriental traditions (except for the Byzantine) according to the form these took in their respective contemporary liturgical books.

A. PREPARATION AND SELECTION OF THE GIFTS
A prominent characteristic of the Oriental rites is the presence of an often quite complex preparation of the gifts before the celebration; the preparation is preceded in turn by the vesting and private prayers *(apologiae)* of the celebrant, the latter being especially noticeable among the West Syrians.

Among the East Syrians the preparation includes not only the bread and wine intended for the Eucharist but even the baking of the bread, which is freshly prepared for each celebration. Among the Copts, at the door to the altar area the celebrant selects the bread and wine from among the gifts carried by the server; he accompanies his action with prayers and commemorations for various intentions. The gifts are then carried in procession around the altar; the bread, wrapped in a silk veil along with the wine, is carried by the celebrant over his head. After this circling the gifts are placed on the altar and are prepared to the accompaniment of a prayer of presentation. The rite used by the Ethiopians is substantially the same, but with prayers that brings out the symbolism of the miracle at Cana. In the rites of both groups the preparation of the gifts includes an epicletic prayer that is consecratory in tone and sounds exactly like the epiclesis in the anaphora.

The West Syrian liturgy connects the presentation rites with a sacrificial vision that is also shared by the Byzantines and with a commemoration of the offerers that takes place at the altar behind closed curtains and is divided (note the Old Testament point of view) into an "Office of Melchizedek" and an "Office of Aaron." Among the Armenians the rite used for the presentation is the tenth-century Byzantine rite of the offertory (πρόθεσις).

The Chaldeans (i.e., West Syrians of Catholic communion) perform a short presentation of the gifts during the entrance rite. The Malabarese Chaldeans prepare the gifts at the end of the Liturgy of the Word, as do the Maronites, among whom the preparation is considerably shortened and an offertory prayer is said before the anaphora.

B. BEFORE THE BIBLICAL READINGS
In the course of time and in all the traditions, the ancient, simple entrance of the assembly into the Church, accompanied by singing and followed by a greeting from the presider, accumulated a great many texts and hymns. It is a well-known fact that in the West, too, the eucharistic rite tended to undergo an expansion of both the entrance and the concluding rituals. Generally speaking, though differently in the different traditions, the present form of these rites has been influenced by the urban stational liturgy or by various services of the Liturgy of the Hours.

That is what happened in the East Syrian rite, where we see a remnant of the morning psalmody, two antiphonal songs, one fixed and one variable, and the hymn τρισάγιον or *Thrice Holy*, each of these with its own prayer. Meanwhile, the procession from the sanctuary to the *bema* (raised platform), which is the architectural center of the church for the Liturgy of the Word, has been eliminated. The West Syrians move on directly from the *sedro* or rite of offering incense (from the Liturgy of the Hours?) to the Old Testament readings, which are separated from the New Testament readings by the hymns ὁμονογενής *Only-Begotten Son* and *Thrice Holy*. In the reformed Mass of the Syrian Maronites there are prayers for approaching the altar, psalmody, a ritual of incensing, the *Thrice Holy*, a psalm of praise with antiphons, and the readings. Among the Copts and the Ethiopians the preparatory prayers of absolution predominate, these being followed by the rite of incense with intercessions, the readings, and the hymn *Thrice Holy* before the gospel. To be noted is the penitential and propitiatory emphasis in the use of incense by the Syrians, Maronites, Copts, and Ethiopians, unlike, for example, the Byzantines, where the incensing has a purely honorific purpose.

In addition to the ancient entrance song from their own tradition, the Armenians have hymns and prayers from the Byzantine ἔναρξις (preliminary part of the liturgy); these are followed by a ritual procession with the book of the gospels and the hymn *Thrice Holy*.

## C. Before the Anaphora

The phrase "rites before the anaphora" refers to everything between the end of the intercessions and the opening dialogue of the Eucharistic Prayer. In the Oriental traditions the rites preceding the anaphora are not concerned with the material preparation of the gifts, since the preparation and presentation of these has already taken place; they are concerned rather with the spiritual preparation of the ministers and the congregation with a view to the offering that takes place in the anaphora. The prayers during this time refer to the gifts and can be even called "prayers of offering," which mention the saint or father to whom the ensuing anaphora is attributed and from whom the verbal formula of preparation comes. It follows that these prayers can by no means be interpreted as an *offertory* in the Western acceptation of the term; rather they are a ritual for the *approach to the altar*. The altar is the place of sacrifice and plays no part during the Liturgy of the Word (consider the East Syrian *bema*), even if this is not true today in all the rites.

In the East, the group of preanaphoral rites usually includes: (a) a material preparation for the Eucharist by a transfer of the gifts, in a procession, from the place of their earlier selection and preparation, the placing of them on the altar where they are covered and incensed; (b) a spiritual preparation or "approach to the altar," in a true and proper sense, that includes a washing of hands, a prayer of approach in which God is asked to make his servants worthy to draw near to the altar and celebrate the sacred mysteries, the *Orate, fratres* dialogue, the profession of faith (as in the Ambrosian rite in the West), and the kiss of peace.

In the West Syrian, Coptic, and Ethiopian rites, since the preparation of the gifts at the beginning of the liturgy now takes place on the main altar, the procession for the transfer of the gifts has disappeared, whereas the Syrian Maronites have revived it in their reform. Among the East Syrians we still see remnants of the ancient rite of the *bema:* the transfer of the gifts is done by the deacons without solemnity, since the only solemn procession had been the entrance procession from the central *bema* to the sanctuary, accompanied by the "rite of the *bema*" in which the main celebrant bows to the right and the left while asking the concelebrants for their prayers and forgiveness. Among the Syrians, Copts, and Ethiopians, the meaning of the approach to the altar is emphasized by the "prayers of the veil" and the kiss of peace. Among the West Syrians the *Orate, fratres* has retained its original function as a formula by which the bishop selects the concelebrating presbyter who alone is appointed to recite the eucharistic anaphora.

The Armenians and Maronites are the only ones who have an offertory prayer, which is perhaps to be attributed to Roman influence; on the other hand, the recitation of the creed, which among the Armenians comes after the gospel, is to be regarded as their own tradition and anterior to the Latinization of their liturgy.

D. BEFORE THE COMMUNION

Like the preanaphoral rites, the preparation for Communion has two phases: a material preparation in the form of the "manual acts" (fraction, commingling, and so on), and a spiritual preparation through prayers, especially (in the Chaldean tradition in particular) the Our Father and others of a generally sapiential tonality. The order of the two phases can vary. Among the Copts and Ethiopians the fraction and signing come before the Our Father, while the other manual acts follow upon the spiritual preparation. In the Armenian and Maronite rites, however, the rites consisting of the fraction, the placing of the particles after the fraction, and the intinction, signing, and commingling, are very complex.

Communion is *always* in both kinds; but only the Copts and Chaldeans distribute Communion in the ancient manner, first the bread and then the chalice separately. The eucharistic bread is leavened, except among the Armenians and Maronites, who use unleavened bread, the last named in the form of a host, due to Roman influence.

The expansion of the original prayer after Communion has given rise to a series of dismissal rites in which later additions to the original structure, consisting of formulas of blessing, have left their deposits, as in the Roman rite. The greeting of the altar is peculiar to the Maronite tradition.

*3. An Example: The Development of Byzantine Eucharistic Rite*
Since the limits placed on this essay make it impossible to trace the development of the eucharistic rite in all the "Oriental" traditions, I am forced to choose just one. Choices of this kind, however, are always painful because every Eucharist of the Christian East has texts and a vision of the celebration that should be known and studied.

I propose, then, the Byzantine tradition, whose rite is, after the Roman, the one most widely used throughout Christendom. Its history and the development of its eucharistic rite are paradigmatic; it is, just like the Roman rite, a concrete example of the development of a liturgical tradition which, though born in a particular place, here the capital of the eastern Roman Empire, has throughout its history come in contact with and embodied various languages, races, and cultures. As a result, it has become in fact a supranational liturgy, the liturgy of the Byzantine Commonwealth.

A. The "Divine Liturgy"
In the Byzantine world the eucharistic celebration is known as the divine liturgy ("liturgy" being understood as "public worship," one of the meanings of the Greek word λειτουργία, which in this context is accurately translated by the German *Gottesdienst* or the English "worship"). One kind of literature has accustomed us to dividing the Byzantine Eucharist and almost all the Oriental Eucharists into a

liturgy of the catechumens and a liturgy of the faithful. But the division is not satisfactory to the extent that these two terms imply precise lines of demarcation in the texts. The "liturgy of the catechumens" is not exclusively such, in the way that the second section belongs exclusively to the faithful. Furthermore, the almost universal practice of the Christian initiation of infants has emptied the distinction of any real meaning.

I prefer, therefore, to adopt the more consistent terms *Liturgy of the Word* and *Liturgy of the Eucharist*.

## B. EARLY PERIOD (FOURTH–FIFTH CENTURIES)

The history of a specifically "Byzantine" Eucharist necessarily begins after the transfer of the imperial capital to the shores of the Bosporus in 313. This Eucharist took shape between approximately 381 and 451, that is, between the first council held in Constantinople (the third ecumenical) and the Council of Chalcedon, which in its Canon 28 assigned to the New Rome (as being the imperial city) a primacy of honor second only to the Old Rome.[2]

The liturgical background in Constantinople was of West Syrian and, in particular, Antiochene origin. This fact is evidenced chiefly by the homilies of John Chrysostom.[3] As has been recently shown, the anaphora that bears Chrysostom's name was in fact a reworking, on antieunomean lines, of the *Urtext* of the Syriac anaphora known as the Anaphora of the Twelve Apostles; this was done by Chrysostom himself during his time as bishop of Constantinople (398–404).[4]

This anaphora, which Chrysostom brought to Byzantium, took its place beside the one already used there: the Anaphora of Basil, which was an expanded version of the primitive Alexandrian text. The moment when these two anaphoras began to have a common redactional history within the same bishopric marked the start of a process by which they became for practical purposes recognized as equal at various points, for example, in the account of institution and the final

---

[2] For a survey of the historical development of the Byzantine tradition see R. F. Taft, *The Byzantine Rite. A Short History* (Collegeville, 1992).

[3] F. van der Paverd, *Zur Geschichte der Messliturgie in Antiocheia and Konstantinopel gegen Ende der vierten Jahrhunderts. Analyse der Quellen bei Johannes Chrsysostomos* (OCA 187; Rome, 1970).

[4] R. F. Taft, "The Authenticity of the Chrysostom Anaphora Revisited. Determining the Authorship of Liturgical Texts by Computer," *OCP* 56 (1990) 5–51.

doxology.[5] It was the same process of equal recognition that the Roman Church would experience after Vatican II with the use of new Eucharistic Prayers other than the Roman Canon.

## C. LITURGY OF THE CAPITAL (SIXTH–SEVENTH CENTURIES)

The ascent of Justinian I to the throne (527–565) marked the start of what scholars agree on calling the "imperial period" of the Byzantine Eucharist, a period characterized by the organization (as at Rome) of a stational liturgy which involved in its circuits not only churches, monks, and clergy, but even the civic life of the city.[6] The Cathedral of Hagia Sophia, built in 532–537, provided an ideal architectural setting for the rite. It was a building intended for the liturgy to be celebrated there: a building characterized by an altar brought forward from the apse, a central ambo, and an outside sacristy (σκευοφυλάκιον).[7]

In the sixth century, and in a departure from previous practice, non-biblical songs (τροπάρια) were added to the psalms that accompanied the entrance of the congregation into the church and the preanaphoral procession for the transfer of the gifts from sacristy to altar. The first such hymn was introduced in 528 and the second in 574.[8]

Borrowing from the catechumenal discipline, Patriarch Timothy (511–517) introduced the Nicene-Constantinopolitan Creed into the preanaphoral rites, thus duplicating the primitive and unique profession of faith contained in the anaphoral story of the divine wonders (the *mirabilia Dei*). Without intending to claim a factual connection, I may point out that in that same sixth century it became increasingly difficult to hear about the *mirabilia Dei* in the anaphora because the celebrant was reciting in a low voice not only the anaphora but other prayers as well, and in particular the "offertory" prayer which introduced the anaphora and made its appearance during this period.

The *Mystagogy* of St. Maximus the Confessor (628–630) not only makes it possible to fill in many details of the celebration[9] but also

---

[5] H. Engberding, "Die Angleichung der byzantinischen Chrysostomusliturgie an die byzantinische Basiliusliturgie," *Ostkirchliche Studien* 13 (1964) 110–22.

[6] J. F. Baldovin, *The Urban Character of Christian Worship* (OCA 228; Rome, 1987).

[7] T. F. Mathews, *The Early Churches of Constantinople: Architecture and Liturgy* (London, 1971).

[8] The two were the well-known hymns were *The Only-begotten* (ὃ μονογενής) and the Cherubikon (ὃ Χερούβικὸς Ὕμνος).

[9] Text in PG 91:657–717.

provides a first interpretation of a liturgy that was evolving. In 624 Maximus' predecessor, Patriarch Sergius, added a final Communion hymn to the Communion psalm. This ended the process of "antiphonalization" of the original responsorial psalmody at the entrance, the transfer of the gifts, and the Communion, at which Psalms 94, 23, and 33 were chanted, with a simple Alleluia as response.[10]

## D. THE FIRST WRITTEN TEXT

In the second half of the eighth century, but before the iconoclast controversy, the earliest known text of the Byzantine Eucharist, namely, the famous euchologion Barberini gr. 336, was copied in the part of southern Italy that was subject to Byzantium. The commentary of Patriarch Germanus (d. ca. 733) is almost contemporary with the euchologion.[11]

The Barberini ms claims Basil as the author of every part of the formulary that bears the name of the bishop of Caesarea, while attributing to Chrysostom only the properly eucharistic prayers, beginning with the prayer of oblation (τῆς προσκομιδῆς). As for the other prayers, all those preceding the proclamation of the biblical readings belong to an Alexandrian and Syro-Palestinian repertory from southern Italy, the area in which the ms originated.[12]

The prayers in the formulary of Basil, along with the commentary of Germanus,[13] confirm the very great influence which the stational liturgy had on the formulary for the Eucharist. Three prayers for three antiphonal psalms precede the prayer accompanying the entrance of the gospel at the beginning of the Liturgy of the Word, while a stational petition follows upon (the homily and) the gospel. These elements soon became fixed parts of the *ordo* even when the liturgy was not a stational liturgy. As a result again of the stational

[10] There is an extensive treatment in R. F. Taft, *The Great Entrance. A History of the Transfer of Gifts and Other Preanaphoral Rites of the Liturgy of St. John Chrysostom* (OCA 200; Rome, 1978²) 53–188.

[11] *L'Eucologio Barberini gr. 336*, ed. S. Parenti and E. Velkovska (BELS 80; Rome, 1985).

[12] "L'evoluzione dei libri liturgici bizantini in Calabria e in Sicilia dall'VIII al XVI secolo, con particolare riguardo ai riti eucaristici," in *Calabria bizantina. Vita religiosa e strutture amministrative* (Atti del primo e secondo incontro di studi bizantini; Reggio Calabria, 1974) 47–59.

[13] R. F. Taft, "The Liturgy of the Great Church: An Initial Synthesis of Structure and Interpretation on the Eve of Iconoclasm," *Dumbarton Oaks Papers* 34–35 (1980–1981) 45–75.

liturgy, the prayer of the faithful was moved from after the readings and, just like the Roman *Kyrie,* placed after the entrance procession, and, still paralleling Rome, the Old Testament readings were dropped.[14]

As the liturgy thus developed in an anthological manner, that is, by amassing elements without any criterion for selecting them, several rites moved in the direction of a real atrophy. The entrance of the celebrants and the congregation into the church became an entrance of the celebrants alone into the sanctuary and altar. Clericalization can also be seen at work in the prayers with the appearance of *apologiae* or private prayers (in the preanaphoral rites and before Communion); these are easily identified because they are addressed to Christ.

The clerical vision of the Eucharist is accentuated in the prayers of the celebrant, now removed from their context, which accompany the prayer of the faithful. Instead of referring to the intentions of the faithful, these prayers, especially in the formulary of Basil, developed apologetic themes of the unworthiness of the celebrants. All this is a sign that the distinction between the Liturgy of the Word and the eucharistic liturgy was being increasingly disregarded.[15]

There was a tendency to duplicate and multiply deaconal litanies under the influence of mixed celebrations combining the Liturgy of the Hours and the Eucharist, one such being the Liturgy of the Presanctified.[16] A prayer of blessing was added to the simple dismissal, "Let us go in peace."

E. THE POST-ICONOCLASTIC REFORM

The re-assertion, in 843, of the legitimacy of depicting the face of Christ on icons as an authentic profession of faith in the incarnation of the word of God produced the conditions for a further revision of the eucharistic liturgy, within the framework of a broader revision of the Byzantine liturgical universe.

Two important interventions directly affected the eucharistic formulary: the "advancement" of the Liturgy of Chrysostom to first place in the euchologion in preference to that of Basil, from which, however, were taken all the prayers before the celebrant's prayer in

---

[14] J. Mateos, *La célébration de la Parole dans la Liturgie byzantine, Etude historique* (OCA 191; Rome, 1971) 25–68.

[15] Taft, *Great Entrance,* 364–69.

[16] Ibid., 311–49.

the liturgy of the catechumens. The formulary of Basil, which at an earlier period had almost certainly been used on Sundays, was gradually reserved for important times of the liturgical year (Lent and Holy Week).[17] At the same time the Anaphora of Chrysostom underwent a textual revision in the interests of equality with that of Basil. Thus, what has been described as a "victory" of the Chrysostom formulary over that of Basil was in fact exactly the opposite.[18]

Since the positive outcome of the iconoclast controversy was to be attributed to the lobbying of the Constantinopolitan monastery of Stoudios, we would naturally expect that henceforth the eucharistic liturgy would increasingly show monastic influences. Beginning in the tenth century, first in Italy and the East and then in Constantinople itself, an office for the communion of the hermits of Palestine (known as τυπικά), which had become part of the Liturgy of the Hours of the Studites (but now lacking any reference to the Eucharist), partly replaced the antiphons of the stational liturgy and partly became an appendix to the dismissal.[19]

The post-iconoclastic reform also slowly altered the architectural arrangement of the church in the direction of a monastic sobriety that would prove harmful to the tridimensional aspect of the celebration. The abandonment of the outside sacristy would also reduce the solemn preanaphoral transfer of the gifts and, earlier, the entrance procession to purely ceremonial acts. With the elimination of the central ambo the liturgy was confined to the presbyteral enclosure.

F. THE ROLE OF MOUNT ATHOS

The occupation of Constantinople by the Franks in 1204 and the establishment of the "Latin empire" and a Latin hierarchy (1204–1261) caused a veritable blackout in the liturgical life of the capital; its reorganization would once again be the work of the monks. Like the Avignon interval in Rome, so in Constantinople the exile of the emperor to Nicaea and the eclipse of the Orthodox hierarchy had as a result the abandonment of the stational liturgy.

[17] A. Jacob, "La tradition manuscrite de la Liturgie de saint Jean Chrysostome (VIIIᵉ–XIIᵉ siècle)," in *Eucharisties d'Orient et d'Occident* 2 (Lex orandi 47; Paris, 1970) 109–38.

[18] S. Parenti, "Osservazioni sul testo dell'anafora di Giovanni Crisostomo in alcuni eucologi italo-greci (VIII–IX secolo)," *EphLit* 105 (1991) 120–54.

[19] Mateos, *Célébration de la Parole,* 68–71.

Except for unimportant elements of ritual, the rite which at this period still showed a certain vitality, with numerous variations according to liturgical regions (Constantinople, the East, Italy), was the πρόθεσίς or preparation and selection of the gifts; one reason for this was the strongly felt symbolism of Christ as Lamb of God and as Suffering Servant of the Old Testament (Isa 53) or, in other words, the biblical typology of the passion.[20]

An end to the multiplicity of alternative celebrations came with Philotheus, a friend and biographer of Gregory Palamas (1300–1379), who was a monk first of Sinai and then of Athos. In order to standardize the eucharistic liturgy in the Athonite monastery of the Great Lavra, he composed a set of rubrics (διάταξις) that had considerable success. In fact, it spread throughout the Slavic Orthodox world in the translation first of Patriarch Eutymius of Tirnovo (1375–1393) and then of Cyprian, Metropolitan of Moscow. The rubrical norms of Philotheos did not, however, put an end to local usages until 1881, especially in southern Italy and in the monastery of Grottaferrata, near Rome. Other sets of rubrics contemporary with that of Philotheus or later than his would continue in use until the advent of printing.[21]

## G. THE WIDELY USED *EDITIO PRINCEPS*

In the setting of the advancement of Greek letters in Late Renaissance Rome and with the patronage of Pope Clement VIII, 1526 saw the publication of the *editio princeps* of the three Byzantine eucharistic formularies.[22] The preface tells us that the work, "intended for all Orthodox Christians," was edited by Demetrios Doukas, a Cretan. We know nothing about the sources he used, but it is probable that in addition to the editor's own choices, the text reflects typically Cretan usages.[23] The publication was very widely circulated and was several

---

[20] M. Mandalà, *La protesi della liturgia nel rito bizantino-greco* (Grottaferrata, 1935).

[21] R. F. Taft, "Mount Athos. A Late Chapter in the History of the Byzantine Rite," *Dumbarton Oaks Papers* 42 (1988) 179–94.

[22] F. Niutta, "Libri greci a Venezia e a Roma," in *Il libro italiano nel Cinquecento: produzione e commercio. Catalogo della mostra* (Biblioteca Nazionale Centrale, Rome, October 28–December 16, 1989; Rome, 1989) 77–98, especially 90; color plate on 88. The text is reproduced in C. A. Swainson, *The Greek Liturgies Chiefly from Original Authorities* (Cambridge, 1884; Hildesheim-New York, 1971) 101–44.

[23] A. Strittmatter, "Note on the Byzantine Synapte," *Traditio* 10 (1954) 75–76.

times reprinted in Venice. The spread of a handy printed text led to the suppression, in Greek circles, of various local usages, although these continued in Russia until 1651, when Patriarch Nikon and the council he convoked approved the revision of the liturgical books along the lines of the Greek texts. This gave rise to the schism of the "Old Ritualist."[24]

The present-day "Byzantine" liturgy is thus the text of the new, eleventh-century Constantinopolitan recension, celebrated according to rubrics set down on Mount Athos in the fourteenth century and in the particular redaction made by a Cretan humanist at the behest of a Roman pope.

## H. A COLLATERAL BRANCH: THE EUCHARISTIC LITURGY IN THE CATHOLIC ORIENTAL CHURCHES

During the period following upon the publication of the widely used *editio princeps*, some Orthodox dioceses of eastern Europe and the Middle East entered into a union with the Roman Church in the Ukraine (1595–1596); the Ukrainians were followed by the Ruthenians (1646), the Rumanians (1698), the Melkites (1724), the Bulgarians (1859–1860), and others groups of lesser size. The entrance of these groups into communion with Rome was accompanied, on the Roman side, by respect and the preservation of the liturgical rite proper to each Church. This was certainly so in the beginning, but with the passage of time changes (still in effect) were introduced into the Liturgy, inspired for the most part by the pre-Vatican II Roman rite. The changes came about either through the activity of western religious there or to the desire of the Greek Catholics to differentiate themselves from the corresponding Orthodox Churches.

Some of the practices introduced, in addition to a general tendency to shorten the liturgical formulary, were: celebrations that were private or without singing; Communion from the reserved Eucharist; the multiplication of celebrations; the use of commercial bread or, in some cases, of hosts; the abandonment of the rite of the ζέον (the hot water poured into the chalice); and, generally, the theology of the epiclesis, which led to a much talked about divorce between the *lex credendi* and the *lex supplicandi*. The Holy See has intervened on several

---

[24] P. Meyendorf, *Russia, Ritual, and Reform. The Liturgical Reforms of Nikon* (Crestwood, N.Y., 1992).

occasions to regulate the Liturgy of these Churches, seeking to make them more traditional and more in keeping with their original tradition; until now it has had little perceptible success.[25]

I. TOWARD A REFORM?

Let me end this brief excursus on the history of the Byzantine eucharistic Liturgy not with "conclusions" that can be taken for granted, but with a question. I do not mean that conclusions cannot be drawn, but simply that at the point where the divine liturgy is today it has not quite finished its developmental journey with what ought to be a liturgical reform. It is the task of a liturgical reform to make the rites more immediately understandable and to restore the ability to communicate which they undoubtedly once had, without needing too many, often unfounded interpretations.

But such a reform, being an expression of tradition, is the task of the individual Churches and their higher authorities, according to the canonical system of each. What I have summarily described is at bottom simply a story of ongoing successive reforms, a history that cannot but continue.

[25] See *Ordo celebrationis Vesperarum, Matutini et Divinae Liturgiae iuxta recensionem Ruthenorum* (Rome, 1953).

## Bibliography

Bornet, R. *Les commentaires byzantins de la Divine Liturgie du VII^e au XV^e siècle.* Archives de l'Orient chrétien 9. Paris, 1966.

Brightman, F. *Liturgies Eastern and Western.* Vol. 1: *Eastern Liturgies.* Oxford, 1896.

Guillaume, D. *Hiératikon.* Vol. 2: *Les divines Liturgies.* Rome, 1986.

Janeras, S. *Bibliografia sulle Liturgie Orientali, 1961–1967.* Rome, 1969.

Mateos, J. *Le Typicon de la Grand Église. Ms. Sainte-Croix N°. 40, 1–2.* OCA 165–6. Rome, 1962–1963.

———. *La célébration de la Parole dans la Liturgie byzantine: Étude historique.* OCA 191. Rome, 1971.

Sauget, J.-M. *Bibliographie des Liturgies Orientales, 1900–1960.* Rome, 1962.

Schulz, H.-J. *The Byzantine Liturgy: Symbolic Structure and Faith Expression.* New York, 1986.

Swainson, C. *The Greek Liturgies Chiefly from Original Authorities*. Cambridge, 1884; New York, 1971.

Taft, R. *The Great Entrance: A History of the Transfer of Gifts and Other Pre-anaphoral Rites of the Liturgy of St. John Chrysostom*. OCA 200. Rome, 1978².

____. "The Pontifical Liturgy of the Great Church According to a Twelfth-Century Diataxis in Codex British Museum Add. 34060." I: *OCP* 45 (1979) 279–307; II: *OCP* 46 (1980) 89–124.

____. *Introduzione allo studio delle Liturgie Orientali*. Rome, 1982.

____. "The Structural Analysis of Liturgical Units: An Essay in Methodology." In *Beyond East and West: Problems in Liturgical Understanding*, 151–64. Washington, 1984. Originally published in *Wor* 52 (1978) 314–29.

____. "Mount Athos: A Late Chapter in the History of the Byzantine Rite." *Dumbarton Oaks Papers* 42 (1988) 179–94.

____. *A History of the Liturgy of St. John Chrysostom*. Vol. 4: *The Diptychs*. OCA 238. Rome, 1991.

Winkler, G. "Die Interzessionen der Chrysostomusanaphora in ihrer geschichtlichen Entwicklung." I: *OCP* 36 (1970) 301–36; II: *OCP* 37 (1971) 333–83.

Enzo Lodi

# 4

# The Oriental Anaphoras

INTRODUCTION

Since the genesis of the Oriental anaphoras has already been explained, this theological discussion will be limited to setting forth the more important stages of the three great traditions in the Oriental rites. A more detailed analysis will be made of the two Byzantine anaphoras of St. John Chrysostom (CB) and St. Basil (BB). As a matter of fact, until the eighth–ninth century, the anaphora of Basil was regularly used in Constantinople, but it was then supplanted by that of Chrysostom; today the anaphora of Basil is used only about fifteen times a year, as compared with the habitual use of the anaphora of Chrysostom. The Greek anaphora of St. James is also used, but only on the titular feast of the saint, October 23 (but by ancient custom it is frequently used on the island of Zante).

In the Church of the Syro-Antiochene rite, the West Syrians have over seventy anaphoras, but the ones actually used are the anaphora of the Twelve Apostles (XII-A) and the Syriac anaphora of St. James. The East Syrian tradition has three anaphoras, those of Addai and Mari, Theodore of Mopsuestia, and Nestorius. Of its many anaphoras the Coptic Church uses the anaphora of Gregory the Theologian (Gregory of Nazianzus), the (short) Coptic anaphora of Basil, and the anaphora of Cyril of Alexandria (which is, in substance, the Greek anaphora of St. Mark). Regarding these anaphoras of the East Syrian and Alexandrian traditions, I shall limit myself, in a short concluding summary, to showing some of their more characteristic elements in a theological comparison with the anaphoras of the Byzantine tradition; for the sake of brevity, however, I shall cite in its entirety only the anaphora of Chrysostom. Since the latter is the one most frequently

77

used in both its Greek version and its Slavic versions, it will be appropriate to take as our starting point the conclusions of scholarly study of its authenticity.

Finally, this brief theological analysis will be limited to the euchological formularies, although for the full understanding of these it would be necessary to combine the analysis with the explanation of the liturgical actions which, along with the word, make up the rites in questions. Some short passages from the "Byzantine Commentaries"[1] will help to bring out the most important aspects.

## I. THE BYZANTINE ANAPHORA
## OF ST. JOHN CHRYSOSTOM

*1. Results of Recent Research into the Authenticity of Anaphora* CB
The results of the last seventy-five years of research, as summed up by the patrologists and liturgists, led to the conclusion that the so-called liturgy of Chrysostom was apocryphal because its present form arose at a period much later than that of the patriarch of Constantinople whose name it bears.[2] The arguments used to cast doubt on the attribution to Chrysostom were: the (spurious) testimony of Patriarch Proclus (434–446); the silence of Leontius of Byzantium who, when accusing Theodore of Mopsuestia in 540 of having dared substitute his own anaphora for that of the Twelve Apostles *(XII-A)* and for the one composed by St. Basil, never so much as mentions a liturgy of Chrysostom; the similar silence of the Synod in Trullo (692) in its canon 32 about the existence of this liturgy of Chrysostom (though it mentions the liturgies of James and Basil).[3] Nor was valid-

---

[1] See R. Bornert, "L'Anaphore dans la spiritualité de Byzance. Le témoignage des commentaires mystagogiques du VIIe au XVe siècle," in *Eucharisties d'Orient et d'Occident* (Paris, 1970) 2, 241–64. For the anaphoral texts in Greek, with Latin translations, see E. Lodi, *Enchiridion Euchologicum Fontium Liturgicorum* (Rome, 1978): Anaphora of Chrysostom, nos. 2896–2901, 1271–81; Syrian Anaphora of the Twelve Apostles, nos. 522–30, 313–21; Anaphora of Basil, nos. 531–41, 317–26; Alexandrian Anaphora of Mark, nos. 542–50, 324–28; East Syrian Anaphora of Addai and Mari, nos. 509–15, 3-1-6.

[2] See *BAR,* 24–41 (liturgy of Chrysostom); 1–14 (liturgy of Basil).

[3] See A. Raes, "L'authenticité de la liturgie byzantine de saint Jean Chrysostome," *OCP* 24 (1958) 5–6; M. M. Solovev, *The Byzantine Divine Liturgy* (Washington, D.C., 1970) 251–95; G. Khouri-Sarkis, "L'origine syrienne de l'anaphore byzantine de saint Jean Chrysostome," *OS* 7 (1962) 3–63; Leontius of Byzantium, *Adv Nest. et Euthich.* III, 19 (PG 86:1368C).

ity allowed to studies aimed at showing the correspondence of this liturgy with the descriptions of the eucharistic liturgy in the homilies of the same saintly Father.

The most interesting studies, however, have been those on the relationship between *CB* and the Syriac anaphora of the *XII-A*,[4] since the present formulary of the latter supposes an earlier Greek text that would, it was said, be behind the text of *CB*. This base text would supposedly have been translated into Syriac, probably toward the sixth century, while at the same time some expressions peculiar to the West Syrian liturgies and some adornments from an older Syriac anaphora were introduced into the model.

G. Khouri-Sarkin saw a sameness between these two anaphoras (the Antiochene anaphora of the *XII-A* and *CB*), and he supposed that Chrysostom used the Antiochene anaphora when he was a priest and instructor of catechumens at Antioch (381–397), and then brought it with him to Constantinople when he was elected patriarch in 398. The new findings which Franz van de Paverd[5] made in 1970 in his reassessment of those studies led him to challenge the hypothesis of a transfer to Constantinople of the anaphora known to Chrysostom in Antioch. His reason: in the fourth-century Church of Antioch there did not yet exist a single anaphora with a definitively set text, as can be seen from the writings of Chrysostom during his time in Antioch.

But a few years later G. Wagner[6] refuted these negative conclusions and developed his thesis of the authenticity of the anaphora of Chrysostom, chiefly by reappraising the arguments based on the silence of the sources mentioned above. He took as his basis the fact, in particular, that the name of the prayer of offering, "Prayer of Offering of St. John" (εὐχὴ τῆς προσκομιδῆς τοῦ ἁγίου Ἰοάννου), as found in the ancient Barberini euchologion,[7] was originally a synonym for

---

[4] H. Engberding, "Die westsyrische Anaphora des Hl. Johannes Chrysostomus und ihre Probleme," *OC* 39 (1955) 33–37.

[5] F. van de Paverd, *Zur Geschichte der Messliturgie in Antiocheia und Konstantinopel gegen Ende des vierten Jahrhunderts. Analyse der Quellen bei Johannes Chrysostomus* (OCA 187; Rome, 1970).

[6] G. Wagner, *Der Ursprung der Chrysostomusliturgie* (LQF 59; Münster W., 1973).

[7] A. Jacob, "La tradition manuscrite de la liturgie de saint Jean Chrysostome (VIIIe-XII2 siècles)," in *Eucharisties d'Orient et d'Occident* 2, 109–38; *BAR*, no. 31, 30–31.

"anaphora"; consequently, this prayer, which is attributed to Chrysostom, is followed by other Eucharistic Prayers that make up an anaphora in the full sense, and these form a single group in the manuscripts. A comparison with the anaphora of the *XII-A* shows (Wagner said) that the name was not of itself proof of antiquity and that the similarity to the name given by Leontius of Byzantium[8] was a mere coincidence.

Wagner concluded, in essence, that not only does it seem impossible to maintain that the Antiochene anaphora is a witness independent of the primitive text of the *CB*, but that in addition all the proofs point to the contrary thesis, that is, the dependence of the Antiochene anaphora on the anaphora of Chrysostom. Therefore, when we take into account also the comparison with the saint's works, the anaphora of *CB* can be said to have been the result of a redaction by Chrysostom, despite the contrary and not easily disputed testimony deriving from the silence of Leontius of Byzantium. The points made in Engberding's work are really not so opposed to Wagner's claim. In fact, when the two anaphoras overlap, the Greek text seems, in general, to have better preserved the original.

The most likely hypothesis, then, is that behind the two anaphoras lies one and the same text, in Greek, which Chrysostom took over, with his own modifications and insertions, thus following a procedure similar to that of Basil in the anaphora attributed to him. Chrysostom can therefore be called the author, in a broad sense, of the anaphora that bears his name; it does not seem impossible, consequently, that features of this anaphora should be reflected in his writings. On the other hand, given the creative freedom that kept any one anaphora from being regarded as fixed and normative before the sixth century, it is not possible to maintain that the anaphora of the *XII-A* should be regarded as representative of the Antiochene Church.

### 2. Analytical Commentary on Anaphora CB

The commentary will follow the structural outline of the anaphora and bring out some more characteristic aspects of this great prayer,

---

[8] See P. De Meester, "Les origines et les développements du texte grec de la liturgie de saint Jean Chrysostome," in *Crysostomika. Studi e ricerche intorno a S. Giovanni Crisostomo* (Rome, 1907) 245–357, especially 260–1; idem, "Liturgie byzantine," *DACL* 6 (1925) 1592.

the name of which (i.e., anaphora) refers to the action of raising up or offering (see Heb 7:27; 13:15). It consists of the following parts: opening dialogue; theological prayer, introduction to the *Sanctus,* christological prayer, account of institution; anamnesis, epiclesis, intercession, doxology, and Amen of the faithful.

## A. DIACONAL ADMONITION

*Deacon:* "Let us rise to our feet in awe, as is right! Let us be attentive to make the holy offering in peace." *Choir:* "Mercy and peace! Sacrifice of praise!"

This admonition to the entire community is of late origin; before the seventh century there was a simple summons to pay attention to the gifts and the act of offering, but subsequently the admonition developed, taking various forms. Germanus of Constantinople (d. 733), in his commentary *History of the Church,*[9] cites these phrases: μετὰ φόβου Θεοῦ (with fear of God) and τῇ ἀγίᾳ ἀναφορᾷ (to the holy anaphora). While in Antioch, Chrysostom cites this phrase: Ὀρθοὶ στῶμεν καλῶς (let us stand upright in goodness).[10]

## B. DIALOGUE

*Priest:* "The grace of our Lord Jesus Christ, the love of God the Father, and the communion of the Holy Spirit be with all of you." *Choir:* "And with your spirit."

These words of blessing are taken from 2 Cor 13:13. To each person of the Trinity is assigned the gift for which we look to him: grace from the Son (John 1:14, 17); love (ἀγάπη) from the Father, who is the source of love for the other persons (in the anaphora of James this phrase comes first), according to Romans 5:5; communion or κοινωνία (see Gal 4:4-6; Rom 8:14) is the special word signifying the presence of the Spirit in the eucharistic community, but it also signifies communion with the Church, because the gift of the Holy Spirit is not only the fundamental means to sacramental participation but

[9] F. A. Brightman, "The Historia Mystagogica and Other Greek Commentaries on the Byzantine Liturgy," *JThS* 9 (108) 392–93.

[10] John Chrysostom, *De incomprehensibili Dei natura contra anomaeos* 4, 5 (PG 48:734); R. Raft, "Textual Problems in the Diaconal Admonition before the Anaphora in the Byzantine Tradition," *OCP* 49 (1983) 340–64.

also the condition for the unity of the members of the body of the Church.[11]

*Priest:* "(Let us raise) our hearts on high!" *Choir:* "They are directed to the Lord." *Priest:* "Let us give thanks to the Lord!" *Choir:* "It is right and just to worship the Father, the Son, and the Holy Spirit, the consubstantial and indivisible Trinity."

The biblical text echoed here is Lam 3:41: "Let us lift our hearts above our hands, to God in the heavens." In other anaphoras we find "spiritually" or "mind and hearts" (Anaphora of James) instead of "hearts."[12] This elevation of the soul to the Lord (see Ps 24:1) is necessary, according to Chrysostom,[13] in order to unite ourselves with the choir of angels and to join the seraphim in singing the hymn *Sanctus* near the Throne of Glory. The appeal to give thanks to the Lord is also mentioned by Chrysostom in his *Commentary on the Letter to the Corinthians* (18, 3).

According to the ancients, this dialogue has three purposes. First, it reminds the community present of the divine plan of salvation, which is as it were summed up in the thanksgiving or blessing that, in the context, the celebrant is giving to the people as he recites the formula. Secondly, it proclaims that the anaphora actualizes the plan of salvation in a sacramental form. Finally, it reminds the community that "God-is-here-with-us" ("Immanuel": see Exod 3:12 where this is said to Moses in view of the Exodus; Matt 1:18: to Mary before the incarnation). In the passage cited Chrysostom says: "During the most awesome mysteries the priest prays for the people and the people pray for the priest."[14]

## C. THEOLOGICAL PRAYER (PREFACE)

*Priest (in a low voice).* "It is right and just that we should celebrate you, bless you, give you thanks, and worship in every place where you rule.

[11] John Chrysostom, *In S. Pentecosten* 1, 4 (PG 50:458); J. Matheos, "L'action du Saint Esprit dans la liturgie de St. Jean Chrysostome," *POC* 9 (1959) 193–208; John Chrysostom, *In 2 Cor. homiliae* 18, 3 (PG 61:527). The response of the faithful is "And with your spirit."

[12] R. Taft, "The Dialogue before the Anaphora in the Byzantine Eucharistic Liturgy. II. The *Sursum corda*," *OCP* 54 (1988) 47–77.

[13] *Sur l'incompréhensibilité de Dieu*, Homily 4 (SCh 28bis) 258–63. = PG 48:734.

[14] J. Lécuyer, "La théologie de l'anaphore selon les Pères de l'Ecole d'Antioche," *OS* 6 (1961) 385–412.

For you are the ineffable, inconceivable, invisible, incomprehensible God who are always the same, the same eternally — you and your only-begotten Son and your Holy Spirit. You have drawn us out of nothing into being, and when we fell, you raised us up and have not ceased to do everything necessary in order to lead us to heaven, and you have given us the gift of your future kingdom. For all this, we give thanks to you and to your only-begotten Son and to your Holy Spirit, for all your blessings which we know and those which we do not know, those manifest and those hidden, but done for our sake. We give you thanks also for this liturgy which you have deigned to accept from our hands, even though you are waited on by thousands of archangels, myriads of angels, the cherubim and the seraphim with their six wings and many eyes, sublime winged beings, *(aloud)* who sing the hymn of victory, acclaiming you, crying out, and saying:"

*Choir:* "Holy, Holy, Holy, Lord of hosts; heaven and earth are filled with you glory. Hosanna in the highest heavens. Blessed is he who comes in the name of the Lord. Hosanna in the highest heavens."

The fact that this first part (preface) of the thanksgiving is spoken in a low voice makes it a kind of unspoken invocation, as Chrysostom says in the third of his *Homilies against the Anomeans*. Ignatius of Antioch writes in his *Letter to the Trallians* 5, 3, that the bishop should remain silent (see also *Eph.* 5, 3). The adverb μυστικῶς (here = "silently") occurs also in the hymn of the Cherubim (the χερουβικόν), but with a different meaning: "We who mystically represent the Cherubim." Until the sixth century all the prayers of the anaphora were recited aloud.[15]

Thanksgiving for "blessings which we know and those which we do not know, those manifest and those hidden, but done for our sake" is found only in the anaphora of Chrysostom (and in the East Syrian anaphora of Nestorius, which derives from it). Therefore this first part of the anaphora (in the western rites "preface" means a prayer "said before" the people, and not a prayer preceding another)

---

[15] See P. Trempelas, "L'Audition de l'anaphore eucharistique par le peuple," in *L'Eglise et les Eglises* (Chevetogne, 1955) 2, 207–8; Eusebius, *The History of the Church from Christ to Constantine* 7, 9, trans. G. A. Williamson (Baltimore, 1965) 291 (Letter of Dionysius of Alexandria to Pope Sixtus); *Novellae* of Justinian, 137; Chrysostom, *Homilies against the Anomeans* IV (PG 48:707).

celebrates the praise of God: the worship, praise (αἰνεῖν), and celebration (ὑμνεῖν) of God in himself, according to the way of apophatic
theology, in which the divine attributes are multiplied, but qualified
by a negative *a-* or *in-*. The words "you and your only-begotten Son
and your Holy Spirit," designating the Trinitarian recipient of this
celebration of praise, are perhaps a later addition, because a moment
later the prayer is addressed to the Father (see the anaphora of
James). In the anaphora of Mark, the Son is mentioned as mediator of
creation and of the offering.

The primary intention of the prayer, namely praise, is accompanied
by another: thanksgiving for the divine works. The commemoration
of the economy of salvation links creation and redemption directly
with the "theological" celebration and with the thanksgiving: "We
give you thanks also for this liturgy."

D. THE TRISAGION (THRICE-HOLY)
The singing of the Trisagion repeats the acclamation of the four living
beings (Rev 4:7-8), whom Isaiah had already seen in his vision (Isa
6:2-3). Germanus of Constantinople has this comment in his *History of
the Church*:

"Just as God speaks invisibly to Moses and Moses to God, so the
priest stands between the two cherubim at the propitiatorium. He
bows because of the glorious splendor of the divinity, which it is not
permitted to contemplate directly. Spiritually, he sees and contem-
plates the heavenly liturgy and the divine splendor of the supersub-
stantial Trinity, the source of life."[16]

Maximus the Confessor in his *Mystagogy* (628/630) assigns a
twofold meaning to the Trisagion. In the broad meaning (γενικῶς)
which it has when uttered by all the faithful, the threefold "Holy" of
this hymn to God signifies their future unity and equality with the
incorporeal, spiritual Powers. It is for this reason that human beings
will be instructed to sing in union with the heavenly Powers and call
"Holy, in a threefold sanctification," the one divinity in three persons;
then humanity will be caught up in an eternal unchanging movement around God.[17] This general (or typical) meaning, which prefig-

[16] Brightman, "The Historia Mystagogica" (note 9, above) 393.
[17] Maximus the Confessor, *Mystagogia* (PG 91:657).

ures the union of human beings with the angels for a common praise of the Trinity in the world to come, also becomes particular (ἰδικῶς), that is, mystical: "By means of the Trisagion, the Word places souls in the number of the angels and grants them the same knowledge which the angels have of the theology that says 'Holy.'"[18]

## E. CHRISTOLOGICAL PRAYER AND ACCOUNT OF INSTITUTION

*Priest (in a low voice).* "Together with these blessed powers, we too, O Sovereign, Friend of humanity, cry out and say: Holy are you, entirely holy, you and your only-begotten Son and your Holy Spirit, Holy are you, entirely holy, and magnificent is your glory. You have so loved this world of yours as to give your only-begotten Son in order that whoever believes in him may not perish but have everlasting life. After he had come and had completed the entire plan [of our salvation] for our sake, on the night in which he handed himself over for the life of the world, taking bread in his holy, pure, spotless hands, after having given thanks, he blessed it, broke it, and gave it to his disciples and apostles, saying:

*(aloud)* "Take, eat, this is my body which is broken for you for the forgiveness of sins." *Choir:* "Amen." *Priest (in a low voice):* "In the same way the cup also, after having eaten, saying *(aloud)*: Drink, all of you, of this: this is my blood of the new covenant, which is being poured out for you and for many for the forgiveness of sins." *Choir:* "Amen."

## F. ANAMNESIS AND EPICLESIS

*Priest (in a low voice):* "Remembering, therefore, this saving commandment and everything that was accomplished for us: the cross, the burial, the resurrection after three days, the ascension into heaven, the sitting at the right hand, the second and glorious coming, *(aloud)* we offer you what is yours from what is yours, in everything and for everything." *Choir:* "We praise you, we bless you, we give you thanks, O Lord, and we pray to you, O our God."

It may be noted that the concluding words, "in everything and for everything (κατὰ πάντα καὶ διὰ πάντα)," which accompany the elevation

---

[18] Ibid., ch. 13 (PG 91:962C).

of the paten and the chalice, refer to the conformity of the liturgical action with the tradition handed down.[19] The words were introduced into the Byzantine liturgy in the time of Emperor Justinian, who had the following sentence sculpted around the altar of Hagia Sophia: "O Christ, your servants Justinian and Theodora offer you your gifts, taken from among your gifts." The uttering of the prayer aloud (ἐκφώνως) would indicate that the liturgy is not a repetition of Calvary but a sacramental contemplation of the ascension, since Christ has gone up to heaven with his sacrifice, as Chrysostom says.[20]

*Priest (in a low voice):* "We offer you also this rational (λογική) and un-bloody (ἀναίμακτος) worship; we pray and beseech you: Send your Holy Spirit on us and on these gifts."

*Deacon:* "Lord, bless this holy bread." *Priest:* "And make of this bread the precious body of your Christ." *Deacon:* "Amen. Bless, O Lord, the holy cup." *Priest:* "And let what is in this cup [become] the precious blood of your Christ" — *Deacon:* "Amen. Bless them both, O Lord" — *Priest:* "by transforming (μεταβολῶν) them through your Holy Spirit" — *Deacon:* "Amen, amen, amen" — *Priest:* "in order that they may become, for those who participate, sobriety of soul, forgiveness of sins, communion in your Holy Spirit, the fullness of the kingdom of heaven, outspokenness in your presence, and not a condemning judgment."

Note that the words "rational worship" at the beginning of the epiclesis refer to the sacrifice of the Word or Logos (Goar's Latin translation, *rationabilis*, does not bring out this meaning). With regard to the epiclesis I also note that N. Cabasilas has compared it with the prayer in the Canon of the Roman Mass: "through the hands of your holy angel to your altar on high (*per manus sancti angeli tui in sublime altare tuum*)."[21] Among the commentaries on these sections of the anaphora I shall cite Germanus of Constantinople, who writes in his *History of the Church:*

---

[19] A. Raes, "κατὰ πάντα καὶ διὰ πάντα. En tout et pour tout," *OCP* 48 (1964) 216–8. (ET in J. Stead, *The Church, the Liturgy, and the Soul of Man: The Mystagogia of St. Maximus the Confessor* [Still River, Mass., 1982].)

[20] P. De Meester, "Les origines" (note 8, above) 340.

[21] Nicholas Cabasilas, *Explication de la Divine Liturgie,* ed. and trans. S. Salaville (SCh 4bis; Paris, 1953) 176–93 (= PG 150:427–34).

"The priest calls upon God the Father because he is fulfilling the mystery of his Son, and the Son is born anew, that is, the bread is changed into his body and the wine into his blood, thus fulfilling these words of the scriptures: 'Today I have begotten you' (Ps 2:7). Then the Holy Spirit, who is invisibly present due to the consent of the Father and the will of the Son, makes known the divine energy: using the hand of the priest as his witness, he signs and consecrates the holy gifts that have been offered, changing them into the body and blood of Christ, our Lord."[22]

Cabasilas says that the consecration (ἁγιασμός), which follows upon the great theologico-christological prayer, is a true sacrifice (θυσία). He writes:

"The priest then personally offers thanksgiving to God; he glorifies him, he praises him together with the angels, he thanks him for all the blessings bestowed by him from the beginning. Finally, he mentions this ineffable and incomprehensible plan of the Savior for us. Then he consecrates the precious gifts, and the sacrifice is completely accomplished."[23]

Cabasilas then locates the epiclesis in a trinitarian context. The Father takes possession of these sacred gifts on the altar by turning them into the body and blood of his only Son; the Son consecrates them by changing them into his body and his blood; and "by means of the hand and tongue of priests, the Holy Spirit consecrates the mysteries."[24]

G. INTERCESSIONS

*Priest (in a low voice):* "We offer this rational worship (τήν λογικήν ταύτην λατρείαν) for those also who have fallen asleep in the faith: first parents, patriarchs, prophets, apostles, forerunners, evangelists, martyrs, confessors, virgins, and all the spirits of the just who have been brought to fulfillment by faith. *(Aloud)* Especially for our most holy, immaculate, more than blessed, glorious Sovereign, Mary, Mother of God and ever Virgin. . . ."

[22] Germanus of Constantinople, *Historia ecclesiastica*, 60 (PG 98:395).

[23] *Explication*, 27 (SCh 4bis, 175; PG 150:425AB).

[24] Ibid., 28 (SCh 4bis, 177–78; PG 150:428B); Simeon of Thessalonike, *Interpretatio Ecclesiae et Liturgiae*, 86 (PG 155: 732–33); idem, *De sacra liturgia*, 99 (PG 155:297A).

*Choir:* "It is truly right to proclaim you blessed, O Mother of God, you who are most blessed, utterly immaculate, and Mother of our God. We exalt you who are more worthy of veneration than the cherubim and incomparably more glorious than the seraphim, and who without any corruption gave birth to the Word of God, being truly the Mother of God."

*Priest (in a low voice):* "For St. John, prophet, forerunner, and baptizer; for the holy, glorious, illustrious apostles; for St. *N.* whose memory we celebrate; and for all your saints. For our petitions: visit us, O God. And remember all those who have fallen asleep in the hope of rising to everlasting life. *(Mention of those he wants to remember.)* Grant them rest there where the light of your face shines on them. We also pray you: Remember, Lord, all the orthodox bishops who correctly dispense the word of your truth; the entire presbytery; the deacons in the Lord, and every priestly order. We also offer this rational worship for the entire world, for the holy, catholic, and apostolic Church, for those who live a pure and devout life, for our most faithful kings, the friends of Christ, and for their courts and their army. Grant them, Lord, a peaceful reign so that we too, in the tranquillity they provide, may live a serene and quiet life, filled with devotion and holiness.

*(Aloud)* "Be mindful first of all, Lord, of our most holy father, the pope of Rome, and of our most blessed patriarch [or most holy metropolitan or archbishop or bishop, N., most dear to God]. Grant to all your holy Churches that they may exist in peace, security, good health and long life, as they rightly dispense the word of your truth."

*Deacon (remembers the living and says aloud):* "And for him who offers these holy gifts, the devout priest N. For the salvation of our most religious kings, who are protected by God, and for the salvation and help of the people here present and of those whom each person has in mind, and of all and of all." *Choir:* "And of all and of all."

*Priest (in a low voice):* "Be mindful, Lord, of this city (or country or monastery) in which we dwell, and of every city and land and of the faithful who dwell in them. Be mindful, Lord, of those at sea, of travelers, the sick, the suffering, the imprisoned, and of their salvation. Be mindful, Lord, of those who bear good fruit and those who do good in your holy Churches, and those who are mindful of the poor. Send your mercies on all of us."[25]

H. Doxology

(Aloud). "And grant that with one mouth and one heart we may glorify and sing the praises of your most venerable and wonderful name: of the Father and of the Son and of the Holy Spirit, now and always and for endless ages." *Choir:* "Amen." *Priest (turning the people, says aloud):* "And the mercy of the great God and our Savior Jesus Christ be with all of you." *Choir:* "And with your spirit."

*3. Theology of the* CB *Anaphora*
Chrysostom's revision of this anaphora has given its first section (down to the account of institution) a unified and also a more logical structure, because all its elements are now linked by the idea, repeated a number of times, of thanks and praise. The first part of *XII-A*, on the other hand, shows prayers that are almost independent of each other. In the *Sanctus* and account of institution of *XII-A* the influence of the West Syrian tradition can be seen.

A. In the First Part of the Thanksgiving, Down to the *Sanctus* *Naming of the Trinity.* The three persons are joined simply by the copulative "and"; according to J. Wagner, this trinitarian formula is not unconnected with the trinitarian controversy of the fourth century in Antioch and would represent the formula defended (ca. 350) by Diodorus (Chrysostom's teacher) and Flavian as the expression of Nicene orthodoxy (see Matt 28:19), as seen in other trinitarian formulas.[26] Praise that is focused on the incomprehensibility of God tallies with the writings of Chrysostom against the Anomeans. This

---

[25] G. Winkler, "Die Interzessionen der Chrysostomusanaphora in ihrer geschichtlichen Entwicklung," *OCP* 36 (1970) 301–36; 37 (1971) 333–83. In Codex Barberini Gr. 336, only the different categories of saints are mentioned; there is as yet no remembrance of the Mother of God. But there is no thanksgiving for the saints, as Cabasilas interprets the text (*Explication*; SCh4bis, 208–12 and 274–95). The solemn invocation of the Mother of God goes back to the beginning of the sixth century. The phrase "It is truly right to proclaim you blessed" introduces a hymn composed at Mount Athos in 980.

[26] For the early symbols of faith see DS 1–6 and 11; for the more complete symbols, DS 40–2.

incomprehensibility of the divine essence and indeed of the entire economy of salvation is such that true "knowledge" (γνῶσις) is "ignorance" (ἀγνωσία), that is, a partial knowledge, because we can say that God is wise and provident but we do not know how he possesses these qualities.[27] As Chrysostom says when commenting on Ps 138:14 (LXX), only the religious wonder born of the experience of faith can thank God for his incomprehensibility (ἀκαταληψία).[28]

*The work of salvation.* This divine action, which is presented here as the focus of the thanksgiving, relates to three stages in the existence of human beings. The first is creation, which is the work exclusively of God who draws things out of nothingness. The second is the human response of sin (the fall) to this initial mercy and to the new mercy that raises up again. The third is definitive salvation and entrance into the kingdom. The text that lies behind this schematic history of salvation is Eph 2:5-7. Chrysostom's favorite word in describing salvation is "to lead up, lift up" (ἀναγεῖ), referring to the elevation of human nature by Christ. With its typical Jewish phrasing ("For all this we give thanks to you"), the end of this thanksgiving speaks of "blessings which we know and those which we do not know"; this is an expression which Chrysostom got, he says, from the prayer of a holy person.[29]

## B. AFTER THE *SANCTUS*

After this acclamation, which is incorporated into the general thanksgiving, the history of salvation is further described in a strictly christological perspective, running from the citation of John 3:16 to the end of the anamnesis. The concrete events in this saving activity are listed in a way that is faithful to the primitive texts (whereas *XII-A* is influenced by the Syriac tradition, which is reflected in the anamnesis addressed to the Son and not to the Father). The emphasis on the glorious aspects of the mystery of Christ can be seen in the use of the words "cross" (σταυρός), "burial" (τάφος), and "sitting at the right hand" (τῆς ἐκ δεξιῶν καθέδρας), which are always understood both as

---

[27] See Chrysostom, *De incomprehensibili* 1, 4 (PG 38:707A).

[28] Idem, *Adversus Iudaeos* 1, 1 (PG 53:404); *De incomprehensibili* 1, 4 (PG 48:705).

[29] Idem, *Hom. X ad Col.* 3 (PG 62:368-9): "I know a man who used to pray thus: 'We give you thanks for all your blessings, of which we are unworthy, from the first day until today, for those we know and those we do not know, for the manifest and the hidden.'"

saving events and as glorious completions.[30] The entire history of salvation converges on the present Eucharist, in virtue of the fact that it is a memorial offered by Christ to the Father. Therefore the formula "We offer you what is yours from what is yours" translates the eucharistic memorial into sacrificial terms. The content of this anamnesis is fundamentally the same as that of the anamnesis in the anaphora of the *Apostolic Tradition*. (In *XII-A* the express mention of the sacrificial element is lacking.)

In the epiclesis, finally, this salvation takes concrete form in a cultic act, inasmuch as the consecration itself, looked at here from the viewpoint of the divine action, is the subject of an expansion. The one reality has two aspects: one emphasizes the visible rite, the other the invisible action. The second part, concerning the participation of the congregation, includes some very meaningful phrases: sobriety of soul[31]; the communion effected by the Spirit (κοινωνία); and outspokenness (παρρησία) before God. The difference from *XII-A* in describing the effects which participation in the Eucharist brings through the mediation of the Spirit (using Johannine categories) shows the originality that marks the intervention of the patriarch.

C. COMMUNION EPICLESIS

R. Taft's study[32] enables us to understand better the theology of Communion present in this postconsecratory epiclesis.

The history of this important part of the anaphora, which, unlike the Roman Canon, places the formulation of the fruits of the Eucharist within the epiclesis to the Holy Spirit, helps us to grasp the significance of the formulary. The graces or fruits of the Eucharist are certainly also mentioned in other parts of the anaphora: in the preanaphoral dialogue, in the doxology of the anaphora, and in the greetings of the precommunion rites (in the introduction to the Our Father and in the late, medieval prayers of preparation for Communion). It

---

[30] Long ago, A. Baumstark, "Zur Geschichte der Chrysostomusliturgie," *Theologie und Glaube* 5 (1913) 109–11, called attention to the reference of these words to glory; see P. Stockmeyer, *Theologie und Kult des Kreuzes bei Johannes Chrysostomus. Ein Beitrag zum Verständnis des Kreuzes im 4. Jahrhundert* (Trier, 1966) 92–116, 230–38. 255–56.

[31] Matheos, "L'action du Saint Esprit" (note 11, above) 200–2.

[32] R. Taft, "The Fruits of Communion in the Anaphora of St. John Chrysostom," in *Psallendum. Miscellanea di studi in onore di J. Pinell I Pons* (SA 105; AL 15) 275–302.

will be enough to refer to the prayer at the preparation of the bread and wine (προσκομίδια), where the fruits are already listed, anticipating what is said in the epiclesis: "And make us worthy to find favor with you in your presence, so that our sacrifice may be pleasing to you and so that the good spirit of your grace may remain on us and on these present gifts and on all your people."

The epiclesis, which follows upon the block made up of the account of institution, the anamnesis, and the offertory, begins with a prayer for the transformation of the gifts; and, assuming that this is granted through the coming of the Holy Spirit on the gifts, the prayer ends with the request for the six fruits of Communion: sobriety of soul, forgiveness of sins, communion in your Holy Spirit, the fullness of the Kingdom of God, outspokenness in your presence, and no condemnatory judgment.

These fruits are received by those who eat and drink, that is, who communicate sacramentally. Let me dwell on only some of them.

*Forgiveness of sins.* This aspect, already mentioned in the anaphora of the *Apostolic Constitutions* (CA, VIII, 12, 39), appears also in the Alexandrian anaphoras (Mark; Serapion; Coptic Mark). The very words of institution in Matt 26:28 (cup poured out for the forgiveness of sins)[33] ensure this effect, and the exclusion from Communion due to serious sins is part of the tradition of the early anaphoras. If the mystery of the cross is presented once again by the Eucharist, then the latter, too, will bring forgiveness of sins.[34] But some more serious sins ("capital" sins) excluded a person being healed by the Eucharist, and it was necessary to have recourse to the discipline imposed by the ministers of the Church; later on, the development of this discipline gave rise to various forms of reconciliation. Chrysostom's emphasis on the necessity of being worthy to approach the cup is proof that the prayer for the forgiveness of sins in the epiclesis is not an invitation to those burdened by serious sins that they should approach the Eucharist without having been cleansed.

*Communion in your Holy Spirit.* The greeting that begins the anaphora already anticipates this communion of the Holy Spirit (2 Cor

---

[33] See 1 Cor 11:27.

[34] See P. Sorci, *L'eucaristia per la remissione dei peccati. Ricerca nel sacramentario Veronese* (Palermo, 1979); C. Blanchette, *Pénitence et eucharistie. Le rapport et la complementarité dans la théologie contemporaine: dossier d'une question controversée* (Rome, 1986).

13:13: ἡ κοινωνία τοῦ Ἁγίου Πνεύματος). While communion in the body of Christ (see 1 Cor 10:16-17) is the first effect of the Eucharist, Chrysostom also relates this work of the Spirit to trinitarian theology: "For the Father and for the Son and for the Holy Spirit the gifts and the power are one."[35] He says that this communion in the body of Christ is "a communion with Christ himself."[36] Thus he writes elsewhere: "Let them, like nursing babies, suck the grace of the Spirit; to participate, through that grace, in the divinity of Christ is to participate also in his communion with the Father and with the Holy Spirit, who share the same divine nature; to receive the Eucharist, then, is to receive the Holy Spirit."[37] This is in fact Paul's thesis in 1 Corinthians 10 and 12:12, where "forming a single body" through the Eucharist is parallel to "being baptized in a single Spirit to form a single body, and we have all been made to drink of the one Spirit."

That the reference here is to a communion "with" the Spirit and not of the Spirit (1 Cor 13:13 — as though the genitive were subjective, meaning, that is, that our mutual communion is caused by the Spirit) is clear from patristic thought and the liturgical texts.[38]

*The fullness of the kingdom.* This fruit refers to the petition in the Our Father: "Your kingdom come." The adjective "heavenly" ("of heaven") is not found in the ancient manuscripts and is a late interpolation in the received text *(textus receptus)*. In fact, the reference is not only to a future kingdom but also to one which is inchoatively present in the communion that is the Church, and of which the messianic eucharistic banquet is a sacrament; see Matt 8:11; Luke 13:29 ("you shall sit at table with Abraham . . . in the kingdom of heaven"). Communion in the Spirit not only unites us to the life of the Trinity; it also unites us to one another in the body of Christ which is the Church. The socio-ecclesial dimension is indispensable in the theology of Communion, according to the original tradition: see Matt 5:23-24: reconciliation before offering at the altar (a text taken over in the *Didache* 14, 1–2). It is to this practice that Pliny

---

[35] John Chrysostom, *In Romanos homiliae* 13, 8 (PG 60:519).

[36] Idem, *In 1 Corinthios homiliae* 24, 2 (PG 61:201).

[37] Idem, *In Matthaeum homiliae* 82, 6 (PG 53:744).

[38] P. Nautin, *Homélies paschales* II. *Trois homélies dans la tradition d'Origène* (SCh 36; Paris, 1953) 28–30; Irenaeus, *Adversus haereses* II, 293 (ed. W. W. Harvey; Cambridge, 1857).

refers in his famous letter to Trajan (*Ep.* X, 96, 7), when he says that believers in Christ "gathered before dawn on an appointed day and committed themselves by a religious oath not to commit any crime, such as theft or robbery or adultery or perjury or a refusal to return what has been borrowed."

*Not a condemning judgment.* The final petition, with its hendiadys (literally, "judgment and condemnation"), speaks of being spared a judgment of guilt, a judgment of condemnation. This petition is out of place in the epiclesis, where it follows all the positive aspects represented by the other fruits of Communion. Does its presence signify a contamination by the precommunion prayer already cited in which this phrase appears (Matheos' thesis)? But it can be maintained that, on the contrary, this precommunion prayer repeats the epiclesis and not the other way round; that the testimony of the manuscripts is reliable; that such a petition occurs also in the Byzantine anaphora of Basil *(BB)* and, in substance, also in the anaphora of Serapion; that in the Syriac version of *XII-A* the epiclesis is expanded to the point of mentioning the final judgment. The reference to Paul's teaching that "whoever receives the Eucharist unworthily receives his own condemnation" (see 1 Cor 11:27-34) is incontrovertible. In the context not of individual guilt deriving from secret sins but of a social ethics calling for a life of communion, we can understand how the need of this discernment of the social body of the community, that is, of the mystical body of Christ, is indispensable.

## II. THE EAST SYRIAN ANAPHORAS

### 1. Three Anaphoras

The Anaphora of Addai and Mari *(A-M)*, used by the Nestorians, Chaldeans, and Malabarese, was composed in Syriac and is characterized by a specifically Syrian parallelism that is modelled on Jewish blessings: the *birkat ha-zan* (1st *ghanta* or section: blessing of the Name of God), the *birkat ha-aretz* (2nd *ghanta:* thanksgiving for the effects of the salvation accomplished by Christ), and the *birkat ha-Yerusalayim* (3rd *ghanta:* intercessions), into which the block containing the account of institution and the epiclesis has been inserted.[39]

---

[39] See B. Botte, "Les anaphores syriennes orientales," in *Eucharisties d'Orient et d'Occident* (note 1, above) 2, 7–24; D. Webb, "La liturgie nestorienne des apôtres Addaï et Mari dans la tradition manuscrite," ibid., 25–50.

The Second Anaphora of Nestorius, which is related to the Anaphora of *CB*, especially through its thanksgiving (with passages taken in large part from *BB*), has an epiclesis matching that of *A-M*, but with the interpolation of a phrase from *CB*: "transforming them [the bread and wine] through your Holy Spirit"; it retains the peculiarity of placing the intercessions after the anamnesis and before the epiclesis.

The Anaphora of Theodore of Mopsuestia has an epiclesis corresponding to that of *A-M*, with the interpolation of the change of the bread and wine into the body and blood of Christ, similar to that in the Anaphora of Nestorius. It is also distinguished by the fact that the account of institution and the anamnesis differ from the traditional ones in that they place the order to eat and drink at the end of the account of institution, which ends with the sentence: "when you assemble. . . ." Since the two Anaphoras of Nestorius and Theodore are compilations based on the two Byzantine anaphoras, being partially translated from the Greek, they will not be analyzed here.

## 2. The Anaphora of the Apostles Addai and Mari

### A. THE FIRST GHANTA
This is addressed to God in the second person, in accordance with Jewish practice, and develops the theme of the blessing of God ("the Name"), Creator of the universe and humanity, whose work is prolonged by the new and more wonderful creation brought about through the redemptive action of Christ. Due to the utterly free character of these works, this first blessing turns into praise. The theology of the Name (see Exod 3:13-16; 6:3) looks primarily to God but also to the Name "that is above every other name," that is, the Name of Christ (Phil 2:9; Eph 1:20-21). Clement of Rome already addresses his prayer of praise to the Name (1 Clem 59, 3). This praise is developed in the commemoration.

### B. THE SECOND GHANTA
In the thanksgiving, the prayer commemorates the blessings of the new covenant, that is, not only the historical events but their effects: incarnation, forgiveness, and knowledge (the same theme is seen into the Benedictus and the Magnificat, which are full of Old Testament echoes). The third section follows upon a conclusion similar to that of the *birkat ha-aretz*: "And for all your graces, we give you praise and honor, now and always through the ages."

## C. The Third Ghanta

This turns into intercession, because it continues to speak of the creative and redemptive work by introducing the festive embolism consisting of the eucharistic institution and the anamnesis. This last fits in naturally with a missing account of institution (as B. Botte has pointed out, and of which we have witnesses in Syria), one that ends with the words: "You shall do this every time you gather in my name." The anamnesis reads as follows: "And we also, your servants . . . who have gathered in your name . . . celebrate the mystery . . . of the passion, death, burial, and resurrection of our Lord and Savior, Jesus Christ." Remembering these divine actions, as the celebrating people faithfully do, they can beseech God to be mindful of his people: "Lord, remember us." In the list of saving events given in the anamnesis of this anaphora there is lacking what is found in all the other Oriental anaphoras, namely, mention of the ascension (after the resurrection), the sitting at the Father's right hand, and the parousia.

In the structure, then, of this anaphora which is made up of three prayers (said aloud), the first and last words of each prayer (*ghanta*) are repeated, and the *ghantas* end with their respective doxologies (*kanuna*). The latter are preceded, depending on the case, by a priestly prayer (of later origin) that is penitential in character and said in a low voice (*kusapa*). Two blocks can be distinguished: the first consists of the thanksgiving and praise for redemption and creation, which, broadly speaking, culminates in the *Sanctus,* is continued in a more detailed commemoration of redemption, and ends in a doxology; the second consists of the various intercessions and includes the anamnesis, epiclesis, and final doxology.

## III. THE ALEXANDRIAN ANAPHORA OF ST. MARK

This anaphora, which since the sixteenth century has been reserved for days of fast and for the Marian month of *kihak* (November 27–December 26 in the Julian calendar) and is celebrated by the Copts (in the Coptic recension attributed to St. Cyril), is proper to the Alexandrian Church. The other two anaphoras used there, the Alexandrian Anaphoras of Basil and of Gregory the Theologian (Gregory of Nazianzus), are of the Antiochene type and were therefore imported. The two characteristic traits of the Anaphora of St. Mark are: the presence of intercessions between the thanksgiving and the *Sanctus,* and the presence of two epicleses, one before and one after the account of institution.[40]

*Introductory dialogue.* The formula used here, "The Lord be with all" (ὁΚύριος μετὰ πάντων) is also used elsewhere. — *Thanksgiving and praise.* The subject of this is the creation of the world and humanity through the mediation of Christ (Wis 9:1; John 1:9). — *Offering of the sacrifice.* The subsequent sacrifice is anticipated here: "through whom [Christ] we offer you the spiritual sacrifice, this unbloody worship," with its allusion to Mal 1:11 and the addition, at the end, of the words "sacrifice" (ἐπιθυσία) and "offering" (προσφορά), which further specify the words of Malachi. The anamnesis lacks a formula of offering, which occurs only at the end of the thanksgiving in the verb "we offer" (προσφέρομεν).

*Intercessions.* These precede the *Sanctus* and are like, in part, to those in the Greek Anaphora of St. James. — *Introduction to the Sanctus.* There is an introduction (citation of Eph 1:21), then a patchwork of biblical texts (Dan 7:10; Ezek 1:5-18; Rev 4:6-8; Isa 6:2-3), and finally a phrase linking the earthly liturgy to the heavenly liturgy of the angels. — *After the Sanctus.* The embolism is based on the word "full" (πλήρης) and not simply "holy" (ἅγιος), as in the Syro-Antiochene anaphoras, in order to make the transition to the (first) *epiclesis:* "Fill this sacrifice with your blessing through the coming of your Most Holy Spirit." — *Account of institution.* This is introduced by the conjunction "because" (ὅτι), referring to the offering expressed in the thanksgiving. — *Anamnesis.* This has three stages: a transition (see 1 Cor 11:25-26), a commemoration which develops the Pauline sentence so as to become a proclamation, and a confession of faith. The mysteries of Christ's life are grouped under these three verbs: "we proclaim," "we confess," "we await."

*(Second) epiclesis.* This longer epiclesis (partly inspired by the Anaphora of Chrysostom) is more developed in comparison with the first, undifferentiated, preconsecratory epiclesis. Two themes are developed: a theology of the Holy Spirit and a listing of the effects of his coming upon the gifts and upon the participants (for this last element see the parallel passage in the Anaphora of St. James). — *Doxology.* This is like that of the other two Alexandrian anaphoras.

---

[40] See R.-G. Coquin, "L'anaphore alexandrine de saint Marc," in ibid., 51–82.

The general character of this anaphora is thus more kerygmatic than theological (as compared, for example, with the Anaphora of Basil). In fact, the initial thanksgiving looks only to creation and simply refers to the mediation of the Word without any mention of the incarnation; the mysteries of the life of Christ that are listed in the anamnesis are not the objects of commemoration but are articles of faith. The *Sanctus,* lacking as it does the additional text of Isaiah 6:3 (Hosanna . . . Blessed . . . ), is purely latreutic, without any emphasis on the theme of glory. As a result, the *Sanctus* lacks any reference to Christ.

## IV. COMPARATIVE SYNTHESIS
## OF THE THREE ANAPHORAL TRADITIONS

A synoptic comparison of the three traditions — the Antiochene-Byzantine, the East Syrian, and the Alexandrian — brings to light the following characteristic traits in each section of the anaphoras.

*The one addressed in the celebration.* In *A-M* it is the divine Name (the addition of the persons of the Trinity is late), which is usually identified with the Father (in *CB* the explicit mention of the Trinity is late), while in *BB* the Trinitarian structure is more explicit. In the Anaphora of Mark the Word is mediator of creation and of the offering.

*Praise of God.* This is the purpose of the celebration. In *CB,* however, thanksgiving for the divine works takes precedence over praise of God in himself; in the Anaphora of Mark the theme of offering predominates over the theme of praise.

*Sanctus.* In *CB* the *Sanctus* seems less appropriately linked to the preceding theme of thanksgiving; this is true also in the Anaphora of *A-M* and in that of Mark. In *BB* the introduction to the *Sanctus* seems to belong to the structure (in the other anaphoras it is a later insertion). In the Alexandrian anaphoras the introduction to the *Sanctus* is peculiar to them; and the *Sanctus,* lacking as it does the second part (Matt 21:9), prepares the way for the sanctification of the gifts before the epicletic prayer.

*The commemoration of the plan of salvation.* It is a unified prayer in the Anaphora of Mark due to the linking of the work of creation and redemption. In the other anaphoras there is a separation between the commemoration of the Old Testament and the commemoration of Christ. In *CB* the commemoration of the works of God is joined directly to the theological celebration (i.e., praise and thanksgiving to

God). In the Anaphora of Mark there is no commemoration of any kind between the *Sanctus* and the account of institution. In the Anaphora of *A-M* the theological commemoration is concerned more with the fruits of God's plan for us than with the plan itself (in God and in time).

The purpose of the christological commemoration, which draws on texts of the Bible, is to introduce the account of institution. In the Antiochene anaphoras the account comes after the commemoration, whereas in the Syro-Chaldean anaphora the account is connected with the remembrance of the fathers and the just, so that the remembrance of Christ is called for by the remembrance of the faithful and vice versa. In the Alexandrian anaphoras, on the other hand, the account comes after the epiclesis, which follows upon the *Sanctus* and before the last and properly so-called epiclesis: thus located in the part devoted to intercession, it acquires a greater relief and value (see the Roman Canon). In the Egyptian tradition, the responses of the faithful to the two parts of the account are ancient; in addition to the Amen there is a twofold profession of faith (in Greek): "We believe, we confess, and we glorify." In the Chaldean rite the priest says, after the account: "And he has left us the commemoration of our salvation, this mystery which we offer in your presence."

*Anamnesis*. In the Alexandrian anaphora this prayer is attached to the Pauline text of Christ's command, while in the Chaldean it is attached to Christ's command as found in the Syrian tradition preserved in the *Diatessaron*: "Do this every time you assemble." In the Byzantine rite (and the Roman), the interior remembering of faith is expressed in a participle (μεμνημένοι = *memores*) that is subordinated to the main verb προσφέρομεν = *offerimus*, thus emphasizing the act of offering. In the Antiochene tradition (Anaphora *BB*) the memorial includes the terrible second coming, thereby indicating that the sacrifice is one of propitiation for sinners. On the other hand, the Alexandrian tradition (Anaphora of Mark) exalts rather the glorious mysteries of Christ (but the Coptic liturgy of Cyril has been influenced by the Syrian tradition). The words "in everything and through everything" (κατὰ πάντα καὶ διὰ πάντα: Byzantine anaphoras) and "and in everything" (καὶ ἐν πᾶσιν: Alexandrian anaphora) refer not to the preceding verb ("we offer") but to the following sentences of thanksgiving and praise; they correspond, though in an adverbial form (κατὰ and διὰ with a temporal and local meaning) to the Latin formula used in the preface ("always and everywhere we give thanks"; *semper et ubique gratias agimus*).

*Offering.* This is the heart of the Byzantine (and Roman) anamnesis and is often linked to the thanksgiving. In the Syrian anaphoras this offering takes first place; to it are then added the pleas for mercy by priest and people.

*Epiclesis.* The thought is expressed in various ways: "(Father,) send the Spirit," in the Syrian and Alexandrian traditions; "Let (the Spirit) come," among the Chaldeans. In the Byzantine anaphoras, the goal of the coming is the offering of the Church, but the Spirit is also invoked upon the ministers ("upon us"). The coming upon the ministers is lacking in the Egyptian and Chaldean anaphoras. The action assigned to the Spirit is expressed by the verb "make" (ποιεῖν) in the Syrian and Alexandrian anaphoras, where, however, other verbs are also used: "show," "bless" (first epiclesis of Mark), and "sanctify" (Chaldean anaphora). The parallelism between these verbs and the account of institution does not lessen the efficacy of the transformative action caused by this sanctification of the gifts. The effects for the faithful are also expressed: holiness in this life (Anaphora of Mark), or as a totality of gifts (as in the Chaldean anaphora): "that this offering may be for us the forgiveness of debts and the remission of sins, the great hope of resurrection from the dead, and new life in the kingdom of heaven together with all those who have been pleasing in your sight."

*Intercessions.* In the Anaphora of *A-M*, the intercessions are uttered before the epiclesis and consist of a more recent prayer of petition (*kusapa;* "Receive . . . and look upon") and an intercession *(ghanta)* for the just ancestors, for the children of the Church, and for all the inhabitants of the earth (see the prayer of Solomon in 1 Kgs 8:56-60). In the Anaphora of Mark the shorter intercessions between the preface and the *Sanctus* and the longer ones later on maintain a degree of connection with the epiclesis and the intentions of the offertory; in the commemoration of the living there is an intercession for the offerers; otherwise the intercessions are based on the celebration of God's mercy and blessings. In this Alexandrian anaphora the two sets of intercessions seems to be a copy of the offertory (see the liturgy of the synagogue). They also reflect the two meanings of the epiclesis: the efficacy of the sacrifice in obtaining the presence of God, who saves and blesses; and the power of the Spirit's sanctifying action to bring the children of God together as at Pentecost.

*Doxology.* In all the anaphoras it celebrates the Name of God, with the addition of descriptive adjectives.

In these three anaphoral traditions — the Byzantine, the East Syrian, and the Alexandrian — we see similarities and differences; the most important visible differences, however, are the intercessions before the anamnesis in the Syro-Chaldean tradition, and the intercessions before the *Sanctus* in the Alexandrian tradition. The ancient *ghanta* in the Anaphora of *A-M* derives from the Jewish tradition, at the point when Solomon invoked the divine presence as he brought the ark into the temple; so now the Church, as the new temple in Christ, invokes the divine favor on the new sacrifice. In the Alexandrian tradition, the intercessions for the holy ones, for the living and the dead, lead up to the *Sanctus,* which in turn opens into the epiclesis, that is, to the coming of the Shekinah with the divine blessings.[41]

[41] E. Lanne, "Les Anaphores eucharistiques de saint Basile et la communauté ecclésiale," *Irén* 55 (1982) 307–8; E. Mélia, "Les Dyptyches liturgiques et leur signification ecclésiologique," in *L'Eglise dans la liturgie* (Rome, 1980) 211–26; H. Paprocki, *Le Mystère de l'Eucharistie* (Paris, 1993) 328–37, who says that the intercessions can be divided into four basic forms: those of Jerusalem (the *ektenia* in the Anaphora of James); Alexandria (the *ektenia* in the Anaphora of Mark); Antioch (in *Apostolic Constitutions* VIII); and the Alexandro-Syrian form (Anaphora of Gregory of Nazianzus).

## Bibliography

Botte, B., and others. *Eucharisties d'Orient et d'Occident. Semaine liturgique de l'Institut Saint-Serge.* LO 46–47. Paris, 1970.

Brightman, F. "The Historia Mystagogica and Other Greek Commentaries on the Byzantine Liturgy." *JThS* 9 (1908) 392–93.

Cabasilas, N. *A Commentary on the Divine* Liturgy. Trans. J. Hussey and P. McNulty. London, 1960 (PG 150:427–34).

Engberding, H. "Die westsyrische Anaphora des Hl. Johannes Chrysostomus und ihre Probleme." *Oriens Christianus* 39 (1955) 33–47.

Lécuyer, J. "La théologie de l'anaphore selon les Pères de l'École d'Antioche." *L'Orient Syrien* 6 (1961) 385–412.

Lodi, E. *Enchiridion euchologicum fontium liturgicorum: Clavis methodologica cum commentariis selectis.* Rome, 1978.

Mateos, J. "L'action du Saint Esprit dans la liturgie de St. Jean Chrysostome." *Proche-Orient Chrétien* 9 (1959) 193–208.

Parenti, S., and E. Velkovska. *L'Eucologio Barbarini (= BAR)*. Rome, 1995.

Raes, A. "κατὰ πάντα καὶ διὰ πάντα." "En tout et pour tout." *OCP* 48 (1964) 216–18.

Wagner, G. *Der Ursprung der Chrysostomusliturgie. LQF* 59. Münster, 1973.

Marcel Metzger

5

# The History of the Eucharistic Liturgy in Rome

The writing down of the Roman liturgy of the first centuries is a difficult undertaking. Duchesne had said this in the past when he commented the notice devoted to Pope Zephyrinus in the *Liber Pontificalis*, "This text is as important as it is obscure and its obscurity is the more regrettable as the ceremonies of the Roman Mass, in the fifth and sixth centuries, are very little known."[1]

In fact, for the historical study of the Roman Mass in the first seven centuries, only a limited documentation is available, in no way comparable to that concerning Jerusalem or Antioch during the same period. No mystagogic catecheses, no sufficient allusions in the homilies and sermons. This led the researchers to exploit the slightest bits of information and formulate a vast number of hypotheses to explain them.

In this article we shall follow the available documents in their chronological order, by giving an account of the institutions alluded to in the earliest testimonies, before having recourse to the *ordines* that describe the eucharistic celebrations.

THE LIMITS OF THE AVAILABLE DOCUMENTATION
The historical documentation on the eucharistic celebrations in Rome from the fifth to the eighth centuries must be handled carefully. Prior to the *Ordo Romanus* I (beginning of the eighth century), which describes the stational Mass on Easter Sunday, we possess no systematic description. A few notices in the *Liber Pontificalis* and, in letters, the answers given by the popes to the questions posed to them, yield

[1] L. Duchesne, *Le Liber Pontificalis*, vol. I, 139, n. 3.

some partial indications. For the seventh and eighth centuries, the sources are more abundant; we do have some liturgical collections reflecting the usages of the time.

The historical worth of the notices found in the *Liber Pontificalis* is dubious. The primary fund of this chronicle dates back to the years 500 to 530 and the notices concerning the popes who lived before that time are rather unreliable. Nevertheless, their depictions of liturgical institutions may attest to customs established at the redactor's time.

As to liturgical books, lectionaries, sacramentaries, and antiphonals of Roman origin, they are intended for the persons having a part in the celebration but they very rarely give directions for use. Since these books preserved ancient traditions, the fact that a given piece is transcribed there does not prove that it was effectively in use. The most revealing example is the listing of stations, which was reproduced throughout generations of Roman books down to the edition of the *Ordo Missae* of Paul VI, whereas the actual stational practice had long been abandoned.

## THE SYNAXES IN THE NEIGHBORHOOD CHURCHES (*TITULI*), SERVED BY *PRESBYTERI*

Between the first and the fifth centuries of our era, the demographic situation of Rome was unique in the whole empire because of the extent of the urban territory and the number of its inhabitants. Rome was the only city whose population approached one million. The perimeter of the city measured 22,300 kilometers and the average distance between two extreme points was 7.5 kilometers. For the sake of comparison, at the end of the fourth century, Antioch had some 200,000 inhabitants, and Constantinople 120,000.

In the beginning of our era, the Jews, who numbered about 50,000, frequented a dozen different synagogues.[2] Similarly, the early testimonies on the Christians in Rome suggest that several communities gathered in private houses to which historians have given the name of "domestic churches."[3] The greetings of Paul, at the end of his Letter to the Romans offer an example of this when he mentions the "church" that gathers in the house of Prisca and Aquila (16:5). All the other Christians greeted by Paul do not seem to be part of this par-

---

[2] R. E. Brown and J. P. Meier, *Antioche et Rome*, Paris 1988, 127 and 135.
[3] Ibid., 178, 205 and 215.

ticular assembly. Among the twenty-five odd names contained in this series of greetings, one notices that five are Latin, and the others Greek. This reflects the cosmopolitan character of the *urbs,* which had attracted people from the different regions of the empire.

In 165, according to the account of Justin's martyrdom recorded in the *Acta Justinii* 3,1, the Christian philosopher answers the prefect Rusticus during the interrogation, "Do you believe that we all assemble in one place? Not in the least; the God of the Christians is not the prisoner of any one location. He is invisible, he fills the heavens and the earth; everywhere, he is adored and glorified by the faithful."[4] Justin gives the address of the assembly he belongs to, but is silent concerning the others. And it is also probable that the Christian assembly he describes in *Apologia* 1,67 must have convened simultaneously in several places.[5]

In the letter that Irenaeus sent to Pope Victor, about 190, at the time of the dispute on the date of Easter, one discerns also an allusion to the existence of several Christian assemblies in Rome. Some of them were Asiatic in origin and followed their own customs, at least with regard to the Easter celebration.[6]

This fragmentary information suggests that, from the beginning, the Christians of the Roman megapolis gathered in several locations. From the fifth century on, the documentation is more copious. It demonstrates that numerous edifices were set apart for the celebrations, in particular those called *tituli,* whose organization was the responsibility of the ecclesiastical administration.

In several of its notices, the *Liber Pontificalis* delineates the institutions of the neighborhood churches in the city of Rome and the initiatives of the popes in that domain. Although their historical worth is dubious for the periods anterior to the fifth century, they are valid at least for the fifth century itself. The attribution of these churches, or *tituli,* to presbyters, is presented as ancient (*PL* I, 126 in the notice on Pope Evaristus at the end of the first century). Their being supplied with a store of liturgical objects is attributed to Pope Urban I

---

[4] P. Franchi de Cavalieri, *Note agiographiche,* Rome 1902 (Studi et Testi) 33–36.

[5] P. Lampe, *Die stadtrömischen Christen in den ersten beiden Jahrhunderten,* Tübingen 1989, 307.

[6] Eusebius of Caesarea, *Hist. eccl.* V, 24, 14–5, *SCh* 41, 70.

(222–230?) (*LP* i, 143). The notice mentions twenty-five chalices and patens, a number that corresponds to that of the *tituli* existing at the time of Innocent I (401–417).

Further on, in the notice concerning Pope Marcellus I (308–309), the *Liber Pontificalis* says, "And he established in the city of Rome, twenty-five *tituli* as dioceses, because of the administration of baptism and penance to those who convert from paganism and because of the tombs of the martyrs."[7] If the twenty-fifth and last *titulus*, St. Vitalis, was set up by Innocent I (401–417), the third of the *tituli* is nevertheless anterior to the beginning of the fourth century. Every one of them had its own membership and its own clergy, as is proved by the acts of the Roman synods[8] of 499 and 595.

## THE SUNDAY SYNAXES IN THE *TITULI* AND THE SENDING OF THE *FERMENTUM*

As far as the Sunday synaxes in the *tituli* are concerned, the most explicit indications are found in the letter of Pope Innocent I to the bishop of Gubbio (March 19, 416) in chapter 5:[9]

"As to the *fermentum* which we send on Sundays to the diverse *tituli* . . . . All our churches are within the walls of the city. On Sunday, as their presbyters are not able to join us because of the people entrusted to their care, the *fermentum* from our Eucharist is therefore sent to them by acolytes so that they will not consider themselves separated from communion with us, especially on that day."[10]

The liturgical institution here described concerns the *tituli*, which the pope clearly defines: churches situated within the city, with presbyters attached to them to serve the people in their care. On Sundays, the Eucharist is celebrated there. As a consequence, the presbyters are busy in their *tituli* and are obviously unable to join the pope.

---

[7] *Et XXV titulos in urbe Roma constituit quasi diocesis, propter baptismum et penitentiam multorum qui convertebantur ex paganis et propter sepulturas martyrum.* LP I, 164.

[8] See the list in *DACL*, art. *Rome*, col. 2901.

[9] R. Cabié, *La lettre du pape Innocent I<sup>er</sup> à Décentius de Gubbio*, Louvain 1973.

[10] *De fermento quod die dominica per titulos mittimus, superflue nos consulere voluisti, cum omnes ecclesiae nostrae intra civitatem sint constitutae. Quarum presbyteri, quia die ipsa propter plebem sibi creditam nobiscum convenire non possunt, idcirco fermentum a nobis confectum per acolytos accipiunt, ut se a nostra communione maxime illa die non iudicent separatos.*

A further proof that the *tituli* were the customary places of the Sunday eucharistic celebration is found in the content of a liturgical book written in the second half of the seventh century, the *Vaticanus Reginensis 316,* or Gelasian Sacramentary. This is a collection of prayers intended for the presbyters in charge of the neighborhood churches, the *tituli.* In book III, I–XVI and XVIII–XXIII are gathered series of Sunday formularies; and it is in this context that the canon was transcribed (III, XVII). By comparison, in the Gregorian sacramentaries, the primary fund concerned the stational celebrations and did not contain any formularies for the Sundays *per annum.*[11]

Pope Innocent's letter evokes a tradition peculiar to the church of the city of Rome, the sharing of the *fermentum* on Sundays in the *tituli.* But the information on this practice is laconic. However, we do find some indications in the *Liber Pontificalis,* which alludes once to it in the notice on Pope Melchiades (311–314) to whom the initiative of this practice is ascribed (*LP* I, 74 and 168). In that notice, the text signals the relationship established by the *fermentum* between two *consecrationes* ("consecrations"), that confected by the bishop and that confected by the presbyters. *Fecit ut oblationes consecratas per ecclesias ex consecratione episcopi dirigerentur, quod declaratur fermentum.* ("He established that the gifts consecrated by the bishop be sent to the churches; this practice is called *fermentum*").

Another notice, that concerning Pope Siricius (384–399), accords a normative character to the practice of the *fermentum* (*LP* I, 86, 11.3–4; 216, 11.3–4); *Hic constituit ut nullus presbiter missas celebraret per omnem ebdomadam nisi consecratum episcopi loci designati susciperet declaratum, quod nominatur fermentum* ("He decreed that no priest should celebrate Mass throughout the week without having received from the local bishop the species consecrated by him; this practice is called the *fermentum*").

As for Pope Innocent I, he justifies this custom by the following argument: the priests of the *tituli,* being unable to join the bishop on Sundays, because of their service to their people, should not feel "excluded from communion with the pope, especially on that day."

---

[11] The canon has been added in a supplement at the beginning of the yearly cycle, in the Hadrianum, and, with Sunday formularies in a further supplement, in the Gregorian P (Padua, D 47). In this last book, the yearly cycle was augmented by the addition of formularies for the Sundays *per annum.*

On the actual ritual of the sending and the receiving of the *fermentum*, little is known. According to Pope Innocent's letter, the *fermentum* is "made" *(confectum)* by the pope, sent by him on Sunday, carried by acolytes, and received by the priests, but only in the *tituli*, for it is not carried outside the walls of the city.

A document from the eighth century mentions the mixing of the *fermentum* in the chalice at the time of the *Pax Domini*. This is a gloss to Pope Innocent's letter, written in a manuscript of Ratisbonne.[12] It describes the use of the *fermentum* during stational Masses in the absence of the pope (we shall come back to this later) and the sending of the *fermentum* to baptismal churches, on Holy Saturday: "On the Holy Saturday of the Pasch, in the baptismal churches, no presbyter will give communion to anyone before the pope sends him a portion of the *Sancta* ("holy gifts," "sacred species") that he himself offered."[13]

The sending of the *fermentum* is described in a more explicit way in a section of the *OR XXX B*, par. 64–5, which also goes back to the eighth century:[14] "And each presbyter dispatches a *mansionarius* of his *titulus* to the church of the Savior (the Lateran) and they wait until the breaking of the *Sancta*, carrying corporals with them. Then comes the subdeacon *oblationarius* who gives them a part of the *Sancta* which the pontiff has consecrated. They receive them in their corporals and each one goes back to his own church and delivers the *Sancta* to the presbyter. He in turn makes a cross with them over the chalice and then places them in the chalice and says *Dominus vobiscum*. And all receive communion as has been said above."[15]

The reception of the *fermentum* has given rise to gratuitous hypotheses on the subject of the Sunday synaxes in the *tituli*. Some have

---

[12] Mabillon, *Iter Germanicum*, in *Analecta vetera*, 2ᵉ éd., 1733, 11; transcribed by M. Andrieu, *Les Ordines romani*, vol. II, 62, and by R. Cabié, *La lettre du pape Innocent Iᵉʳ*, 52.

[13] *Sabbato sancto paschae nullus presbyter per ecclesias baptismales neminem communicat antequam mittatur ei de ipsa Sancta quam obtulit dominus papa.*

[14] M. Andrieu, *Les Ordines romani*, vol. III, 474.

[15] *Et transmittit unusquisque presbiter mansionarium de titulo suo ad ecclesiam Salvatoris et exspectant ibi usquedum frangitur Sancta, habentes secum corporales. Et venit oblationarius subdiaconus et dat eis de Sancta, quod pontifex consecravit, et recipiunt ea in corporales et revertitur unusquisque ad titulum suum et tradit Sancta presbitero. Et de ipsa facit crucem super calicem et ponit in eo et dicit: Dominus vobiscum. Et communicant omnes sicut superius.*

identified these Sunday synaxes as liturgies of the presanctified, thinking that the presbyters of the *tituli* would not have celebrated the eucharistic action but merely engaged in a consecration by contact with the pope's *fermentum*.[16] But the available documentation in no way authorizes any hypothesis of this sort. On the contrary, in the notice devoted to Pope Melchiades mentioned above, the *Liber Pontificalis* applies the vocabulary of the *consecratio* and the *missa* to the Eucharist celebrated by the presbyters *(oblationes consecratas per ecclesias:* "the oblations consecrated in the churches"). Besides, the liturgical texts recorded in the Gelasian Sacramentary offer complete formularies for all Sundays and for the eucharistic action.

## THE STATION

Roman liturgical books from the seventh and eighth centuries bear the mark of the stational organization: it is attested in common by the Gregorian sacramentaries, the W Epistolary, the P, L, S Evangelaries, the Roman antiphonals. Indeed, in the titles of some sixty Masses, they specify in what church the synaxis was held. But this institution antedates the seventh century.

Whereas the Sunday synaxes *per annum* gathered the inhabitants of the neighborhoods in the various *tituli*, the *statio* aimed at assembling the Christian people as a whole in the same place around the pontiff for the Sunday celebration. All the faithful and the clergy of all the *tituli* were invited. This assembly gathered, station after station, in the *tituli* of the neighborhoods and in the more spacious basilicas situated outside the area of the *tituli*, having neither clergy nor congregation of their own. The six basilicas were the Lateran, St. Mary Major, Holy Cross, St. Peter's in the Vatican, St. Paul, and St. Lawrence (outside the Walls).

This organized mobility of the church of Rome throughout some thirty places of worship prevents us from applying to the Lateran the medieval notion of "cathedral." In the vast urban network of Rome, no one basilica occupied a central position. The residential areas were scattered around the urban center, that is a vast zone occupied by temples and public buildings which, until the seventh century, Christians

---

[16] See P. Nautin, "Le rite du fermentum dans les églises urbaines de Rome," *EphLit* 1982, 514–22; *Actes du XIe congrès international d'archéologie chrétienne*, Coll. de l'École française de Rome, 123 (1989) 930.

avoided frequenting. The great Constantinian basilicas are either far from the center — this is the case of the Lateran — or outside the walls. In the documents, the adjective *cathedralis* is never used when speaking of any of the Roman churches. To designate the Lateran, the pope says, *nostra ecclesia* ("our church").[17]

## THE STATIONAL INSTITUTION
## AND THE URBAN EVOLUTION OF ROME

Concerning the stational institution, the earliest testimonies go back to the fifth century. The twenty-fifth *titulus* was established under Pope Innocent I (401–417) (*LP* I, 220, 1. 9). The same number of twenty-five reappears in the notices of the *Liber Pontificalis* when it mentions the renewal of the liturgical furnishings that had been pillaged by the invaders. After the sack of Rome by Genseric (455), Pope Leo I replenishes the stores of the *tituli* from the treasury of the great basilicas (*LP* I, 239).

Afterwards, Hilarius (461–468) restores the appointments of the great basilicas to which he affects *ministeria* ("vessels used by the eucharistic ministers") on a stable basis (*LP* I, 243–5). For the stations, he sets up a "rotating service" of *ministeria*: "In the city of Rome, he arranged for sacred vessels to circulate through the established stations: a gold scyphus for the stations, twenty-five silver scyphi for the *tituli*, twenty-five silver plates, fifty silver ministerial chalices. He stored all these objects in the Constantinian Basilica and in St. Mary."[18]

These figures correspond to the number of the *tituli*, whose priests are present at the stations. The sacred vessels were destined for the wine of the Eucharist; they were stored in the Lateran and at St. Mary's. The fifty chalices (twenty-five plus twenty-five) corresponded to the groups of communicants, men and women separately, of the twenty-five *tituli*. There is no mention of patens; these were brought by the priests of the *tituli*, according to the notice of the *Liber Pontificalis* on Zephyrinus (see below).

That these vessels were kept at the Lateran or St. Mary proves that they were not destined for the regular service of each *titulus*, but that

---

[17] See A. Chavasse, *La liturgie de la ville de Rome*, 263–4.

[18] *In urbe vero Roma, constituit ministeria, qui circuirent constitutas stationes scyphum aureum stationarium . . . , scyphos argenteos XXV per titulos . . . , amas argenteas XXV . . . , calices argenteos ministeriales L . . . Hic omnia in basilica Constantiniana vel ad sanctam Mariam constituta recondit. LP I, 244, 1. 24.*

they were to be available at the time of these gatherings that the stations were. The haste with which the store of sacred vessels was replenished after the plunders shows the importance of the stational institution at that time.

The stational organization corresponds to the topographic and demographic state of the church of Rome in the fifth century. At that period, the population was still approaching the million and lived in all the residential neighborhoods of the city. But, in the sixth century, this situation was profoundly upset by the plague and the Gothic War: after the sack of the city, the deportations, and the ravages of famine and epidemics, the population fell to about ten thousand inhabitants grouped in a small agglomeration to the west of the city and in the Plain (Campus Martius). Immense areas were abandoned or reclaimed for agriculture, within what was left of the walls. As a result, a disjunction occurred between these new neighborhoods and the stational institution established prior to this great upheaval. Nevertheless, the church of Rome continued to journey from station to station over this devastated territory as the sermons of Pope Gregory I (590–604) attest, because they contain the topographic identification of the stations.

## DAYS OF STATION
According to the liturgical documentation of the seventh and eighth centuries, people gathered at the station for the major solemnities (Christmas with its threefold celebration, Epiphany, Easter, and Pentecost), for the paschal cycle (from Septuagesima to the Saturday after Easter), the week of Pentecost, and the fasts of the seventh and tenth months. Outside the walls, the pontiff could convene the church of Rome for the celebration of the *natalicia* ("birthdays," that is, days of death) of the saints in the basilicas where they were buried. Liturgical books contain formularies for such celebrations, sometimes for several anniversaries on the same day, in places distant from one another. But we do not know anything about the frequency of these ceremonies which depended on the wish of the pontiff.

## THE STATIONS DURING LENT
In a first phase, in Rome as in the neighboring churches of the East and Milan, the Lenten ferias were aliturgical; their synaxes ended with the *Oratio fidelium,* a practice that remained in use on Good Friday. These synaxes became eucharistic at the latest before 530, and

perhaps even before the close of the fifth century, at the time when Hilarius (461–468) systematized the internal structure of the liturgical station *per constitutas stationes* ("through established stations") according to the text from the *Liber Pontificalis* quoted above. In the antiphonals, we find twenty-six ferias, from the Wednesday of Quinquagesima to the Friday before Palm Sunday, twenty-six antiphons *ad communionem* ("for communion"), drawn in order from Psalms 1 to 26. They correspond, each week, to ferias 2, 3, 4, 6, and 7, Thursdays being excepted.[19]

These ferial eucharistic synaxes were stational. Topographically, the arrangement of the Lenten stations corresponds to the distribution of the population of the city before the destructions brought about by the Gothic War, in particular before 545. The ferial synaxes became eucharistic "owing to the organization of the Lenten stations expressly intended for its pastoral impact."[20]

The Roman liturgical books of the seventh and eighth centuries give us a clue as to how extensive was the stational organization: twelve Sundays and fifty-four week days. But these indications continued to be written in the following generations of liturgical books, at periods when and in places where the practice was no longer in force or even had ever been held.[21] By contrast, the *OR* III, par. 1 (end of the eighth century) mentions only four big feasts on which the presence of all the presbyters of the *tituli* at the Mass celebrated by the pope was required: Easter, Pentecost, St. Peter, and Christmas. In the *OR* IV, par. 2 (also end of the eighth century), this list is augmented by the addition of four other days: Epiphany, Holy Saturday, Monday after Easter, and Ascension.

THE CELEBRATION OF THE STATIONAL MASS
In the two notices concerning Popes Zephyrinus (198–217) and Urban I (222–230), the *Liber Pontificalis* supplies two additional indications on a rite observed at the Mass celebrated by the pope. Because they allude to the twenty-five *tituli,* these pieces of information show they pertain to the time of Pope Innocent I (401–417). Here are these notices:

[19] They became eucharistic only under Gregory II (715–731).
[20] A. Chavasse, *La liturgie de la ville de Rome,* 44.
[21] The *Missale Romanum* has reprinted these indications down to the edition of Paul VI.

"Zephyrinus made a regulation concerning the church. In the church, glass patens held by ministers are placed before the priests, as the bishop celebrates Mass, with all priests standing in front of him; this is how the Mass must be celebrated. With the only exception of what the episcopal law prescribes, the clergy will remain standing, present to the whole service. Then, from this consecration, the presbyter will receive from the bishop's hand the consecrated crown (the bread made in the shape of a crown) to be distributed to the people."[22]

"Urban ordered all the utensils used in worship to be made of silver and he supplied twenty-five silver patens."[23]

According to these notices, the stational Mass is instituted to gather together bishop, clergy, and people; it is an action of the Church properly ordered. It is the bishop who celebrates the Mass. When both texts speak of the priests attending the celebration, only patens are mentioned. For the wine, the *ministeria* ("vessels used by the eucharistic ministers") were those of the bishop, which, as we saw above, were restored by Popes Leo and Hilarius after the plundering, and deposited in the Lateran and St. Mary Major.

The *Ordines romani* enable us to complete the picture. The *OR* I (end of the seventh century) describes the stational Mass presided by the pope, without speaking of the patens placed in front of the *sacerdotes* ("priests"), but all the other indications agree with the notice on Pope Zephyrinus. We shall come back to this later on.

The *OR* II (ca. 750) explains what is done when the stational Mass is celebrated by someone replacing the pontiff, whether bishop or presbyter. This person cannot act in everything as the pontiff does; he cannot use the cathedra (pars. 2 and 3) and, at the *Pax Domini,* he must place in his chalice a fragment of the bread consecrated at a previous Mass celebrated by the pontiff (par. 6). The gloss in the manuscript of Ratisbonne, already quoted above, makes explicit the kinship of this rite with that of the *fermentum:*

---

[22] *Et fecit constitutum de ecclesia et patenas vitreas ante sacerdotes in ecclesia et ministros supportantes, donec episcopus missas celebraret, ante se sacerdotes adstantes, sic missae celebrarentur; excepto quod ius episcopi interest tantum, clerus sustineret omnibut praesentes; ex ea consecratione de manu episcopi iam coronam consecratam acciperet presbiter tradendam populo.* LP I, 60 and 139.

[23] *Hic fecit ministeria sacrata omnia argentea et patenas argenteas XXV posuit.* LP I, 62 and 143.

"Concerning the *fermentum* of which (Innocent) speaks, the Roman custom is that, from the Masses sung at the Lord's Supper on Holy Saturday, the holy day of Easter, Pentecost, and the holy day of the Lord's Nativity, some [consecrated bread] be kept through the whole year, and everywhere in the stations; and if the pope himself is not present at Mass, some of it be deposited in the chalice when "The Peace of the Lord be always with you" is pronounced. . . . This is called *fermentum*. However, on the Holy Saturday of the Pasch. . . ."[24]

As for the *OR* III (after 750), what it describes is no longer the station but vast assemblies for the big feasts, Easter, Pentecost, St. Peter, Christmas. The *prebyteri cardinales* are convoked to these celebrations. Each one accomplishes in his own right the same actions as the pontiff accomplished in the past in his function of head:

"The cardinal priests must join with (the assembly), each one holding a corporal in hand, and the archdeacon comes and gives three offerings to each one. When the pontiff comes to the altar, they surround him on the right and the left and speak the words of the canon together with him, while holding the offerings, not placing them on the altar, so that the pontiff's voice may better be heard, and they simultaneously consecrate the body and the blood of the Lord, but only the pontiff signs the cross on the altar on the right and the left."[25]

## THE EUCHARISTIC ROMAN RITUAL, ACCORDING TO THE INDICATIONS ANTERIOR TO THE *ORDINES*

The first complete descriptions of the ceremonies of the Mass are found in these *Ordines romani*. They concern the celebrations

---

[24] *De fermento quod dicit (Innocentius) mos est Romanis, ut de missa quae cantatur in caena domini et in sabbato sancto et in die sancto paschae et in pentecosten et in natali domini die sancto, per totum annum servaretur, et ubicumque per stationes, si ipse papa ad missam praesens non fuerit, de ipsa missa mittitur in calicem, cum dicit: Pax domini sit semper vobiscum . . . Et hoc dicitur fermentum. Tamen sabbato sancto paschae nullus presbyter . . .*

[25] *Habent colligendas presbiteri cardinales, unusquisque tenes corporalem in manu sua et venit archidiaconus et porregit uniquique eorum oblatas tres. Et, accedente pontifice ad altare, dextra levaque circumdant altare et simul cum illo canonem dicunt, tenentes oblatas in manibus, non super altare, ut vox pontificis valentius audiatur, et simul consecrant corpus et sanguinem domini, sed tantum pontifex facit super altare crucem dextra levaque. OR III, § 1.*

presided by the pope or his substitute, but say nothing about the Masses celebrated by the priests in their *tituli*. From that period only occasional information has reached us and it deals with some parts of the celebration.

*1. The Introduction of the* Kyrie Eleison

The introduction of the *Kyrie eleison* into the Roman Mass is known to us through canon 3 of the Council of Vaison in 529.[26] The letter of Pope Gregory I to John of Syracuse (in 598, *Ep* IX, 25) attests that the *Kyrie* is said alternatively by the clergy and the people, and that the invocation *Christe eleison* is peculiar to the Romans. The pope distinguishes the *cotidianae* ("daily") masses which comprise *Kyrie* and *Christe,* and exceptional celebrations — perhaps those featuring the *Laetania,* for instance April 25 — with the litany's three *Kyrie* in the beginning and the end. The *Ordines Romani* IV, 20 and XV, 16 limit the number of the *Kyrie-Christe* to nine.

*2. The Readings and the Homily*

A list of books attributed to a rural church in the vicinity of Tivoli (25 kilometers from Rome), in a charter of foundation going back to 471, already supplies an early indication on the readings at Mass: *Item codices, evangelia IIII, apostolorum, psalterium et comitem* ("Similarly, books, the four Gospels, the apostles, the psalter and the *comes*").[27] The *comes* was a repertory of the pericopes to be read.

Concerning the choice of pericopes, one finds some allusions in the *Homilies on the Gospel* by Gregory the Great. These were preached in 590–592 and published in 593; numbering forty, they each are preceded by the pericope commented upon. Elements of the cycle of readings then in use in the church of Rome are discernible, at a period when Advent still had six Sundays.[28]

Other clues on ancient cycles of readings are found in lectionaries dating from the seventh and eighth centuries, because these collections have preserved groups of pericopes attesting to practices in force in the sixth century. The *Comes of Würzburg* (nos. 214–55) has recorded a series of forty-two pericopes that might have been used on the forty-two Sundays celebrated in the *tituli*. Likewise, the evangelaries *CapEv*

[26] Text in *CCIL* 148 A, 79, l. 35–41; *SCh* 353, 190–91.
[27] Text in L. Duchesne, *Le Liber Pontificalis,* vol. I, CXLVI s.
[28] See A. Chavasse, *La liturgie de la ville de Rome,* 123 s. and 131.

have kept a group of ten pericopes, organized on the basis of a geographical selection, for these gospel passages deal with the different places of Jesus's ministry. However, the rediscovery of these organized groupings at a later date suggests that before the lectionaries of the seventh and eighth centuries, there did not yet exist one general and unified plan *de circulo anni* ("for the entire yearly cycle").[29]

That the homily was a current practice is attested by the activity of the popes, among whom Leo I (440–461). As for Gregory I (590–604), some of his homilies were improvised, others were dictated in advance and read by a notary.[30]

### 3. Psalmody in Connection with the Readings
In a notice whose interpretation is difficult, the *Liber Pontificalis* ascribes to Pope Celestine I (422–432) initiatives concerning, it seems, the psalms associated with the readings: "And he decided that the one hundred and fifty psalms of David would be psalmodied before the sacrifice, what had not been done previously, except that the letter of the blessed Paul and the holy gospel were read." The second edition specified that this psalmody of all the psalms should be done with antiphons.[31]

### 4. From the Oratio Fidelium to the Deprecatio
The *Oratio fidelium* ("Prayer of the faithful") or *Orationes solemnes* ("Solemn Orations") has survived in the office of Good Friday. In this formulary, invitations and orations give a large place to the praise of God and the recollection of God's providence. This *Oratio* was in use in both aliturgical and eucharistic synaxes, during the third, fourth, and fifth centuries. Then it disappeared from the eucharistic celebrations. It seems to have been supplanted by the *Deprecatio Gelasii* which focuses more on the human situations and personal dispositions of the petitioners. The circumstances that best explain the adop-

---

[29] IDEM, "Les lectionnaires romains de la messe du VIIᵉ siècle, au *Missale Romanum* (1570) . . . ," in *EO* 11 (1994), 282 s.

[30] IDEM, *La liturgie de la ville de Rome*, 121 s.

[31] P. Jeffery, "The Introduction of Psalmody into the Roman Mass by Pope Celestine I (422–433): Reinterpreting a Passage in the Liber Pontificalis," in *ALW* 26 (1984) 147–65. *Et constituit ut psalmi David CL ante sacrificium psalli [antephonatim ex omnibus], quod ante non fiebat, nisi tantum epistula beati Pauli recitabatur et sanctum Evangelium. LP* I, 88 and 230.

tion of the *Deprecatio* must be sought in the institution of the ferial Lenten stations, which was treated of above.[32] The adoption of the *Deprecatio Gelasii* may explain that, in the Mass formularies, there was added a second oration before that said over the gifts; this could have been an *oratio post precem*, an oration said by the priest as a conclusion to the *Deprecatio*. This second oration is present in 73 percent of the Mass formularies of the temporal cycle in the collection called Leonine Sacramentary, and 82 percent in the Gelasian; but the Gregorian sacramentaries and the *Ordines romani* do not include the *Deprecatio Gelasii*.

### 5. The Liturgical Objects Used for the Eucharist

In the *Liber Pontificalis*, the notices devoted to a few popes of the fourth and fifth centuries describe what were the *ministeria*, or vessels, attributed to basilicas in Rome, for the eucharistic celebration. These lists attest to the organization established for the reception of the gifts and the service of Communion in the large assemblies. Four kinds of *ministeria* are mentioned:

—*patena*, a plate for the Communion at the liturgies;
—*amulae*, large containers to receive wine offerings;
—*scyphi*, large vases for the wine destined for the eucharistic offering;
—*calices ministeriales*, smaller cups used at the time of Communion.

For the Communion from the cup, the consecrated wine was poured into these smaller Communion vessels, one for men, the other for women.[33]

### 6. Elements of the Eucharistic Prayer

In his letter to Decentius (March 19, 416), Pope Innocent I speaks of the proclamation of the names of those faithful who have brought the offerings; he specifies that the Roman custom was to make this proclamation during the holy mysteries *(per sacra mysteria)*.

In 538, Pope Vigilius alludes to the embolisms introduced in the canon on big feasts (Easter, Ascension, Pentecost, Epiphany, feasts of saints): "As to the arrangement of prayers for the celebration of Mass,

---

[32] B. Capelle, 1939 article reprinted in *Travaux liturgiques*, II, Louvain 1962, 142–4; P. de Cleck, *La prière universelle dans les liturgies latines anciennes*, Münster 1977, 95, 144; A. Chavasse, *la liturgie de la velle de Rome*, 38–45.

[33] See indications in *LP* on the *tituli*.

we make no difference for any time, any feast, but we consecrate always in the same manner the gifts offered to God. In order to celebrate the feasts of Easter, the Ascension of the Lord, the Epiphany, and the saints of God, we add distinct paragraphs proper to those days; through which we commemorate the holy solemnity or the saints whose anniversaries we celebrate."[34]

The two letters of Innocent I and Vigilius designate the Eucharistic Prayer by the word *Prex*. The same vocabulary is also found in the book called the Leonine Sacramentary and in the Gelasian Sacramentary, in which the title of the Mass formularies, *Orationes et Praeces*, announces the orations and the first part of the canon *(Vere dignum)*. These two books have recorded many *Vere dignum* (there are still two hundred and sixty-eight of them in the Leonine), this variable part of the Mass having for a long time allowed the Roman celebrants to express, within the eucharistic action, the pastoral concerns of the time; this is the case in particular of the Masses of Popes Gelasius I and Vigilius.

*7. The* Our Father

In the time of Pope Gregory I (590–604), the *Our Father* was part of the Mass, but Gregory changed its place, by joining it to the canon. He explains his reasons in a letter to John of Syracuse: "Here is why we recite the Lord's prayer immediately after the prayer (the canon): the apostles' custom was to consecrate the sacrifice by the sole prayer of offering. And I saw a great incongruity in saying over the oblation a prayer composed by some scholarly person and in not saying over the body and blood of our Redeemer that which he himself composed and which tradition has transmitted to us."[35]

---

[34] *Ordinem quoque precum in celebritate missarum nullo nos tempore, nulla festivitate significamus habere diversum, sed semper eodem tenore oblata Deo munera consecrare. Quoties vero Paschalis aut Ascensionis Domini et Pentecostes et Epiphaniae Sanctorumque Dei fuerit agenda festivitas, singula capitula diebus apta subiungimus, quibus commemorationem sanctae solemnitatis aut eorum facimus quorum natalicia celebramus; cetera vero, ordine consueto prosequimur.* PL 69, col. 18.

[35] *Orationem vero dominicam idcirco mox post precem dicimus, quia mos apostolorum fuit, ut ad ipsam solummodo orationem oblationis hostiam consecrarent. Et valde mihi inconveniens visum est, ut precem, quam scholasticus composuerat, super oblationem diceremus et ipsam traditionem, quam Redemptor noster composuit, super eius corpus et sanguinem non diceremus.* Ep. IX, 12, PL 77, col. 956 s.; *Registrum* 9, 26, Hartmann-Ewald, t. 2, 59–60.

118

## 8. The Kiss of Peace

In his letter to Decentius, Pope Innocent I explains that the kiss of peace follows the Eucharistic Prayer. He contrasts the Roman practice with that of other places and justifies it by presenting this rite as an expression of the consent of the people to the mysteries being celebrated.[36]

On the moment when the kiss of peace is exchanged, Pope Innocent's custom differs from what Justin records in his *Apologia* I, 65, where he attests that this rite followed the universal prayer and therefore preceded the Eucharistic Prayer. Why this change? The practice of the *fermentum* might explain it. As was said above, on Sundays in the *tituli*, and at the stational Mass in the pope's absence, the *fermentum* was brought in and deposited in the chalice before the greeting *Pax Domini*. The kiss of peace took place then after the *fermentun* had been received from the absent pope; it was a confirmation of the pope's communion with the local assembly.

### THE CEREMONIES DESCRIBED IN THE *OR* I

The *Ordines romani* have recorded the unfolding of the rites; they were written not to guide the practice of the Roman officiants, but to provide information. The *Ordo* I describes the stational Mass (par. 24) celebrated in St. Mary Major on Easter Sunday (par. 15). It was written before the end of the seventh century. The shorter recension, which is the earliest, is limited to the description of the celebration, whereas a longer recension added to it a listing of the Roman ecclesiastical and liturgical institutions, the order of the procession from the residence at the Lateran to the church of the station, and the inventory of the *ministeria*, books, and vessels brought for the celebration (pars. 1–23). The books to be used are called *Gospels* (pars. 22, 30–51, 59), *Apostle* (par. 20), and *Cantatorium* (par. 57).

In general, the ceremonies described agree with the directions given in the books intended for the stations: they are the common fund of the Gregorian sacramentaries, that is the *Hadrianum*, the manuscript of Padua, and that of Trent (respectively *GrH, GrP,* and *GrT*), the epistolary represented by the *Comes of Würzburg,* the evangelary recorded in the *Capitulares (CapEv),* and the Roman antiphonals.

---

[36] See R. Cabié, *La lettre du pape Innocent I à Decentius de Gubbio*, 20–22.

Before depicting the synaxis, the *OR* I deals at length with the welcoming of the pontiff. The entire clergy, among which bishops[37] and priests, waits for the pope in the church. He proceeds to the *secretarium* ("sacristy") to vest, while the archdeacon sees to the preparation of the evangelary. The pontiff has control of the celebration; the names of the readers and psalmists are subject to his approval, and throughout the celebration he directs the succession of the actions (pars. 37, 40, 48, 50, 52, 77, 85, 104, 117, 121, 124) with the assistance of the archdeacon (pars. 30, 77, 105, 108, 124). The ministers are numerous both for the singing (*scola*, for instance pars. 5, 44, 52) and the actions (deacons, subdeacons, acolytes). Incense and candles are used (pars. 41, 46, 59, 125).When the schola begins the antiphon *ad introitum* ("for the entrance") (par. 44), the pontiff and his ministers leave the sacristy and enter the church (pars. 44–6). The texts of these antiphons have been kept in the antiphonals.

Two acolytes show the pontiff a box *(capsa)* containing the *Sancta* of a previous Mass. The pontiff venerates them and examines them; if they are too many, he has some deposited in the reserve (par. 48).

During the doxology concluding the psalm (*Gloria Patri,* . . . par. 50), the pontiff prays before the altar, then he kisses the book of the Gospels and the altar and goes to his seat. The schola repeats the antiphon and sings the *Kyrie eleison* (par. 52, *laetania*). Then comes the *Gloria in excelsis* (par. 53) if the liturgical time authorizes it. The pontiff addresses a *Pax vobis* to the people and proclaims *Oremus* and the oration (par. 53).

There is mention of one reading, the "Apostle," done by the subdeacon (par. 56; see par. 20); of a responsory for which the *cantatorium* is used; and of the Alleluia (par. 57). Some Roman liturgical books preserved the listings of the pericopes drawn from the apostolic writings, for instance the *Comes of Würzburg;* some others have preserved the text of the responsories, for instance the M Cantatorium, and, afterwards, the antiphonals. The reading from the Gospel is introduced by a procession with the evangelary and followed by rites of veneration, with a greeting by the pontiff and the *Oremus* (pars. 59–65). The evangelaries *CapEv* contain lists of gospel pericopes arranged according to the cycle of the stational celebrations.

[37] On the bishops ministering in the stational synaxes and in the Roman basilicas, see A. Chavasse, *La liturgie de la ville de Rome,* 337–42.

Then, the text of the *OR* I goes directly to the preparations for the eucharistic action, indicating that the deacons place a table cloth (*corporale*, par. 67) on the altar. Afterwards, it describes the vast movement of the *Offertorium* which comprises the bringing of the gifts — wine and bread — and their reception. The bringing of the gifts involves the whole assembly, in a given order: men, women, pontiff, bishop, priests, deacons, and so on. The reception involves the ministers, from the pontiff who comes down to receive them (pars. 69, 74) down to the acolytes, each degree cooperating according to its status. The reception of the wine offerings is done with the aid of large containers, the *scyphi*, mentioned in the inventories of the *Liber Pontificalis* (see above). The pontiff goes back to his *cathedra* and washes his hands (par. 76) while the other ministers complete the reception of the gifts (pars. 72–6).

Once the reception of the gifts is completed, the archdeacon washes his hands, oversees the preparation of the altar (pars. 77–8), pours the wine (par. 79) and the water (*fons*, par. 80) into the pontiff's chalice.

The pontiff goes to the altar on which are placed his offerings (par. 83) and his chalice (par. 84). Then he motions to the schola to stop the singing (par. 85) whose antiphonals have preserved the texts. The act of offering ended (*finito offertorio*, pars. 86, 87), the other ministers take their places (pars. 86–7) and the initial dialogue of the canon begins. This collective gesture of *offertorium* is not comparable to a procession of offering, featuring the carrying of the gifts from the sacristy to the altar, as in other liturgies (Eastern, Gallican). There is no mention of any oration *super oblata* ("over the gifts").

Bishops and priests are silent, heads bowed, while the pontiff says the canon alone (par. 86). At the moment of the *Per ipsum*, the archdeacon lifts up the chalice while the pontiff touches the side of the chalice with the gifts (pars. 89–90). Here, the writer of the *Ordo* backtracks to explain that the subdeacon holds the paten during the canon. Then gives it to a deacon for the fraction (pars. 91–97).

After the greeting *Pax Domini*, the archdeacon gives the kiss of peace to the first bishop. This rite continues according to the ordering of the assembly (*per ordinem*, par. 96). The pontiff begins the fraction by breaking one piece that he leaves on the altar and returns to his seat (pars. 97–98). Acolytes bring in sacks of bread to the bishops and the priests for the fraction, while deacons break the other gifts of the pontiff[38] (pars. 103–4). The schola sings the *Agnus Dei* (par. 105).

The pontiff receives Communion at his seat. After making three signs of the cross, he places the fragment already bitten into the chalice presented by the archdeacon and from which he then takes Communion (par. 107). Bishops and priests receive Communion from the pontiff's hand, whereas the first bishop and the deacons take charge of the Communion from the cup (an action expressed by the verb *confirmare* (pars. 107, 114, 116, 118). The priests "give Communion to" and "confirm" the people (par. 116). The schola sings the Communion antiphon and the psalm until the pontiff signals to it to sing the *Gloria Patri* (par. 117). After Communion, the archdeacon announces the next station.

After Communion, the pontiff sits down and washes his hands, then goes back to the altar for the final oration (*ad complendum*, par. 123). One of the deacons announces the dismissal (*Ite, missa est*, par. 124).

THE WITNESS OF THE BOOKS SENT FROM ROME
Liturgical books of Roman origin are known to us through the ways they were received and adapted outside of Rome. They attest both to Roman usages and to the adaptations they received outside of Rome. Each one for its part is a witness to the eucharistic ceremonies in the city of Rome. Only the Gelasian Sacramentary reflects the liturgy of the *tituli*. The other books known to us concern the stational celebrations.

We already have stressed the contribution of the lectionaries when we spoke of the *OR I*. According to the *Comes of Würzburg*, the gospel reading was preceded by only one reading, except on Wednesdays and Fridays in weeks when fast was held (Ember Days), Holy Week, and the Vigil of Pentecost. For this first reading, the Sunday pericopes are taken from the New Testament; the ferial ones and some vigils of the Sanctoral from the Old Testament.

The Mass formularies in the Gregorian Sacramentary have retained variable prayers said by the celebrant presiding at the stational Mass: an oration preceding the readings (a piece without a title), an oration

---

[38] Some authors have attempted to explain why there is no mention of the *fermentum* in this *Ordo*. In fact, as what is dealt with here is the stational Mass, the presbyters of the *tituli* are in attendance; therefore, on that day, the rite of the *fermentum* would be pointless.

over the gifts *(Super oblata*, which has no place in the *OR* I as we have already noted), occasionally a preface and specific formulations for the canon *(Hanc igitur)*, a postcommunion *(Ad complendum)*, and, during Lent, an oration over the people *(Super populum)*. When it was received in Frankish lands, the *Hadrianum* Gregorian contained, in the beginning of the volume, a brief *Ordo missae*, and then the text of the canon,[39] the *Our Father* and its embolism *(Libera nos)*; there is also a mention of the *Agnus Dei* introduced into the Roman Mass by Pope Sergius I (687–701) as we shall see later.

The books of chant have preserved on the one hand the three antiphons the *OR* I speaks of *(ad introitum*, for the *offertorium*, and for Communion), on the other — in the *cantatorium* — the responsory following the reading.

The only known witness to the liturgy of the *tituli* is the Gelasian Sacramentary. We have explained above the presence, in 82 percent of the Mass formularies, of a second oration. In the Gelasian, the canon was written after the formularies for the Masses *per annum*, from the *Sursum corda* to the *Pax Domini* with the *Our Father* and its embolism (nos. 1242–1259). The canon does not contain the *Memento* of the dead, which is in agreement with the directions of the *OR* VII, 16 and XV, 128–30 which exclude the commemoration of the dead at Sunday Masses.[40] The *Agnus Dei* is likewise absent from the Gelasian Sacramentary, a sign that its text predates Pope Sergius's innovation.

## THE EVOLUTION OF THE ROMAN LITURGY ABOUT THE EIGHTH CENTURY

The practice of holding eucharistic liturgies was extended by Pope Gregory II (715–731) to days hitherto aliturgical, in particular the Thursdays in Lent *(LP* I, 402). These innovations are recorded in the Gregorian sacramentaries, whereas they are absent from the Gelasian. Besides, the Sanctoral received additional feasts under successive pontificates, for example, nine feasts between Boniface IV (608–615) and Theodore I (642–649).

The decisions of Pope Sergius I (687–701) pertain to the Mass ceremonies themselves. On the one hand, they concern the singing of the

---

[39] The oldest copy does not have the *Memento* of the dead.

[40] M. Andrieu, *Les Ordines romani*, vol. II, 274–78; C. Giraudo, *Preghiere eucaristiche per la Chiesa di oggi*, Roma e Brescia 1993, 225–40.

*Agnus Dei,* inserted at the time of the fraction. "He established that at the moment of the fraction of the Lord's body, the *Agnus Dei qui tollis peccata mundi, miserere nobis* ("Lamb of God who take away the sins of the world") be sung by clergy and people,"[41]

On the other hand, Pope Sergius extended the *laetania* to four feasts. "He established that on the days of the Annunciation of the Lord, of the Dormition and the Nativity of the Mother of God and always virgin Mary, and of St. Symeon, which the Greeks call Ypapante, a litany would depart from St. Hadrian and that the people would come to St. Mary."[42]

We already alluded to the procession called *laetania* when speaking of the *Kyrie eleison.* Here, the text of the *Liber Pontificalis* indicates the place of gathering, the church of St. Hadrian, and the place of celebration, St. Mary Major. These detailed regulations are recorded in the Gregorian sacramentaries.[43]

The introduction of the *Gloria in excelsis Deo* into the eucharistic celebrations is signaled in several documents. In the notice devoted to Pope Symmachus (498–514) the *Liber Pontificalis* reports that the singing of this hymn had been extended to all Sundays and to the *natalicia* ("dates of martyrdom") of the martyrs.[44] The *OR* specify that this practice was reserved for the pope: in his absence, the hymn was omitted when the substitute was a priest (*OR* II, 9). However, the same document mentions the paschal exception: "The *Gloria in excelsis Deo* is not said by a presbyter, except on Easter Sunday."[45] This tradition is explained in the *OR* XXX B, par. 64, in connection with a text on the priests presiding at the baptismal celebration in the *tituli* during the Easter night:[46] "On this night, the cardinal priests are not

---

[41] *Hic statuit ut tempore confractionis dominici corporis* Agnus Dei, qui tollis peccata mundi, miserere nobis *a clero et populo decantetur. LP* I, 376.

[42] *Constituit autem ut diebus Adnuntiationis Domini, Dormitionis et Nativitatis sanctae Dei genitricis semperque virginis Mariae ac sancti Symeonis, quod Ypapanti graeci appellant, letania exeat a sancto Hadriano et ad sanctam Mariam populus accurrat. LP* I, 376.

[43] *Oratio collecta ad Sanctum Hadrianum,* n° 123, *Item ad missa ad Sanctam Mariam Majorem,* n° 124.

[44] *Hic constitutit ut omni die dominico vel natalicia martyrum Gloria in excelsis ymnus diceretur. LP* I, 263.

[45] . . . *preter Gloria in excelsis Deo, quia a presbitero non dicitur nisi in pascha.*

[46] M. Andrieu, *Les Ordines romani* vol. III, 474.

present, but each one says Mass in his *titulus* and he has the right to sit in the chair and to say the *Gloria in excelsis Deo.*"[47]

When speaking of the bishops celebrating in St. Peter's, the notice devoted to Pope Stephen III (768–772) in the *Liber Pontificalis* also speaks of the singing of the *Gloria in excelsis* on Sundays: "He decreed that every Sunday the solemnities of the Mass would be celebrated at the altar of the blessed Peter by the seven cardinal priests who are attached to the Lateran and that the *Gloria in excelsis* would be sung."[48]

## THE MELDING OF THE TWO FORMS
## OF THE ROMAN LITURGY

It has been observed above that, according to documents from the end of the eighth century, there was a reduction in the number of stations, while the books still retained the enumeration of some sixty of them, twelve Sundays and fifty-four ferias. In the *OR* III, only four big feasts remain listed.

In parallel fashion, the content of the liturgical books derived from the stational service goes beyond the needs of this institution. In the body of the *GrH* and *GrT* Gregorian sacramentaries one finds, written about 680, the formularies of the sixty stations, augmented by six Sunday formularies without station: octave of Easter and Pentecost, the Sunday following the fast of the *Menses VII and IX* ("seventh and ninth months"), and the first and second Sundays of Advent. These two books also offer Sunday formularies, but as a supplement outside of the calendar. On the contrary, in the *GrP* Gregorian, the cycle comprises not only the station days and the six Sundays without station, but also the other thirty-four Sunday formularies of the year. Obviously this book has combined the formularies of the two forms of the Roman liturgy, those of the stational liturgy and those of the *tituli.*

The coordinated functioning of the stations and the Sunday synaxes in the *tituli* was adapted to the Roman situation of the fifth century, in an overpopulated city. But it was out of harmony in a

---

[47] *Ipsa nocte, omnes presbiteri cardinales non ibi stant sed unusquisque per titulum suum facit missa et habet licentiam sedere in sede et dicere Gloria in excelsis Deo.*

[48] *Hic statuit ut omni dominico die, a septem episcopis cardinalibus ebdomadariis qui in ecclesia Salvatoris observant, missarum solemnia super altare beati Petri celebrarentur et Gloria in excelsis Deo ediceretur.* LP I, 478.

much smaller area with many fewer residents. This explains the combination of the celebrations in the *tituli* and the stations into one single grouping *de circulo anni* ("throughout the year"). Now this new arrangement suited well the transalpine Churches which had imported the Roman books.

## THE ROMANO-FRANKISH *ORDINES*

The Frankish clerics of the eighth and ninth centuries regarded the liturgy of Rome as a model to imitate. They came to Rome to observe it, as is attested by the end of the *OR XIX* (pars. 33ff.). The writer exhorts the critical reader to: "overcome his laziness and imitate so many priests, fathers, devout monks; let them make like them the pilgrimage to Rome, or at least dispatch there a faithful messenger."[49] These observations are recorded in the Romano-Frankish *Ordines* which purport to describe the Roman liturgy for the benefit of transalpine Churches.

The *OR III* to *X*, then *XV* and *XVII* present adaptations of the Roman eucharistic liturgy to episcopal and monastic churches outside Rome. In their transcriptions of the ceremonies of the Mass, they depend on *OR I* which they copied, more or less faithfully, making selections with a view to render the Roman ritual practicable in other churches. They also incorporated Frankish and Germanic traditions concerning the composition of the clergy, the orientation of the buildings and the place of the episcopal throne (for instance, *OR IV*, 18, 35), the episcopal blessing before communion (for instance *OR V*, 72), certain liturgical vestments (*OR VIII*), and so on. Nevertheless, the non-Roman traditions are presented as though they had been followed in Rome.

In its presentation of the papal Mass, inspired by the *OR I*, the *OR IV* describes at greater length the movements of the acolytes and of the members of the schola, and what follows the synaxis, the way in which the ministers take off their liturgical vestments (pars. 93–94) and take some refreshment (pars. 95–96). As to the *OR V*, it integrates some practices of the Frankish Churches such as the singing of the sequence (*jubilatio, quam sequentiam vocant* (par. 31) ["the joyous song which they call sequence"]), of the *Credo in unum* (par. 40) and the

---

[49] *vadat sibi ipse Roma aut, si piget, misso suo fideli in suo loco transmittat et inquirat diligenter . . .*

rite of the *Orate fratres* at the end of the *offertorium* (par. 56). There is a mention of the oration over the gifts, and it is specified that it is said in a low voice as is also the case for the canon: *dicta oratione super oblationes secreta et episcopo alta voce incipiente: Per omnia . . . . Tacito intrat canonem* (par. 58 ["when the oration over the gifts has been said and the bishop is intoning *Per omnia* in a loud voice, . . . he enters the canon in silence"]). The *OR* VII supplies the text of the canon and indicates in the proper places postures and rites, among which the signs of the cross.

The *OR* IX adapts the Roman Mass of the *OR* I to the celebration by a bishop. After the *Credo in unum*, the bishop receives the gifts of bread and wine first from the men then from the women (pars. 21–27). The *OR* X deals with the Mass celebrated by a bishop in a cathedral church having regular canons. It is mentioned that the bishop preaches after the gospel (pars. 30–32). The bishop also receives the gifts (par. 38) and then recites a formula of blessing drawn from the Gallican liturgy: "Come, almighty Sanctifier, and bless this sacrifice prepared for you who live and reign for ever and ever."[50]

The *OR* XV (end of the eighth century) contains two Mass rituals. First it describes the pope's Mass (pars. 12–65) and adapts it to the transalpine Churches. This first Mass has the ritual of the reception of the gifts as does the *OR* I. The second ritual (pars. 121–51) concerns the celebration of the Mass by a priest, in different circumstances: in monasteries, a city, a town, on Sunday, during the week, at solemnities, publicly with the participation of the clergy or with two ministers, or even only one (par. 121). The writer fictitiously gives Rome as the place where all this applies. He speaks of the Introit antiphon, with its psalm and doxology, then of the *Kyrie* (pars. 121–23). The *Gloria in excelsis* is said by the priest on Sundays and Saints' feasts (par. 124), and is omitted during Lent (par. 152). In this second ritual, there is no mention of the reception of the gifts. These are prepared before the celebration of the Mass in the *sacrarium* ("sacristy"): the wine is poured into the chalice and the loaves are placed in "towers" *(turres)* or on a paten. After the gospel, these gifts are processionally brought to the altar, while the antiphon *Laudate Dominum* is sung three times — a Gallican custom.

---

[50] § 46: *Veni, sanctificator omnipotens, aeterne Deus, benedic hoc sacrificium tibi praeparatum, qui vivis et regnas in saecula saeculorum.*

The *OR* XVII was composed for the priests of a monastery. In its description of the Mass (pars. 17–63), it depends on the *OR* I and the *OR* XV. The Roman ceremonies have been simplified. For the offertory, the two practices described in the *OR* XV, the one for the pope's Mass and the other for the priest's Mass, are offered in the *OR* XVII as suitable respectively for the presence or the absence of people at the monastery celebrations (pars. 38–43): when the people are present, one adopts the rite of the reception of the gifts, derived from the *OR* I; in monasteries where lay people do not have access, the gifts are prepared in the sacristy and brought out in procession. In this *OR* XVII, one also finds the early form of the *Orate fratres* (par. 45), and the specification that the oration over the gifts is said in a low voice.

## THE EVOLUTION OF THE ROMAN LITURGICAL BOOKS

Once they crossed the Alps, the liturgical books of Roman origin evolved. They were adapted, reworked, and given complements. This appropriation gave rise to new books, the Gelasian sacramentaries of the eighth century, and various forms of the Gregorian sacramentaries, either corrected or supplemented. In a subsequent phase, the books destined for different functions were joined to form one single book for the celebration of the Mass, the Missal, which combined the epistolary, the evangelary, the antiphonal, and the sacramentary.

The four books were first grouped together into one volume, one after the other by simple juxtaposition with occasional modifications in order to have them agree with one another.

Later on the four books were dismantled and their contents fused into a new arrangement, that of the Missal. The Missal presents complete Mass formularies, placed according to the order of the Mass, and offering, one after the other, introit antiphon, oration, epistle, gradual, Alleluia or tract, gospel, offertory antiphon, secret *(super oblata)*, Communion antiphon, postcommunion, and, when appropriate, an oration over the people *(super populum)*.

This new book was suited to the celebration of private Masses, without a congregation, in which the priest performed alone all the ministerial functions. Later on, custom and written norms made the Missal the indispensable instrument for the celebration of Mass.

## THE APOLOGIES IN THE *ORDO MISSAE*

The Sacramentary of *Angoulême*, a Gelasian of the eighth century, contains — but outside the *Ordo missae* — a penitential prayer said by the priest before Mass: *Incipit accusatio sacerdotis quomodo se ante altare accusare debeat* (formulary CXLVIII, no. 064) ("Here begins the accusation which the priest must make before the altar"). The invocation is addressed to Christ; the priest acknowledges his unworthiness at the moment of celebrating the sacrifice and asks that the wounds made by sin be healed, for the good health of the assembly (*familia tua*, "your family"). Such personal penitential prayers said by the priest, called apologies, grew more numerous in the sacramentaries of the tenth and eleventh centuries and became part of the *Ordo missae*. A sacramentary of St. Denis has seventy-five of them. After the twelfth century, the number of theses apologies diminishes.[51]

These prayers are private in character; they are written in the first person; the priest intercedes for himself, acknowledging his unworthiness at the moment he exercises his priestly ministry. These formulations betray a separation between the priest and the assembly and an overly sacrificial conception of the Mass. Their appearance, frequency, then their regression have been shown to be linked with the evolution of the penitential discipline during the same period and to the practice of penitential commutations through the celebration of Masses for the dead.

The *Ordo missae* retained some apologies at certain moments of the celebration — chiefly at the beginning of Mass, at the offertory, and at the time of Communion — down to the *Missale romanum* of 1570.

THE EVOLUTION OF THE FORMS OF THE CELEBRATION
Outside of Rome, the celebration of Mass according to the Roman custom was possible only through the application of written rules. From that time on, the history of the Roman Mass outside of Rome is one and the same thing as the history of liturgical books, and therefore the history of the written tradition, which had become that of the Missal.

From the material viewpoint, the content of the Missal is that of the Roman books, with the adaptations and reworkings the books underwent when they were accepted in the transalpine regions, and then repeatedly transcribed. But the formation of the Missal has led to another conception of the liturgy, because of the passage from the oral

---

[51] See A. Nocent, "Les apologies dans la célébration eucharistique," in *Liturgie et rémission des péchés* (Conf. S. Serge 1973), Rome 1975, 179–96.

tradition to the written rule. Indeed, in Rome itself, at least up to the Carolingian period, the celebrations were organized by oral tradition. As we have said above, according to the *OR* I, the pope and the archdeacon gave the necessary instructions during the course of the action and the other ministers knew their functions. On the contrary, outside of Rome, the Roman usages have been disseminated and imposed by an overwhelming recourse to writing, to such an extent that the written rules superseded the customs preserved by the living memory of the local communities.

With the advent of the Missal, the ceremonies of the Mass became fixed in their main lines.[52] Subsequent modifications concerned not so much the ritual itself than the way it was to be applied, through the multiplication of Masses, the variety of the forms of celebration (pontifical Mass, solemn Mass, private Mass), the theology of the Eucharist, the decline of the reception of Communion, the curtailment of the participation of the faithful, and the spreading of devotions.

The organization described in the *Ordines romani* has been maintained for the essential, but the preference given to personal piety has developed at the expense of collective actions such as the movements associated with the bringing in and the reception of the gifts, the kiss of peace, and the Communion. Whereas the early evocations of the Roman eucharistic celebration show it to be an action of the whole local Church, by contrast, at the end of the Middle Ages in the West, the "Roman" Mass was understood as a ritual to be performed, with hardly a suggestion of its ecclesial context. The point of reference has become the private Mass and no longer the celebration presided by the bishop. The reform of the Ordinary of the Mass at Vatican II has clearly broken with this state of affairs and the eucharistic celebration of the Roman liturgy has, in a very large measure, become again an action of the whole local church, in which the universal Church is present.

[52] Cf. C. Folsom, "The Liturgical Books of the Roman Rite," *Handbook for Liturgical Studies*, vol. I, 245–314.

## Bibliography

Among the most authoritative works, we shall signal especially the editions of Roman texts and documents accompanied by substantial introductions and notes, and some outstanding works.

Andrieu, M. *Les Ordines Romani du haut moyen-âge.* 5 vols. Spicilegium Sacrum Lovaniense 11, 23, 24, 28, 29. Louvain, 1931–1961.

Chavasse, A. *Le Sacramentaire gélasien: Sacramentaire presbytéral en usage dans les titres romains au VII^e siècle.* Tournai, 1958.

____. *Le Sacramentaire dans le groupe dit "gélasiens" du VIII^e siècle.* 2 vols. Instrumenta patristica 14A–14B. Steenbruge, 1984.

____. *La liturgie de la ville de Rome du V^e au VIII^e siècle.* SA 112. Rome, 1993.

____. *Les Lectionnaires romains de la Messe au VII^e et au VIII^e siècle: Sources et dérivés.* 2 vols. SFS 22. Fribourg, 1993.

Duchesne, L. *Le Liber pontificalis: Texte, introduction, et commentaire.* 2^nd ed. by C. Vogel. 3 vols. Paris, 1955–1957.

Klöckener, M. *"Sakramentarstudien zwischen Fortschritt und Sackgass."* ALW 32 (1990) 207–30.

Vogel, C., and R. Elze. *Le Pontifical romano-germanique du dixième siècle.* 3 vols. ST 226, 227, 229. Rome, 1963–1972.

The earliest testimonies concerning the history of the Roman Mass have been gathered in:

Leclercq, H. "Messe." *DACL* 11, cols. 701–66.

For a long time Jungmann's important study has been the reference and basis for the knowledge of the Eucharistic liturgy. However, the perspectives of historical research have evolved and, following global studies of the eucharistic liturgy juxtaposing pieces of information obtained from different Churches, researchers have now been paying closer attention to the development proper to each Church and, for Rome, to the twofold organization of the stational liturgy and the liturgy of the *tituli.*

Jungmann, J. *The Mass of the Roman Rite: Its Origins and Development.* Trans. F. Brunner. Christian Classics. Westminster, Md., 1986. Reprint 1992. Originally published New York, 1951–1955.

Michael Witczak

# 6

# The Sacramentary of Paul VI

## INTRODUCTION

The Sacramentary of Pope Paul VI is both traditional and reformed. It is traditional because it continues the Roman Church's following of the command of Christ to "Do this in memory of me" (Luke 22:19; 1 Cor 11:24-25) in continually developing ritual form. It is reformed because the bishops of Vatican II together with Pope Paul VI consciously decided to adapt the Roman rite to the changed conditions of the day.

The history of the celebration of the Eucharist appears elsewhere in this volume. But here it will be helpful to recall the liturgical movement and the papal initiatives of the twentieth century regarding liturgy. St. Pius X, who coined the phrase "active participation" in his 1903 *motu proprio* on sacred music, also issued the encyclical *Divino afflatu* in 1911, which led to changes in the Roman Missal published by Benedict XV in 1920.

The liturgical movement contributed a deepened liturgical theology and knowledge of history, and a conviction that full, active participation in the liturgy would enrich the Christian life of every member of the Church. The movement was academic, pastoral, and social in its concerns, and it prepared for the changes of Pius XII in the ritual of Holy Week (1951 and 1955), the simplification of the rubrics (1955), and finally to John XXIII's new Roman Pontifical (1960) and Roman Missal (1962).

But John XXIII had also called a council in 1959, and it was clear that the reform of the liturgy would be a part of its agenda.

Chapter 1 of the Constitution on the Sacred Liturgy (*Sacrosanctum Concilium* = *SC*; 4 December 1963) contains the "General Principles for the Renewal and Promotion of the Sacred Liturgy." Most notable is the theology of the liturgy which is rooted in the plan of salvation history that God has for us in Christ (nn. 5–6) and the theology of the manifold presence of Christ in the celebration of the liturgy (n. 7), whether it be in the person of the minister celebrating, in the word proclaimed, or in the community gathered in Christ's name. The liturgy, while not the whole of Christian life, is its source and summit (n. 10). The aim of the whole reform is the active participation of the faithful in liturgical celebration (n. 14). Since the liturgy is by nature a public action, public celebration is the preferred form (n. 26), and the various ministers should each perform only their own proper work (n. 29). The Scriptures are to have a more extensive role in liturgical celebration (nn. 33; 35,1). To foster active participation, a role is given to the languages of the people (n. 36), and the liturgy should be adapted to the culture and genius of the various peoples (nn. 37–40).

These general norms were then applied to the celebration of the "Mystery of the Most Holy Eucharist" (chapter II). The chapter begins with a brief summary of the theology of the celebration of the Eucharist which is not a systematic treatment of the Eucharist, but rather gives a range of understanding of the richness of this paramount Christian sacrament (n. 47). At such a great mystery, the faithful cannot be mute spectators, but rather active participants (n. 48). To accomplish this, the fathers decreed the following.

The order of Mass is to be revised to facilitate participation, especially eliminating things not helpful and restoring elements lost over time that would aid in understanding and participating in the Mass (no. 50).

The Scriptures are to be read more abundantly over the course of several years (no. 51). The homily is to be restored as an integral part of the celebration of Mass (no. 52). The general intercessions or prayer of the faithful is to be restored to the celebration (no. 53). The vernacular language can be used, especially for readings and prayers (no. 54).

At Communion, on special occasions, the people can receive Communion under both species of bread and wine (no. 55).

The celebration of Mass is to be understood as a single celebration in two parts, the Liturgy of the Word and the Liturgy of the Eucharist, which form but a single act of worship (no. 56). The people must be catechized to understand the importance of this.

Finally, concelebration by priests is to be permitted on various occasions (nn. 57–8).

Clearly this is a major shift from the reformed medieval order of Mass enshrined in the Roman Missal of 1570. For that reason, Paul VI wasted no time in beginning to implement the reforms decreed by the fathers of the council.

## THE CONSILIUM FOR THE IMPLEMENTATION OF THE CONSTITUTION ON THE SACRED LITURGY

On January 25, 1964, Paul VI issued the Apostolic Letter *Sacram liturgiam*, in which he began the work of implementing the Constitution on the Sacred Liturgy. He announced the formation of a special commission to oversee the work of reform. This later came to be known as the Consilium for the Implementation of the Constitution on the Sacred Liturgy.

Study groups were quickly established. For the celebration of the Eucharist, there were seven study groups, with several additional groups for elements shared jointly with the liturgy of the hours. The study groups were: Ordinary of the Mass; Biblical Readings for Mass; "Prayer of the faithful or general intercessions"; Votive Masses; Songs at Mass; General Structure of the Mass; and Concelebration and Communion under Both Kinds. The joint study groups included: Particular Rites during the Liturgical Year; Revision of Commons; Prayers and Prefaces; and Rubrics of the Breviary and Missal.

As can be seen from this brief list, the reform was comprehensive and complex. A good overview of the details can be found in Bugnini's work listed in the bibliography.

The progress of the work of the Consilium can be seen in the three Instructions that it issued. The First Instruction (*Inter oecumenici*, 26 September 1964) gave the first step of the reform, especially allowing the readings to be read in the vernacular, the restoration of the general intercessions, and some simplifications of the rubrics. The reforms were to begin on the first Sunday of Lent in 1965. The Second Instruction (*Tres abhinc annos*, 4 May 1967) cautions that the reform must be overseen by the apostolic see, and includes some further simplifications. The Third Instruction (*Liturgicae instaurationes*, 5 September 1970) continues the cautious note about liturgical innovation, and encourages the use of the new books that have been published. The details of the reform will be dealt with as they occur in our treatment of the Order of Mass.

The main fruit of the reform was the publication of the Order of Mass (6 April 1969), the Order of Readings (25 May 1969; second typical edition with a new introduction, 21 January 1981), the Roman Missal with all its texts (26 March 1970; second typical edition, 27 March 1975), and the Lectionary (30 September 1970).

## THE SACRAMENTARY OF PAUL VI

The sacramentary is divided into several parts. The first part of the book contains introductory material: the decrees of the Congregation for Divine Worship (1970 and 1975), Paul VI's Apostolic Constitution *Missale Romanum* (3 April 1969), and the General Instruction of the Roman Missal (1969, emendations in 1970, 1972, 1975 and 1991). In addition, the General Norms for the Liturgical Year and Calendar are included with the General Roman Calendar. The sacramentaries of some of the particular churches include other documents in this section, such as the Directory for Masses with Children, and the special norms and appendices for that country.

The next part of the sacramentary is the *Proper of Seasons,* which contains the prayers for the liturgical seasons of Advent and Christmas, Lent and Easter, as well as for ordinary time and solemnities of the Lord in the general calendar. In the center of the sacramentary is the *Order of Mass with a congregation* (383–476). This is followed by the *Order of Mass without a congregation* (477–86) for celebrations when no assembly is present, but only a single minister. There is a brief appendix with options for various formulas at the beginning of Mass and for the penitential rite, and for introducing and concluding the prefaces, and the acclamations after the consecration of the Eucharistic Prayer (487–92). Also relating to the *Ordo Missae* are the solemn blessings and prayers over the people (493–511).

The next section is the *Proper of Saints* (513–661) with all the special texts for the feasts and memorials of specific saints. This is completed by the Common of Saints with prayers for saints who do not have a complete set of formularies for their celebrations (663–726). There follow the prayers for *Ritual Masses* (727–82) for the celebration of the sacraments and other rituals of the Church; *Masses and Prayers for Various Needs and Occasions* (783–854); *Votive Masses* for

various devotional celebrations of Mass (855–77); and *Masses for the Dead* (879–914).

The sacramentary concludes with an *Appendix* containing the rite of blessing and sprinkling holy water (917–20), samples of the prayer of the faithful (921–31), and the rite to commission special ministers of holy Communion (931). A series of prayers for preparation for Mass (931–4) and thanksgiving after Mass (934–7) follow, taken mostly from earlier sources. There are the melodies for the singing of the texts of the Mass (939–78), and finally some indices and the table of contents (979–99).

The sacramentary is more than just a listing of its materials. The real contents of the sacramentary can be discovered only when it is celebrated. The following commentary attempts to explicate the celebration of the Eucharist according to the Sacramentary of Paul VI.

### 1. *The General Structure of the Mass*

The introductory materials of the sacramentary follow the method used in the documents of Vatican II: first, they articulate the theological basis of the topic, and then go on to practical implications and norms. The Apostolic Constitution of Paul VI begins by placing the reformed sacramentary within the tradition of the Latin Church and the reforms called for by the Council of Trent and implemented by Pope St. Pius V (1570). Paul VI goes on to mention the reform work of Pope Pius XII (1939–1958), and the call for the reform of the liturgy by Vatican II (1963). The Pope mentions the main changes in the new sacramentary: the presence of the General Instruction of the Missal, which is a new kind of document, not just giving rubrical directives, but placing them within a theological and ritual context. He mentions as particularly noteworthy the new Eucharistic Prayers which enrich the tradition by placing three new prayers alongside the Roman Canon which had been the sole prayer in the West for more than one thousand years. The simplifications of the celebration of Mass did not preclude the addition of the homily as an ordinary part of the celebration, of the general intercessions, and of the penitential rite at the beginning of Mass. The enrichment of the lectionary is also noteworthy. The prayers of the Missal have an even greater variety and number than in the past. The new sacramentary also gives a place for the adaptation of the celebration of Mass to the cultural expression of the various peoples of the Church.

Between the publication of the Apostolic Constitution (3 April 1969) together with the *Order of Mass* (6 April 1969) and the appearance of the sacramentary (26 March 1970), it became necessary to add an Introduction *(Prœmium)* to the General Instruction of the Roman Missal. The Introduction makes three major points. First, the reformed Missal is part of the ongoing faith of the Church and continues today what began at the Last Supper and on the cross of Christ: the sacrifice of praise, of thanksgiving, and of propitiation and satisfaction. In addition, the new Missal is part of the uninterrupted tradition of that faith, based on the "pristine norm of the Fathers," as the Missal of 1570 was. Finally, the new Missal is adapted to the needs of the day by its use of the vernacular and its enrichment in the variety and number of the prayers.

The General Instruction of the Roman Missal continues with chapter 1: "The Importance and Dignity of the Celebration of the Eucharist" (nn. 1–6). These first paragraphs lay out the theology of the celebration of the Eucharist as described in the rest of the sacramentary. This theology is rooted in that of the Constitution on the Sacred Liturgy as well as other conciliar documents. The celebration of the Eucharist is placed in its soteriological and christological context where it is seen as the center of the life of the Church, a joint act of Christ and his people where the whole mystery of God's salvation in Christ is recalled throughout the course of the year. The Eucharist is to be celebrated in such a way that all in the Church may receive the full benefit of participation.

Chapter 2 of the General Instruction, "The Structure of the Mass and its elements and parts," is crucial for understanding the reasons for the shape of the celebration of the Eucharist. The chapter is divided into three parts: the general structure of the Mass, the various elements of the Mass, and the individual parts of the Mass.

The General Structure of the Mass (nn. 7–8) is rooted in the action performed by Jesus at the Last Supper. There is a litany of names and descriptions given to the celebration: the Lord's Supper, the Lord's Memorial, the eucharistic sacrifice, the perpetuation of the sacrifice of the Cross. Each of these names captures an aspect of this rite where we encounter Christ present in the gathered assembly, in the person of the priest, in the word proclaimed, and sacramentally and continually in the eucharistic species (*SC* 7). This presence is celebrated in the two basic parts of the Mass: the Liturgy of the Word and the Liturgy of the

Eucharist, which are so closely connected that they form but a single act of worship. There are also rites to begin and end the celebration.

This understanding of the Mass, that it is two basic parts, is not new. For centuries, people had been used to think of the Mass in terms of the "Mass of the Catechumens" and the "Mass of the Faithful." Later medieval theology had further understood the Mass as an introductory period of instruction followed by the celebration of the mystery, which was in three major parts: the Offertory, the Consecration, and the Communion. This way of understanding the Mass has been set aside by this approach to its structure. There are two main parts, word and Eucharist, and they are one act of worship, where one encounters Christ in a variety of modes. This is a major shift in thinking about the structure of the celebration.

The chapter mentions the elements that form this general structure (nn. 9–23): the word, which is God speaking to us, Christ announcing his good news, then explained in the homily. The prayers (nn. 10–3), foremost of which is the Eucharistic Prayer, the high point of the whole celebration, and the opening prayer (collect), prayer over the gifts, and prayer after Communion are the key "presidential prayers," where the priest speaks in the language of prayer to God on behalf of the gathered faithful. The nature of the presidential role is such that the one leading must speak to be heard and lead the congregation to fruitful participation.

Other formulas occurring during Mass help highlight the communal and dialogical nature of the celebration: acclamations and responses, the penitential rite, the profession of faith, the general intercessions, and the Lord's Prayer (nn. 14–9). In addition, there are some texts which stand by themselves, such as the *Gloria,* the Gospel acclamation ("Alleluia"), the *Sanctus,* the memorial acclamation, and the hymn after Communion. Other texts accompany actions, such as the entrance song, the offertory song, the *Agnus Dei,* and the Communion song. Texts are to be said or sung in a way that allows for understanding and participation (n. 18). Music is crucial for good celebration (n. 19): while not everything need be sung, more solemn days demand more singing. The people should learn parts of the Ordinary, especially the Creed and the Lord's Prayer, in Latin for situations when people from various places and languages are celebrating together. The gestures and postures of the Mass (nn. 20–2) should be uniform to facilitate the spirit of unity among participants.

These include standing, sitting and kneeling at appropriate times. Gestures and postures should also be adapted to the various cultures as appropriate. Finally, silence needs to be a part of every celebration to allow time for reflection and prayer (n. 23). These are the building blocks of the celebration of the Eucharist.

The next section, on the individual parts of the Mass, is the first of a series of descriptions of how to celebrate the Mass. It gives the structure and meaning of the various sections of the Mass (nn. 24–57). The second description comes in chapter 4, on the various forms of celebrating Mass, which describes how these various structural elements are actually performed: first in a regular Mass with the people (the "typical form," nn. 77–152); then when Mass is concelebrated by several priests (nn. 153–208); then finally for Mass without people present. The form upon which all the others are based is the "typical form" of Mass celebrated with the people. This is a change from the Roman Missal of 1570 where the basic form described in the *Ordo Missae* and the *Ritus Servandus* was the private Mass to which were added the elements of the solemn Mass. The third description comes in the Order of Mass, placed in the center of the sacramentary between the celebrations of the Church's year and the celebrations of the saints. It lays out the entire celebration integrating the rubrics and the prayer texts in a continuous form (385–476, numbered 1–145). We will come back to these three complementary descriptions in the next section where we analyze the celebration of the Eucharist in the Sacramentary of Paul VI.

Between chapter 2 on the structure of Mass and chapter 4 on the celebration of Mass is the description of the offices and ministries of the Mass (chapter 3, nn. 58–73). After a reminder that each person in the celebration functions only in his or her own role (n. 58, citing *SC* 14, 26, and 28) so that the mystery of the Church be revealed, the ministry of the ordained then follows (nn. 59–61) speaking of the roles of the bishop (n. 59), presbyter (n. 60), and deacon (n. 61). The role of the assembly is then explained (nn. 62–4), rooting their action in their sacerdotal character and seeing it as a share in the action of the priest (n. 62, citing *SC* 48).

The choir is seen as part of the People of God, assisting the faithful to participate in song (n. 63). The cantor or leader of the schola must be present to help the people in their singing parts (n. 64). Other ministers, including acolytes (n. 65) and lectors (n. 66; both terms are used in the technical sense of those who have been officially installed by the bishop), the psalmist, and other ministers (n. 69: commentators, servers, and those who take up the collection) round out the ministers who might participate in the celebration. In larger communities, it may be helpful to have someone to oversee the celebrations (n. 69). The role of women as ministers is the subject of the adaptations made by the local conference of bishops (n. 70). The roles of ministers are to be adapted to the concrete circumstances of the celebration: if there are several ministers, roles can be divided among them (n. 71); and a single minister can fulfill several roles (n. 72). Finally, good celebration needs preparation on the part of the ministers (n. 73) so that each minister knows what the other is doing.

The General Instruction concludes with chapters that deal with some very concrete concerns. Chapter 5 explains how churches should be organized for the celebration of Mass. Some general principles (nn. 253–6) introduce the chapter. They focus on the need for a church suitable for celebrating the divine mysteries in a way that is worthy and beautiful (n. 253) and adapted for the active participation of the people (n. 254). The church should be solemnly dedicated and this should be celebrated regularly in the parish (n. 255). The diocese should have a commission to help parishes accomplish this (n. 256). The chapter then goes on to detail the needs of the church in its various parts: the nave of the church (n. 257); the presbyterium (n. 258; this is also called the sanctuary); the altar (n. 259–67); altar decorations (n. 268–70); the chair for the priest celebrant (n. 271; also called the presidential chair) and chairs for the ministers; the ambo, or place where the word is proclaimed (n. 272); the place of the people (n. 273); the place of the schola and organ and other musical instruments (nn. 274–5); the reservation of the Blessed Sacrament (nn. 276–7); images for the veneration of the faithful; and finally, general dispositions of the sacred place (nn. 279–80).

Chapter 6 gives the prescriptions for the things required for the celebration of Mass: bread and wine (nn. 281–6: while their quality must follow certain norms [unleavened bread and grape wine], they must also have the appearance of food); general norms for the furnishings of church: that they be noble and simple, adapted to the artistic genius of the people of the area (nn. 287–8); sacred vessels (nn. 289–96); vestments (nn. 297–310); and other furnishings (nn. 311–2).

Chapters 7 and 8 explain the choice of the various formulas for the celebration of Mass. These choices should be prepared ahead of time, and must be made in the light of the needs of the people and not solely according to the piety of the celebrant (n. 313). The rules are then given for choosing texts according to the various seasons and days (nn. 314–6), for readings (nn. 317–20), prayers (nn. 321–3) and music (n. 324). There are special rules for Masses for various needs and occasions (nn. 326–34) and Masses for the dead (nn. 335–41).

*2. The Celebration of Mass According to the Sacramentary of Paul VI*

A. PREPARATIONS BEFORE MASS

For a good celebration, certain things must be prepared ahead of time. This includes, as was noted above, that the ministers be prepared for their roles, and that the celebrant have ensured the preparations for the Mass of the day, including readings, prayers, and songs, and have communicated this with the appropriate ministers (n. 73). The "typical form" includes the participation of the priest celebrant, an acolyte, a lector and a cantor. A deacon can function in any of the forms (n. 78).

The altar must be covered ready for the celebration with a white cloth. On or near the altar should be two, four or six candles (or even seven if a bishop is celebrating). These can be carried into the presbyterium (sanctuary) in procession. A cross, too, should be on or near the altar, and may also be carried in the procession (n. 79). Prepared near the priest's chair should be the sacramentary and a book with the songs. At the ambo should be the lectionary. At the credence table (a side table where things for the celebration are kept) should be the chalice, corporal, purificator, the things for washing the celebrant's hands, a plate for the Communion of the faithful, and extra bread, if needed. There can also be, if they are not on the table from which the faithful will present the gifts, the paten with bread and a vessel with wine. The chalice should be covered by a veil which can always be white. In the sacristy, the vestments are laid out for the various ministers.

The requirements and explanations of the various objects is given elsewhere in the General Instruction. The purpose here is to describe the proper way of celebrating the Eucharist.

B. THE INTRODUCTORY RITES

The Introductory Rites (as well as the Preparation of the Gifts and the Communion Rite) could be described in the simplest terms as a procession accompanied by a song and concluded by a prayer. Yet the Introductory Rites (and the other two) have had a convoluted history and have a complex structure.

Today, the Introductory Rites have six major parts: the entrance song, the greeting, the penitential rite, the *Kyrie*, the *Gloria*, and the opening prayer or collect. These six elements have a multiple task: to prepare the gathered people to hear God's word and to enter fully into the mystery of the Eucharist (n. 24). One of the innovations of the Sacramentary of Paul VI is found in this section. The previous Missal never gave the meaning of the rites, but only explained what should be done. The General Instruction of the Roman Missal provides the basic meaning of each of the rites. These explanations can serve as a basis for evaluating the celebrations of communities and for giving catechesis about the meaning of the Mass.

*Analysis of the Introductory Rites*
*People.* The rites involve all the people from the start of the celebration. Except for the entrance procession and greeting of the altar which concern only the presider and ministers, every other element of the introductory rites is communal. The presider greets the people and they respond. He invites them to examine their lives, and they offer the penitential rite. All join together in the *Kyrie* and *Gloria*. The presider invites the people to pray, which they do in silence, after which he collects their prayers in the collect, to which they respond "Amen." This way to begin Mass is fundamentally different from the Missal of 1570, where the initial part of the celebration included only the priest and ministers until the *Kyrie*.

*Verbal elements.* Exploring the verbal elements reveals that, unlike the Roman Missal of 1570, there are no private prayers in the Introductory Rites. All the prayers and other texts are public.

The entrance song has an antiphon given in the sacramentary.[1] It is very thematic during the seasons of Advent/Christmas and Lent/Easter, and of a more general character for Ordinary Time. If

---

[1] The *Liber Pontificalis* indicates that the Introit was added to the *Order of Mass* by Pope Celestine I († 432), though the notice generally is considered to lack historical foundation. It is included in the *OR* I as a responsorial piece of music to accompany the entrance procession. Eventually it included an antiphon, a psalm verse, the *Gloria Patri*, and the repetition of the antiphon. Generally, it set the theme and tone for the celebration.

the antiphon is not sung with its psalm, schola and people alternating, another song can be substituted. This song is given great weight by the GIRM: to open the celebration, to help unite the community, to present the mystery of the season or day, and to accompany the procession of the ministers. Hence the text must be one that can bear all this responsibility and the melody one that can foster participation.

The Sign of the Cross and the greeting are the first words exchanged between the presider and the people.[2] The Sign of the Cross, a typical way to begin prayer, was proposed as a silent gesture in the experimental *Missa normativa*. Its advantage is to avoid a second beginning after the entrance song. Speaking of the words can have the effect of cutting the entrance song off from the rest of the celebration, making it seem more a prelude than the effective beginning of the Mass.

The greeting has three forms from which to choose. In its simplest form, it is the biblical phrase, "The Lord be with you" (Ruth 2:4; Luke 1:28), with the response, "And also with you." Other formulas, given as options, are taken from the Pauline letters: "The grace of our Lord Jesus Christ, the love of God, and the fellowship of the Holy Spirit be with you all" (2 Cor 13:13; also used in some Eastern Eucharistic Prayers); and "Grace and peace of God our Father and the Lord Jesus Christ be with you" (Rom 1:7; Gal 1:3; 1 Cor 1:2; 2 Cor 1:2; Eph 1:2; Col 1:3; 1 Thess 1:2; 2 Thess 1:2). This second can have the response "Blessed be God, the Father of our Lord Jesus Christ," but this is seldom used since the greeting itself is similar to the first, and there is nothing to cue the people to this longer response. The bishop's greeting is "Peace be with you," the phrase used by Jesus with the disciples in the upper room after his resurrection (John 20:19, 21, 26).

The penitential rite has a fairly complex verbal structure in four parts. (a) There is the option of introducing the Mass briefly *(brevissimis verbis)*. This is to help orient the people to the celebration of the day, much in the way that the entrance song is intended to do. If the song has functioned effectively in this way, it would not be necessary to say anything at this point. Unfortunately, this brief introduction can become a miniature homily, which is not at all its meaning.

---

[2] The greeting formularies, seemingly originally of Semitic origin, are first attested in the late fourth and early fifth century in the writings of Augustine (*De civitate Dei* 22,8,22) and John Chrysostom (*In Matt. Hom.* 12,6).

(b) The presider introduces the penitential act. The formula given can be adapted to the circumstances of the season, the community, and the form of the penitential act being used (GIRM n. 11). (c) After a period of silence comes the "general confession." The form actually given in the *Order of Mass* (n. 3) is the formula for general confession *Confiteor*, a prayer of apology originally part of the private preparation of the priest.[3] Two other optional forms are given in an appendix (487–8; integrated into the *Order of Mass* in vernacular sacramentaries). The first is an adaptation of Psalm 85:8. The second is a series of three invocations directed to Christ. The first invocation is concluded with *Kyrie eleison*, the second with *Christe eleison*, and the third with *Kyrie eleison*. (d) All three of these forms are concluded with the absolution. The *Confiteor* and first option are general forms of confession, expressing a sense of personal sinfulness and begging God's mercy. The *Kyrie* form, however, has a much different character. First, the text given in the appendix of the Sacramentary is a model, and other similar invocations can be used. Second, in addition to being a changeable form, it also has the character of praising Christ for his merciful actions rather than being a petition for mercy. In this respect it is more similar to the *Gloria* than to the penitential rite. Third, it differs from the first two options in that it is not followed by the *Kyrie*, which is included as the conclusion of the invocations. All in all, this third option constitutes a different act from the first two.

In place of the Penitential Rite on Sundays there is the optional *Ordo ad faciendam et aspergendam aquam benedictam* provided in an appendix at the end of the sacramentary. The prayers have more the character of a reminder of baptism rather than of a rite of purification. This is especially true of the prayer for use during the Easter season, which adapts the prayer of blessing water for baptism. The baptismal motif of the prayers makes the inclusion of the absolution at the end seem out of place. The accompanying antiphons include the traditional texts: *Asperges* outside of Easter time and the *Vidi aquam* for Easter time from the 1570 Missal, but also include other options.

---

[3] The origins of the penitential rite seem to be the prayers of apology found in Frankish and Germanic sources as early as the eighth century (*Sacramentary of Amiens*) and flourishing especially in the ninth and tenth centuries. These prayers were originally personal prayers of preparation for the priest and ministers to be recited in the sacristy and on the way to the altar.

The *Kyrie* is a chant sung after the penitential rite, originally immediately after the Introit.[4] If it is integrated into the penitential rite, it is not repeated separately. The *Kyrie* is a litany acclaiming Christ and pleading for his mercy.

The *Gloria*, an ancient hymn of praise, is based on the angelic praise at the birth of Christ.[5] It is prescribed for use on Sundays, solemnities, and feasts outside of Lent and Advent. The text is a venerable one praising God and begging peace for those of good will. It heaps up praises to the Father, then begs the merciful attention of the Son, with the Holy Spirit. It is a pure act of praise, with no other action or gesture accompanying it.

The collect, or opening prayer, has a complex structure: the priest celebrant invites the people to pray; there is a moment of silent prayer; and, the celebrant offers the prayer on behalf of all, who respond with "Amen." The prayer text has a form which typically begins with the invocation of God by name. This name is extended by mentioning some attribute of God or some action that he has performed on our behalf. In the light of this, we ask God to continue to act for us, petitioning God to do some specific thing, oftentimes also mentioning the motive for that action. The prayer concludes through the mediation of Christ and in the unity of the Holy Spirit. The people ratify the prayer with their "Amen." The collect is the key prayer of the introductory rites.[6] It brings them to a close and leads to the Liturgy of the Word. The texts of the prayer express the richness of our experience with God and the variety of our needs. They articu-

[4] The origins of the *Kyrie* are not clear. It may well be the remnants of the litany sung in procession from the church where the people gathered (the *collecta*) to the place of the celebration (the *statio*). It may also be the remnant of the litanic general intercessions moved to the beginning of the Mass around the time of Gelasius († 496) or Gregory the Great († 604). See the work by Baldovin noted below for an overview of the issues.

[5] The *Gloria*, first used in the celebration of Lauds, found its way into the celebration of the bishop's Mass by the sixth century, first only at Christmas (*LP* 1:253), then Sundays and martyrs' feasts (*OR* XXXIX, 27; Andrieu *OR* IV, 285; priests could use it at the Easter Vigil and their Mass of installation after ordination). Finally, it was allowed to priests whenever bishops could use it by the end of the eighth century (*OR* XV; Andrieu, *OR* III, 121).

[6] The collect seems to have entered the celebration of Mass during the fifth century and is found in the earliest sacramentaries (*Ve, GeV*, the Gregorian tradition).

late the nuances of the liturgical season, or beg for the strength to emulate the heroism of the saints, or offer to God the earth in its variety through various sacramental celebrations, funerals, and other prayers for various needs and occasions.

*Gestures, postures and objects.* The Introductory Rites are primarily action and hence are full of movement and objects. The fundamental posture is standing.

The gestures include the procession of the ministers through the church to the altar, symbolizing the approach of God's people. This procession can be simple, with only a minister and the reader accompanying the presider, or it can be solemn, including incense, cross flanked by candles, other ministers, concelebrants, and a deacon carrying the book of the Gospels.

The altar emerges as a central symbol of the celebration. It is reverenced by a bow, venerated with a kiss, and can be incensed. It is the throne of the book of the Gospels until that book is taken to the ambo to be read during the gospel procession.

The chair serves as the place from which the presider directs the Introductory Rites, the Liturgy of the Word, and the Concluding Rites.

The Sign of the Cross and the gesture of greeting reveal the community also as a sign of Christ's presence, and these gestures will be repeated at key moments throughout the celebration. The Sign of the Cross gathers the person under the Trinity to participate in the celebration. The greeting gesture includes all present as members of Christ's body and symbol of his presence "where two or three are gathered together" (Matt 18, 20).

The *orans* gesture, arms spread wide, hands uplifted in openness and supplication, will be the gesture of prayer throughout the celebration. Here it is used in the opening prayer for the first time to lift our gathered prayers to God.

*Open Question on the Introductory Rites*
Some conferences of bishops have petitioned for a simplification of the Introductory Rites. This simplification would be done in a way analogous to what is proposed already in the *Directory for Masses with Children*. After the entrance song and the greeting, there would be one introductory element: either the penitential rite (in one of its three forms), or the rite of blessing and sprinkling holy water, or the *Kyrie*, or the *Gloria*. Finally, there would always be the opening

prayer. Others have proposed that there be a ferial order of Mass where a similar kind of simplification would occur on days other than Sunday.[7]

C. THE LITURGY OF THE WORD

The Liturgy of the Word is one of the two major parts of the celebration of the Mass, so closely bound to the eucharistic liturgy that it forms a single act of worship (GIRM 17–8). The Liturgy of the Word is fundamentally a dialogue among God, who speaks of his salvific will; Christ, who is present in the proclaiming of his Gospel, offering spiritual nourishment; and people who respond, also with God's own word in the psalm and offer prayers for the whole world.

There are two basic structures for the Liturgy of the Word, one for Sundays and solemnities, and one for weekdays and feasts.

*Analysis of the Liturgy of the Word*
*People.* The variety of ministers in the celebration of the "typical form" of the Mass is one of its characteristics. The reader proclaims the texts of the readings before the gospel. The psalmist leads the community in the responsorial psalm. A deacon reads the gospel, or a concelebrant does, if there is no deacon. If neither is present, the priest celebrant himself reads it. The celebrant gives the homily, then leads the community in the profession of faith and directs the general intercessions. It is important to note that the minister of the gospel is ideally someone other than the presider. The one who preaches, normally the presider, is subject himself to hearing the word before preaching it. The petitions are announced by the deacon or another minister.

*Verbal elements.* The readings constitute the heart of the Liturgy of the Word. As the GIRM says, God is speaking to his people, Christ proclaims his gospel (*SC* 33). The people use the words of Scripture to respond to the offer of salvation and spiritual nourishment they have received.

The dynamic of the Liturgy of the Word is a profound one. God is speaking. This takes place through the medium of the words of the

---

[7] For the simplified Introductory Rites, see International Commission on English in the Liturgy, *Second Progress Report on the Revision of the Roman Missal* (Washington, D.C.: 1990) 93–95. The German *Meßbuch* (1975) provides the option of substituting a penitential song or a *Glorialied* for elements of the introductory rites. On the ferial order, see Chupungco, in the bibliography.

readings. The Old Testament readings are offered as the story of God's plan of salvation fulfilled in Christ, the New Testament readings as the living out of that promise, and the gospel passages as the presence of Christ himself speaking to us. The richness of this communication is detailed in the section of the *Handbook* dealing with the lectionary, but it is one of the jewels of the whole liturgical reform, the basis of most lectionary reforms in the various Christian communions.

After proclamation and reflection, there is response. The responsorial psalm has the function of allowing us to use the words of Scripture to respond to God's word to us. The sequence, used in the celebration of Easter, Pentecost, Corpus Christi, and Our Lady of Sorrows, is a poetic text celebrating the feast with its own rhythmic and rhyme schemes. The gospel acclamation gives us the words to acclaim the presence of Christ in his word. The Creed puts the words of reading and reflection into the inherited language of baptismal faith. The general intercessions form a response in prayer, where the word proclaimed and reflected upon becomes the source of our prayerful concern for the Church and all in the world, whatever their needs. And finally, the response to the word takes its full shape in the celebration of the eucharist.

*Gestures, postures, objects.* The postures of the Liturgy of the Word reflect this fundamental dynamic. The community sits to hear the word proclaimed, to reflect in silence, to respond in the responsorial psalm, to hear the homily. The community stands to acknowledge Christ's presence in the gospel and to act in professing faith and praying to God for those in need in the general intercessions.

The gestures of the Liturgy of the Word focus primarily on the reading of the gospel. The book of the Gospels, which had been placed on the altar at the beginning of Mass, must be carried to the ambo. This procession can have great ceremony. Incense is prepared, the deacon is blessed, and the book is carried by him, accompanied by incense and acolytes with candles, to the place where the word will be proclaimed. After greeting the people and announcing the reading, the deacon incenses the book of the Gospels. At the end of the reading, he kisses the book. Posture, procession, and gesture all combine to declare that the gospel is the privileged moment of proclamation in the Liturgy of the Word.

Virtually the whole Liturgy of the Word can be sung. The readings can be chanted as a solemn form of proclamation. This is more frequently done for the proclamation of the Passion on Passion/Palm Sunday and Good Friday, but can be done any time, using a simple form of chant. This way of doing the readings highlights that this is ritual proclamation, not simply sharing a story. The responsorial psalm almost requires singing. The psalms themselves were composed to be sung, and this is clearly the preferred way of utilizing them. The gospel acclamation is omitted if not sung. The Creed can be sung, as can the general intercessions. It would seem best to use the principle of progressive solemnity articulated in the General Instruction of the Liturgy of the Hours (n. 273), using more singing the more solemn the day is.

*Open Questions on the Liturgy of the Word*
Some problems have emerged in the celebration of the word. Some have to do with the reform of the content of the lectionary, and are taken up in that section of this volume. Others have to do with the celebration of the word. A significant concern is the preparation of the readers for their ministry. Catechesis in both the Bible and the techniques of reading are essential for this ministry to have its full impact.

Silence needs to become a part of celebration. This requires catechesis in the meaning and use of silence and the courage to allow time for reflection. Silence helps create a sense of God's presence working in the people through the power of the Holy Spirit, and can do much to mitigate the criticisms that the revised order of Mass is too busy and without moments of silence for awe before God's presence.

There is a problem in the relationship between the Old Testament readings and the New Testament, especially the Gospels. This is taken up in the section on the lectionary. But it is experienced in the celebration of the word, especially in the ceremony surrounding the gospel. Is God's word a single word to us, or are there privileged moments? There are some who propose not using the book of the Gospels and not using the options of incense and candles so as not to "overemphasize" the gospel at the expense of the other readings.[8]

The homily must move beyond historical critical exegesis and become a true expression of the meaning of God's word for this com-

---

[8] See National Liturgical Office (Canada), "Pastoral Notes on the Use of the Book of the Gospels," *National Bulletin on Liturgy* 27:137 (Summer 1994) 115–25.

munity in this celebration today. Holding in tension all three poles: the word proclaimed, the liturgical season, and this community of believers in their own existential moment, will allow the homily to be the moment of integration and deepening it is meant to be. It also must serve as a moment of transition from word to sacrament, and from ritual to life.

The challenge of the general intercessions is that they be both general and yet an expression of this particular community's response in prayer to the word that has been proclaimed. On the one hand, the petitions should not become a list of local concerns. On the other hand, they should not just be taken from an anonymous source written by someone for general use. These resources, while helpful, should be adapted by the local community to express their own particular understanding of the general needs of the Church and the world in the light of these readings.

## D. THE LITURGY OF THE EUCHARIST (GIRM 48)

The GIRM dedicates one paragraph to a general overview of the Liturgy of the Eucharist. It makes an analogy to the Last Supper of Christ, when he instituted the paschal banquet and sacrifice, which is now celebrated continually by the priest. The actions of that Last Supper are found in all the accounts of it in the Scriptures: he took bread and wine, blessed them, broke the bread, and gave them to the disciples. Hence the celebration of the Liturgy of the Eucharist follows this fourfold action: "taking" in the preparation of the gifts; "blessing" in the Eucharistic Prayer; and "breaking" and "giving" in the Communion Rite.

### 1) PREPARATION OF THE ALTAR AND GIFTS

The Preparation of the Altar and Gifts corresponds to the Lord's "taking" of bread and wine at the Last Supper. The focus is on the material gifts: on the bread and wine, which will become none other than Christ's own body and blood given for us, and on the offering of gifts for the Church and the poor, which extends the reality of the body of Christ beyond the ritual. There is likewise emphasis on presenting the gifts by the people, manifesting their self-offering, and acceptance by the presider, to prepare them for the sacrifice.

In simplest terms, the Preparation of the Gifts can be seen as a procession with gifts accompanied by song and concluded with prayer. The experimental *Missa Normativa* had attempted to return to a rite that was virtually wordless, with the only public prayer being the prayer over the gifts. The actual rite we have returns to some of the characteristics of the 1570 Missal. But it seems impossible to avoid offering language here. The bread and the wine, once they are presented, have no other function than to become Christ's body and blood for us. The action we are performing is the necessary prelude to the great Eucharistic Prayer that will follow, and the actions and prayers absorb some of the meaning of that which will follow. The whole rite has a transitional character, ending the Liturgy of the Word and beginning the Liturgy of the Eucharist.

*Analysis of the Preparation of the Altar and Gifts*
The renewed rite of the Mass, first of all, changes the name of this part of the Mass. It is now not called the Offertory, but the Preparation of the Gifts. The name change has not been effected completely, since the GIRM still makes reference to the Offertory (nn. 21, 50).

*People.* Rather than being regarded as just the action of the priest as in the former Missal, preparation of the gifts is a ritual that involves the whole community. The schola leads the community in the singing of the offertory song. Ministers prepare the altar. Often others take up a collection of money or other objects for the needs of the Church and the poor. Representatives of the community present the bread and wine, and these other gifts.

*Verbal elements.* The texts of the Preparation of the Gifts are very different from the former ones.[9] The Offertory song is no longer a prescribed text, but can be chosen from any suitable text. Despite the reference to the antiphon in the GIRM (n. 50), no text is given. The prayers for placing the bread and wine on the altar are new compositions. Originally, the experimental *Missa Normativa* had proposed two brief texts to be said privately by the priest. One was an adaptation of the *Didache (Sicut hic panis erat dispersus et collectus factus est unus,*

---

[9] The origin of the prayers during the preparation of the gifts is similar to the origins of the prayers during the introductory rites. The original prayer was the prayer *super oblata*, as found in *OR* I. During the eighth and ninth centuries, apologies were added to the offertory. This is part of a tendency to attach a prayer to every rubric. See B. Luycks, *De oorsprong van het gewone der Mis*, De Eredienst der kerk 3 (Utrecht-Antwerp, 1954; German tr. "Der Ursprung der gleichbleibenden Teile der heiligen Messe *[Ordinarium Missae]*," *Priestertum und Mönchtum, Liturgie und Mönchtum* 29 [Maria Laach, 1961] 72–119).

*ita colligatur ecclesia tua in regnum tuum. Gloria tibi in saeculum).* The text with the wine was Proverbs 9:1-2, on Wisdom's banquet. This same experimental order included no text for adding water to the wine, and omitted the invitation to prayer *(Orate, fratres).* Paul VI intervened directly in all these areas. His main concern was for participation for the people. Hence he required prayers that would involve a response of the people, and the maintenance of the *Orate, fratres.*

The actual way that the prayers is proposed is curious. If the offertory song is being sung, then the presider says the prayers quietly, and there is no response by the people, who are singing. If there is no song, he *may* say the prayers aloud, which indicates that it is not necessary that he do so. The people may make a response, indicating that this too is optional. The Consilium had proposed a rite in which the basic action was simple and clear: preparing the altar and placing the gifts upon it with prayer. The new prayers, beautiful adaptations of the Jewish *berakah,* complicate the action somewhat. The texts proposed in the experimental liturgy spoke of unity and preparation; the new texts praise God for creation and for giving us bread and wine to offer, a return, obliquely, to the language of offering that was so dominant in the former Missal of 1570.

The *Orate, fratres,* maintained from the former rite, is an extended introduction to the Prayer Over the Gifts. This latter prayer, while simpler in structure than the Opening Prayer, still follows the classic Roman style. It often does not begin with invoking God's name, but with the petition of the prayer. Often, the motivation for the prayer is omitted. The prayer is an effective transition from the Preparation of the Gifts and its emphasis on accepting the material gifts of bread and wine, to the offering that will take place in the great Eucharistic Prayer. Its vocabulary is rich in words that evoke both the material gifts and offering.

There are also additional private prayers in the Preparation of the Gifts. When the deacon or presider adds the water to the wine, he says quietly *Per huius aquae et vini mysterium,* an abbreviation of the earlier prayer. The prayer of apology *In spiritu humilitatis* is maintained from the earlier Missal. The washing of the hands is accompanied by a verse from Psalm 51 instead of the verses from Psalm 25. All three of these private prayers have been maintained from the medieval custom of attaching prayers to rubrics and actions which offer a spiritual interpretation of what is taking place.

*Gestures, postures, objects.* The Preparation of the Gifts is primarily action. There is a collection of money and other objects for the needs of the Church and the poor. Water is added to the wine, probably continuing the Mediterranean custom of drinking watered wine.

The presider bows during the apology *In spiritu humilitatis,* taking on the posture of humility, and continues in the same spirit in the washing of the hands (which originally served the practical function of cleaning the presider's hands after collecting the gifts of the people). He opens his hands in greeting when inviting the prayer of the people *(Orate, fratres),* and uses the *orans* gesture in leading the people in the prayer over the gifts.

Those not involved in the actions of collection, presentation, and preparation usually sit until the prayer over the gifts.

Incense can be used as part of the preparation of the gifts, after they have been placed on the altar with prayer. The presider incenses the bread and wine, then the altar. The deacon or another minister incenses the presider and then the people. Hence all are honored and included in the offering being made.

2) THE EUCHARISTIC PRAYER

The Eucharistic Prayer corresponds to the second of the three actions of Jesus that lay the basis of the Liturgy of the Eucharist. It is the prayer *par excellence,* the center and apex of the whole celebration (n. 54). The prayer is led by the priest on behalf of the people, whom he calls to join together in a prayer of praise offering the eucharistic sacrifice.

The prayer has the following structure (n. 55). The first element is the Thanksgiving, usually called the Preface in the Roman tradition (55a). This is the part of the prayer that through the centuries has traditionally expressed the sentiment of thanks to God for his wonderful deeds on our behalf, the marvels of salvation which he has done for us. This prayer is concluded by a reference to angels and the worship taking place eternally in heaven in which we participate, and there follows the *Sanctus,* which is sung by all (55b). The next element identified is the *epiclesis* (from the Greek word ἐπίκλησις which means "invocation"), in which the Church invokes God's power upon the bread and wine offered by those present to consecrate them into Christ's body and blood (55c). The institution narrative and consecration follows, using Christ's own words to accomplish the eucharistic sacrifice, and to command the apostles to continue this act in memory of him (55d). The *anamnesis* (from Greek ἀνάμνησις, meaning "memorial") forms the next section of the prayer, in which the Church follows Christ's command, remembering the facets of his paschal mystery, his death, resurrection and ascension (55e). The description in the GIRM is unclear at this point, but the acclamation of the people after the institution narrative has an anamnetic character, and may be included as part of this structural element of the prayer. The Offering is the next element (55f), recognizing that our very act of offering is done in the context of memorial, and that we offer not only the victim but ourselves. The Intercessions (55g) continue the prayer of the offering, making explicit the ways that the unity that is ours through participating in communion finds expression in the Church throughout the world, with the dead, and in union with all the saints. Finally, the prayer concludes with the Doxology (55h), glorifying God and ratified by the "Amen" of all the people.

### Analysis of the Eucharistic Prayer

The sacramentary contains four Eucharistic Prayers: the Roman Canon (Eucharistic Prayer I); a short Eucharistic Prayer with its own preface (which can however be replaced by another preface) based somewhat on the Eucharistic Prayer in the *Apostolic Tradition* (Eucharistic Prayer II); a medium length Eucharistic Prayer, using the variable prefaces, which was a new composition (Eucharistic Prayer III); and a longer Eucharistic Prayer based on the eastern Antiochene tradition, offering a more complete survey of salvation history with a fixed preface (Eucharistic Prayer IV).

*People.* In each of the four prayers, the role of the people and various ministers is the same. The presider introduces the prayer with the dialogue and the people respond. The priest continues with the preface, and the people join in the acclamation at its end. The priest continues with the prayer through the institution narrative, and then introduces the memorial acclamation, which the people sing. The priest then continues through the doxology, and the people respond with "Amen." The prayer is the prayer of all, led by the presider and punctuated with acclamations.

*Texts.* The Dialogue is a formal yet festive beginning to the prayer, recognizing Christ's presence in the gathered assembly (*Dominus vobiscum*), inviting all into the action of the prayer (*Sursum corda*), and introducing the theme of the prayer (*Gratias agamus Domino Deo nostro*).

Many prefaces were added to the Sacramentary of Paul VI. From the fourteen prefaces that were in the last edition of the *Roman Missal of 1570*, the new book has a total of 87 prefaces.

The prefaces begin and end fairly stereotypically. The introductory text, or protocol, continues the final response of the dialogue of the people: *Dignum et iustum est. — Vere dignum et iustum est . . .* and sets the theme of thanksgiving to God through Jesus Christ. The body of the preface then praises God for some aspect of his saving work in our midst, whether for the mystery of salvation being commemorated in the liturgical year, the heroism of the saint being remembered, or the way God participates in human life as in the ritual prefaces. The end of the preface leads the community to recognize its participation in praise with the heavenly community: *Et ideo cum angelis et archangelis . . .* leading to the text of the *Sanctus*.

The *Sanctus* has been a part of the Eucharistic Prayer tradition from early on. It is made up of two phrases from scripture: Isaiah 6:3, the vision of God's majesty surrounded by the angels; and the cry of the crowd on Palm Sunday: "Hosanna, blessed is he who comes" (Matt 21:8). It combines our earthly worship with the recognition that our action is one with meaning beyond just the present time.[10]

The Roman Canon is venerable. The first complete texts come from the seventh–eighth century (*Bobbio Missal, Stowe Missal, Missale Francorum, Gelasianum Vetus*), but it has roots that go back to the late fourth century, when Pope Damasus (366–384) seems to have presided over the transition from Greek to Latin in the Roman liturgy. St. Ambrose cites a text very similar to the heart of the Roman Canon in his *De Sacramentis*, which can be dated about 390. This ancient prayer is famed for its incomparable use of the tools of rhetoric and *cursus*. Its theology of acceptance of the sacrifice and of the unity of the local community with all those who have preceded us is eloquently pleaded throughout the prayer. But there are likewise problems with it.

We know that the prayer has had additions. Leo the Great (440–461) and Gregory the Great (590–604) are both credited with adding phrases. The memento for the dead was originally only used at funeral Masses. In general, the prayer seemed to be more a series of prayers tacked together rather than a literary and theological

---

[10] For a recent survey on the history of the *Sanctus*, see B. Spinks, *The Sanctus in the Eucharistic Prayer* (Cambridge, 1991).

whole. The list of saints is one exclusively of saints venerated in Rome. The Holy Spirit is mentioned only in the final doxology, unlike in the eastern tradition in which the Holy Spirit is prominent as a prime actor in the consecratory action of the prayer. The limited number of prefaces resulted in an impoverishment of the themes of the prayer. Especially when the decision was made to translate the prayer into the vernacular, it was difficult to recapture the powerful Roman rhetoric in another verbal idiom.

The main contributions of the Roman Canon to the scheme outlined above are: the variable preface tradition now greatly enriched; and the first *epiclesis* of the prayer *Quam oblationem*. It is this first *epiclesis* that becomes the dominant characteristic of the new prayers. A significant difference, as we will see, is that the Roman Canon's *epiclesis* is not pneumatological.

The basic structure of the Roman Canon seems to be that of balanced sets of prayers before and after the words of institution. The opening preface and *Sanctus* balances with the closing praise of the doxology. The initial prayer for acceptance of the offerings *(Te igitur)* is balanced by the final plea for blessing *(Per quem haec omnia)*. The initial prayers commending the living and the first list of saints ( . . . *in primis quae tibi offerimus pro* . . . and *Memento, Domine* . . . and *Communicantes*) pairs with the commendation of the dead and a second list of saints *(Memento etiam* . . . and *Nobis quoque peccatoribus)*. The preliminary offering and first *epiclesis (Hanc igitur* and *Quam oblationem)* balance the prayers after the institution narrative *(Supra quae propitio* . . . and *Supplices te rogamus)*. All these prayers center on the heart of the prayer where we find the institution narrative and *anamnesis (Qui pridie* . . . , *Simili modo* . . . , and *Unde et memores)*.

The Second Eucharistic Prayer was designed to be short and clear in structure. It is based on the anaphora found in the *Apostolic Tradition* and bears resemblance to the theology of Hippolytus of Rome. A comparison of the two prayers shows that the use of the Roman structure (found in GIRM 55) radically alters the prayer. After the introductory dialogue, the new prayer uses the typical Roman preface introduction *Vere dignum et iustum est* instead of the original *Gratias tibi referimus*. The new prayer omits much of the introductory part of the older prayer that could be considered theologically problematic or difficult. It then radically alters the structure of the older prayer by introducing the *Sanctus*, which was not in the *Apostolic Tradition*. Yet another radical shift in the structure is the insertion of a first *epiclesis* after a brief transitional phrase *(Vere sanctus es)*. The words of the institution narrative have been made identical in all of the new prayers except for their introductory phrases. Also a major shift from the structure of the earlier prayer is the presence of the memorial acclamation by the people. The prayer of *anamnesis* and offering is very similar to the original prayer, except for the retouching of the *epiclesis* which now speaks exclusively of the fruits of communion and no longer of the Spirit coming upon the gifts. The intercessions in Eucharistic Prayer II are also a novelty, not found in the *Apostolic Tradition*. Finally, the doxology, which like the institution narrative is the same in all the new prayers, has been changed from the strong ecclesiological sense of the original *(cum sancto Spiritu in sancta Ecclesia tua,* with the Holy Spirit in your holy Church). The brevity and clarity of structure of this prayer have given it a privileged place in the celebration of the Mass since its appearance.

The Third Eucharistic Prayer is a new composition meant to use the variable prefaces and be of medium length. It is based on a study and proposal of C. Vagaggini (see bibliography). After the dialogue, preface and *Sanctus,* it continues, as does Eucharistic Prayer II, with a phrase that continues the theme of the *Sanctus (Vere sanctus).* The transitional section leading to the first *epiclesis* is a rich blend of Trinitarian theology *(Vere Sanctus es, Domine . . . per Filium tuum . . . Spiritus Sancti operante virtute)* with a clear exposition of God's provident love *(vivificas et sanctificas universa),* for the Church *(populum tibi congregare non desinis)* which is offering this sacrifice *(oblatio munda offeratur nomini tuo,* a citation of Mal 1:11). There follows the institution narrative which begins with the Pauline motif: *Ipse enim in qua nocte tradebatur.* The *anamnesis* is enriched, speaking not just of the passion, resurrection and ascension, but adding to these traditional elements of the *anamnesis,* the words *praestolantes alterum eius adventum.* This prayer is rich in sacrificial language that does not just refer to the sacrificial character of Christ's own death, but also to our participation in the offering here and now *(offerimus tibi, gratias referentes, hoc sacrificium vivum et sanctum).* The Communion *epiclesis* also maintains this sacrificial character, asking that our participation in the victim's death make us one body and one spirit in Christ *(agnoscens Hostiam, cuius voluisti immolatione placari).*

The Fourth Eucharistic Prayer was composed to provide a longer prayer that would treat in a more synthetic way the whole history of salvation. It is based in the Alexandrian Anaphora of St. Basil. It begins with an inseparable preface. God is praised as holy Father (*Pater sancte*) throughout the prayer, echoing John 17. The preface first treats of the theme of God's creative glory (*inaccessiblilem lucem inhabitans . . . creaturas tuas benedictionibus adimpleres*). The preface turns to the world of the angels in a much more integrated way than the typical Roman preface, which leads naturally to the acclamation of the *Sanctus* (*coram te innumerae astant turbae angelorum . . . te incessanter glorificant. Cum quibus . . . confitemur, canentes: Sanctus . . .*). The prayer continues the story of salvation, beginning with God's creation of human beings, continuing through the fall, and gift of the covenant and the continual work of the prophets. Christ then appears as the culmination of this history, *completa plenitudine temporum:* Christ's salvific actions in the incarnation, his life on earth, and his dying and rising complete the memorial of God's actions and lead to his gift of the Spirit that we might live for him. This summary of the whole of salvation history leads to the consecratory *epiclesis* and the account of the Last Supper. This latter is introduced by a reminiscence of John 13 (*cum hora venisset ut glorificaretur a te, Pater sancte*). The institution narrative is the same as in the other prayers, with the interesting note that the cup was "filled with wine, *ex genimine vitis repletum.*"

Eucharistic Prayer IV, in addition to the mentioning of the death of Christ mentions also his "descent among the dead, *descensum ad inferos*," his resurrection, ascension to the right hand, and as a separate element added to these traditional ones, again a reference to "his coming in glory, *ipsius adventum in gloria.*" Here as in the third prayer, the coming in glory is treated differently since the death, resurrection and ascension are events which have already happened and the second coming is yet to occur. The Offering is unique in the Roman prayers, in that here it says, "we offer you his body and blood, *offerimus tibi eius Corpus et Sanguinem*," rather than the more typical "we offer these gifts, this living bread and saving cup." The liturgical tradition has been careful to link our offering to the sacramental signs rather than to the underlying reality, which is more normally put in terms of Christ's own self-offering.

*Other Eucharistic Prayers Added Since 1970*
The fours prayers just discussed formed part of the original text of the sacramentary published in 1970 and in the second typical edition

in 1975. However, several other prayers have been added to the repertory of Eucharistic Prayers. These are the two Prayers for Masses of Reconciliation, three Prayers for Masses with Children, and the Prayer for Various Needs (also known as the Prayer of the Swiss Synod). The Prayers for Masses with Children and Masses of Reconciliation were published in late 1974 and soon were translated and in use throughout the world. At first approved for three years only, the permission was extended in 1977 for another three years, and in 1980 for an indefinite period. Not found in the 1975 *Missale Romanum*, they can usually be found in an appendix of the vernacular sacramentaries.

The so-called Swiss Synod Prayer was originally composed for a national synod in Switzerland and approved in 1974. Over the next thirteen years, churches from twenty-nine nations requested permission to use it. Finally, in 1991, an official Latin version of the prayer was issued for the whole Church. The Latin changes some elements of the original prayer, and subsequent editions must take the Latin text into account.

All these prayers follow the fundamental outline of a Eucharistic Prayer found in GIRM 55. It is worth noting that the prefaces in all these prayers are not variable but rather a necessary part of the prayer they begin.

Eucharistic Prayer for Masses with Children I is designed to help the children to learn the *Sanctus* in an inverted order. Hence throughout the preface, the *Sanctus* is divided into parts, and then combined at the end. After the initial dialogue, the prayer continues with praise of God for the beauty of the earth, then the second phrase of the *Sanctus*, *Pleni sunt caeli et terra gloria tua*. The preface continues, praising God for his gift of Jesus who saves us, which leads to *Benedictus, qui venit in nomine Domini*. The preface lists all those who join in praise, including the pope and the bishop, after which follows the first part of the *Sanctus*.

Eucharistic Prayer for Masses with Children II makes provision for additional acclamations throughout the prayer. After the initial dialogue, the preface lauds God for the varieties of ways that God shows love for us. Each of the four elements of praise are capped by an acclamation which leads to the *Sanctus*, sung by all. During the elevation of the consecrated host and the chalice, the children sing the acclamation, *Iesus Christus pro nobis tradetur*. There follows the anamnesis and offering prayed by the presider, with the acclamation *Gloria et laus Deo nostro* or *Te laudamus, te benedicimus, tibi gratias agimus.* After the Communion *epiclesis* and the intercessions, there are three further acclamations, *Unum corpus sint ad gloriam tuam!*[11]

Eucharistic Prayer for Masses with Children III was designed to have variable parts for the seasons of the year, analogous to the *Communicantes* of the Roman Canon. These variable parts are placed in the preface, in the *Post Sanctus* before the first *epiclesis,* and in the intercessions. While the original intention was to provide variations for several celebrations and seasons, only variations for the Easter season were published. On the other hand, the Italian sacramentary provides variations for Advent, Christmas, and Lent, as well as Easter.

Eucharistic Prayer for Masses of Reconciliation I begins with the dialogue and then continues with a preface that lays out the dilemma of human relationship with God: God is ever faithful, calling us to respond, yet we sin. This celebration is another opportunity to respond to God's call to reconciliation. There follows a long transitional section leading to the institution narrative which continues the theme of return to the Father *(Cum vero perissemus nec tibi appropinquare valeremus, summo nos dilexisti amore).* The prayer continues with the *anamnesis* and offering which highlight Christ as the source of peace and reconciliation. The Communion *epiclesis* asks in particular that division be excised *(ut virtute Spiritus Sancti congregentur in unum Corpus in quo omnis auferatur divisio).*

The Eucharistic Prayer for Masses of Reconciliation II begins, after the normal dialogue, with a beautiful recounting of God's way of bringing about peace among the human family. There are two sets of three images that portray God's work: the Spirit changes our hearts, God's power is at work, when divisions cease and unity and peace take over. The *Post Sanctus* insists on the role of Jesus in this powerful work of bringing peace with another three-fold flourish (Jesus is the *sermo,* the *manus,* and the *via,* that leads to peace). The Eucharist is conceived of as the celebration of reconciliation received from God through Jesus. The *anamnesis,* offering, and Communion *epiclesis* continue with their refrain of reconciliation. The intercessions pray for

---

[11] Here we are citing the Latin text of the prayers. However, the prayers were not originally written in Latin, nor ever intended to be celebrated in Latin. Rather, the Latin text is for study purposes only.

the Church, in communion with the saints, and in the hope of a world where all will be joined *ad perpetuae unitatis convivium.*

The Eucharistic Prayer for Various Needs is a single prayer with four sets of variable parts. The four variable sections are the preface and the intercessions, with four themes: the Church on the way of unity *(Ecclesia in viam unitatis progrediens),* God guides the Church on the way of salvation *(Deus Ecclesiam suam in viam salutis conducens),* Jesus, way to the Father *(Iesus via ad Patrem)* and Jesus, the compassion of God *(Iesus pertransiens benefaciendo).*

After the initial dialogue, the prayer continues with its thematic preface, each of which reflects on the pilgrim character of the Church, whether it be the Church's own journey or the leadership it has in Christ. Because the prayers are focused on the Church as a theme, they tend to speak eventually of the Church today, abandoning the preface as a place for the recitation of God's marvelous deeds in the past, which we use as a basis for our prayer today to beg God's action through the Holy Spirit. Each of the prefaces leads to the *Sanctus* and then to the invariable *Post Sanctus,* which continues the theme of the Church on the way *(qui semper illis ades in itinere vitae)* and makes reference to the disciples on the road to Emmaus (Luke 24:31ff: *sicut olim pro discipulis nobis Scripturas aperit et panem frangit).* The intercessions take up again the four themes in a variable section which focuses on the unity of the Church in the world today. Then there is a return to the invariable section for intercessions for the dead and a prayer to be one with the saints *(Concede nos quoque, terrena exacta peregrinatione, ad aeternam pervenire mansionem).*

*Open Questions on the Eucharistic Prayer*
Participation in the Eucharistic Prayer is manifold. The opening dialogue sets the stage for a prayer that fully engages all present. The *Sanctus,* memorial acclamation, and Amen at the end of the doxology punctuate the prayer with exclamation points of praise and presence. The children's prayers go even farther, with multiple acclamations to facilitate a sense of participation by all in the prayer. Yet the modern sensibility does not seem comfortable with a prayer said only by one person. The Eucharistic Prayer, rather than the center and high point of the celebration can seem a hiatus between a dynamic homily and the act of Communion. While a more prayerful and energized proclamation of the prayer by the presider can help the people enter, and

acclamations and other sung forms can help foster a sense of partici-pation, perhaps the main problem is an assembly unused to having someone speak on its behalf at great length.

The texts of the prayers have been analyzed by many commenta-tors at length from a number of perspectives: structural, theological, liturgical, literary, etc. The prayers are not without fault in any of those areas, yet at the same time they offer a variety of ways of pray-ing eucharistically today, new to the Roman rite. While extensive and rigorous criticism on all these levels and more remains a necessity, there is also the need to appreciate the variety and depth of the prayers that have so far been produced.

The gestures of the Eucharistic Prayer have been simplified. Yet they share the same tendency toward allegorization and dramatiza-tion that has been inherent since they began entering the Roman Canon in the early middle ages. When one takes the bread and cup at the word "takes" in the institution narrative, and bends a little to "bless" them, one wonders why the bread is not broken at the same time — and some priests actually do break it during the words of in-stitution! But rather than chide overly dramatic presiders, perhaps it would be better to ask about the wisdom of these gestures. Since the Eucharistic Prayer is the blessing, to be followed later by the break-ing and giving in Communion, why are gestures necessary at all? Standing prayerfully using the *orans* gesture for the entire prayer could emphasize that this is prayer and avoid suspicions of magic.

Concelebration is also a problem with the co-recitation of the words sometimes obscuring the central role of the presider, and the gestures confused between indication and invocation. Unfortunately, in some cases, concelebration is experienced not as a manifestation of the church in its diversity of orders, but as a division between clergy and laity.

3) THE COMMUNION RITE (GIRM 56; 110–22; 136–8; 146–7; 192–206; 240–52; OM 125–40)

The Communion Rite corresponds to the action of the Lord at the Last Supper, when, after having blessed the bread, he broke it and gave it to his disciples and did the same with the cup. This rite, then, like the Introductory Rites and Preparation of the Gifts, can be char-acterized as fundamentally an action, a procession with song, con-cluded by a prayer.

*Analysis of the Communion Rite*

*People.* The presider leads the people in participation. He invites the people to join in the Lord's Prayer and extends it with the embolism that follows. After praying for peace on behalf of the community, he also shares that peace with those around him. All the people do the same. The presider takes the lead in breaking the bread and preparing the chalices for Communion. After a period of quiet personal preparation, he invites the people to share in Communion and gives out Communion. He leads the community in silent adoration after Communion, and sums up the prayers of the community in the prayer after Communion.

The other ministers such as a deacon or acolyte assist in the preparing of the Eucharist for Communion, may help distribute Communion, and help in the cleansing of the vessels after Communion. It is not unusual to have some in the church give directions to the people to assist in the smooth unfolding of the Communion procession. The schola may lead the singing of the Communion song, which is processional music reinforcing the community's action. They can also be involved in the singing of the *Agnus Dei* during the breaking of the bread and in a hymn of praise after Communion.

*Verbal elements.* The texts of the Communion Rite are varied. Some are public prayers. The Lord's Prayer is said in common by all. Phrases such as "give us this day our daily bread," and "forgive us as we forgive" make it an ideal prayer in preparation for Communion. The theme of the Lord's Prayer is continued by the embolism of the priest *(Libera nos)* which takes up the last phrase of the Lord's prayer and asks for peace, one of the main themes of the prayers before Communion. The prayer for peace is an adaptation of a prayer of apology that has been in use since the ninth century *(Domine Iesu Christe, qui dixisti)*. This is one of the few prayers of the Mass not directed to the Father. The prayer is followed by the greeting of peace, made by the presider, and the invitation to share a sign of peace, made by the deacon if he is present.

The *Agnus Dei*, ideally sung, is a litany done by all. It can be extended as long as needed for the breaking of the bread; it ends with another call for peace, *dona nobis pacem.*

The priest invites all to Communion with a text adapted from John's Gospel (1,29) and the book of Revelation (19:19). Difficulties

164

with this text (*ad cenam Agni vocati sunt*) have led to different ways of translating it in the various countries.[12] During Communion, each person is told, "The body of Christ. — Amen. The blood of Christ. — Amen." During the Communion procession, the antiphon is sung. The text often is taken from the Gospel of the day, highlighting the unity of the two tables of the word and of the Eucharist.

The final public text of the Communion Rite is the prayer after Communion. This prayer follows the simpler style we saw in the prayer over the gifts. It particularly focuses on the theme of participating in the benefits of Communion. It also stands as the transition between Communion and the whole ritual action of the Mass and the dismissal and return to ordinary life.

There are also a number of non-public texts prayed during the Communion Rite. They are all remnants of the medieval custom of prayers of apology which gathered around the beginning of Mass, the Offertory, and the Communion Rite. The first is a text for the mingling of a particle of the host in the chalice (*Haec commixtio*). For the presider's personal preparation, there is a choice of one of two texts, both of which were part of the repertory of prayers of apology. These two with the prayer adapted as the preparation for the sign of peace were all part of the *Roman Missal* of 1570. When he receives Communion, the presider recites silently *Corpus Christi . . . Sanguis Christi custodiat me in vitam aeternam*. Finally, after Communion as part of the purifying of the vessels, the presider says quietly, *Quod ore sumpsimus . . .* The purpose of these silent prayers is to help the presider keep his attention focused on the meaning of what he is doing.

---

[12] The German translation attempts to keep the reference to the wedding feast of the Lamb: *Seht das Lamm Gottes, das hinwegnimmt die Sünde der Welt. R. Herr, ich bin nicht würdig, daß du eingehst unter mein Dach aber sprich nur ein Wort, so wird meine Seele gesund. – Selig, die zum Hochzeitsmahl des Lammes geladen sind.* The latter is an optional addition by the priest.

In Italian, the text is: *Beati gli invitati alla Cena del Signore. Ecco l'Agnello di Dio che toglie i peccati del mondo.*

It is similar in Spanish: *Éste es el Cordero de Dios, que quita el pecado del mundo. Dichosos los invitados a la cena del Señor.*

The French is the same as the Italian: *Heureux les invités au repas du Seigneur! Voici l'Agneau de Dieu, qui enlève le péché du monde.*

The English language text is: "This is the Lamb of God who takes away the sin of the world. Happy are those called to his supper."

*Gestures, postures, objects.* The fundamental gesture of the Communion Rite is the procession itself. Unlike the entrance procession, which involves the presider and the ministers of the celebration, and the procession at the preparation of the gifts, which involves representatives of the community, this procession involves all those who will participate in Communion. They are members of the body of Christ receiving the body of Christ.

The basic posture of the whole rite is standing, though after Communion, the assembly can sit for the hymn of praise (GIRM, n. 21).

The presider extends his hands in the *orans* gesture for the Lord's Prayer, the Prayer for Peace, and the Prayer after Communion. In some communities, the whole assembly joins the presider in the *orans* gesture during the Lord's Prayer. The sign of peace is a gesture that recognizes our fundamental unity as members of Christ's body. Coming as it does between the Lord's Prayer, recited by all together, and the breaking of the bread, the sign of peace is part of a whole repertoire of prayers and gestures that emphasize the unity that binds us as brothers and sisters.

The act of receiving Communion, whether by the ancient form of receiving in the hand or in the medieval custom of receiving on the tongue, is an intimate gesture of receiving the Lord into ourselves. The GIRM emphasizes that the ideal form of Communion is to receive from hosts consecrated at the same Mass, so that the unity of the sacrificial action can be perceived (n. 56h).

The GIRM gives a whole section to explaining Communion under both kinds (nn. 240–52). Communion under the form of both bread and wine is a fuller form by reason of its sign value: a meal is made up of food and drink; at the Last Supper, Jesus and the disciples partook of both bread and wine. Our participation under both forms shows forth that fullness more completely. Numerous cases are listed when Communion under both kinds can be given, mainly special and sacramental celebrations and concelebrations, but ultimately, the local bishop can give permission for special circumstances. In some countries, Communion can be shared under both kinds at all community Masses, including on Sunday.[13] Four modes are described for sharing Communion under the form of both bread and wine: drinking directly from the chalice; intinction of the host into the conse-

---

[13] This is the case, for instance, in the United States of America.

crated wine; Communion using a golden straw (a custom from the papal court of the Middle Ages); using a spoon (similar to the eastern custom). Since most churches do not have golden straws or spoons, the most common ways are drinking directly from the chalice and by intinction. Drinking from the chalice best seems to maintain the symbolism of the action.

The purification of the vessels, which used to take place at the center of the altar, now can take place at a side table or in the sacristy after Mass. If done after Mass, the vessels are covered at the side table.

*Open Questions on the Communion Rite*
The ritual flow of the rite is complex. It consists of three actions that speak of the union that will be ours most fully in the reception of Communion: the common praying of the Lord's Prayer, the sign of peace, and breaking of the bread. The sign of peace, while venerable in this place in the Roman rite, is experienced by many as breaking the flow of the action, especially if it becomes prolonged. Some have suggested moving the rite of peace to the beginning of the Preparation of the Gifts, where it is in most other rites, as a way of preparing for the whole Liturgy of the Eucharist (see Matt 5:23-24).

The mingling of the host in the chalice is an ancient custom and found in most of the rites of the Church. While its meaning historically in the Roman rite is clear (namely, the *fermentum* sent from the pope's Mass to the other churches in the city), when it is not part of the Communion sent from the bishop's Mass, it is more difficult to understand. It usually, then, is given a spiritualized interpretation, as in the accompanying text, or an allegorical one, symbolizing the resurrection because it represents the reunion of Christ's body and soul.

Communion under both kinds remains an important part of the participation in the Eucharist. As it does make manifest the fullness of the action under the form of signs, it is important that communities pay attention and take opportunities when this will be a real possibility. Related to this is the desire of the Church that the faithful receive from hosts consecrated at that Mass. This highlights the unity of the action and the full participation in the one sacrifice of Christ. Allowing the sacramental symbols full room to express their meaning remains an ongoing task for our communities.

## E. The Concluding Rite

The Concluding Rite, which concludes the celebration of Mass and is part of the transition from liturgy to ordinary life, is of the utmost simplicity.

### Analysis of the Concluding Rite

*People.* The whole assembly is blessed and sent forth in the conclusion. Having been nourished at the table of the word and the table of the Eucharist, they go out to live what they have experienced. The presider leads the community in this action by blessing them. The deacon calls them to receive the blessing and sends them forth.

*Texts.* There are only public texts in the conclusion. The announcements, mundane as they may seem, begin to articulate the concrete ways in which the eucharistic community will live out its membership in the body of Christ. The blessing forms a trinitarian conclusion, analogous to the trinitarian Sign of the Cross at the beginning of Mass. There are two more extensive forms of blessing, both introduced by the greeting by the presider and the deacon's (or in his absence, the presider's) invitation to *Inclinite vos ad benedictionem*, "Bow your heads and pray for God's blessing." The solemn blessing is a series of three invocations of God over the community, each text concluded by an "Amen" by the people. This is taken from a Gallican custom of episcopal blessing. The prayer over the people is an ancient Roman prayer, found in the earliest sacramentaries. After the presider's greeting and the invitation by the deacon, the presider continues with the prayer, which follows the same basic pattern as the prayer over the gifts and the prayer after communion. Both the solemn blessing and the prayer over the people are concluded with an explicit blessing formulary: *Benedicat vos omnipotens Deus . . . .*, "May almighty God bless you."

The final text is the dismissal, done by the deacon if present, otherwise by the presider. The only formula given is, *Ite, missa est. - Deo gratias.*

*Gestures.* The posture of the Concluding Rite is simply standing. Gestures include bowing of the head by those being blessed, the extension of the hands in blessing when the solemn blessing or prayer over the people is used, and the gesture of the Sign of the Cross, made over the people by the presider, and those present making it on themselves.

Announcements tend to move about. They have been done before Mass, after the gospel, after Communion, and in the place given in the rubrics. The value of doing them at the place in the rubrics is that it is part of the transition from Mass to life, and the events of the community need to be seen as flowing from the Eucharist.

The solemn blessing, while often powerful, is sometimes pastorally difficult because the people do not know when to respond with "Amen" at the end of each blessing. The translations need to be done in such a way that the people can participate fully in the blessings and give their full assent. The decision was made to include a specific text of blessing after the solemn blessings and prayers over the people. While this is a familiar gesture, it continues to imply that blessing is more a gesture rather than text.

There is no provision made for a concluding song in the Roman rite, nor has there ever been. Yet it has become common in many places to accompany the procession of the ministers out with a song. This seems to respond to a popular need, and it does create a sense of inclusion with the opening song. It may give more weight to the conclusion than the rite calls for.

## CONCLUSION

The Sacramentary of Paul VI is traditional — it continues the Roman rite's living out of the command of Jesus, "Do this in memory of me." The sacramentary is also reformed, providing a celebration that requires full, active conscious participation of the people who are nourished by the banquet of Christ's word and his body and blood.

The task of living this reformed tradition is one well begun and requiring continued work in the future.

## Bibliography

### I. THE CONCILIAR REFORM OF THE LITURGY

#### Source

Vatican II, Constitution on the Sacred Liturgy, *Sacrosanctum Concilium*, December 4, 1963. *AAS* 56 (1964) 97–138. See *EDIL* I:1, 1–27; *DOL* 1.

## Commentaries

"Commentaire complet de la Constitution conciliare sur la Liturgie." *MD* 77 (1964) 3–221.

Jungmann, J. "Einleitung und Kommentar" [on the Constitution on the Sacred Liturgy]. *LThK*, supplementary vol. 1 (1966) 10–109.

Sodi, M. "Vent'anni di studi e commenti sulla 'Sacrosanctum Concilium.'" *Costituzione liturgica "Sacrosanctum Concilium": Studi*. Ed. Congregation for Divine Worship. BELS 38. Rome, 1986.

## II. THE CONSILIUM FOR THE IMPLEMENTATION OF THE CONSTITUTION ON THE SACRED LITURGY

### Sources

Paul VI. Motu proprio *Sacram liturgiam* (25 January 1964). *AAS* 56 (1964) 139–44. *EDIL* 1:7, 41–4. *DOL* 20.

Sacred Congregation of Rites. [First] Instruction on the Proper Implementation of the Constitution on the Sacred Liturgy, *Inter Oecumenici* (26 September 1964). *AAS* 56 (1964) 877–900. *EDIL* 1:12, 50–78. *DOL* 23.

_____. Second Instruction on the Proper Implementation of the Constitution on the Sacred Liturgy, *Tres abhinc annos* (4 May 1967). *AAS* 59 (1967) 442–8. *EDIL* 1:66, 296–302. *DOL* 39.

Sacred Congregation for Divine Worship. Third Instruction on the Proper Implementation of the Constitution on the Sacred Liturgy, *Liturgicae instaurationes* (5 September 1970). *AAS* 62 (1970) 692–704. *EDIL* 1:132, 703–13. *DOL* 52.

### Studies

Bugnini, A. *The Reform of the Liturgy 1948–1975*. Trans. M. J. O'Connell. Collegeville, Minn., 1990.

Lengeling, E. "Liturgiereform 1948–1975: Zu einem aufschlussreichen Rechenschaftsbericht." *ThRv* 80 (1984) 265–84.

## III. THE SACRAMENTARY OF PAUL VI

### Source

Sacred Congregation for Divine Worship. *Missale Romanum ex decreto sacrosancti Oecumenici Concilii Vaticani II instauratum auctoritate Pauli PP. VI promulgatum*. Rome, 1970, 1975.

### Studies

Brovelli, F., and F. Dell'Oro. "Rilettura critica dell' 'Ordo Missae' attuale." *RL* 62 (1975) 491–513.

Cabié, R. *The Eucharist.* Vol. 2 of *The Church at Prayer,* ed. A. G. Martimort. Trans. M. J. O'Connell. Collegeville, Minn., 1986.

Carminati, G. "Una teoria semiologica del linguaggio liturgico: Una verifica sull 'Ordo Missae.'" *EphLit* 102 (1988) 184–233.

Chupungco, A. "Toward a Ferial Order of Mass." *EO* 10 (1993) 11–32.

DeClerck, P. "L 'Ordo missae' de Vatican II: Ses innovations et sa réception." Conférences Saint-Serge, XLIᵉ Semaine d'Études Liturgiques. Paris, 1994. BELS 79. Rome, 1995.

Emminghaus, J. *The Eucharist: Essence, Form, Celebration.* Rev. ed. Collegeville, Minn., 1992.

Lengeling, E. *Die neue Ordnung der Eucharistiefeier: Allgemeine Einführung in das römische Messbuch.* Reihe Lebendiger Gottesdienst Heft 17/18. 4ᵗʰ ed. Münster, 1973.

Marsili, S., A. Nocent, and others. *La liturgia, Eucaristia: Teologia e storia della celebrazione. Anàmnesis* 3/2.

"La nouvelle liturgie de la Messe." *MD* 100 (1969) 8–122.

"L'Ordo Missae." *MD* 192 (1992).

Stensvold, A. "Sacred Communication: An Analysis of the Structure of Communication in the Mass." *QL* 68 (1987) 167–74.

### 2. The Introductory Rites

#### Studies

Aldazabal, J. "Los domingos, aspersión." *Ph* 28 (1988) 246–51.

Baldovin, J. F. "Kyrie Eleison and the Entrance Rite of the Roman Eucharist." *Wor* 60 (1986) 334–47.

Bierritz, K.-H. "Zeichen der Eröffnung." *Zeichen: Semiotik in Theologie und Gottesdienst.* Ed. R. Volp. Munich and Mainz, 1982.

Dacquino, P. "I saluti liturgici nel nuovo rito della messa." *Not* 6 (1970) 254–57.

Farnes, P. "El acto penitencial de la Misa." *Ph* 28 (1988) 235–45.

Heinz, A. "Ein anderer Ort für den Bussritus." *LJ* 39 (1989) 109–26.

Jilek, A. "Der Eröffnung der Messfeier." *LJ* 39 (1989) 127–54.

Krosnicki, T. "Grace and Peace: Greeting the Assembly." *Shaping English Liturgy,* 93–106. Ed. P. Finn and J. Schellman. Washington, 1990.

Maas-Ewerd, Th. "'Brevissimis verbis' in die Messfeier einführen: Zu einer Frage liturgischer Praxis." *Klerusblatt* 67 (1987) 321–26.

Searle, M. "Semper Reformanda: The Opening and Closing Rites of the Mass." *Shaping English Liturgy,* 53–92. Ed. P. Finn and J. Schellman. Washington, 1990.

Wagner, J. "Reflexionen über Funktion und Stellenwart von Introitus, Kyrie und Gloria in der Messfeier." *LJ* 17 (1967) 40–47.

### 3. The Liturgy of the Word

#### Studies

Houssiau, A. "Le service de la Parole." *QL* 65 (1984) 203–12.

Lengeling, E. "Zur Neuausgabe der Leseordnung für die Eucharistiefeier." *Dynamik im Wort, Lehre von der Bibel, Leben aus der Bibel*, 385–411. Stuttgart, 1983.

Melloh, J. A. "The General Intercessions Revisited." *Wor* 61 (1987) 152–62.

*Il Messale Romano del Vaticano II: Orazionale e Lezionario.* 2 vols. Quarderni di Rivista Liturgica, n.s., 6–7. Turin, 1981, 1984.

Nübold, E. *Entstehung und Bewertung der neuen Perikopenordnung des römischen Ritus für die Messfeier an Sonn- und Festtagen.* Paderborn, 1986.

Pacik, R. "Der Antwortpsalm." *LJ* 30 (1980) 250–61.

"La preghiera dei fedeli." *RL* 74 (1987) 1–141.

Verheul, A. "Le pourquoi et le comment du Service de la Parole." *QL* 66 (1985) 203–17.

———. "Le psaume responsorial dans la liturgie eucharistique." *QL* 73 (1992) 232–52.

Zimmerman, J. "The General Intercessions: Yet Another Visit." *Wor* 65 (1991) 306–19.

### 4. The Liturgy of the Eucharist

#### a. Preparation of the Altar and Gifts

#### Studies

Janicki, J. *Le orazioni "super oblata" del ciclo "de tempore" secondo il "missale Romanum" di Paolo VI: Avviamento ad uno studio critico-teologico.* Rome, 1977.

Jilek, A. "Diakonia im Herrenmahl; Sinndeutung des Opfergangs aus der Stiftung der Eucharistie." *LJ* 36 (1986) 46–57.

———. "Symbolik und sinngerechte Gestaltung der Eucharistiefeier: Dargelegt am Beispiel der Gabenbereitung." *LJ* 38 (1988) 231–48.

Krosnicki, T. "'Mixtio aquae cum vino': A Case of Moral Unity." *EphLit* 104 (1990) 182–86.

———. "Preparing the Gifts: Clarifying the Rite." *Wor* 65 (1991) 149–59.

Keifer, R. "Preparation of the Altar and the Gifts or Offertory?" *Wor* 48 (1974) 595–600.

McManus, F. R. "The Roman Order of Mass from 1964–1969: The Preparation of the Gifts." *Shaping English Liturgy*, 107–38. Ed. P. Finn and J. Schellman. Washington, 1990.

Molin, J. B. "Depuis quand le mot 'offertoire' serait-il à désigner une partie de la messe?" *EphLit* 77 (1963) 357–80.

Raffa, V. "Le orazioni sulle offerte del Proprio del Tempo nel nuovo Messale." *EphLit* 84 (1970) 299–322.

Rasmussen, N. K. "Les rites de la présentation du pain et du vin." *MD* 100 (1969) 44–58.

b. The Eucharistic Prayer

Studies

Albertine, R. "Problem of the (Double) Epiclesis in the New Roman Eucharistic Prayers." *EphLit* 91 (1977) 193–202.

_____. "The Epiclesis Problem: The Roman Canon (Canon I) in the Post-Vatican Liturgical Reform." *EphLit* 99 (1985) 337–48.

_____. "The Post Vatican Consilium's (Coetus X) Treatment of the Epiclesis Question in the Context of Select Historical Data (Alexandrian Family of Anaphoras) and the Fragment of 'Der Balyzeh.'" *EphLit* 102 (1988) 385–405.

Ashworth, H., and others. *Preghiere eucaristiche: Testo e commento.* Quaderni di Rivista Liturgica 11. Turin, 1969.

Brandolini, L. "Le nuove preghiere eucaristiche (Rassegna bibliografica)." *EphLit* 83 (1969) 278–85.

DeJong, K. W. "Questions à propos de la double épiclèse." *QL* 68 (1987) 256–76.

Fossas, I. M. "'Manu dextera . . . ad panem et ad calicem extensa' — Historia de una controversia." *EO* 9 (1992) 201–16.

Heinz, A., and H. Rennings, eds. *Gratias Agamus: Studien zum eucharistischen Hochgebet: für Balthasar Fischer.* Freiburg, 1992.

Kavanagh, A. "Thoughts on the New Eucharistic Prayers." *Wor* 43 (1969) 2–12.

Krosnicki, T. "Manu . . . ad panem et ad calicem extensa: A Unitive Gesture." *EO* 7 (1990) 61–67.

Lamberts, J. "The Elevation During the Eucharistic Celebration: Too Much of a Good Thing?" *QL* 75 (1994) 135–53.

Levesque, P. "Eucharistic Prayer Position: From Standing to Kneeling." *QL* 74 (1993) 30–42.

Mazza, E. *Le odierne preghiere eucaristiche.* 2 vols. Bologna, 1984.

McKenna, J. "The Epiclesis Revisited: A Look at Modern Eucharistic Prayers." *EphLit* 99 (1985) 314–36.

Nocent, A. "L'unité de la prière eucharistique avec sa doxologie." *EO* 11 (1994) 133–52.

"Prière Eucharistique." *MD* 191 (1992).

Vagaggini, C. *The Canon of the Mass and Liturgical Reform.* Trans. P. Coughlin. Staten Island, N.Y., 1967.

_____. "Les nouvelles prières eucharistiques." *MD* 94 (1968).

Wegman, H. "The Rubrics of the Institution Narrative in the Roman Missal 1970." In *Liturgia: Opera Divina ed Umana,* 319–28. BELS 28. Rome, 1982.

## Other Eucharistic Prayers Added Since 1970

### Sources

Sacred Congregation for Divine Worship. *Preces eucharisticae pro missis cum pueris et de reconciliatione* (1 Nov. 1974).

Sacred Congregation for Divine Worship and the Sacraments. *Prex eucharistica quae in missis pro variis necessitatibus adhiberi potest. Decretum, Praenotanda. Textus. Not* 27 (1991) 388–99.

### Studies

Bugnini, A. *The Reform of the Liturgy 1948–1975.* Trans. M. J. O'Connell. Collegeville, Minn., 1990.

Giraudo, C. *Preghiere eucaristiche per la chiesa di oggi: Riflessioni in margine al commento del canone svizzero-romana.* Rome and Brescia, 1993.

Mazza, E. *La odierne preghiere eucaristiche.* 2 vols. Bologna, 1984.

### c. The Communion Rite

#### Studies

Augé, M. "A proposito della comunione sulla mano." *EO* 8 (1991) 293–304.

Béraudy, R. "Les rites de préparation à la communion." *MD* 100 (1969) 59–71.

Bohl, H. *Kommunionempfang der Gläubigen: Probleme seiner Integration in der Eucharistiefeier: Eine liturgiewissenschaftliche Untersuchung.* Disputationes theologicae 9. Frankfurt, 1980.

Bugnini, A. "Sulla mano 'come in trono.'" *Not* 9 (1973) 289–96.

Gallagher, P. A. "The Communion Rite." *Wor* 63 (1989) 316–27.

Krosnicki, T. *Ancient Patterns in Modern Prayer.* SCA 19. Washington, 1973.

Lopez, J. "La comunión bajo las dos especies." *Ph* 28 (1989) 296–305.

Raffa, V. "Le orazioni dopo la Comunione e la riconciliazione." *Not* 26 (1990) 533–65.

Taft, R. "Receiving Communion — A Forgotten Symbol?" *Wor* 57 (1983) 412–18.

Verheul, A. "L'ordonnance de la communion, selon le nouvel Ordo Missae." *QL* 53 (1972) 119–33.

____. "Le 'Notre Père' et l'Eucharistie." *QL* 67 (1986) 159–79.

## 5. The Concluding Rite

### Studies

Borella, P. "La benedizione della messa." *A* 43 (1967) 7–36.

Krosnicki, T. "New Blessings in the Missal of Paul VI." *Wor* 45 (1971) 199–205.

Lehmann, W. "Ite, missa est." *Bibel und Liturgie* 40 (1967) 66.

Moeller, E. "Les bénédictions solennelles du nouveau missel romain." *QL* 52 (1971) 317–25.

Adrien Nocent, O.S.B.

7

# The Roman Lectionary for Mass

INTRODUCTION

"Lectionary" is a general term that refers to the book containing the biblical pericopes, that is the scriptural passages to be read during the Liturgy of the Word at Mass (the term also refers to the biblical and patristic readings of the Divine Office). From its origin as a simple marginal note placed next to the biblical text, the lectionary developed in two stages:

1. *Capitularia*. The notes originally placed next to the biblical text were collected into lists in which the individual passages to be read were indicated with the first word *(incipit)* and the last word *(desinit)*. We have manuscripts, now edited, with marginal notes, which date from a period that goes from the seventh to the fourteenth century.[1]

A capitulary can be either a *Capitulare lectionum*, if it contains lists of the non-gospel readings, or a *Capitulare evangeliorum*, if it contains a list of the gospel passages. Before the Bible was divided into chapters and verses, this was the only practical system by which Scripture passages could be used in the liturgy.

2. A lectionary properly so-called is a collection of the texts that originally were only noted in the margins of the Bible. It may be either an Epistolary, or *Apostolus*, for the non-gospel pericopes, or an Evangelary for the gospel pericopes. Although these two collections form two separate books, they may be combined. The *Comes* or *Liber comitis* contains the epistolary pericopes but also at times those of the evangelary.[2]

---

[1] *CapEv*, XXXV–XXXVI.

[2] To facilitate study and reading, we give the various names proposed by Klauser, *CapEv*. LXXXI–CXX. For the Epistolarium: *Apostolus, Comes, Liber comitis,*

It is essential that we study the contents of the *Lectionary for Mass*, since it enables us to identify a celebration's distinctive characteristics and to understand its theology and spirituality. We cannot go into the details of the study of lectionaries, which is a complicated subject. Here we will give enough information to enable students to work by following the guidelines and consulting the specialized books mentioned.

The *Lectionary for Mass* of Vatican II must be studied in a different way. In the earlier lectionaries, the texts to be proclaimed before the gospel can be treated separately from the gospel texts, since they were composed independently of each other. But in the lectionary of Vatican II, the readings for feasts and Sundays (except for the Sundays in ordinary time) have a certain deliberate connection among themselves.

## THE MASS LECTIONARY PRIOR TO VATICAN II

### A. Collections of Pre-Gospel Readings

The first of these is the *Lectionary of Victor of Capua* from the mid sixth century, around 546.[3] Although this lectionary is not Roman, it allows us to guess what might have been the readings used in Rome, now that we have come to know more about the close ties between the liturgy of Benevento and Capua and that of Rome.

1. The first type of lectionary dates from the end of the sixth century and is adapted in part to the early Gelasian Sacramentary. Our only witness is the *Comes of Würzburg*.[4]

---

*Epistolare, Liber epistolarum, Epistolarium, Epistolium, Collectarium, Liber epistolarum, Lectionarius.* For the Evangeliarium: *Evangelium excerptum, Evangeliare, Evangelistale, Evangelistarium, Liber/Libellus/Ordo evangelii, Evangeliarum plenarium.* For the single Mass lectionary (which sometimes joins the epistolary and evangelary): *Comes, Epistolae cum evangeliis, Lectionarius, Liber comitis, Liber lectionum, Liber comicus.* The meaning of the terms *Comes, Liber comitis, Liber commicus* is not very clear; apparently it does not mean "companion" (A. Wilmart, "Le comes de Murbach," *RBén* 30, 1913, 26), but rather *book* of pericopes, *comma* meaning "section" or "pericope."

[3] Fulda, Landesbibl. Codex Bonifacianus 1. Datable to 545: Ed. E. Ranke, Codex Fuldensis, Leipzig 1868, 165–68; G. Morin, *Lectiones ex epistolis paulinis excerptae, quae in ecclesia Capuana saec. VI legebantur. Analecta Maredsolana 1,* append. V, Maredsous 1893. Th. Klauser, op. cit., XXXI, 9 (note 35).

[4] Library of the University of Würzburg, Cod. M.P. th. F. 62. Ed. G. Morin, "Le plus ancien lectionnaire ou Comes de l'Eglise romaine," *RBén* 27, 1910, 41–74. (Do not confuse the epistolary and evangelary that are joined in the same codex but do not necessarily go together).

This book was certainly used in Rome, since it contains six masses *In Natale Papae* and presupposes a day of fasting in preparation for this feast. Although the manuscript was written between 730 and 750, it puts us in touch with the liturgy of the sixth and seventh centuries. As a matter of fact it does not contain the celebrations introduced in the seventh century. But we do still find the prophetic readings, already suppressed by the time of Gregory the Great and listed in the book after the New Testament readings. Advent still consists of five or six weeks etc. But there are also seventh-century traces: the readings for the week after Pentecost, whose Monday and Wednesday readings were fixed by Gregory the Great.

Folios 2v–10v give the titles of 255 epistles with *incipit* and *desinit* (*Capitolare epistolarum vel lectionum*). According to Chavasse, the last part of the collection (nn. 214–55) contains forty-two pericopes from the letters of Paul, listed according to their order in the *Vulgate*. These pericopes are for the Sundays after Pentecost and the Sundays between January 1 and the first Sunday of Lent.[5]

2. The second type of lectionary comes from before ca. 626 and is adapted to the Gregorian Sacramentary. Our only witness is the *Comes Alcuini (Comes ab Alcuino ordinatus* or *Epistolary of Alcuin)*. This title is incorrect, since the collection was already known 150 years prior to the corrections made at the time of Charlemagne. It was composed during the pontificate of Honorius (625–638), freely uses the *Comes of Würzburg,* and seems to be Gregorian in structure. It reached France under Charlemagne, and a supplement was added thanks to the work of Abbot Helisachar of St. Richier in Picardy. In the preface to the supplement, Alcuin is mentioned by name: *Hunc codicem ab Albino politum atque emendatum.* This recalls the monastic chronicle for 831: *Lectionarius plenarius a supradicto Albino ordinatus.*[6] Since it contains Masses for Thursdays of Lent, which are not Roman in origin, the collection must have left Rome before the time of

---

[5] A. Chavasse, "Les plus anciens types du lectionnaire et de l'antiphonaire de la messe," *RBén* 62, 1952, 1–91; C. Vogel, *Introduction aux sources de l'histoire du culte chrétien au moyen âge,* Spoleto 1966, 279–328.

[6] A. Wilmart, "Le lectionnarie d'Alcuin," *EphLit* 51, 1937, 136–97. Concerning the author of the preface, see G. Morin, "Une rédaction inédite de la préface au Supplément au Comes d'Alcuin," *RBén* 29, 1912, 341–48. Ed. of preface: A. Wilmart, *EphLit* 51, 1937, 164–65.

Gregory II (715–731).[7] The title *Comes ab Albino* is not found in the manuscripts but was written by Tommasi, who took these words from the manuscript's preface. In fact, Alcuin did not really adapt or arrange the book; he merely made a few revisions.

We have one ninth-century manuscript[8] of the lectionary without supplement, written for the church of Cambrai, and one manuscript with supplement from the first half of the ninth century.[9] This *Supplementum* contains sixty-five Old Testament readings but gives only some non-gospel readings from the New Testament. According to Chavasse, the *Supplementum* has taken the form of an evangelary of type Π *(pi)* and was revised in 627.[10] It is safe to say that the document we know under Alcuin's name is really a Roman document.

3. The third type of lectionary is from the eighth century. It includes numerous as-yet-unidentified manuscripts, which Chavasse has grouped into two families. Family A originated in Rome around 900. Family B apparently originated in France and seems to have adapted the family A lectionaries to the eighth-century Gelasian Sacramentary.[11]

Among the many family B manuscripts, we mention the *Comes of Murbach* from the end of the eighth century, thus later than that of Alcuin. It contains only the *incipit* and *desinit* of the readings, derived from a lectionary that contained the full text.[12]

We also mention the *Comes of Corbie*, which contains the same readings found in the Murbach.[13] This document is Franco-Roman.

---

[7] Idem, "Un missel grégorien," *RBén* 26, 1909, 281–300; A. Dold, *Vom Sakramentar, Comes und Capitulare zum Missale* (Textse und Arbeiten A 34) Beuron 1943.

[8] Cambrai, Bil. Munic. Cod. 553: Ed. A. Wilmart, "Le lectionnaire d'Alcuin," *EphLit* 51, 1937, 136–97. (Text only in Bibl. Eph. Lit: II, Rome, 1937).

[9] Paris, B.N. cod. Lat. 9452: Ed. A. Wilmart, "Le lectionnaire d'Alcuin," *EphLit* 51, 1937, 151–68.

[10] For a description of the evangelary types Π, Λ and Σ, see T. Klauser, *Das römische Capitulare Evangeliorum*, I: Typen; C. Vogen, *Medieval Liturgy*, 342–44; *Introduction aux sources*, 323–27.

[11] A list of witnesses from families A and B may be found in C. Vogel, *Introduction aux sources*, 326–27.

[12] Besançon, Bibl. Munic. Codex 184, late eighth-century. A. Wilmart, "Le Comes de Murbach," *RBén* 30, 1913, 25–9. Idem, *DACL* 5, 316–21; 908–14.

[13] St. Petersburgh, State Lib., Cod. Q.v. 1/16, verso 772–780. Ed. and bibl. W. H. Frere, *Studies in Early Roman Liturgy*, III, Oxford 1935, 1–24 (N.B: Frere mistakenly places the manuscript in the tenth century).

4. Finally there is the *Lectionary of the Missal of 1570*. This seems to be a revision of the *Comes of Alcuin*. Chavasse's most recent work helps us understand the origin of this lectionary. Although it depends on the Murbach, it has not kept the readings for Wednesdays and Fridays envisioned by the latter.[14]

### B. Collections of Gospel Readings

After the work of Frere, Klauser renewed the study of the evangelaries. After examining about a thousand manuscripts, he classified the evangelaries into four types. The first three are Roman in origin: Π (645), Λ (740), Σ (755). The fourth is Franco-Roman and depends on Π.[15] The *Capitulare evangeliorum of Würzburg* belongs to type Π.

Hesbert, after studying the manuscripts of the Benevento tradition, concluded that the evangelaries are of two types, similar to the families of epistolaries.[16]

Chavasse distinguishes three types. The first is Gelasian, the second Gregorian, and the third is eighth-century Gelasian, which is subdivided into two families.[17]

We shall use Chavasse's conclusions, indicating when he agrees with Frere and Klauser in order to facilitate reference to these works.

Type 1 hypothetically belongs to the Gelasian family. Although the *Capitulare of Würzburg* contains Gelasian traces (16 Sundays after Pentecost; 10 Sundays after Epiphany, although six would suffice), we do not have an evangelary manuscript from this era.

Type 2, pure Roman, belongs to the Gregorian family, which originated ca. 645. It corresponds to Frere's "ancient" type and to Klauser's family Π. The principal manuscript is the Würzburg and the pericopes are gospel texts (ff. 10v–16v), unrelated to the list of epistle pericopes in the same manuscript and from a different era. The *Capitulare*

---

[14] A. Chavasse, *Les lectionnaires romains de la Messe au VIIᵉ et au VIIIᵉ siècle: Sources et dérivés*, Tome II: Synpotique général: Tableaux complémentaires, Fribourg.

[15] *CapEv*, 1–172.

[16] R. J. Hesbert, "La tradition bénéventaine dans la tradition manuscrite," *Paléographie musicale* 14, 1936, 60–479. Idem, "Les séries des dimanches après la Pentecôte," *LMD* 46, 1956, 35–39.

[17] A. Chavasse, "Les plus anciens types du lectionnaire et de l'antiphonaire de la Messe," *RBén* 62, 1952, 1–91.

*evangeliorum* reflects the Roman *consuetudo* ca. 650 and seems to have been drawn up at the time of Vitalian (652–672).

Not yet mentioned are the Thursdays of Lent. The exact title is *Incipiunt capitula lectionum evangeliorum de circulo anni.* It begins with the Midnight Mass for Christmas. The lectionary, on the other hand, begins with the Vigil of Christmas.[18] According to Chavasse, the manuscripts of the *Capitulare* are divided into two types. In the eighth century two families would derive from this *Capitulare:* Λ and Σ, both Gregorian but different in their sanctoral. The Treviri manuscript is an important example of type Λ.[19] Various manuscripts exist of Chavasse's type 2, which is the same as Klauser's type Σ or Frere's *Standard Type.*[20]

Type 3 consists of two new families: A and B. During the eighth century there were two families, Π and Σ. At the same time, two other families came into existence. Around the year 700, family A originated in Rome. It fixed the gospel pericopes for the Sundays after Pentecost and the Sundays after Epiphany. In 746, in the Frankish territories, family B came into existence. It added the missing pericopes. Family B is the same as Klauser's type D or Frere's *Vitus-Type.* There are several witnesses of this type.[21]

For the sake of completeness, we should mention the plenary Mass lectionaries, that is those with complete texts, not simply the *incipit* and *desinit.* We have the following complete lectionaries:

The *Lectionary of Verona* or *Monza* from the eighth or ninth century. It is certainly Roman, even though it was written outside Rome and begins with the Vigil of Christmas. This lectionary is complete.[22]

The *Lectionary of the Palimpsest Sacramentary of Monte Cassino* from the end of the eighth century. The readings are given in full after the orations for the Mass.[23]

---

[18] C. Vogel, *Introduction aux sources,* 314, other manuscripts of type 2.

[19] Ibid., 314: Treviri, Stadbl. codex aureus, that is 22, ff. 1611–1711, ca. 800. Other manuscripts are mentioned.

[20] Ibid., 314: Paris B.N. nouv. acq. lat. 1588, Autun, ca. 800.

[21] Ibid., 315.

[22] Ibid., 316. Ed. and Bibl. R. Amiet, "Un comes carolingien inédit de la Haute Italie," *EphLit* 73, 1959, 333–67; DACL V, 335–42; XIII, 2107.

[23] Ibid., 319. Monte Cassino, Bibl. dell'Arciabbazia cod. 271 (olim). Ed. A. Dold, *Vom Sakramentar, Comes und Capitulare zum Missale.*

The *Lectionary of Chartres* from the first half of the ninth century.[24]
For this lectionary we have only a few fragmentary manuscripts.[25]

Lists of witnesses to these liturgical books can be found not only in the aforementioned works by Chavasse, Frere, Hesbert, Klauser and Vogel, but also in the works of Botte, Gamber and Martimort.[26]

## THE MASS LECTIONARY AFTER VATICAN II

The Constitution on the Liturgy laid down the general principle that the liturgy should provide a more ample, more varied and more suitable selection of readings from both Old and New Testaments.[27]

The renewal of the readings has caused us to return to the practice of one book for the priest's prayers, the sacramentary, and one or two books for the pre-gospel and gospel readings.[28]

The starting point for choosing the readings was the choice of gospel. In other words, beginning with the gospel pericopes, the council fathers wished to choose corresponding readings. They wished to restore the most ancient practice of three readings for Sundays and feasts: from the Old Testament, from the writings of the apostles and from the gospel. But they meant to choose so as to create a certain link among the readings. This desire cannot be supported by tradition. We know that, except in a few special cases, the book of readings and the book of Gospels were composed independently. But it seemed (and rightly so) that today's mentality, at least the European, tends to expect a certain logic in the readings, a certain unity of celebration. It did not seem right to ignore these modern wishes, the result of a certain culture and logic that perhaps did not feel this way in the past.

The number of biblical passages could not be increased without recourse to yearly cycles of readings. At this point, contrary views

[24] Ibid., 317–18. Chartres, Bibl. Munic. cod. 248 (olim 32). Ed. and bibl. A. Wilmart, "Remarques sur un lectionnaire de Chartres, copié à Tours." *Comptes-rendus de l'Académie des Inscriptions et Belles Lettres de Paris*, XIII, 1925, 290–98.

[25] Ibid., 315–17.

[26] B. Botte, in E. Dekkers, *Clavis Patrum*, 2nd ed. Steenbrugge 1961, nn. 1947–1994. An exhaustive inventory of the biblical pericopes in the order of their liturgical use in the epistolaries and evangelaries. A. G. Martimort, *Les lectures liturgiques et leurs libres. Typologie des sources du moyen âge occidental*, Brepols 1992, 23–7; 29–32; 34–42.

[27] SC 24; 35; 51.

[28] *Lectionarium, Missale Romanum*, Vatican City 1970; *Ordo Lectionum Missae*, ed. typica altera, Vatican City 1981.

could legitimately arise regarding the Sundays during the year. These were called "ordinary," perhaps a rather unhappy term in some languages where it means unimportant or trivial or commonplace. Generally, the group working on the composition of the lectionary, Coetus XI, agreed that there be a semi-continuous reading of one gospel for these Sundays, choosing the other readings in relation to the gospels read each Sunday. Others would have liked to create four cycles, one for each evangelist. But there were two obstacles to this. The Gospel of John was traditionally read during Lent and the Easter season, and they did not want to abandon this tradition. Thus it did not seem proper to repeat this gospel another time. Moreover, they could not see how they could find enough texts from the letters of the apostles and the Old Testament to go with the whole Gospel of John. In the end they decided on three cycles, one for each synoptic gospel, while John was left to the times traditionally envisioned for its reading. Thus cycle A was created with the Gospel of Matthew, cycle B with the Gospel of Mark, cycle C with the Gospel of Luke.

But when it was time to conclude and start to choose readings corresponding to the selected gospel passages, it was proposed that the second reading be continuous, seeing that the people were relatively unfamiliar with the letters of the apostles. The proposal was accepted without opposition. But this decision, despite its catechetical thrust, was flawed because it was incompatible with the basic decisions. A continuous reading of the letters of the apostles assured that they would hardly ever be in harmony with the first reading and the gospel, often not even minimally. Strangely, no one noticed this rather serious drawback, and the decision was not questioned. Today this disadvantage is more deeply felt, both by the one who must prepare the homily and by all who listen to the proclamation of the word.

When choosing passages for the continuous gospel reading, texts were sometimes encountered that were too difficult. It was decided to assign these passages to weekdays, when the congregation is often better prepared and more able to understand than the Sunday assembly, which consists of people with widely varying levels of knowledge and religious formation.

For feasts and the Sundays of Advent, Lent and Easter, three cycles were envisioned and the option of two harmonized pre-gospel readings. (Lent was restructured, dropping Septuagesima, Sexagesima and Quinquagesima; it consists of five Sundays before Palm Sunday).

The weekday readings follow the principle of continuous reading. (A reading from the Old or New Testament is begun and continued without break, except for a few brief interruptions in some cases). There is no attempt to harmonize these two readings: Old Testament or letters of the apostles and the gospel. Only two cycles are envisioned for the weekday readings.

We should note the attempt to find a responsorial psalm after the first reading to correspond to the contents of the reading. For the Alleluia, a verse was often chosen from the gospel that follows, in this way serving to announce it.

This entire arrangement was not accomplished without objections and differing ideas. Some, for example, arguing from modern advertising methods, wanted to have only the *ipsissima verba Christi* proclaimed in a single sentence. This could have made a deep impression on the hearers. After long discussion, the idea was not accepted for various reasons. First, the liturgy cannot go into the technical details of a text's composition, determining the *ipsissima verba Christi* and separating them from what the evangelist wrote. A gospel is already, at least in part, a composition involving the free and inspired choice of the evangelist. Thus it seemed that any further choice in the manner of determining the text to be proclaimed must be excluded. Finally, from a liturgical point of view, it would have been rather strange to have the deacon walk to the ambo to proclaim a single sentence.

The Coetus had consulted at least five hundred people, pastors, specialists, etc. for the composition of the new lectionary. The numerous responses were all studied. Someone, for example, wished to remove the words *In illo tempore* at the beginning of the gospel. They had been introduced later in the evangelaries. According to the Constitution on the Liturgy, it is Christ himself who still proclaims his gospel today. This request was accepted.

The Coetus also had to consider the arrangement of the lectionary for the major seasons. For example, what about Advent? Here they had to consider the history of the creation of Advent and its late introduction in Rome at the end of the sixth or beginning of the seventh century (whereas elsewhere it was already celebrated in the fifth century), considering that in Rome the feast of the Nativity had been created at the beginning of the fourth century. The Roman liturgy for the end of the liturgical year was more conscious of the parousia as a conclusion to salvation history, and the final Sundays of the year emphasized the last day. Preparation for Christmas was of lesser importance; everything revolved around Easter. Advent recalled a twofold reality: the Lord's coming on the last day and his coming in the flesh for our salvation. This twofold view had to be preserved. For this reason, in the present lectionary the first two Sundays of Advent evoke our waiting for the coming of the last day, and the other two Sundays focus on the Lord's coming in the flesh.

Added to this problem of how to structure a liturgical season was that of the desired harmony among the readings. There was the danger of perhaps creating an artificial and forced harmony, with the risk of distorting the meaning of one of the Scripture texts. They had to think in terms of a link that was very broad yet real. In general, this problem has been well resolved. But use of the lectionary presupposes an understanding of typology and of liturgical meaning which, although not contrary to the purely exegetical sense, does go beyond it. Here is an example from the first Sunday of Lent, cycle A. This cycle is always to be used in churches where there are catechumens preparing for baptism at the Easter Vigil. The catechumens are presented for entrance into the Church and reception of the sacraments of Christian initiation. All of us are invited to think again of what we wish to achieve through the Church we have entered. The Church is realistic and is not afraid to remind the catechumens of their state of sin and disorder; for this reason, the story of creation and the fall is proclaimed in the first reading (Gen 2:7-9; 3:1-7). But the Church cannot remain trapped in a negative vision. To anyone who wishes to enter the Church, to all of us who have entered, she proclaims Christ's victory over the spirit of evil, a victory already foreshadowed in the story of the temptations in the desert (Matt 4:1-11). The concrete application, a synthesis, is provided in the second reading (Rom 5:12-19): where sin abounded, grace abounded. The connection among the readings is easy to see, but this connection flows from a liturgical-spiritual reading of the texts. Exegetically speaking, the three readings are not connected at all. On the other hand, the connection is not so much material but is broadly conceived.

It seems the lectionary offers new riches unknown to the Church in the past, and thus 85 percent of Scripture is included in the Mass lectionary of Vatican II.

But we cannot say the lectionary is perfect; there are still some defects that will have to be corrected. This does not mean the work was not well done, only that the work has its limitations like every human work. New optional readings could be provided for ordinary Sundays, more in harmony with the other two. Sometimes the choice of verses that begin or end a passage could be rearranged; the beginning and end of some passages are not always well chosen. The omission of verses in a passage, the option of a second shorter reading, might also be discussed. This system of choosing fragments of Scripture and juxtaposing them in order to bring out some point seems at times to push the boundaries of objectivity. It appears to be a kind of "scholastic" use of Scripture.

These reflections, which may not be shared by all, are not meant to deny the profound value and riches of our lectionary, which in fact is used, in whole or in part, by other Christian Churches.

## Bibliography

Chavasse, A. "Les plus anciens types du lectionnaire et de l'antiphonaire romains de la messe." *RBén* 62 (1952) 1–94.

____. "Aménagements liturgiques, à Rome, au VII<sup>e</sup> et VIII<sup>e</sup> siècle." *RBén* 99 (1989) 75–102.

____. "Évangéliaires, épistoliers, antiphonaire, sacramentaire: Les livres romains de la messe au VII<sup>e</sup> et VIII<sup>e</sup> siècle." *EO* 6 (1989) 177–255.

____. "Le regroupement des formulaires annuels pour la messe dans les livres du VII<sup>e</sup> et du VIII<sup>e</sup> siècle." *EO* 7 (1990) 335–42.

____. *La liturgie de la ville de Rome au V<sup>e</sup> au VIII<sup>e</sup> siècle*, 109–46. SA 112; AL 18. Rome, 1993.

____. "Après Grégoire le Grand. L'organisation des évangéliaires au VII<sup>e</sup> et VIII<sup>e</sup> siècle." *La liturgie de la ville de Rome*, 147–52. SA 112; AL 18. Rome, 1993.

____. *Les lectionnaires romains de la messe au VII<sup>e</sup> et VIII<sup>e</sup> siècle*. Vol. 1: *Procédés de confection*. Vol. 2: *Synoptique générale: Tableaux complémentaires*. SFS 22. Fribourg, 1993.

Frere, W. H. *Studies in Early Liturgy*. Vol. 3: *The Roman Epistle–Lectionary*. ACC 32. Oxford-London, 1935.

____. *Studies in Early Liturgy*. Vol. 2: *The Roman Gospel–Lectionary*. ACC 30. Oxford-London, 1934.

Godu, G. "Epîtres–Evangiles." *DACL* 5.5, 245–344; 852–923.

Hesbert, J. "La tradition bénéventaire dans la tradition manuscrite." *Paléographie musicale* 14 (1936) 60–479.

\_\_\_\_. "Les séries d'evangiles des dimanches après la Pentecôte." *MD* 46 (1956) 35–59.

Klauser, Th. *Das römische Capitulare Evangeliorum, I Typen.* LQF 28. Münster, 1935.

Martimort, A.-G. *Les lectures liturgiques et leurs livres: Typologie des sources du moyen âge occidental.* Fasc. 64. Brepols, 1992.

Vogel, C. *Medieval Liturgy: An Introduction to the Sources.* Rev. and trans. W. Storey and N. Rasmussen. Washington, 1986.

Domenico Sartore, C.S.J.

# 8

# The Homily

INTRODUCTION

Vatican II, continuing and interpreting the Church's earliest tradition, gave us essential teachings on the homily, which, more than any other form of Christian preaching, is the "proclamation of God's wonderful works in the history of salvation, the mystery of Christ ever made present and active in us, especially in the celebration of the liturgy" (*SC* 35).

The new experience of Church that has grown in recent decades in the Christian people has led both pastors and laity to reconsider the homily in all Christian rites, especially the eucharistic celebration, where it is related to the two tables of the word of God and the body of Christ and where it points the way to Christian involvement by communities and individuals.

We can sum up by saying that the homily, in the full sense of the term, is one of the ways of proclaiming the word, a hermeneutic moment of actualization and ecclesial interpretation, closely linked to the celebration of a Christian assembly.

*1. The Homily in Christian Tradition*

Etymologically speaking, "homily" means a conversation, colloquy or informal discourse (in the NT, see Luke 24:14; Acts 20:11, 24:26; 1 Cor 15:33). Ignatius of Antioch urged Polycarp to preach (ὁμιλίαν ποίειν) against the heretics. Origen calls his commentaries on Scripture ὁμιλίαι. In the fourth century *homilia* becomes a common term referring to all forms of preaching by the Church, especially within the context of a liturgical celebration.[1] Corresponding to this Greek

---

[1] R. Grégoire, "Omelia," *DPAC* II, 1983, 2467–2472.

term are the Latin *tractatus* and *sermo*. Augustine speaks of these informal discourses, "which the Greeks call *homilias*."[2]

## THE WITNESS OF JUSTIN MARTYR
The first apology of Justin contains one reliable bit of information, which is very old (150), about the homily at Mass:

"On the day called Sunday all gather in the same place, whether they live in the city or in the country. The memoirs of the apostles or the writings of the prophets are read for as long as time allows. When the reader has finished, the president delivers a discourse (λόγος), urging and exhorting us to imitate these good examples. . . ."[3] *(This is followed by the general intercessions and then the celebration of the Eucharist).*

Based on this evidence, written in Rome by a layman originally from the Hellenistic East, three things seem to be already traditional by the middle of the second century: Celebration of the Eucharist in the early Christian communities is preceded by the Liturgy of the Word; the word at Mass is actualized in the homily; this λόγος is delivered by the same person who presides over the entire celebration.

## PRE-HISTORY OF THE CHRISTIAN HOMILY
Like other elements of the Christian liturgy, this particular form of preaching, which saw an amazing development during the patristic era, is rooted in Judaism, especially in the synagogue worship of Jesus' time.[4] This consisted essentially of a Liturgy of the Word composed of four parts: (a) reading from the Torah, (b) reading from the prophets, (c) homily, (d) prayer.

The synagogue homily, a reflection of the entire biblical tradition, is completely original with respect to other cults. It is associated with the word and its special importance for these people, among whom it is constantly re-actualized in the face of new events and the demands of

---

[2] Augustine, *Epist.* 224, 2 (Opere di S. Agostino XXII), Rome 1974, 650: ". . .tractatus populares, quos Graeci homilias vocant"; C. Mohrmann, "Praedicare-tractare-sermo," *Etudes sur le latin des chrétiens,* II, Rome 1961, 63–72.

[3] Justin Martyr, *I Apologia,* 67, 3–5, A. Hänggi - I. Pahl, *Prex eucharistica,* (SF 12), Freiburg/Switzerland 1968, 70–1 (Greek and Latin text).

[4] See. C. Perrot, "La lecture de la Bible dans les synagogues au premier siècle de notre ère," *MD* 126 (1976) 24–41.

fidelity to the covenant. Two texts give us a very good idea of the function of the synagogue homily and sum up its history. Neh 8:18 tells us how Ezra "read from the book of the law of God," interpreting and explaining its meaning so that everyone could understand the reading. Luke 4:21 recounts the words with which Jesus, in the synagogue at Nazareth, introduces his commentary on the reading of Isa 61:1-2: "Today this scripture passage is fulfilled in your hearing."

Synagogue worship concludes with prayers and psalms. It is a response to the word proclaimed and actualized, an expression of the dialogue between the God who reveals himself and the people which manifests its fidelity to him.

In the New Testament we find many elements that lead into the Christian homily. The Christ event is the interpretive key to all of salvation history and the new age that flows from his Passover. Every word of Jesus is filled with allusions to the ancient Scriptures. The apostles examine the Old Testament for words and events that are fulfilled in the mystery of Christ. The first Christian communities express their faith awareness that Christ is present among them through the Word and sacraments of the Church. The Acts of the Apostles constantly give us a glimpse of Paul as he "converses" with his communities assembled in the name of the Lord. Traces of the early Christian *haggadah* can be seen especially in the various Johannine texts, in 1 Corinthians and in 1 Peter.

THE PATRISTIC HOMILY
We have already considered the precious witness of Justin. It is an essential reference point for an already established liturgical practice, one that would be confirmed by all subsequent liturgical tradition.

Between the second and third centuries we already begin to have the first "documented" Christian homilies: the homily of Pseudo-Hippolytus[5] and the paschal homily of Melito of Sardis.[6] A study of the homiletic method used in the two texts shows that three steps are involved: (1) reading of the sacred text, (2) detailed explanation of what has been read, and (3) contemplation of the mysteries in their realization.[7]

[5] R. Cantalamessa, *L'omelia 'in Sanctum Pascha' dello pseudo-Ippolito di Roma*, Milan 1967.

[6] Melito of Sardis, *Sur la Pâque et fragments*, SChr 123, Paris 1966.

[7] R. Cantalamessa, op. cit., 434.

The chief sources for this first Christian homiletic practice can be seen in the Jewish *Passover Haggadah*,[8] a typical example of Jewish homiletics, and in various New Testament passages already cited. The style and language of these two early texts clearly shows the influence of the mystery religions and a keen awareness of the signs of the times, shown in a strong desire to proclaim the things of God in human terms.[9]

We come to the fourth and fifth century via Origen and Cyprian. It is the golden age of the Fathers of the Church, among whom we meet the great homilists Basil, John Chrysostom, Ambrose, and Augustine.

Rather than pausing to analyze especially important pages from these and other masters, we offer a few notes on this literary genre, typically Christian, which Leclercq describes as "an informal conversation by a pastor of souls with his people, during a liturgical action, on a biblical text suggested by the liturgy."[10] The noted medievalist stresses that the homily's essential elements derive from the fact that it is given during a liturgical action. These elements are: (1) *topic:* the Christian mystery, which must be shared and lived by the community; (2) *audience:* usually uneducated people, including many catechumens who already believe but must be helped to a deeper understanding and assimilation; and (3) *speaker:* not one of the laity, more or less educated, but someone who has received the sacrament of orders: a bishop, presbyter, or deacon, whose very person serves to emphasize the essential connection between preaching and the Christian celebration.[11]

An extremely serious crisis occurred in Christian preaching at the end of the fourth century. So seductive was the rhetoric in vogue in contemporary society that the homily was in danger of losing its simplicity and authenticity. But it was saved by the example of the two greatest homilists of the early Church, St. John Chrysostom and St. Augustine. Their systematic reflections on Christian preaching were profound and stimulating: in the treatise *On the Priesthood* and in Book IV of *De doctrina christiana* respectively.[12]

---

[8] See *Sédèr haggadah sèl Pèsah, seu ordo narrationis Pasquae* in A. Hänggi - I. Pahl, 13–34.

[9] R. Cantalamessa, op. cit., 434.

[10] J. Leclercq, "Le sermon, act liturgique": *MD* 8 (1946) 27–46; we are quoting the text as given in *Liturgie et les paradoxes chrétiens* (LO 36), Paris 1963, 208.

[11] Ibid., 210.

[12] Ibid., 211–12.

Toward the end of the patristic age in the West, two great popes also left us important homiletic models that would be very influential in the future: St. Leo the Great (+ 461), whose magnificent sermons are full of theological and liturgical inspiration, and St. Gregory the Great (+ 604), whose simple and direct commentaries on Scripture are predominantly moral in their inspiration.

Christian preaching declined in the high Middle Ages, although a strong patristic influence remained. Selected texts from the Fathers, arranged according to the liturgical year in special collections (homilaries), were read. From the twelfth century on, preaching saw various revivals, but it became more and more detached from the liturgy. It was interpreted in succession by different oratorical genres which belong more to the history of sacred oratory than to that of the genuine biblical-liturgical homily. The homily followed the historical ups and downs of the rest of the liturgy until Vatican II.

### THE TEACHINGS OF VATICAN II

The liturgical movement called renewed attention to the original meaning and practice of the homily. Also influential were the biblical and patristic renewal. Among the more important results reached by scholars, we might recall Leclercq's study mentioned earlier. He rediscovers the liturgical nature of homiletic preaching in light of the Fathers. There is also Vagaggini's reflection which sees the homily, understood as an integral part of the liturgical action, as "the supreme actualization of Christian preaching."[13]

With regard to current mentality and pastoral practice, in the years after Vatican II the situation of the homily was highly problematic almost everywhere. The so-called Sunday sermon was downplayed or often totally neglected. Other times it was becoming so long that it lasted the entire Mass, which was celebrated by another priest. Sometimes it was given after Mass. It was utterly devoid of liturgical inspiration. Usually it was seen as an "explanation of the gospel," but often it dealt with other subjects, sometimes planned by individual dioceses or suggested by scholars.[14]

---

[13] C. Vagaggini, *Il senso teologico della liturgia*, Rome 1956, 683–84.

[14] See G. Fesenmayer, "L'omelia nella celebrazione eucaristica," G. Barauna, *La Sacra Liturgia rinnovata dal Concilio*, Turin (Leumann) 1964, especially 415–20.

The *Caerimoniale episcoporum* stated that the homily should normally be given *de evangelio currenti*. If it was of an extraordinary nature, it was to be postponed until the end of Mass.[15] Canon 1345 of the *Codex juris canonici* (1917) hoped that at all feastday Masses there would be "an explanation of the gospel or some part of Catholic doctrine."

In order to give some organization and coherence to homiletic preaching, many dioceses prepared "preaching syllabuses," often designed with no reference to the liturgy or the proclaimed word.

At Vatican II the statement prepared by the preparatory commission on the subject of the homily was generally well received. Those few Fathers who spoke referred generally to its obligatory nature, which was insisted upon, and to the question of preaching syllabuses, which were not covered in *SC* but taken up later in the Instruction *Inter oecumenici* (1964).[16]

The teaching of *Sacrosanctum concilium* begins in n. 24:

24. "Sacred Scripture is of the greatest importance in the celebration of the liturgy. For from it are drawn the lessons which are read and which are explained in the homily. . . ."

35 (2). "The most suitable place for a sermon ought to be indicated in the rubrics, for the sermon is part of the liturgical action whenever the rite permits one. The primary source of the sermon, moreover, should be scripture and liturgy, for in them is found the proclamation of God's wonderful works in the history of salvation, the mystery of Christ ever made present and active in us, especially in the celebration of the liturgy."

52. "By means of the homily, the mysteries of the faith and the guiding principles of the Christian life are expounded from the sacred text *(ex textu sacro)* during the course of the liturgical year. The homily is strongly recommended since it forms part of the liturgy itself *(pars ac-*

[15] *Caeremoniale episcoporum*, Book I, ch. 22,2,5, editio tertia post typicam, Turin-Rome 1948, 62. Here is the text: 2. "Sermo regulariter fiat de Evangelio currenti. . . . 5. Si vero habendus est sermo extraordinarius . . . non debet infra Missam fieri, sed illa finita. . . ."

[16] See "Konstitution über die heilige Liturgie. Enleitung und Kommentar von J.A. Jungmann," *LTK*, 1966, Bd III, 54–5; SCR, "Instructio 'Inter oecumenici' ad executionem constitutionis de sacra Liturgia recte ordinandam," *AAS* 56 (1964) 877–900: nn. 53–55.

*tionis liturgicae).* In fact, at those Masses which are celebrated on Sundays and holydays of obligation, with the people assisting, it should not be omitted except for a serious reason."

The Instruction *Inter oecumenici* (1964) deals with three questions that came up in the council debate: obligatory nature, *ex textu sacro,* preaching syllabuses.

53. "There shall be a homily on Sundays and holydays of obligation at all Masses. . . ."

54. "A homily on the sacred text means an explanation, pertinent to the mystery celebrated and the special needs of the listeners, of some point in either the readings from sacred Scripture or in another text from the Ordinary or from the Proper of the day's Mass."

55. "Because the homily is part of the liturgy for the day, any syllabus proposed for preaching within the Mass during certain periods must keep intact the intimate connection with at least the principal seasons and feasts of the liturgical year, that is, with the mystery of redemption."

The introduction to the second typical edition of the 1975 *Roman Missal of Paul VI (IGMR),* gives an authoritative summary of all earlier documents that refer to the homily, adding a clarification in n. 42:

"The homily should ordinarily be given by the priest celebrant."[17]

The 1981 typical edition of the *Ordo lectionum missae,* n. 24, recalls the most important teachings concerning the homily, describing it more briefly as "part of the Liturgy of the Word." But it adds some important directions:

"Whether the homily explains the biblical word of God proclaimed in the readings or some other texts of the liturgy, it must always lead the community of the faithful to celebrate the eucharist wholeheartedly, 'so that they may hold fast in their lives to what they have grasped by their faith.' From this living explanation, the word of God proclaimed in the readings and the Church's celebration of

---

[17] *Missale Romanum* ex decreto Sacrosancti Oecumenici Concilii Vat. II instauratum, auctoritate Pauli PP. promulgatum, ed. typica altera, 1975: Institutio generalis.

the day's liturgy will have greater impact. But this demands that the homily be truly the fruit of meditation, carefully prepared, neither too long nor too short, and suited to all those present, even children and the uneducated."[18]

Besides these documents that deal typically with the liturgy, two post-conciliar documents should also be cited. The 1975 apostolic exhortation of Paul VI, *Evangelii nuntiandi,* n. 43, speaks of the homily as "a form of preaching, which is specifically included in the celebration of the Eucharist from which it derives an especial strength and force."[19] Finally, there is the 1979 apostolic exhortation of John Paul II, *Catechesi tradendae,* n. 48, which describes the homily as "catechesis given in the setting of the liturgy, especially in the Eucharistic assembly." He invites his readers to respect and take advantage of its proper cadence, "within the whole circle of the liturgical year."[20] Both documents say that the homily should be carefully and appropriately prepared in accord with its special nature.

SUMMARY

Recovery of certain aspects of the patristic homily and analysis of the most important conciliar and post-conciliar documents on the homily allow us to sketch in a preliminary way the distinguishing features of this eminent form of Christian preaching:

— the etymology, which describes it as an "informal conversation," stressing its easy and popular style;

— the patristic concept of the homily in relation to its liturgical role and its essential parts (topic, audience, speaker);

— *ex textu sacro:* as an actualization of the Word;

— *pars actionis liturgicae:* its liturgical and mystagogical character;

— its *purposes:* relationship to the word, the mystery celebrated and the assembled community;

— an *efficacious instrument* of evangelization and special form of catechesis in a liturgical context;

---

[18] *Missale Romanum* ex Decreto Sacrosancti conc. Oecumenici Vat. II instauratum, auctoritate Pauli PP. VI promulgatum, *Ordo Lectionum Missae,* ed. typica altera, 1981.

[19] Paulus PP. VI, "Adhortatio apostolica *Evangelii nuntiandi de evangelizatione in mundo huius temporis,*" n. 43, *AAS* 58 (1976) 1008–125.

[20] John Paul II, "Adhortatio apostolica *Catechesi tradendae,*" *AAS* 71 (1979) 1277–340.

— need for careful *preparation*, with attention to the word, the celebration and the experience of the Christian people.

## 2. *Christian Preaching in the Full Sense*

### CHRISTIAN PREACHING

As used in the New Testament, the verb *predicare* (κηρύσσειν / εὐαγγε-
λίζεσθαι) means to announce the coming of salvation, to solemnly
proclaim that Jesus Christ is Lord and Savior. This apparent restric-
tion of what we normally mean by preaching focuses on the basic object of all Christian proclamation: the Easter message. Preaching in a
Christian sense will be, first of all and always, a proclamation of the
word. It is the ordinary way that leads to faith: "Faith comes from
what is heard, and what is heard comes through the word of Christ"
(Rom 10:17).

The closing statement of Mark's Gospel, "They went forth and
preached everywhere, while the Lord worked with them. . . ."
(16:20), is echoed in the Church's most recent teaching: "Christ is
present in another manner, equally true, when the Church preaches,
since the gospel it preaches is the word of God, which is proclaimed
in the name and by the authority of Christ, the incarnate Word, and
with his help."[21]

### A THREEFOLD DIVISION

Early tradition, like the magisterial documents and recent authors,
uses various terms for the different forms of Christian preaching. We
prefer to stick to a basic typology in which Christian preaching,
understood in a general sense, takes three basic forms: (1) *evangelization* (κήρυγμα), the first proclamation of the Christian message in
order to arouse faith, (2) *catechesis,* more systematic teaching aimed at
believers in order to make their faith more active and aware, and (3)
*homily,* special catechesis in the context of a liturgical action, closely
connected with the word and rites.[22]

---

[21] Paul VI, Encyclical "Mysterium fidei de doctrina et cultu SS. Eucharistiae," n.
14, *AAS* (1965) 753–74.

[22] D. Grasso, "Evangelizzazione, Catechesi, Omelia," *Gregorianum* 42 (1961)
242–67. See also the Italian Bishops Conference (CEI), "Il rinnovamento della catechesi," Rome 1970, n. 22. This important Italian document presents the homily in
this way: "The homily is an integral part of the liturgical action and takes on its
movements and characteristics. Through the homily the designated minister

Paul VI sees the homily as "a powerful and most suitable instrument of evangelization."[23] The *General Catechetical Directory* presents the homily as "the liturgical form of catechesis."[24] John Paul II states that "the homily takes up again the journey of faith put forward by catechesis and brings it to its natural fulfillment," describing it as "one of the benefits of the liturgical reform."[25]

The traditional structure we have proposed is widely accepted. It offers a full vision of Christian preaching and shows well how it culminates in the homily. But the homily does not exhaust every aspect of preaching, nor is it always totally distinct, in the concrete, from the other two forms.

Complex pastoral realities also make it hard to clearly distinguish the various forms of Christian proclamation. The primary need becomes evangelization, and the baptized, who as a rule have received the sacrament without a true catechumenate, must be continually reinitiated into the faith and more deeply formed in the Christian life.

### 3. The Homily as Part of the Liturgical Action

We have already noted that rediscovery of the homily as a *pars actionis liturgicae* came from a revisitation of early Christian tradition, the liturgical movement with its pastoral research, and the teaching of *SC* 52. In the celebration of the Eucharist above all, but also in the other Christian rites, the homily is not simply an accessory or a digression,

---

proclaims, explains and pays tribute to the Christian mystery being celebrated, that the faithful might receive it intimately into their life and be disposed to bear witness to it in the world. The homily derives its topics and themes primarily from Sacred Scripture and the liturgical texts of the Mass or sacrament being celebrated. In the course of the liturgical year the homily illustrates the mysteries of faith and the norms for Christian living, always with reference to Christ's paschal mystery. It takes into account the liturgical action that is going on, and it assumes a distinct tone: kerygmatic, doctrinal, moral or apologetic, depending on the particular needs of the faithful present" (n. 29).

[23] Paul VI, *Evangelii nuntiandi*, n. 43.

[24] Sacred Congregation for the Clergy, *General Catechetical Directory*, Turin (Leumann) 1971. While stressing in n. 71 that the various forms of the ministry of the Word are closely linked in reality, it distinguishes between evangelization or missionary preaching, which is intended to arouse the first act of faith, and catechesis, "whose purpose is to reawaken people to a conscious and active faith by means of suitable instruction." It notes that this catechesis also has *a liturgical form*.

[25] John Paul II, *Catechesi tradendae*, n. 48.

nor simply an explanation of the readings. A certified part of a Christian celebration, that actualizes the word and fosters participation by the community, helping it express in its life what it has celebrated in the mystery.

## THE TEACHING OF THE FATHERS

Our direct knowledge of the patristic homily *infra missam* is not all that great, nor have the Fathers left us a complete theory in this regard. They give us a few elements that can serve as an introduction to this particular form of Christian preaching:

— the *moment* of the homily which is linked to the end of the Liturgy of the Word and introduces the Liturgy of the Eucharist;

— the meaning of the fact that the *same minister* delivers the homily and presides at the Eucharist, as St. Augustine emphasizes;[26]

— the *word-sacrament* relationship which is explored by the Fathers;[27]

— the concrete *links* found in some patristic homilies between the biblical introduction and the euchological conclusion;[28]

— the *mystagogical homily*, sometimes used in the context of the same celebrations.[29]

## WORD AND SACRAMENT

Our liturgy is completely sacramental. In particular, the Eucharist is the commemorative and prospective representation of salvation, the sacramental encounter with Christ yesterday, today and forever. The homily is located at the meeting-point between the word proclaimed and Church's signs, which converge to accomplish among us the *Mysterium fidei*, the total event of our redemption. The event is prolonged and expressed in all the Church's liturgical actions, whether they are linked to temporal rhythms or to concrete situations in human life.

[26] Augustine, *Sermo* 214, 1 (Opere di S. Agostino XXXII/1), Rome 1984, 218: "[Nos] qui iam ministrantes altari, quo accessuri estis, assistimus, nec ministerio sermonis vos fraudare debemus. . . ."

[27] Y. Congar, "La relatione tra il culto o il sacramento e la predicazione della parola," *Con* 4 (1968) 67–79.

[28] See A. Olivar, *La predicación cristiana antigua*, Barcelona 1991, 515–27.

[29] See D. Sartore, "Mistagogia ieri e oggi: alcune pubblicazioni recenti," *EO* XI (1994) 181–99; E. Mazza, "Saint Augustin et la mystagogie," *Mystagogie: pensée d'aujourd'hui et liturgie ancienne*. Conférences Saint Serge. XXXIX semaine d'études liturgiques (BELS 70) Rome 1993, 202–26.

The homily helps us constantly renew this faith experience. It gives us a deep and living experience of that mysterious reality which the Church today has rediscovered in the words of Leo the Great: "Our Redeemeer's visible presence has passed into the sacraments."[30]

## THE MINISTER OF THE HOMILY

Ever since the testimony of Justin, we observe that at the eucharistic celebration the homily is normally reserved to the same minister who presides, in continuity with his pastoral ministry within the community: a bishop, presbyter or even a deacon (who also belongs to the Church's hierarchy, although at a lower level).

The close link between the two tables at the eucharistic celebration is also seen in the fact that the Church entrusts the sacrament of the Word and the sacrament of the Eucharist, which form a single act of worship, to the same minister.

The presidential and magisterial nature of the homily at the Eucharist has remained a constant in tradition, although there have been important exceptions in the East.[31] In the West, preaching the homily has always been considered a presidential function.

Scholars, however, raise certain questions about the possibility of lay people sharing in the homily by reason of their royal and prophetic priesthood, although subordinate to and in collaboration with the hierarchy:

— we might ask if the present way of exercising the presidential function in the homily is the only one, or whether there may be alternatives, such as community preparation, presentation of introductory starting points, contributions by specialists, personal witness; the celebrant might also give a short homily, followed by questions or guided discussion, etc.;

— we believe there should be no question as to the homiletic nature of preaching by a religious or lay person delegated to preside at various rites (including the Sunday celebration without a priest);

— in exceptional cases, when the priest was unable to preach at a liturgical celebration, lay people have been asked to do this, with an appeal to the temporary or subsidiary nature of the role.

---

[30] Leo the Great, *Sermo 61 de Ascensione Domini: SChr* 74 bis, p. 278.

[31] See P. Siniscalco, *Attività e ministeri della parola nella Chiesa antica*, Brescia 1978, especially 100–3.

In any case, it seems essential that lay people be able to share with their pastors responsibility for the word in a specific context, and that this collaboration maintain a secular character in keeping with the secular character of the laity themselves.[32]

## HOMILY AND CELEBRATION

A homily, seen as part of a liturgical action, cannot be isolated from the entire celebration in which it occurs and which it interprets. Its preparation and delivery must begin from the scripture readings (see below). It must be coordinated with the admonitions, the penitential rite and the general intercessions. It takes on the rhythms and features of an actual celebration and is able to draw inspiration from individual ritual or euchological elements or refer to them (see below), all in the context of a unitary and harmonious vision. A correct understanding of the homily, besides affecting its content and methods, would also suggest that it not be so long that it disrupts the rhythm of the liturgical action and compromises its overall effect.

## THE MYSTAGOGICAL TASK OF THE HOMILY

Since the homily is "part of the liturgical action" and at its service, the task of the homily is said to be mystagogical, especially in three senses:

— linked to a celebration and situated at a specific moment between word and ritual, it introduces the mystery celebrated and is itself the instrument and form of its accomplishment;

— addressed to a Christian community assembled for a specific liturgical experience, it promotes its full and active participation;

— it brings out certain elements of the celebration as symbolic, capable of arousing faith and fostering Christian experience.

## 4. Based on the Sacred Text

When speaking of the homily as a *pars actionis liturgicae*, we mentioned another of the Council's statements which we will now try to explain: the homily is given *ex textu sacro*.

This expression, especially if we compare it with the Church's past practice, means first of all that the homily is a commentary on the biblical readings of a particular liturgical celebration. By its nature it

---

[32] See D. Sartore, "Omelia," *Enciclopedia di pastorale. 3. Liturgia*, Casale M. 1988, 170–75.

is linked to the word of God proclaimed within the Christian assembly, and it is explained and actualized in this setting — not only the gospel, but also the Old Testament readings, the letters of the apostles and the scriptural chants that accompany them. It must faithfully interpret the biblical texts in their exegetical sense and in their original context; it must show how the liturgical action "becomes a new event and enriches the word itself with new meaning and power."[33]

With its rich content and new structure, the *Lectionary of Vatican II* is in many ways very important for a correct understanding of the homily in the Church today:

— first, according to the directives of *SC* 35, the reading of the word of God today is "more ample, more varied and more suitable";

— new criteria for selection and links between the readings, which should be known and properly used, favor an overall interpretation;

— the constant presence of the Old Testament, besides offering pages filled with faith and life experiences, introduces the Christian community to a historic-salvific vision inspired by the divine pedagogy and centered on the mystery of Christ, in which our Christian life and the liturgical rites that are part of it take on a deeper meaning;

— the question of planned homiletic cycles, which was brought up again by some on the basis of *Inter oecumenici* 55, needs to be dealt with using the thematic arrangement already found in the present order (semi-continuous reading, selection of passages that are linked, the liturgical year etc.), in view of a broader and more vital catechesis of a historical-liturgical nature.

The introduction to the *Missal of Paul VI*, echoing the document cited above, says that the homily "should develop some point of the readings or of another text from the Ordinary or from the Proper of the Mass of the day, and take into account the mystery being celebrated and the needs proper to the listeners" (*IGMR* 41). These directions, we believe, could be spelled out better in two ways. The homily is in a special way an explanation of the readings, especially the gospel; but in special cases it can also present individual elements of the celebration (texts, gestures, signs). Through frequent use, these will perhaps remind us to emphasize and actualize the biblical-liturgical message in a Christian celebration.

[33] See *Ordo Lectionum Missae*, ed.typ.altera, 1981, n. 3.

## 5. The Problem of Actualization

Certain gains, which we can call definitive, enable us to approach better the problem of the homily today. But many questions, by no means incidental, still remain. They are the object of lively discussion on the part of scholars, pastors and the laity themselves. We will deal only with the liturgical actualization of the word. It is a problem that touches on the purpose of the homily and is rooted in the question of hermeneutics. Preaching must be able to take the word in its original power and meaning and translate it into ever new expressions, courageously using it to confront the most dramatic aspects of our constantly changing culture and the crisis in which people find themselves today.

To aid in such a demanding task, the Bible itself provides us with an actual paradigmatic model of the homily. A process of continual re-actualization runs through the entire book according to a method that can provide us with exciting models.[34] We need only think of Deuteronomy with respect to the Old Testament books that preceded it, to the developments in the books of Isaiah and Daniel. The word of God remains for ever, and in the rite it is presented again in relation to new events and cultic celebrations.[35]

This biblical fact is prolonged in the age of the Church:

— the homily can be a powerful aid in expressing and explaining the full meaning of a cultic celebration in a Christian community's "today," giving it a unitary interpretation and proposing a global hermeneutic;

— various events in the Church's life — historical-social, cultural, individual or family in nature — define new hermeneutical contexts and help to identify the experience in which the mystery of Christ is actualized through word and sacrament.

Homiletic preaching is certainly harmed when too many preachers are unable to go beyond the abstract and general nature of stereotyped forms. These prevent the word of God from again becoming an "event" and from being even today "living and effective, sharper than any two-edged sword" (Heb 4:12).

## 6. The Homily as a Form of Communication

We have shown from various perspectives the homily's liturgical and ecclesial nature. This fact modifies the conditions under which we

---

[34] See F. Dreyfus, "L'actualisation à l'intérieur de la Bible." See Bibliography.
[35] See Bibliography: Sociological Aspects.

can speak of its reception within the Christian assembly or evaluate the effectiveness of the preacher (see Augustine's concept of the "interior teacher").

But we cannot neglect a series of considerations based on the human sciences. Here are some starting points.

The homily is a particular form of Christian preaching, but at the same time it is *a process of human communication* with its particular rules. As such it must be studied, especially in relation to its function and effectiveness. It requires a well-planned system of checks as well as contributions from other disciplines. It must seek proper methods and techniques of expression.[36]

In particular, the homily, as a form of communication, needs to be considered on the basis of its three essential components: the transmitter (preacher), the message (content), and the receiving subject (recipients of the word). Its functions (persuasive, reinforcing, ideological, etc.) also need to be examined.[37]

The homily undergoes a series of *conditionings* that can compromise its effectiveness:

— historical conditioning: the persistent mindset of homilists and faithful regarding the "sermon";

— professional conditioning: the attitude of the preacher toward the audience; traditional style, tone of voice, lack of connection with the assembly;

— technical conditioning: refusal to consider at all the contributions of human communication;

— psychological conditioning: illusion of holding the audience's interest; little attention to the public and its needs;

— sociological conditioning: heterogeneous assembly, the preacher's particular mentality and social status, monologue without feedback;

— religious conditioning: insufficient evangelization of the faithful; lack of deep conviction, insufficient doctrinal preparation and cultural sensitivity on the part of the preacher.

Regarding the *language* of the homily: whether or not it is understandable (words used, short sentences, clear structure and expres-

---

[36] See S. Burgalassi, "Aspetti psico-sociologici della predicazione," *Rivista italiana di sociologia* 3 (1965) 51–112.

[37] See AA.VV., "Ricerca interdisciplinare sulla predicazione," Bologna 1973; see various views in *Servizio della Parola* n. 270 (1995).

sion); type of persuasion adopted (teaching, information, statement, example, objection, positive or negative judgment, invitation, command, prohibition, proposition, etc.); general tone (positive or negative); habitual attitude toward the audience (authoritarian, detached, cordial, fraternal).

## 7. Conclusion: Toward an Adequate Preparation and Evaluation of the Homily

The relative improvement in homiletic practice (and thus in appreciation of the homily) observed since Vatican II is the fruit of more careful preparation by preachers, sustained by a livelier faith awareness and a clearer sense of professionalism.

In conclusion, we would like to offer some methodological suggestions for preparing and evaluating a homily, either individually or as a community (e.g., in the context of a liturgical group). This conclusion will also allow us to summarize quickly the various notes on the homily collected in these pages, supplementing them with some other elements we think are important. There are five points:

### HOMILY PREPARATION CAN BEGIN WITH A PRELIMINARY LOOK AT THE THREE READINGS

Preliminary approach and analysis of the three passages (literary genre: narrative, parable, hymn, exhortation etc.); identify key terms, most important sentences, special difficulties.

### THE TRIPLE CONTEXT: EXAMINE THE BIBLICAL CONTEXT OF THE THREE READINGS

Study the liturgical context (liturgical year — choice of the three texts and connections among them; see also the responsorial psalm); relation to the celebration and to the liturgical texts and rites. Identify the community/existential context: What crisis is touching the life of the community? What problems does it feel the most? What expectations? What hopes is it living? What concrete situation involves the faithful? In short, who is being addressed?

### CONTENT OF THE HOMILY

What themes are suggested by the readings and by the celebration? Isolate a central theme and develop it through reflection/actualization in relation to the three contexts; pick a small unit that can be enriched through assimilation and resonance; pay more attention to a major theme, an element that can pull together the various aspects already mentioned.

STRUCTURE OF THE HOMILY

It should have a significant beginning, a series of deeper reflections in the middle, an appropriate conclusion. There can be different approaches, suitably varied: biblical, liturgical, existential etc. The middle part (deeper exploration from one or more angles: biblical, liturgical, doctrinal, social — against the background of Christian hope). Presentation of a short summary and a pointed ending.

EVALUATION OF THE HOMILY

At times it can be very useful to evaluate our way of preaching: personally or with a representative group, occasionally or systematically, looking at individual homilies or cycles of homilies.

It seems to us that three points are to be stressed above all, omitting other elements we have already dealt with sufficiently:

With regard to content, we might ask: How faithful is it to the Bible? How is it related to the celebration? How much attention does it pay to the community's life and present situation? What themes have been covered? What main theme have we explored?

In particular: What subjects come up too often in our homilies? Which are seldom treated? Which are habitually neglected?

With regard to actualization: What areas of life do we normally mention? Personal? Family? Church? Social? Socio-political?

With regard to language: Is it simple or hard to understand? What attitude toward the audience does it show? What kind of discourse? What is the overall tone?

## Bibliography

I. PREACHING

Grasso, D. "Evangelizzazione, Catechesi, Omelia. Per una terminologia della predicazione." *Gregorianum* 42 (1961) 242–67.

_____. *L'annuncio della salvezza.* Naples, 1965.

Schlier, H. "L'annuncio nel culto della Chiesa." *Il tempo della Chiesa*, 802–29. Bologna, 1965.

Vagaggini, C. *Theological Dimensions of the Liturgy.* Trans. L. Doyle and W. Jurgens. Collegeville, Minn., 1976.

## II. THE PATRISTIC HOMILY

Leclercq, J. "Le sermon, acte liturgique." *MD* 8 (1946) 27–46. Also in *Liturgie et paradoxes chrétiens*, 205–16. LO 36. Paris, 1965.

Mohrmann, Chr. "Praedicare–Tractare–Sermo." *MD* 39 (1954) 97–107.

Olivar, A. *La predicación cristiana antigua.* Barcelona, 1991.

## III. STUDIES ON THE HOMILY

AA.VV. "El arte de la homilia" (Dossiers CPL 3). Barcelona, 1984.

Burke, J. "Witness to Faith: The Homily." *American Ecclesiastical Review* 163 (1970) 184–95; 270–81; 318–26.

Della Torre, L. "Omelia." *NDL* 923–43.

Gelineau, J. "L'homélie, forme plénière de la prédication." *MD* 82 (1965) 29–42.

Giglioni, P. "L'omelia rinnovata e le esigenze dell'annuncio della parola di Dio." *RL* 61 (1984) 41–49.

Lebrun, D. "L'homelie redevenue acte liturgique?" *MD* 177 (1989) 121–47.

Motl, J. R. "Homiletics and Integrating the Seminary Curriculum." *Wor* 64 (1990) 24–29.

## IV. BIBLICAL ASPECTS

Dreher, B. "Esegesi e predicazione." *Conc* 10 (1971) 78–94.

Dreyfus, F. "L'actualisation à l'intérieur de la Bible." *RB* 83 (1976) 161–202; 86 (1979) 6–58, 14–193, 322–84. See also 82 (1975) 321–58.

Llopis, J. "Exégesis biblica y homilia litœrgica." *Ph* 66 (1971) 527–41.

## V. SOCIOLOGICAL ASPECTS

Debarge, L. "Le prédicateur et son auditoire." *MelScRel* 29 (1972) 162–84.

Houtart, F. "Le discours homilétique et la dimension politique de la foi." *LeV* 28 (1973) 409–14.

Lodi, E. "Aspetti sociologici dell'omelia." *RL* 52 (1970) 584–614.

Orlandoni, G. "La predicazione omiletica: Analisi sociologica del processo di comunicazione." *Lat* 43 (1977) 175–91.

Turner, F. *La communication prédicationelle.* Louvain, 1967.

## VI. LAY PARTICIPATION IN THE HOMILY

AA.VV. *La predicazione dei laici: Comunicazione della fede e nuovi ministri della parola.* Brescia, 1978.

Lodi, E. "L'omelia partecipata dai laici." *RPL* 40 (1970) 264–77.

Nicolas, J. H. "Les laïcs et l'annonce de la Parole de Dieu." *NRT* 93 (1971) 821–49.

Jan Michael Joncas

# 9

# Musical Elements in the *Ordo Missae* of Paul VI

The following treatment of the musical elements in the *Ordo Missae* of Paul VI will be limited to the documentation found in *MR1975* and explanatory documents associated with it (e.g., *IGMR, OLM, DMP, MuS*). Adaptations of this order of Mass intended for particular language groups or regions cannot be analyzed here, although such adaptations are a prime instance of liturgical inculturation.

Employing a six-unit division of the Order of Mass (Introductory Rites, Liturgy of the Word, Preparation of the Gifts, Eucharistic Prayer, Communion, and Dismissal Rites), this treatise first deals with the musical elements in each major unit. It then discusses each of the elements within the unit, providing official documentation, an analysis of its ritual function(s), a listing of the participants, and (a) suggested format(s).

## I. MUSICAL ELEMENTS IN THE INTRODUCTORY RITES

"The parts preceding the Liturgy of the Word, namely, the entrance song, greeting, penitential rite, *Kyrie, Gloria,* and opening prayer or collect, have the purpose of a beginning, introduction, and preparation.

The purpose of these rites is that the faithful coming together take on the form of a community, and prepare themselves to listen to God's word and celebrate the Eucharist properly" (*IGMR* 24).

These programmatic statements clearly indicate the extent, purpose, and function of the entire panoply of rites prior to the first reading. In addition to the rites listed in *IGMR* 24, a "Rite of Blessing and Sprinkling Holy Water" may replace the penitential rite and *Kyrie* (cf. Appendix to the *MR1975*); the *General Instruction of the*

*Liturgy of the Hours* 93–8 indicates how the psalmody of a particular hour may be integrated with the Introductory Rites.

Insofar as these rites are initiatory, introductory, and preparatory *(characterem . . . exordii, introductionis et praeparationis),* they are less important than, e.g., the proclamation of the Scriptures or the Eucharistic Prayer. Any musical elaboration should not over-emphasize the Introductory Rites to the detriment of those elements that bear greater ritual weight. At the same time, the Introductory Rites have three clearly defined functions: after the faithful have physically assembled, these rites (1) evoke their communion with Christ and one another in the Holy Spirit, (2) prepare them as a liturgical assembly to hear and ponder the living word of God, and (3) dispose them to celebrate the Eucharist worthily. Thus musical elaboration of any or all of the components of the Introductory Rites must be judged on how well they accomplish these tasks for the particular assembly gathered for worship.

*1. Entrance Song* (Antiphona ad introitum)
"After the people have assembled, the entrance song begins as the priest and ministers come in. The purpose of this song is to open the celebration, intensify the unity of the gathered people, lead their thoughts to the mystery of the season or feast, and accompany the procession of the priest and ministers.

The entrance song is sung alternatively either by the choir and the congregation or by the cantor and the congregation; or it is sung entirely by the congregation or by the choir alone. The antiphon and psalm of the *Graduale Romanum* or the *Simple Gradual* may be used, or another song that is suited to this part of the Mass, the day, or the season and that has a text approved by the conference of bishops" *(IGMR* 25–6).

*IGMR* 25 presupposes that the faithful have already physically assembled before the entrance song begins. Thus the entrance song is not the vocal equivalent of an instrumental or choral prelude played as the assembly convenes, but is a first act of corporate sung worship.

The four functions listed for the Entrance Song in *IGMR* 25 may in practice set up certain tensions. Although the entrance song "opens the celebration" in a common act of sung prayer, the Sign of the Cross and greeting are frequently perceived as the actual ritual beginning of the liturgy. "Intensifying the unity" of the gathered faithful through the entrance song becomes problematic when the repertoire chosen is unfamiliar to a significant proportion of the assembly, when the assembly has not been provided with adequate rehearsal or participation aids to join in the singing, or when the language, volume, style, etc., of the song is alienating. "Leading the assembly's thoughts to the mystery of the season or feast" presupposes that the entrance song has some connection with the Scriptures to be proclaimed, the homily that will be preached, and the particular focus of the celebration's euchology. Thus general praise, gathering, or thanksgiving hymns, while possible choices for an entrance song, seem less appropriate. "Accompanying the procession of the priest and ministers" suggests that the entrance song functions not so much as the initial corporate expression of prayer as "music accompanying (ministerial) movement." From this perspective the music should cease when the activity ceases. It should be noted that *DMP* 34 seems to expand the opening procession from the simple movement of priest and ministers to the sanctuary area by adding the children themselves to the opening procession.

The official documentation states that the entrance song may be sung in a responsorial format with choir or schola intoning a refrain and singing verses to which the assembly responds with an invariant refrain. Alternatively, the entrance song could be sung *in directum* by the assembly as a whole or by a choir without vocal participation by the assembly. The documents do not suggest that a soloist sing the entrance song without participation by assembly and/or choir.

Two formats are suggested for the entrance song. Given the musical complexity of the *Antiphona ad introitum* in the *Graduale Romanum*, it seems unlikely that this could be sung except by trained cantor(s) and choir. It has the advantages of a text frequently related to the feast and season being celebrated and the beauty of the Gregorian musical tradition; it has the disadvantages of being too musically complex for the average assembly to sing (presuming that congregational singing of the song is a value). The fact that the text is in Latin has the advantage of connecting the assembly to a millennium-long worship-music tradition and could unite an assembly composed of many vernaculars; on the other hand, few present worship assemblies would know the meaning of the Latin text without a printed translation or prior preparation. The antiphon and psalm of the *Graduale Simplex* is generally less musically complex than the *Antiphona ad introitum* of the *Graduale Romanum* but would probably still demand trained cantor(s) and choir for its execution; the advantages and disadvantages of singing the Latin text have already been noted.

It should be noted that in celebrations in the vernacular, chants unrelated to the suggested *antiphona ad introitum* are frequently performed; formats include congregational psalmody, litanies, and metrical hymnody.

### 2. Opening Dialogue

"After the entrance song, the priest and the whole assembly make the sign of the cross. Then through his greeting the priest declares to the assembled community that the Lord is present. This greeting and the congregation's response express the mystery of the gathered church" (*IGMR* 28).

*IGMR* 28 clearly indicates the two functions of the Opening Dialogue: (1) the ritual *recognition* that all the rites that follow are done in the presence of God manifest in Christ Jesus present in the Holy Spirit in the gathering of the Church; and (2) the *establishment of the "proclamation-response" pattern* characteristic of Roman Catholic Christian worship.

The opening dialogue is alternated between the priest as proclaimer and the assembly as a whole as respondent. *MR1975* does not indicate that servers or choir may make the responses "on behalf of" the assembly.

Although *MuS* 29 indicates that the "priest's greeting and the congregation's response" belongs to the "first degree" of solemnity at a sung Mass (i.e., that it must always be sung when elements of the second and third degree of solemnity are sung), this prescription applies to a sung Mass in Latin. In vernacular celebration, this element would normally be spoken.

### 3. Rite of Blessing and Sprinkling Holy Water
Although no mention is made of the rite in *IGMR*, an appendix to *MR1975* provides the rubrics, rationale, texts and ceremonies for a "Rite of Blessing and Sprinkling Holy Water" as part of the Introductory Rites:

"The rite of blessing and sprinkling holy water may be done at all Lord's Day Masses, even those that are anticipated in the evening hours of Saturday, in all churches and oratories. This rite takes the place of the penitential rite performed at the beginning of Mass."[1]

These rubrics radically change the character of this ritual as it had been performed at Roman rite Eucharist prior to Vatican II. First of all, the *Asperges/Vidi Aquam* rite had been considered a pious exercise *prefixed to* the formal liturgy, rather than an actual *part of* the Eucharist. This was shown by the change in the presiding minister's vesture from a cope (a non-sacerdotal garment) worn during the sprinkling to a chasuble (a properly sacerdotal garment) assumed by the priest before reciting the Prayers at the Foot of the Altar. The present rite does not call for any change in vesture on the part of the presiding minister. It situates the ritual as part of the Introductory Rites after the liturgy has already begun with the entrance song, veneration of the altar, and greeting of the people. Secondly, the *Asperges/Vidi Aquam* ritual used to be limited to the principal Sunday Mass, the so-called "high," "sung" or "choir" Mass. The present rubrics indicate that it may be used at any or all of the Lord's Day Eucharists whatever their degree of solemnity. Thirdly, the *Asperges/Vidi Aquam* ritual had been reserved to the pastor or superior of the community. The present rubrics indicate that any priest may preside over the rite. Fourthly, the *Asperges/Vidi Aquam* ritual had been limited to the principal church-building in a parish or religious community. The present ritual indicates that it may be done with any gathering of the faithful on the Lord's Day.

The fundamental structure of the rite is five-fold. First, there is a short address by the priest to the assembly indicating the purpose of the rite. As with most monitions, this text should probably be spoken rather than sung. Second, the priest blesses the water with a spoken prayer. Three alternative texts are provided, two for Sundays outside of Paschaltide, and one for use during Paschaltide. The importance of this blessing prayer could be emphasized by chanting it, possibly to the same tones used for the preface. Third, the priest may bless salt and mix it with the blessed water. This seems to be a secondary ritual for use when the water itself is impure. Since it is an optional secondary ritual, the text should probably not be emphasized by chanting. Fourth, the priest sprinkles the blessed water on himself, the ministers, clergy, and the assembly. During the sprinkling a chant is

---

[1] *MR1975*: 917.

sung by cantor, choir, and/or the assembly. *MR1975* suggests seven possible texts and notes that other appropriate songs might be substituted.[2] Since the amount of time needed for the sprinkling will vary with the number of people, the chant accompanying the sprinkling should be "open-ended" (e.g., mantra, verse-refrain, litany). A fixed anthem or hymn form would not be appropriate. Finally, the rite is concluded as the priest offers a short prayer before the "Glory to God" (if prescribed) is sung.

*4. Penitential Rite*

The penitential rite in the Introductory Rites at Eucharist is not an abbreviated form of the sacrament of reconciliation. Rather it functions as a ritual purification of the assembly as it undertakes its corporate worship of God.

*MR1975* notes roles for the presiding minister (opening exhortation, concluding "absolution" text) and full assembly (silent prayer, vocal recitation of texts) in the penitential rite. The invocations of the troped *Kyrie* may be made by the priest or a "suitable minister." These invocations could be sung by priest, deacon, or cantor with assembly (and choir) responding in song. The priest's opening exhortation should probably be spoken, but the concluding "absolution" text might be chanted, especially if the troped *Kyrie* is sung.

Three options appear in *MR1975* for the Penitential Rite. After an opening exhortation addressed to the assembly by the priest and a brief pause for silent recollection, the community may (1) recite together a corporate confession of sin (an adaptation of the *MR1570's Confiteor*), (2) interchange some versicles and responses with the priest, or (3) respond to the troped invocations of a *Kyrie* litany. All three options would be concluded with an "absolution" prayer spoken by the priest.

---

[2] Outside of Paschaltide *MR1975* recommends that Ps 50:9, Ezek 36:25-26, or 1 Pet 1:3-5 be sung; during Paschaltide it recommends the singing of Ezek 47:1-2, 9, Dan 3:77, 79, 1 Pet 2:9, or an ecclesiastical composition: *E latere tuo, Christe*. It does not limit the singing to these texts, however; other appropriate songs might be sung. *MR1975* does not specify if the song(s) during the sprinkling should be sung by cantor, choir, assembly, or any combination thereof.

In the *MR1570* the priest was directed to sprinkle the altar three times with the blessed water before sprinkling himself and the other members of the assembly. He also intoned the chant the choir sang during the sprinkling: *Asperges Me* (Ps 50:9) on Sundays outside of Paschaltide (but without the *Gloria Patri* during Lent) or *Vidi Aquam* (based on Ezek 47:1-2, 9) during Paschaltide.

Option (1) would not normally be sung. Option (2) might be sung since versicle/response interchange appears in "call-response" form. Option (3), the troped *Kyrie* with responses in Greek or in the vernacular, may be sung, especially since it is cast in litanic form. The sample trope-texts provided in the Sacramentary (called *invocationes* in *MR1975*) are all addressed to Christ.[3] Trope-texts other than those provided should not become mini-homilies or an extended examination of conscience, but remain statements about Christ's merciful goodness evoking an acclamatory response of praise. Although three invocations are provided as a model in the Sacramentary this number may be increased for musical or pastoral reasons. Singing trope-texts in various living languages with the *Kyrie/Christe eleison* refrain sung in Greek by the assembly may be a way of unifying diverse ethnic groups within a single worshiping assembly.

### 5. Lord, Have Mercy

"The *Kyrie* begins, unless it has already been included as part of the penitential rite. Since it is a song by which the faithful praise the Lord and implore his mercy, it is ordinarily prayed by all, that is, alternately by the congregation and the choir or cantor.

"As a rule each of the acclamations is said twice, but, because of the idiom of different languages, the music, or other circumstances, it may be said more than twice or a short verse (trope) may be interpolated. If the *Kyrie* is not sung, it is to be recited" (*IGMR* 30).

When the "Rite of Blessing and Sprinkling Holy Water" or the psalmody of one of the Divine Office's hours has not replaced the penitential rite and the penitential rite has employed options (1) (corporate *Confiteor*) or (2) (psalmic verses), the *Kyrie eleison* litany follows as the next liturgical unit in the Introductory Rites. Historically the "Lord, have mercy" litany has had two functions in a certain amount of tension with each other. Originally the text was an *acclamation* shouted as part of pagan emperor worship. It entered Christian liturgy when the honors bestowed on civic figures began to be assumed into Christian worship. Its second function was as an *expression of supplication* and as such served as a response to various sets of intercessions.

---

[3] Some medieval commentators saw the *Kyrie, Christe, Kyrie* invocations as addressed to God the Father, God the Son, and God the Holy Spirit respectively.

By its configuration in *MR1975* in relation to the penitential rite, it has assumed a more distinctly *penitential/purificatory* aspect.

*MR1975* lists the six-fold "Lord have mercy" litany in versicle-response format. Presumably the priest would speak the versicles with the assembly responding in unison. However *IGMR* 30 seems to emphasize its character as a musical event, suggesting that the versicles could be sung by priest, deacon, cantor or choir, as long as the assembly sings its response. Although the six-fold format is printed as the norm when the "Lord have mercy" is recited, the number of repetitions may be increased for musical or pastoral reasons.

We have already indicated that the "Lord have mercy" is in "call-response" litanic form, with the versicles articulated by priest, deacon, cantor or choir to which the assembly responds. Such a format presupposes that the assembly is vocally engaged in singing the *Kyrie eleison*. Musical settings in which the assembly has no vocal role are inappropriate.

*6. Glory to God*

"The *Gloria* is an ancient hymn in which the Church, assembled in the Holy Spirit, praises and entreats the Father and the Lamb. It is sung by the congregation, or by the congregation alternately with the choir, or by the choir alone. If it is not sung, it is to be recited either by all together or in alternation.

"The *Gloria* is sung or said on Sundays outside Advent and Lent, on solemnities and feasts, and in special, more solemn celebrations" (*IGMR* 31).

*IGMR* 31 defines the "Glory to God" as a trinitarian hymn of praise and supplication. As a hymn it is a "closed form," exhibiting a distinct progress of thought. This development may be obscured in musical settings which treat the opening phrase as a detachable recurring refrain. Liturgical history indicates that it only gradually entered the Roman rite Eucharist, most probably migrating from use at Morning Prayer in the Liturgy of the Hours. The fact that its use is restricted to celebrations of higher festivity indicates that it is a secondary element in the Introductory Rites.

Although *IGMR* 31 seems to suggest that the vocal participation of the assembly in the singing (or recitation) of the "Glory to God" is preferable, it notes that the text may be sung by a choir without the assembly's vocal participation. It does not suggest that it may be performed as a solo by the cantor. The custom of *MR1570* in which the *Gloria* was intoned by the presiding priest has been abrogated: it may be intoned by priest, cantor, choir, or sung without intonation by choir and/or congregation.

By defining the "Glory to God" as a hymn (i.e., a religious textual-musical unity involving congregational participation) one would expect that (like the Gospel Alleluia in the Liturgy of the Word) it would be omitted if not sung. It is therefore somewhat surprising that *IGMR* 31 directs that it be recited if it is not sung. Perhaps the alternation format (including alternation by gender or location in congregational recitation) can maintain the *Gloria's* poetic character even when it is spoken.

### 7. Opening Presidential Prayer

The most important element of the Introductory Rites, the collect exhibits three functions. First, it *completes* the Introductory Rites with an act of prayer. Second, it *gathers* the private intentions of the individuals making up the liturgical assembly into a corporate request. Third, it *announces* a thematic focus for the celebration.[4]

*IGMR* 32 notes roles for the presiding minister (invitation to prayer, verbally pronouncing the collect) and for the assembly as a whole (silent prayer, spoken/sung "Amen" to conclude the collect). They do not suggest that servers and/or choir may substitute for the vocal participation of the assembly.

The collect may be sung to a very simple chant-tone (little more than a reciting tone with slight inflections, even simpler than the Preface tones). The assembly would respond with an equally simple recto tono or inflected "Amen" in unison. *MuS* 29 considers the chanting of the collect to belong to the "first degree of solemnity" in the sung Mass. As we have noted above, however, this directive applies to the sung Mass in *Latin*. In vernacular celebrations, the collect would normally be spoken with a spoken congregational response.

---

[4] This last function should not be over-emphasized. The "theme" of every Eucharist is the celebration of the paschal mystery; however particular aspects of this mystery are emphasized during the various liturgical seasons and individual celebrations, aspects that find concise expression in the collect.

## II. MUSICAL ELEMENTS IN THE LITURGY OF THE WORD

### 1. Non-Psalmic Proclamations of Scripture

"The readings, taken from the approved editions, may be sung in a way suited to different languages. This singing, however, must serve to stress the words, not obscure them. On occasions when the readings are in Latin, they are to be sung to the melody given in the *Ordo cantus Missae.* . . .

"Even if the gospel itself is not sung, it is appropriate for *The Lord be with you, A reading from the holy gospel* . . . , and at the end *The Gospel of the Lord* to be sung, in order that the assembly may also sing its acclamations. This is a way both of bringing out the importance of the gospel reading and of stirring up the faith of those who hear it.

"At the conclusion of the other readings, The word of the Lord may be sung, even by someone other than the reader; all respond with the acclamation. In this way the gathered assembly pays reverence to the word of God it has listened to in faith and gratitude" (*OLM* 14, 17, 18).

One needs to distinguish the liturgical dialogues that introduce and conclude the proclamation from the actual proclamation of the Scriptures.

Before the non-gospel readings the lector verbally informs the assembly of the source of the reading. This is not a genuine liturgical dialogue, but simply an announcement not needing to be enhanced by singing. In contrast, the gospel reading is preceded by a genuine liturgical dialogue. The deacon (or priest) gives the greeting "The Lord be with you" to which the assembly replies "And also with you." If this interchange was chanted in the Introductory Rites it would probably be appropriately chanted here, but as was earlier noted, in vernacular celebrations such greetings would normally be spoken. The deacon's announcement of the source of the gospel text seems primarily informational (like the lector's) but since it calls for a community acclamation of praise to Christ, it might be sung.

In contrast both non-gospel and gospel readings are concluded with an acclamatory dialogue: the lector announcing "The Word of the Lord" to which the assembly responds "Thanks be to God" or the deacon announcing "The Gospel of the Lord" to which the assembly responds "Praise to you, Lord Jesus Christ." (It is interesting to note that *MR1975* presents the same text for lector and deacon [*Verbum Domini*] which is not so much a sentence, as an exclamation-cue for the assembly's acclamation [*Deo gratias/Laus tibi, Christe*].) Even if the interchanges before the gospel were not sung, it might be appropriate to sing these post-reading acclamatory dialogues especially in celebrations of high solemnity. The legislation notes that they may be initiated by a cantor rather than the lector or deacon.

The chanting of the Scriptures themselves is not primarily informational or acclamatory but proclamational. Some historians suggest that the "reading-tones" of Latin-rite cantillation developed in a time prior to electronic amplification to guarantee that the text of the Scriptures would be heard in large worship spaces. Others hold that simple cantillation was a form of "solemnizing" public proclamations. In any event, the communication of the verbal text was primary. In vernacular celebrations with electronic amplification of the scriptural proclamations, the purpose of chanting the readings in order to hear the text disappears. However, on certain feasts the readings might be chanted in order to signal solemnity. Best of all would be circumstances in which chanting part of the text would clarify for the hearers its literary structure (e.g., chanting the poetry and speaking the prose insertions in the Prologue of the Gospel of John or Isaiah's commentary on the "Song of the Vineyard").

As already noted, the introductory material before the non-gospel readings would be announced by the reader. The liturgical dialogue before the gospel would be initiated by the deacon (or in his absence by a priest, preferably the priest who will proclaim the gospel *other than* the presider). The Scriptures themselves would be proclaimed by a reader for the non-gospel readings or deacon (or priest) for the gospel reading. The acclamations after the non-gospel readings might be initiated by the reader (spoken or sung) or a cantor (sung). After the gospel reading the acclamations might be initiated by the deacon (spoken or sung) or a cantor. In any case the responses to the introductory and concluding dialogues should be made by the entire assembly speaking or singing. The documents do not suggest that a cantor or choir make the responses "on behalf of" the assembly.

Chants for the acclamations surrounding the readings appear in *MR1975*: (1) a formula for *Verbum Domini/Deo gratias* following the first reading, (2) a formula for the same text following the second reading, (3) three formulae for the dialogue prior to the gospel, and

(4) two formulae for the *Verbum Domini/Laus tibi, Christe* dialogue after the gospel (941–2).[5]

## 2. *Responsorial Psalm*

"After the reading comes the responsorial psalm or gradual, an integral part of the Liturgy of the Word. The psalm as a rule is drawn from the lectionary because the individual psalm texts are directly connected with the individual readings: the choice of psalm depends therefore on the readings. Nevertheless, in order that the people may be able to join in the responsorial psalm more readily, some texts of responses and psalms have been chosen, according to the different seasons of the years and classes of saints, for optional use, whenever the psalm is sung, in place of the text corresponding to the reading.

"The psalmist or cantor of the psalm sings the verses of the psalm at the lectern or other suitable place. The people remain seated and listen, but also as a rule take part by singing the response, except when the psalm is sung straight through without the response.

"The psalm when sung may be either the psalm assigned in the lectionary or the gradual from the *Graduale Romanum* or the responsorial psalm or the psalm with Alleluia as the response from *The Simple Gradual* in the form they have in those books. . . ." (IGMR 36).

"If the psalm after the reading is not sung, it is to be recited" (IGMR 39).

"As a rule the responsorial psalm should be sung. There are two established ways of singing the psalm after the first reading: responsorially and directly. In responsorial singing, which, as far as possible, is to be given preference, the psalmist or cantor of the psalm sings the psalm verse and the whole congregation joins in by singing the response. In direct singing of the psalm, there is no intervening response by the community. Either the psalmist or cantor of the psalm sings the psalm alone as the community listens or else all sing it together.

"The singing of the psalm, or even of the response alone, is a great help toward understanding and meditating on the psalm's spiritual meaning.

---

[5] Formulae for the chanting of the readings *in Latin* may be found in Paolo Ferretti, *Estetica gregoriana dei recitativi liturgici*, ed. Pellegrino Ernetti, Quaderni dei Padri Benedettini di San Giorgio Maggiore-Venezia, 3 (Venezia-Roma, 1964) 13–34.

"To foster the congregation's singing, every means available in the various cultures is to be employed. In particular use is to be made of all the relevant options provided in the Order of Readings for Mass regarding responses corresponding to the different liturgical season.

"When not sung, the psalm after the reading is to be recited in a manner conducive to meditation on the word of God.

"The responsorial psalm is sung or recited by the psalmist or cantor at the lectern. . . .

"Among the chants between the readings, the psalm after the first reading is very important. As a rule the psalm to be used is the one assigned to the reading. But in the case of readings for the common of saints, ritual Masses, Masses for various needs and occasions, votive Masses, and Masses for the dead the choice is left up to the priest celebrating. He will base his choice on the principle of the pastoral benefit of those participating.

"But to make it easier for the people to join in the response to the psalm, the Order of Readings lists certain other texts of psalms and responses that have been chosen according to the various seasons or classes of saints. Whenever the psalm is sung, these texts may replace the text corresponding to the reading" (OLM 20–2, 89).

"Verses of psalms, carefully selected in accord with the understanding of children, or singing in the form of psalmody or the Alleluia with a simple verse should be sung between the readings. The children should always have a part in this singing, but sometimes a reflective silence may be substituted for the singing.

"If only a single reading is chosen, the singing may follow the homily" (DMP 46).

The *psalmus responsorius seu graduale* (one of the *cantus inter lectiones occurentes*) is usually called the "responsorial psalm," but this translation could be misleading on two accounts. First, although the gradual-texts appointed to be sung during the Liturgy of the Word are generally from the canonical psalter, on occasion Old Testament or New Testament canticles appear; in other words, although this text is always taken from Sacred Scripture, the gradual-text is not always a (canonical) psalm. Second, the term "responsorial" has led some commentators to suggest that the purpose of this element of the Liturgy of the Word is responsorial, i.e., "to respond to the first reading." However, the term "responsorial" more properly refers to the structure of this text as presented in the Lectionary for Mass, i.e., "with a response provided for the assembly to sing." Therefore the gradual is not a meditation song nor do its texts only refer back to the first reading. Rather it is a scriptural proclamation executed in song by a cantor or choir with assembly joining in the proclamation, much as the other readings are scriptural proclamations executed (usually) in speech by a lector with the assembly joining in the dialogues before and after their proclamation.

The proper minister of the responsorial psalm is a cantor (much as the proper minister of the scriptural readings is a lector and the proper minister of the proclamation of the gospel is a deacon). Just as the gospel may be proclaimed by a priest (preferably not the presider) in the absence of a deacon, so the responsorial psalm may be proclaimed by a lector, server, or priest in the absence of a cantor. As will be detailed below, the responsorial psalm may also be sung by a choir/schola and/or by the assembly.

Many options exist in the official documentation for the text and format of the responsorial psalm. Pride of place is given to the "proper psalm and proper refrain" printed in the lectionary for a given set of readings. If learning a new sung psalm-refrain at each liturgical gathering is too difficult for a given assembly, *LM* 174 indicates that it is possible to substitute a seasonal refrain, thus giving a "proper psalm and seasonal refrain" format. If learning a new musical setting of the psalm-text at each liturgical gathering is too difficult for the cantor, *LM* 175 indicates that a seasonal psalm may be substituted, thus giving a "seasonal psalm with seasonal refrain" format. In addition to these options from the lectionary, one could sing the proper gradual (in Latin) from the *Graduale Romanum*. Like the *antiphona ad introitum,* its execution demands trained cantor(s) and choir; vocal participation by the assembly would be unlikely. The "common psalm and refrain/Alleluia" (in Latin) from the *Graduale Simplex* uses a psalm-tone formula for the psalm-verses rather than the ornate melodies of the *Graduale Romanum,* but would still probably require trained cantor(s) and choir for its execution. The responsorial psalm as an "integral part of the Liturgy of the Word" is a proclamation-in-song of the Word of God; thus other ecclesiastical compositions or secular texts are inappropriate substitutes.

*IGMR* 36 explicitly notes two formats for executing the responsorial psalm: "responsorial" (cantor singing verses and assembly singing refrain) and "direct" (psalm sung straight through without refrain). In fact at least six formats are conceivable:

1) "Solo direct" singing involves a cantor singing the entire psalm-text *without* a recurring refrain-intervention by the assembly. The text might be sung to a simple (Gregorian-style) psalm tone, a "pulsed" (Gelineau-style) formula, or as a through-composed art-song. The advantage of this format is that the text could be clearly articulated by a single voice; the disadvantages are that it may obscure the structure of the canonical psalm, lead to undue vocal display on the part of the soloist, or reduce the assembly to passive listening.

2) "Choir direct" singing involves the schola singing the entire psalm-text *without* a recurring refrain-intervention by the assembly. The text might be sung to a simple (Gregorian-style) psalm-tone, a harmonized (Anglican chant) recitation formula, a "pulsed" (Gelineau-style) formula, or as a through-composed anthem. This format eliminates the disadvantages of undue vocal display in the "solo direct" format, but might also obscure the text unless the choir has clear diction; the other disadvantages of the "solo direct" format remain.

3) "Assembly direct" singing involves the entire assembly singing the entire psalm-text *without* a recurring refrain. The text might be sung to a simple (Gregorian-style) psalm-tone, a "pulsed" (Gelineau-style) formula, or a hymn-tune with a metrical psalm-paraphrase text (e.g., Genevan Psalter). A disadvantage to this format is that it demands textual and musical literacy on the part of the assembly and printed resources for all to facilitate their singing; the advantages include having the entire assembly actively involved in executing the entire psalm-text.

4) "Responsorial" singing involves having a cantor or schola sing the psalm-verses *with* a recurring invariant refrain sung by the assembly. The advantage of this format is that musical and textual literacy is not demanded from the assembly (since the refrain can be learned "by rote") and yet they can be actively engaged in vocally executing part of the text; a disadvantage is that the recurring refrain may not mirror the progress of thought in the canonical text.

5) "Alternating" singing (sometimes called "antiphonal," i.e., where the liturgical assembly is split into groups who alternate singing strophes of the psalm) exhibits the same techniques, advantages, and disadvantages as "assembly direct" singing considered above. One additional advantage to this format is that the assembly

would not be vocally over-taxed since one half of the assembly would remain silent while the other half is singing.

6) In addition to the five formats mentioned above, "mixed or experimental" formats (which could involve reciting psalm-verses over musical accompaniment) have also been attempted, with or without a recurring refrain sung by the assembly.

It should be noted that some theorists are questioning the preference for the responsorial format enshrined in the lectionary. They argue that forcing all psalm-texts into a format with an invariant recurring refrain does violence to their canonical form (and thus their progress of thought and actual message). They also note that the brevity of the refrains intended to facilitate the assembly's participation may actually hinder it, since the refrains are seldom memorable textually or musically.

### 3. Gospel Acclamation

"As the season requires, the Alleluia or another chant follows the second reading.

"a. The Alleluia is sung in every season outside Lent. It is begun either by all present or by the choir or cantor; it may then be repeated. The verses are taken from the lectionary or the *Graduale*.

"b. The other chant consists of the verse before the gospel or another psalm or tract, as found in the lectionary or the *Graduale*."

"When there is only one reading before the gospel:

"a. during a season calling for the Alleluia, there is an option to use either the psalm with Alleluia as the response, or the responsorial psalm and the Alleluia with its verse, or just the psalm, or just the Alleluia.

"b. during the season when the Alleluia is not allowed, either the responsorial psalm or the verse before the gospel may be used. . . . If not sung, the Alleluia or the verse before the gospel may be omitted" (*IGMR* 37–9).

"The Alleluia, or, as the liturgical season requires, the verse before the gospel, is also a 'rite or act standing by itself.' It serves as the assembled faithful's greeting of welcome to the Lord who is about to speak to them and as an expression of their faith through song.

"The Alleluia or the verse before the gospel must be sung and during it all stand. It is not to be sung only by the cantor who intones it or by the choir, but by the whole congregation together. . . .

"The chant between the second reading and the gospel is either specified in each Mass and correlated with the gospel or else it is left as a choice to be made from those in the series belonging to a liturgical season or to one of the Commons.

"During Lent one of the acclamations from those given in the text of the Order of Readings may be used, depending on the occasion. This acclamation is made before and after the verse before the gospel" (*OLM* 23, 90–1).

The gospel acclamation exhibits two primary functions. It may serve as an accompaniment to the procession with the evangelary (a *movement-accompaniment* function) or as a communal greeting of the proclaimed gospel (an *acclamatory* function). It is interesting to note that the essentially musical character of the gospel acclamation has been clarified in the official legislation since *IGMR*. Originally the documents specified that the gospel acclamation *might* be omitted if not sung; now the documents direct that the gospel acclamation *should* be omitted if not sung. The substitution of a non-Alleluia acclamatory text during Lent reflects an ancient tradition of "fasting" from the Alleluia during the penitential Forty Days. Some theorists, however, have questioned its appropriateness since every eucharistic celebration (even during Lent) bears the marks of paschal joy.

The gospel acclamation is sung as a dialogue between cantor and assembly. A choir may substitute for the cantor if they can intelligibly execute the text of the gospel verse. The choir may also support the cantor and assembly by adding vocal harmonies to their melody.

The format presupposed by the documents involve four moments: (1) the cantor intones a refrain, (2) the assembly repeats the refrain, (3) the cantor chants the gospel verse, (4) the assembly repeats the original refrain. Variations on this format include having the choir extend the refrain through vocal polyphony after the assembly has sung it or prefacing the cantor's intonation with an instrumental fanfare. In some communities the lector reads the gospel verse if no cantor or choir is available to chant it; in order to preserve the essentially musical quality of the gospel acclamation, instrumental music might be played underneath this recitation to bridge between the sung acclamations as well as cue the assembly.

### 4. Sequence

"Sequences are optional, except on Easter Sunday and Pentecost" (*IGMR* 40).

There is considerable debate among musicologists about the origin and development of the sequence. Although an earlier standard theory posits that the sequence developed as Latin or vernacular tropes added to the melodies of the jubilus (an extended melisma on the final syllable of the word Alleluia) to help singers remember these ornate melodies, contemporary scholarship has strongly challenged this assertion. In medieval Missals sequences tend to appear after the Alleluia for feast days. Their popularity seems to reach its height in the twelfth and thirteenth centuries. The *MR* 1570 eliminated all but four: (1) *Victimae paschali laudes* for Easter Sunday, (2) *Veni Sancte Spiritus* for Pentecost, (3) *Lauda Sion* for Corpus Christi, and (4) *Dies irae* for funerals. A fifth Marian sequence, the *Stabat Mater,* was added to the Roman Missal when the feast of the Seven Sorrows of Our Lady was extended to the universal Church by Benedict XIII.

Four sequences have been retained in *MR1975,* but they have been repositioned to *before* the gospel Alleluia. Thus they do not appear to be processional music to accompany the movement of the evangelary. Since only the Easter and Pentecost sequences have been made obligatory, perhaps they should be considered the equivalent of a festival "Hymn of the Day," i.e., a closed (hymnic) form intimately tied to the theme of a great solemnity.

Some commentators have seen in the development of the sequence a genuinely "popular" form of liturgical singing, an eruption of folk-art in the midst of a clericalized musical liturgy. However, since many of the sequences were in Latin and exhibited a fairly wide-ranging and sophisticated musical structure, it seems more likely that they were developed and sung by monastic choral groups. Thus in pastoral practice today they might be sung in Latin to the original chants by choir or schola (perhaps with a printed vernacular translation for the assembly) or they might be sung to a familiar hymn-tune by the entire assembly in a metrical paraphrase.

A peculiarity of at least some of the early medieval sequences is a doubling of strophes: unlike a metrical hymn where each verse is sung to the same tune, the melodies of the sequences change as the texts of varying metrical patterns occur, but these patterns (unlike the non-recurrent free patterns of chant) frequently appear in sets of two (cf. *Victimae paschali laudes*). This has led some commentators to suggest that the strophes of the sequence were sung in alternating format by the monastic choir: side-to-side or men's vs. boys' voices. If the Latin sequences with their melodies are chosen in pastoral practice, perhaps the choir/schola might sing the initial melody with the assembly repeating the same melody to a new text, thus allowing them to hear the melody before they are asked to sing it.

*5. Profession of Faith*

Present liturgical documents present the Profession of Faith as the assembly's response to the proclaimed (remembered) and preached (actualized) word of God. Announcing the text in common becomes a way by which the assembly commits itself once again to the lived implications of its baptismal faith.

Although many dramatic choral musical settings of the Creed stemming from the baroque, classical, and romantic periods survive in which the various narrative moments in the text are mirrored with musical "word-painting," their appropriateness in the reformed liturgy is questionable since the documents describe the Creed as the assembly's profession of faith, made in union with the ordained presider. Although choir and congregation may alternate sections of the Creed, the choir may not sing the Profession of Faith "on behalf of" the assembly. No particular roles for presbyter, deacon, or cantor is indicated.

The present official legislation offers three formats/texts for the Profession of Faith: (1) the Nicene-Constantinopolitan Creed as the "usual" form for Sundays and solemnities, (2) the Apostles' Creed for use in Masses with Children, and (3) an interrogatory form for use at the Easter Vigil and when initiation sacraments are celebrated in the context of Eucharist.

Restrained musical settings of format one (modeled on the Gregorian Credos) involving the assembly's vocal participation are possible, but in vernacular celebrations the text is usually spoken. Likewise the recitation of the Apostle's Creed in format two with children would normally be spoken. Some composers, taking their cue from the interrogatory format (3), have offered musical settings of the Creed in which the assembly is given an assent-refrain and a cantor/choir sings declarations of the Creed as verses.

## 6. General Intercessions

"The congregation takes part in the general intercessions while standing and by saying or singing a common response after each intention or by silent prayer" (OLM 30–1).

Both elements of the term "general intercessions" help to define the function of the Prayer of the Faithful. As *intercessions* these are supplicatory and petitionary prayers made by the baptized on behalf of all creation. These prayers arise from the assembly's commitment to extending Christ's priestly work through space and time until the kingdom arrives in fullness. They are thus not praise, thanksgiving, confessional, or reparation prayers, nor are they reprises of the homily or a bulletin board for community affairs. They are *general* in the sense that only after engaging the great ecclesial, political and social needs of its world does the assembly concentrate on its own needs.

Although a traditional Roman form of the Prayer of the Faithful remains in the solemn intercessions of the Good Friday liturgy, the regular structure in the reformed Roman rite involves three categories of participants: (1) the presider who calls for and concludes the prayer, (2) a deacon, cantor, or assisting minister who announces the intentions, and (3) the assembly who responds to the intentions, usually with an invariable vocal refrain.

The presidential call for prayer would probably be best recited as a simple *monitio* to the assembly. His concluding prayer, however, might be chanted in the same style as the other presidential prayers. The intercessions with refrain would be sung as a litany. The simplest form would involve a deacon or assisting minister reciting the intercession, the cantor singing a "cue-formula" (e.g., "Let us pray to the Lord"), and the assembly responding with its sung refrain (possibly supported by choral harmony). A slightly more complex form would have the cantor singing the intercession, either *recto tono* or with slight vocal inflections, before the cue-formula. It should be noted that many settings involve the assembly (and choir) overlapping its response "Lord . . ." with the last word "Lord" of the cue-formula. This strongly emphasizes the call-response litanic form.

## III. MUSICAL ELEMENTS IN THE PREPARATION OF THE GIFTS

"To the first degree of solemnity for the sung Mass belongs: . . . c. in the liturgy of the eucharist — the prayer over the gifts; . . . to the third degree belong: . . . d. songs for the presentation of the gifts.

"In some places there is the lawful practice, occasionally confirmed by indult, of substituting other songs for the entrance, offertory, and communion chants in the Graduale. At the discretion of the competent territorial authority this practice may be kept, on condition that the songs substituted fit in with those parts of the Mass, the feast, or the liturgical season. The texts of such songs must also have the approval of the same territorial authority" (*MuS* 29, 31, 32).

There is debate concerning the function of the Preparation of the Gifts in *MR1975* and consequently debate concerning the music to be used during these rites. *IGMR* refers to this complexus of texts and ceremonies as the Preparation of the Gifts *(praeparatio donorum),* although in practice many people still refer to them as the "Offertory of the Mass."[6] The single piece of vocal music associated with this panoply of rites in *IGMR* 50 and *MuS* 31–2 is called the "song/antiphon for the offertory" *(cantus/antiphona ad offertorium),* although in practice this music has been called the "Offertory hymn/song." Interestingly, *MuS* 31 places the *cantus ad offertorium* in a different category than the Entrance and Communion pieces which are explicitly termed "songs for the entrance and communion *processions" (cantus ad processiones introitus et communionis).* This is probably due to the fact that, although *IGMR* 49 encourages a procession by the faithful with the gifts, such a procession remains optional. Therefore the translation of *cantus/antiphona ad offertorium* as "presentation song" is probably the most accurate: although the

---

[6] The official responses to the questions "What is the correct meaning of the 'Offertory Rite'?" and "Does it not seem that the 'Offertory Rite,' by suppressing the prayers that had accompanied the offering of bread and wine, has been impoverished?" as found in *Not* 6 (1970) ##25–6, 37–8 are very instructive in this regard.

music may accompany a genuine offertory procession, its primary function is to cover the transfer and placing of the gifts on the altar.

Examining the texts and ceremonies in *MR1975* for the Preparation of the Gifts leads us to posit three functions for this portion of the liturgy: (1) preparing the altar (the *IGMR* presumes that only the evangelary [and possibly some candles] has been placed upon the altar before this point in the liturgy), (2) preparing the eucharistic elements (possibly including blessing prayers for bread and wine modeled on Jewish *berakoth* recited in dialogue between priest and assembly; a text accompanying the mixing of water and wine; and an incensation of gifts, altar, ministers and assembly), and (3) preparing the ordained presider (including a ritual hand-washing and the *Orate fratres* dialogue) for the Eucharistic Prayer. The music employed could highlight one or more of these functions. If there is a genuine procession with the gifts, the music employed should be "movement music," selected by the same criteria that we have noted above for the music to accompany the opening procession of the ministers in the Introductory Rites. Improvisatory instrumental music or open-ended vocal music structures would probably be the most appropriate.

The collection of money or gifts for the poor or church should take place prior to the presentation of the gifts and be accompanied by the same music. Perhaps the bread and wine blessing prayers with their concluding congregational acclamation "Blessed be God forever" could be chanted. The Prayer over the Gifts could likewise be chanted, especially if the other presidential prayers are. It is also possible to cover this complexus of ceremonies with music: an instrumental piece, a choral anthem, possibly a solo song. In some communities the singing of a congregational hymn is a well-established custom. As long as the texts do not emphasize "offering" thematics (proper to the Eucharistic Prayer) this might be appropriate. Finally, having no music at all during the Preparation of the Gifts may provide time for the assembly to keep silence together, ponder the Liturgy of the Word, and emphasize by contrast the importance of the sung elements of the Eucharistic Prayer.

Depending on the functions of the Preparation of Gifts emphasized and the genre of music chosen, the participants may be instrumentalists, vocal soloists, choir, assembly or any combination of the above.

It should be clear that sung participation by the assembly during the Preparation of the Gifts is not a high priority.

If the *antiphona ad offertorium* from the *Graduale Romanum* is chosen to accompany the presentation of the gifts, its execution will involve the same participants and format that we noted above for the *antiphona ad introitum*: choir/schola and/or cantor(s). If other processional music is chosen to accompany the presentation of the gifts, it should be in "open" format (e.g., refrain/verse, litany, mantra) so that it can be easily coordinated with the duration of the rites.

IV. MUSICAL ELEMENTS IN THE EUCHARISTIC PRAYER
The rubrics associated with *MR1570* directed that the dialogue before the preface, the preface itself, and the concluding phrase of the Canon *(per omnia saecula saeculorum)* be audibly spoken or sung by the celebrant. The rest of the Canon text was to be pronounced inaudibly *(secrete)* except for the phrase "Nobis quoque peccatoribus" whose three words were pronounced in a slightly raised voice. Special rubrical instructions marked the words of consecration: they were to be pronounced "inaudibly, distinctly and attentively" *(secrete, distincte, et attente)*. In contrast, *MR1975* directs that all of the texts of the Eucharistic Prayer are to be pronounced audibly, whether spoken or sung; it emphasizes that even the words of the Lord in the Institution Narrative are to be pronounced "distinctly and openly, as the nature of the words requires" *(distincte et aperte, prouti natura eorundem verborum requirit)*. Thus the overarching principle for the vocal performance of the Eucharistic Prayer in the reformed Roman rite is that any musical elaboration of the text would respect its ritual importance, its vocal executants, and its structure.

*1. Preface Dialogue*
In *MR1975* a standard three-element preface dialogue begins the Eucharistic Prayer. *MuS* 29c assigns the singing of the preface dialogue to the "first degree" of musical participation, i.e., always to be done if other parts of the Mass are sung. As was noted above, this prescription applies only to Masses celebrated *in Latin,* although the directive would indicate the importance of chanting this dialogue even in vernacular celebrations.

A single presidential voice (bishop or presbyter) pronounces the versicles and the assembly as a whole responds. There is no provision for servers, schola or choir to respond "on behalf of" the assembly.

MR1975 provides both simple and solemn tones for the preface dialogue[7] corresponding to those in MR1570. If the preface dialogue is chanted, one presumes that the preface and *Sanctus-Benedictus* will be chanted as well.

## 2. Preface

The Preface itself comprises three distinct rhetorical elements: (1) a standardized protocol, expanding on the last phrase of the preface dialogue, announcing that it is "truly right and just, proper and salutary" to praise God, (2) the body, in which the particular reasons for praising and thanking God in the celebration are enumerated, and (3) a standardized eschatocol, usually mentioning the connection between the earthly liturgy and its heavenly participants, that makes a transition to the *Sanctus-Benedictus*. *MuS* 29c assigns the singing of the Preface to the "first degree" of musical participation.

Since the text of the Preface is part of a major presidential prayer, no provision is made for chanting it by other members of the assembly (e.g., deacon, cantor). In episcopal and/or presbyteral concelebration, the principal celebrant remains the solo vocal executant of the Preface text.

MR1975 provides both a simple and a solemn cantillation-formula for chanted Prefaces. Both cantillation-formulae have initials and finals on A with a reciting tone on C, exhibiting a range of only four notes; completely tied to speech rhythm, these chants are well-suited to non-musically trained celebrants. However, applying the same cantillation-formulae to the three structural elements of the Preface may obscure the rhetorical movement of the text.

## 3. Sanctus-Benedictus

"Acclamation: joining with the angels, the congregation sings or recites the *Sanctus*. This acclamation is an intrinsic part of the Eucharistic Prayer and all the people join with the priest in singing or reciting it" (*IGMR* 55b).

"At its [the Preface's] conclusion, he [the priest] joins his hands and sings or says aloud with the ministers and the people the *Sanctus-Benedictus*" (*IGMR* 108).

---

[7] MR1975: 943, 945.

*MR1570* allowed the first half of the *Sanctus* texts (through the first *Hosanna in excelsis*) to be sung by the schola or choir while the priest celebrant prayed *sub voce* the texts of the Canon up to the consecration. After the consecration, the schola or choir would resume the singing of the *Sanctus* (from *Benedictus qui venit* through the second *Hosanna in excelsis*) while the priest celebrant continued *sub voce* the rest of the Canon texts until the *per omnia saecula saeculorum* that concluded the Doxology. The *Sanctus-Benedictus*, thus performed as two movements of a "Mass suite," functioned ritually as an aural overlay on the inaudible presidential prayer.

In contrast *MR1975* directs that the entire *Sanctus-Benedictus* be sung before the priest celebrant continues with the rest of the Eucharistic Prayer texts and *MuS* 29c assigns the singing of the *Sanctus-Benedictus* to the "first degree" of musical participation.

Since this acclamation belongs to the entire liturgical assembly (priests and people together), it would be inappropriate for it to be sung only by the schola, choir, or a soloist. Some contemporary settings assign the *Hosanna in excelsis* to the assembly, with the other sections of the *Sanctus* sung by choir or soloists; while not expressly forbidden in the rubrics, this practice seems to contravene the intention of *IGMR* 55b in directing that the congregation sings or recites the *Sanctus*.

### 4. Post-Sanctus, (First) Epiclesis, Institution Narrative

Only bishops and presbyters vocally execute these elements of the Eucharistic Prayer. While no chants for the *Post-Sanctus* or (First) *Epiclesis* appear in *MR1975*, the Institution Narratives of Eucharistic Prayers I–IV are musically elaborated.[8] In addition to heightening the impact of the proclamation of these texts by a single voice, chanting these elements may also help to unify the voices of episcopal and/or presbyteral concelebrants with the principal celebrant.

Two pastoral issues arise from this practice. First, by chanting only some sections of the Eucharistic Prayer, is the ritual unity of the text diminished? (Perhaps responding to this concern, the monks of the Abbey of St. Pierre de Solesmes have published with official approval an *Ordo Missae in cantu* in which the entire (Latin) texts of Eucharistic Prayers I–IV have been set to musical notation.) Second, by using the

---

[8] *MR1975*: 946–47, 950, 951–2, 953–54.

233

same cantillation-formulae (fundamentally recitation on A with occasional descents to G) for differing elements of the Eucharistic Prayer text, is its movement of thought obscured?

### 5. *Memorial Acclamation/Anamnesis*

*MR1975* provides for a spoken or sung congregational intervention after the Institution Narrative. The principal celebrant calls for the Memorial Acclamation with the exclamation *Mysterium fidei;* both a simple and a solemn tone appear for its vocal execution.[9] In *MR1975* three possible texts are provided for the assembly,[10] although only the first appears with musical embellishment.[11] It should be noted that the congregational intervention is in a certain sense textually redundant; in episcopal and/or presbyteral concelebrated Masses without the participation of other members of the faithful, the Memorial Acclamation is omitted.

The simple cantillation-formula provided for portions of the Institution Narrative also appears for the extended Anamnesis-Offering texts of Euchristic Prayers I–IV.[12]

### 6. *(Second)* Epiclesis, *Offering, Intercessions*

*MR1975* does not provide chants for these elements of the Eucharistic Prayer, although it does not forbid chanting them; the simple alternation of A and G assigned to portions of the Institution Narrative and the Anamnesis might be continued here.

In some vernacular celebrations, a further congregational intervention of supplication (e.g., "Hear us, O Lord") is inserted among the various requests in the intercessions of the Eucharistic Prayer.

### 7. *Doxology and Amen*

In contrast to *MR1570* where only the concluding phrase of the Doxology was spoken or sung audibly, *MR1975* provides both a simple and a solemn tone for the entire text of the Doxology. *MuS* 29c assigns it to the "first degree" of musical participation. In celebrations with a single priest celebrant, chanting the Doxology heightens its ritual weight; in episcopal and/or presbyteral concelebration it could also unify the various voices.

[9] *MR1975:* 947, 951, 952, 954.
[10] *MR1975:* 492.
[11] *MR1975:* 948, 951, 953, 955.
[12] *MR1975:* 948–9, 951, 953, 955.

The congregational response "Amen" is assigned to the entire liturgical assembly. It is inappropriate for servers or choir to make the response "on behalf of" the congregation. In pastoral practice this "Amen" is frequently repeated and/or embellished with harmonies to signal its importance.

Although it is not recommended, it would be possible to speak the Doxology and still sing the "Amen" response.

## V. MUSICAL ELEMENTS IN THE COMMUNION RITES

### 1. Lord's Prayer

"To the first degree of solemnity for the sung Mass belong . . . in the Liturgy of the Eucharist . . . the Lord's Prayer, with the invitation and embolism . . .

"The congregation should join the priest in singing the Lord's Prayer. When it is in Latin, it is sung to the traditional melodies; the melodies for singing it in the vernacular must have the approval of the competent territorial authority" (MuS 29, 35).

The Lord's Prayer is prayed by the assembly as the baptized disciples of Jesus; the presider introduces the prayer and concretizes the final petition for peace in an extended verbal insertion. No special roles are indicated for cantor or choir, although the choir might support the assembly's singing with harmony as long as they do not substitute for the singing of the congregation.

The format of the Lord's Prayer in the present eucharistic liturgy comprises four elements: (1) a call to prayer by the presiding minister, (2) the text of the prayer vocally expressed by the assembly, (3) an "embolism" (verbal insertion) by the presiding minister, and (4) a concluding doxology by the assembly. The call to prayer is addressed to the assembly and would normally be spoken, although on solemn occasions it might be sung. The Lord's Prayer text itself could be recited or sung by the assembly, but if sung its character as community prayer should be emphasized; elaborate musical settings as well as those that do not mirror the progression of thought of the text are inappropriate. The embolism is addressed to God (the Father) and would normally be spoken if the text of the prayer was spoken or chanted if the prayer was chanted. The concluding doxology (as an acclamation) should normally be sung. Even if the presiding minister chooses to recite the call to prayer and the embolism, instrumental music might be played underneath both texts (or just the embolism) to unify this liturgical unit and to provide the assembly with cues for their singing.

## 2. Rite of Peace

"To the first degree of solemnity for the sung Mass belong . . . in the Liturgy of the Eucharist . . . the greeting 'May the peace of the Lord'" (*MuS* 29).

The presiding minister begins the rite by a verbal dialogue with the assembly. The deacon (or in his absence, the presiding minister) may invite the assembly to exchange their individual sign of peace and unity in both text and gesture. There are no special roles suggested for cantor or choir during the Rite of Peace.

The Rite of Peace as presently celebrated involves three elements: (1) In a formal dialogue, the presiding ordained minister wishes the peace of Christ to the assembly and the assembly responds "And also with you" in unison, (2) a deacon or the presiding minister may invite the assembly to both verbalize and offer a gesture of peace and love among themselves, (3) the presiding minister offers such a gesture and text to the deacon or server as the assembly engages the rite. *MR1970/1975* does not suggest that the presiding minister leave the altar area to exchange the text/gesture with assembly-members (although it does not forbid such an action), nor does it suggest that the assembly wait to offer their text/gesture until the sign has been "brought" to them from the altar. Notice that (2), not (3), is optional: *pro opportunitate* the deacon or presiding minister may omit *inviting* the assembly to exchange a sign of peace, but the sign of peace is *always* to be exchanged among the faithful as part of the communion rites at every Eucharist.

The formal dialogue between presiding ordained minister and the assembly would normally be spoken, although on some solemn occasions it might be sung recto tono or to a simple chant. The diaconal directive instructing the assembly to exchange a sign of peace would be spoken, as would the texts spoken among the assembly-members.

## 3. Fraction Rite

"During the breaking of the bread and the commingling, the *Agnus Dei* is as a rule sung by the choir or cantor with the congregation responding; otherwise it is recited aloud. This invocation may be repeated as often as necessary to accompany the breaking of the bread. The final reprise concludes with the words, *grant us peace*" (*IGMR* 56c, e).

"To the second degree of solemnity for the sung Mass belongs the . . . *Agnus Dei* . . .

"Because it accompanies the breaking of the bread, the *Agnus Dei* may be repeated as often as necessary, especially in concelebrations and it is appropriate as well for the congregation to have a part in it, at least by singing the final *Grant us peace*" (*MuS* 29, 34).

The function of the Fraction Rite is to prepare the consecrated elements for individual reception. Since the reformed eucharistic rites direct that the faithful receive communion, as far as possible, from bread and wine consecrated at that Mass, the breaking of the eucharistic bread and the pouring out of the consecrated wine into individual chalices may take some time, especially during Sunday Mass. The chant that specifies the meaning of these actions is the litany "Lamb of God."

The breaking of the eucharistic bread and pouring out of the consecrated wine may be done by the presiding minister, deacon, and/or eucharistic ministers. The chant is sung by cantor or choir and assembly in call/response format. The choir may also support the congregational singing with vocal harmonies.

Although the *MR1975* prints a three-fold form of the *Agnus Dei* ("Lamb of God, you take away the sins of the world:" followed by "have mercy on us" twice and concluded by "grant us peace"), it also notes that the invocations may be repeated as many times as is necessary to accompany the actions of the Fraction Rite. Some musical settings offer other invocations in addition to "Lamb of God" (e.g., "Prince of Peace," "Bread of Life," "Paschal Cup") and/or other tropes in addition to "you take away the sins of the world" ("you call us to the banquet of life," "you suffered for the life of the world," "you give yourself in love to us all"). It is important that the final cue be clearly marked musically and/or textually so that the assembly knows it should sing "grant us peace" to conclude the chant.

### 4. Communion Music

"During the priest's and the faithful's reception of the sacrament the communion song is sung. Its function is to express outwardly the communicants' union in spirit by means of the unity of their voices, to give evidence of joy of heart, and to make the procession to receive Christ's body more fully an act of community. The song begins when the priest takes communion, and continues for as long as seems appropriate while the faithful receive Christ's body. But the communion song should be ended in good time whenever there is to be a hymn after communion.

"An antiphon from the *Graduale Romanum* may also be used, with or without the psalm, or an antiphon with psalm from *The Simple Gradual* or another suitable song approved by the conference of bishops. It is sung by the choir alone or by the choir or cantor with the congregation. . . .

"After communion, the priest and people may spend some time in silent prayer. If desired, a hymn, psalm, or other song of praise may be sung by the entire congregation" (*IGMR* 56i, j).

"To the third degree of solemnity for sung Mass belong . . . songs . . . for communion. . . .

"In some places there is the lawful practice, occasionally confirmed by indult, of substituting other songs for the . . . communion chants in the *Graduale*. At the discretion of the competent territorial authority this practice may be kept, on condition that the songs substituted fit in with those parts of the Mass, the feast, of the liturgical season. The texts of such songs must also have the approval of the same territorial authority. . . .

"Any one of the parts of the Proper or the Ordinary in a low Mass may be sung. Sometimes it is even quite appropriate to have other songs . . . at the communion. . . . It is not enough for these songs to be 'eucharistic' in some way; they must be in keeping with the parts of the Mass and with the feast or liturgical season" (*MuS* 31a, 32, 36).

"Everything should be done so that the children who are properly disposed and who have already been admitted to the eucharist may go to the holy table calmly and with recollection and thus take part fully in the eucharistic mystery; if possible, there should be singing, suited to the children, during the communion procession" (*DMP* 54).

One should distinguish *Communion processional* music from *post-Communion thanksgiving* music. The first is music that accompanies the motion of communicants to and from their Communion stations; the function of this processional music is to facilitate their movement in good order, to specify the meaning of their action as Holy Communion, and to connect the experience of communing in consecrated bread and wine with the particular facet of the paschal mystery being celebrated at the liturgy. The second is music made or listened to by the assembly in common as a means of expressing their thanksgiving for the gift of Communion, articulating their united adoration of their eucharistic Lord, and prolonging their communion with one another in Christ.

If the *antiphona ad communionem* from the *Graduale Romanum* or the *Graduale Simplex* is chosen as communion processional music, it will most probably be sung by cantor(s) and choir without congregational participation as we have noted above. Litanies and psalms or songs with refrains would involve the assembly on the responses and cantors and/or choir on the verses. No particular musical roles are assigned for presiding minister or deacon during the communion processional, since it is presumed that they will be ministering Holy Communion. Similarly, the Roman documents neither mandate nor forbid solo instrumental music during and/or after Communion.

Metrical hymns that involve assembly-members carrying hymnbooks during the Communion procession are *not* recommended since the communicants should have their hands free to receive the consecrated bread and to accept the chalice (if they so choose). Mantras, litanies, or verse/refrain songs with short, memorable responses make better Communion processionals. Any music chosen for the procession should be "open-ended" so that it may coordinate with the actual length of the communal motion. Instrumental or choral music during the procession might also be appropriate although the Roman documents do not specify these options.

Music after Communion may involve litany-, psalm-, or hymn-singing. The Roman documents neither suggest nor forbid choral or individual singing in the time after Communion. Instrumental music after Communion may also support communal meditation and thanksgiving.

*5. Prayer After Communion*

"To the first degree of solemnity in the sung Mass belongs: . . . the prayer after communion" (*MuS* 29c).

The function of the Prayer after Communion is to bring the Communion rite to a conclusion. This presidential prayer normally petitions God to extend the fruits of Holy Communion into the on-going lives of the communicants.

Like the other two minor presidential prayers (Opening Prayer, Prayer over the Gifts), the Prayer after Communion is prayed by the presiding minister in the name of the assembly and the assembly as a whole signifies its assent through its vocal "Amen" at the conclusion of the prayer. No special roles are indicated for deacon, cantor, or choir.

As with the Opening Prayer and the Prayer over the Gifts, the Prayer after Communion comprises four elements: (1) the presiding minister calls for the assembly to pray in silence, (2) the assembly prays in silence, (3) the presiding minister recites the prayer over the gifts, and (4) the assembly concludes the prayer with "Amen." As we have noted before, these texts would normally be spoken, but in circumstances where the other presidential prayers are chanted, it would be appropriate to chant the Prayer after Communion as well.

## VI. MUSICAL ELEMENTS IN THE CONCLUDING RITES

### 1. Greeting and Blessing

Query: "In the Instruction on music in the liturgy no. 29 c, do the dismissal formularies to be sung include the priest's blessing?"

Reply: "According to the recently reformed rite the final dismissal of the Mass consists of the greeting of the congregation, the blessing, and the dismissal. According to the rubrics presently in force, which reserve the singing of the blessing to a bishop, the greeting would be sung, the blessing recited, and the dismissal also sung. The incongruity of such a procedure, however, is obvious — the most important element, the blessing, would have the least solemnity. . . . Therefore in view of the new arrangement of the elements of the rite of concluding the Mass, it seems proper in the interest of uniformity for a priest also to sing the blessing at a sung Mass. . . ."[13]

The function of the greeting is to indicate that a new liturgical unit has begun (similar to its function in the Introductory Rites and before

---

[13] *Not* 3 [1967] 300, no. 105.

the Preface of the Eucharistic Prayer). The blessing serves as a commissioning of the assembly: God is invoked to empower the baptized to live out in their daily lives the implications of the Christian faith they have celebrated in Eucharist.

The presiding minister greets and blesses the assembly in his role as mediating spokesperson for both the assembly to God and God to the assembly. The deacon cues the assembly's common action. The assembly verbally expresses its acceptance of the blessing-commission by inclining their heads or bowing and reciting or singing "Amen."

The blessing can take one of three formats: (1) In the simple form, the presiding minister blesses the people with a trinitarian formula to which the people respond "Amen." (2) In the solemn blessing form, the deacon (or in his absence, the presider) calls for the assembly to bow their heads; the priest, with hands extended over the group, normally prays three benedictions addressed to the assembly and concludes with the trinitarian formula, to each of which the congregation responds "Amen." (3) In the "prayer over the people" format, the deacon likewise calls for the assembly to bow; however, the priest prays a single collect-style oration normally addressed to the Father and concludes with the trinitarian formula, to both of which the assembly responds "Amen."

The diaconal directive as a motion-cue would normally be spoken rather than sung. The solemn benedictions or prayer over the people could be distinguished from the trinitarian blessing by singing one and reciting the other.

### 2. Dismissal

"To the first degree of solemnity for the sung Mass belongs: . . . the final dismissal" (*MuS* 29c).

The dismissal is the formal conclusion of the liturgical assembly. If another liturgical function is to follow immediately the dismissal is omitted.

Historically it was the deacon's responsibility in the Roman Rite to dismiss the liturgical assembly. His formula *Ite, missa est* signified that the liturgical gathering was concluded and the people were free to go. Many vernacular translations of *MR1975* supplement the juridical formula with missionary themes: e.g., "Go in peace to love and serve the Lord." In the absence of a deacon, the presiding presbyter offers the dismissal to which the assembly responds "Thanks be to God."

Like the liturgical greetings, normally in vernacular celebration the dismissal would be recited rather than chanted. However solemn seasons could be emphasized by the chanting of the dismissal formula, especially during Eastertide when "Alleluia" could be appended to both the dismissal and its response.

### 3. Concluding Music

While the Roman rite developed antiphons to accompany the procession of the ministers at the beginning of the Eucharist, there is no evidence for a corresponding musical element to cover their exit. Thus any concluding music is not regulated by universal Roman liturgical norms.

The functions of the concluding music include: (1) accompanying the movement of the ministers and assembly from the assembly-space, (2) providing a festive aural environment to conclude the ritual action, and (3) possibly inviting the assembly to confirm in song their acceptance of the commission proffered in the solemn blessing or prayer over the people.

No particular roles are indicated in the liturgical books for concluding music. If concluding music is played it may involve instrumentalists, choir, and/or assembly. It does not seem an appropriate time for solo cantorial singing.

Three patterns for the concluding music seem to have developed in vernacular celebrations. (1) Following the Roman rite liturgical books, in the first pattern no further music is played after the (diaconal) dismissal. The ministers and people leave the assembly-space in silence. While this is faithful to the Roman liturgical books, some communities find such a conclusion to the Eucharist too abrupt. (2) The second pattern is to play instrumental music or to sing a choir anthem as a "recessional" as the ministers and people disperse. The assembly is not invited to join vocally in the music-making. Such a pattern provides a festive conclusion to the Eucharist without calling for further participation from the assembly. (3) The third pattern is to ask the assembly to remain for the singing of a final hymn. Some of the same tensions that we have listed above in reference to the entrance song could be in evidence in such a practice. While some communities have a long-standing custom of vigorous final hymn-singing, many will leave during the singing of a final hymn in response to the (diaconal) dismissal.


## Bibliography

1. GENERAL

Deiss, L. *Spirit and Song of the New Liturgy.* Cincinnati, 1970.

Keifer, R. *To Give Thanks and Praise: General Instruction of the Roman Missal with Commentary for Musicians and Priests.* Washington, 1980.


2. INTRODUCTORY RITES

Francis, M. "Uncluttering the Eucharistic Vestibule: The Entrance Rites Through Time." *Liturgical Ministry* 3 (Winter, 1994) 1–12.

Hannon, K. "Gathering Rites." *The New Dictionary of Sacramental Worship,* 491–4. Ed. P. Fink. Collegeville, Minn. 1990.

Witczak, M. "The Introductory Rites: Threshold of the Sacred, Entry into Community, or Pastoral Problem?" *Liturgical Ministry* 3 (Winter, 1994) 22–27.


3. LITURGY OF THE WORD

Ashworth, H. "The Prayer of the Faithful." *Liturgy* 37 (July 1968) 67–72.

Keifer, R. *To Hear and Proclaim: Introduction to the Lectionary for Mass with Commentary for Musicians and Priests.* Washington, 1983.


4. LITURGY OF THE EUCHARIST

Dallen, J. "The Congregation's Share in the Eucharistic Prayer." *Wor* 52 (July 1978) 329–41.

Foley, E., and M. McGann. *Music and the Eucharistic Prayer.* American Essays in Liturgy 8. Washington, 1988.

Gelineau, J. *The Eucharistic Prayer: Praise of the Whole Assembly. A Search for a Celebratory "Model" for "Making Eucharist Together."* Washington, 1985.

Joncas, M. *Hymnum tuae gloriae canimus: Toward an Analysis of the Vocal Expression of the Eucharistic Prayer in the Roman Rite: Tradition, Principles, Method.* Rome, 1991.

_____. "The Assembly's 'Ownership' of the Eucharistic Prayer: Why and How." *Today's Liturgy* 16/3 (May–September 1994) 5–11.

Kay, M., ed. *It Is Your Mystery: A Guide to the Communion Rite.* Washington, 1977.

Keifer, R. "Preparation of the Altar or Offertory?" *Wor* 48 (August–September 1974) 595–600.

Marchal, M. "Peccatores ac Famuli: The Roman Preparation of the Gifts and Altar Reconsidered." *SL* 16 (1986–1987) 73–92.

McManus, F. R. "The Roman Order of Mass from 1964 to 1969: The Preparation of the Gifts." *Shaping English Liturgy: Studies in Honor of Archbishop Denis Hurley*, 107–38. Washington, 1990.

Schneiders, M. "Acclamations in the Eucharistic Prayer." In *Omnes Circumadstantes: Contributions Toward a History of the Role of the People in the Liturgy*, 78–100. Kampen, 1990.

Senn, F., ed. *New Eucharistic Prayers: An Ecumenical Study of Their Development and Structure.* New York and Mahway, N.J., 1987.

Smolarski, D. *Eucharistia: A Study of the Eucharistic Prayer.* New York and Ramsey, N.J., 1982.

5. CONCLUDING RITES

Krosnicki, T. "New Blessings in the Missal of Paul VI." *Wor* 45 (April 1971) 199–205.

6. MUSICAL ISSUES

Bauman, W. *The Ministry of Music: A Guide for the Practicing Church Musician.* 2nd ed. Washington, 1979.

Duchesneau, C., and M. Veuthey. *Music and Liturgy: The Universa Laus Document and Commentary.* Washington, 1992.

*The Milwaukee Symposia for Church Composers; A Ten-Year Report.* Washington, 1992.

Sotak, D. *Handbook for Cantors.* Chicago, 1988.

[United States] Bishops' Committee on the Liturgy. *Music in Catholic Worship.* Washington, 1972; rev. ed. 1983.

[United States] Bishops' Committee on the Liturgy. *Liturgical Music Today.* Washington, 1982.

Gabriel Ramis

**10**

# The Eucharistic Celebration in the Non-Roman West

There is no doubt that the spirit of each liturgy has developed from its *Ordo Missae*, which is the culmination of all liturgical-sacramental celebration. From it unique celebrations have been formed, each one different from the others. But although we can highlight the distinctive characteristics of the *Ordo Missae* of each of the Western liturgies, we cannot forget the fidelity of each to the fundamental elements of the celebration that are common to all liturgies: the proclamation of the Word of God, the presentation of the gifts, the eucharistic anaphora, the rite of peace, and the distribution of communion. The uniqueness of the *Ordo Missae* of the different liturgies comes from the distinct distribution and organization of each one of these elements.

A study of the *Ordo Missae* of each of the Western liturgies will illustrate for us the eucharistic celebrations of the Christian West.

AFRICAN LITURGY

Although we do not have any documentation of the African liturgy, we still can form through the works of Cyprian, Optatus of Milevis, and above all those of Augustine, an *Ordo Missae* that most certainly corresponds to the *Ordo Missae* of the fourth-century African liturgy.

Saxer, Cabrol, Bishop, Gamber, Casati, and Gutierrez have outlined an *Ordo Missae* beginning with the works of Cyprian, Optatus of Milevis, and Augustine. All these hypotheses are coherent, and from them we are able to present the African *Ordo Missae*.

Entrance procession with singing of a psalm[1]
Greeting of the celebrant[2]
Old Testament reading
Psalm
Reading of the New Testament Apostle
Gospel reading
Reading of the passion of the martyr
Alleluia
Homily
Dismissal of the catechumens[3]
Prayer of the faithful
Offertory psalm (offertory)
Diptychs
Prayer *post nomina*
Rite of peace[4]
Eucharistic anaphora
Breaking of the bread[5]

[1] Cabrol and Gamber hypothetically propose this beginning of the Mass.

[2] All the authors except Cabrol think that the Mass begins with a greeting from the celebrant: we can deduce this initial greeting even in the work of Optatus of Milevis.

[3] Some authors, like Bishop and Gamber, think that the psalm was recited after the apostolic reading, not after the prophetic reading, because the prophetic, or Old Testament reading, was not always read. From Optatus of Milevis we cannot prove the existence of a psalm. However, Cyprian hints of its existence. In this first part of the Mass we must highlight the reading of the passion of the martyr. Cabrol notes this possibility beginning with the Council of Carthage III; according to the outline of Optatus, this reading takes place after the gospel. Cabrol and Bishop are the only authors who do not mention the homily. The following parts of the Mass are the most difficult to order.

[4] All the authors except Cabrol consider the prayer of the faithful. Bishop proposes two hypotheses for this part of the Ordinary of the Mass. In the first he considers the offertory with its psalm after the prayer *Post nomina;* in the second he thinks that the prayer *Post nomina* is the prayer *Super oblata.*

| diptychs | offertory with psalm prayer |
| *Post nomina* | diptychs |
| offertory with psalm | prayer *Post nomina* = prayer *Super oblata* |

According to Saxer, following Cyprian, the kiss of peace took place before offertory, whereas the other authors place it after the antiphon. Neither Cabrol nor Casati considers the prayer *Post nomina.* Gamber proposes that the offertory comes after the prayer of the faithful.

[5] Cabrol does not consider the breaking of the bread, and Casati presents it as a possibility.

Lord's Prayer
Rite of peace
Communion with Psalm 33
Prayer of thanksgiving

## AMBROSIAN LITURGY

We have various indications of the *Ordo Missae* of the Ambrosian liturgy. The first and oldest is that of St. Ambrose, although he only refers to the Liturgy of the Word; the last and most recent is that of the Ambrosian Missal of 1981.

*1. The Testimony of St. Ambrose*
Ambrose tells us that in the eucharistic celebration there are three readings: "First the Prophet is read, then the Apostle, and finally the Gospel."[6]

The Canon of the Mass must certainly be that of *De sacramentis*, since this is the one that Ambrose commented on, and it corresponds to the oldest form of the Roman Canon.

During the offertory, the gifts placed upon the altar are covered with a veil called sindon; from this probably comes the title *Super sindonem* for the prayer that is recited at the offertory.

*2. The* Ordo Missae *of Beroldus*
The *Ordo Missae* that Beroldus describes for us corresponds to the Mass celebrated by the bishop, but he does not describe it completely, ending at the recitation of the Creed.

Procession from the sacristy to the altar
The subdeacons first make an incensation before the altar in the form of a cross.
The archbishop makes his confession.
The director of the schola begins the *Ingressa*.[7]
After the *Ingressa*, the archbishop or priest says: *Dominus vobiscum*.
The *Gloria in excelsis* follows.
The *Kyrie* (three times)
Prayer over the people
The lector for the week ascends the pulpit and reads the lesson, having received the archbishop's blessing.

---

[6] Ambrose, *In Psalmum CXVIII* 17, 10 (PL 15, 1448).
[7] As its name indicates, the *Ingressa* is the song that accompanies the entrance procession, although some think that it refers to an introductory song to the readings.

After the lesson, a boy from the schola ascends the pulpit to sing the
Psalmellus.[8]

The subdeacon reads the epistle from the pulpit.

The notary sings the *Alleluia* in the pulpit. After the verse, the same
notary says *Alleluia*; then the director of the schola sings melodies
with the boys' choir.

The deacon, with the subdeacons and incense, goes in procession to
the pulpit. The canon deacon says at the side of the altar: *Parcite
fabulis.* Two attendants say in an elevated voice: *Silentium habete.*
The deacon bows before the archbishop for the blessing. Then he
begins to read the gospel.

After the gospel, if there are any feasts in the following week, the
deacon announces them from the pulpit.

The deacon goes up to the altar and kisses it.

Meanwhile, the archbishop or priest says: *Dominus vobiscum,* and the
choir says the *Kyrie* three times.

The chief lector begins the antiphon after the gospel at once.

The archbishop or priest returns before the altar and again greets it;
the deacon says: *Pacem habete,* and the choir responds: *Ad te
Domine.*

Then the archbishop or the priest and the deacon kiss the altar; he
greets it again and says the prayer over the sindon.[9]

The bread and wine are prepared and offered to the archbishop by
the deacon.

Then the director of the schola sings the offertory song.

The offering of the gifts?

The washing of hands

Private prayers for the offering of the chalice

Incensation of the altar

Recitation of the Creed

With these words the description of the Mass celebration ends:
"The Mass is completed in order, with the director of the schola, with
the boys' choir, singing the office to the end."[10]

[8] This is the song between readings.

[9] According to some authors, this should be the concluding prayer of the
prayer of the faithful.

[10] M. Magistretti, ed., *Beroldus sive Ecclesiae Ambrosianae Mediolanensis Kalendar-
ium et Ordines* (Milan, 1894) 46–53.

248

3. *The* Expositio Missae Canonicae
A manuscript of the eleventh century from the University of Mont-
pellier offers us an outline of the Ambrosian *Ordo Missae.*

If anyone is a catechumen, let him leave.
*Ingressa* (Introit)
*Gloria in excelsis*
Antiphon
Old Testament reading
Epistle
Alleluia
Gospel
Prayer over the people
Prayer over the sindon
Prayer over the gifts
Eucharistic Anaphora
 Dialogue
 Preface
 Canon
Lord's Prayer
Embolism *(Libera nos quaesumus)*
Kiss of peace
Deacon: *"Offerte vobis pacem."*
Final prayer[11]

4. *The* Ordo Missae *of the Ambrosian Missal of 1981*
Following the principles of the liturgical reform brought about by
Vatican Council II and in accordance with *Sacrosanctum Concilium*
(no. 4), the Church of Milan revised its liturgical books. In 1981 the
new Ambrosian Missal was published, and in it was proposed the
following *Ordo Missae:*

Opening Rites
 *Ingressa*
 Incensation *(pro opportunitate)*
 *In nomine Patris et Filii . . .*
 Greeting
 Penitential act

[11] A. Wilmart, "Une exposition de la messe ambrosienne," *JLw* 2 (1922) 47–67.

*Gloria*
Prayer over the people

Liturgy of the Word
    Blessing of the lector
    First reading: Old Testament
    (Reading of a martyr's passion on his or her feast)
    Second reading: Acts of the Apostles, Letters of the Apostles
    Alleluia
    Blessing of the deacon
    Gospel (incensed *pro opportunitate*)
    Antiphon after the gospel (while this antiphon is being sung, the
        altar is prepared [corporal, purificator, sacred vessels])
    Prayer of the faithful
    Conclusion of the prayer of the faithful
    Concluding prayer

Liturgy of the Eucharist
Rite of peace *(pro opportunitate)*. This rite can be celebrated before
    communion.
Offering of bread and wine or other gifts by the faithful
The priest offers the bread and wine.
Incensation of the altar and the gifts *(pro opportunitate)*
Washing of hands
Creed
Eucharistic Prayer
    a) Roman Canon (Ambrosian version)
    b) Eucharistic Prayer II (from Roman Missal)
    c) Eucharistic Prayer III (from Roman Missal)
    d) Eucharistic Prayer IV (from Roman Missal)
    e) Eucharistic Prayer V (Ambrosian)[12]
    f) Eucharistic Prayer VI (Ambrosian)
Communion Rite
    Breaking of the bread while the *confractorium* is sung[13]

[12] The fifth and sixth prayers are old Ambrosian Eucharistic Prayers that have
been recovered. They are different from the Roman-Ambrosian Canon, the Canon
of the De sacramentis.

[13] This is the song that accompanies the rite of the breaking of the bread.

Lord's Prayer
Prayer before the sign of peace
*Pax et communicatio Domini nostri Iesu Christi sit semper vobiscum.*
(Rite of peace *pro opportunitate*)
Communion
While Holy Communion is being distributed, the *Transitorium*[14] is
 sung.
Prayer after Communion

Concluding Rite
 *Dominus vobiscum.* ℟. *Et cum spiritu tuo.*
 *Kyrie* (three times)
 Blessing
 Dismissal[15]

## GALLICAN LITURGY
The studies of the Gallican rite (Thibaut, Porter, Cabrol and Pinell)
have proposed the reconstruction of an *Ordo Missae* according to the
information they acquired from various sources. Following these authors, we propose the reconstruction of the *Ordo Missae.*

Antiphon *ad praelegendum*
The deacon says: *Silentium facite.*
*Dominus sit semper vobiscum.*
Trisagion (Greek and Latin)
*Kyrie* (sung by three boys )
*Benedictus* (called "Prophecy")
Collect after the Benedictus[16]
Old Testament reading from the Prophets[17]

---

[14] This is the song that accompanies the communion of the faithful, as they
come forward to receive it, "in transit" from one part of the church to another.

[15] *Missale Ambrosianum iuxta ritum sanctae Ecclesiae Mediolanensis. Ex decreto
Sacrosancti Oecumenici Concilii Vaticani II instauratum, auctoritate Ioannis Colombo,
Sanctae Romanae Ecclesiae Presbyteri Cardinalis, Archiepiscopi Mediolanensis promulga-
tum* (Milan, 1981).

[16] During Lent the *Benedictus* (prophecy) and the *Collectio post prophetiam* were
omitted, and they were substituted by the hymn *Sanctus Deus Archangelorum.*

[17] During Eastertime the Apocalypse is read and, in memory of the martyrs, the
*passio* (according to Porter) is also read.

Blessings (Psalm?)
Reading from the Letters of the Apostles[18]
Gospel reading[19]
Homily
Prayers of the faithful[20]
Collectio after the prayer
Dismissal of the catechumens and penitents
The deacon says: *Silentium facite.*
Offertory procession[21]
Preface[22]
Collectio
Diptychs[23]
Collectio *Post nomina*[24]
Collectio at the kiss of peace
Kiss of peace

Eucharistic Anaphora
Dialogue
Preface (*Contestatio* or *Immolatio*)[25]
*Sanctus — Benedictus*
*Post-Sanctus*
Missa secreta (Narration of the institution)
*Post secreta* or *Post mysterium*

---

[18] According to Thibaut, during Eastertime either the Acts of the Apostles or the Apocalypse is read. During Lent the historic books of the Old Testament are read. On the solemnities of the martyrs the *passio* is read. Following this, the *Benedictiones* continue, and once they are finished, *pueri intonant: Benedictus qui venit in nomine Domini.* The song of the *Benedictiones* must be a memory of the conversion and baptism of King Clovis.

[19] The gospel is carried in a procession while the Trisagion is sung again; after the gospel reading the *Sanctus* is sung.

[20] These prayers are done while kneeling.

[21] During the procession, the *sonus* is sung and ends with the singing of the *Alleluia*. The offerings are covered with a veil.

[22] Thibaut thinks that the form *praefatio Missae* is the prayer of the veil.

[23] In the moment in which the names of the dead are recited, the veil covering the offerings is removed (Thibaut).

[24] According to Porter, this should be the offertory prayer.

[25] This is the form in which the eucharistic anaphora begins, and it ends with the recitation of the *Sanctus*. It corresponds to the Hispanic *Illatio* and to the Roman *Praefatio*.

Breaking of the bread[26]
Lord's Prayer
Blessing of the people
The deacon invites the communicants
Antiphon *ad accedentes* (Psalm 33)[27]
Post-Communion (thanksgiving prayer)
Collectio
Completion of the Mass[28]

## HISPANIC LITURGY

*1. The* Ordo Missae *of Isidore*
In his work *De ecclesiasticis officiis*, St. Isidore describes and comments on the *Ordo Missae*. In this treatise Isidore only comments on the forms of the Eucharistic Prayer in a general manner, and he does not write anything at all about the first part of the Mass, the proclamation of the Word of God.

The first of these, the Prayer of Admonition, is addressed to the people.
*Post nomina.* The second invocation to God is that he mercifully accept the prayers of the faithful and their offerings.
The third prayer is recited for those who are offering or for the faithful deceased.
*Ad pacem.* The fourth prayer is offered after this for the kiss of peace.
The fifth is the *illatio* offered at the sanctification of the oblation . . . and *Hosanna in excelsis* is sung.

---

[26] The pieces are arranged in the form of a cross *Antiphona ad confractionem*.

[27] This antiphon is called *trecanum*, and it accompanies the communion of the faithful. As its name indicates, it is sung while the faithful draw near *(accedentes)* to receive Communion. The name *trecanum* refers to the number of the psalm that is sung, Psalm 33.

[28] J-B. Thibaut, *L'ancienne liturgie gallicane* (Paris, 1929) 23–75. Thibaut comments on the Gallican Mass following the *Expositio brevis antiquae liturgiae gallicanae in duas epistolas digesta* of Germain of Paris (PL 72:83–98), but this work comes after Germain. It is from the seventeenth century, and although it describes the Gallican liturgy for us, we cannot ignore the influence of Visigothic and Byzantine elements in the rite from the time it was written. F. Cabrol, "Les origines de la liturgie gallicane," *RHE* 26 (1930) 951–62; W-S. Porter, *The Gallican Rite* (London, 1958).

*Post sanctus — post pridie.* Then the sixth prayer follows the confection of the sacrament.

*Pater noster.* The last of these is the prayer with which our Lord taught his disciples to pray.[29]

## 2. The Ordo Missae *from Liturgical Sources*

Besides our information from Isidore, liturgical sources naturally give us the complete *Ordo Missae*, but always together with a Mass formulary. The following is the *Ordo Missae* that has been formed from these sources.

*Praelegendum*[30]
*Gloria in excelsis* (on Sundays and feasts)
Trisagion (on solemnities)
Prayer after the *Gloria*[31]

Old Testament
Passion of martyrs[32]
Blessings[33]
*Psallendum*[34]
*Clamor*[35]
The Apostle
Gospel[36]

---

[29] Isidore, *De ecclesiasticis officiis,* 15 (PL 83:752–53).

[30] Etymologically, it is sung before the readings, in other words, as an entrance song, the same as the Ambrosian *Ingressa*.

[31] According to tradition B, this introductory part is omitted on weekdays and the Sundays of Lent. Tradition A substitutes this part with three antiphons on weekdays and the Sundays of Lent.

[32] After the prophecy, on the feast of the martyrs the last part of the *passio* is read; all of the other part already has been read at Matins.

[33] The song of the three youth is in the third chapter of the Book of Daniel is called *Benedictiones*. The *Benedictiones* are also sung in the Gallican liturgy. They are said only on Sundays and on the feasts of the martyrs.

[34] This is the song between readings that corresponds to the Ambrosian *Psalmellus*. According to tradition A, the *Psallendum* is substituted for another song called *threni* in some feasts during Lent; in tradition B, it is substituted on all the feasts of Lent. They are inspired songs in the book of the prophet Jeremiah, also called *threni*.

[35] This is a verse that is sung in a very solemn manner, united to the *Psallendum* on the solemnities.

[36] For the gospel reading a procession is done with candles, the cross, and incense; in the Easter Vigil the gospel is read by the bishop.

Homily
*Laudes*[37]
Prayers of the faithful [38]
Sacrifice (offertory song)[39]

Prayer of admonition
Diptych for the Church
Diptych for the ministers of the Church, the saints, sometimes for
  those offering, and for the dead
Prayer *Post nomina*
Prayer before the kiss of peace
Blessing at the kiss of peace
Deacon's admonition
Antiphon at the kiss of peace

*Illatio*[40]
Introductory dialogue
*Sanctus*
*Post Sanctus*
Narration of the institution[41]
*Post pridie*
Doxology

Song at the breaking of the bread — *confractio*
Profession of faith (according to tradition B, the profession of faith
  takes place before the breaking of the bread)
Introduction to the Lord's Prayer
The Lord's Prayer
Embolism
*Sancta sanctis*, commingling
Song at the commingling (on feasts)

---

[37] During the time of Lent the verse is sung without the *Alleluia.*

[38] The *preces* are only said during Lent.

[39] This is the song that accompanies the offering of the gifts.

[40] This is the form in which the eucharistic anaphora begins, concluding with the singing of the *Sanctus;* it corresponds to the Gallican *Contestatio* or *Immolatio missae* and to the Roman Preface.

[41] The text is taken primarily from 1 Cor 11:23-26. The people respond *Amen* to the words of the blessing of the bread and chalice. At the end all proclaim: *Sic credimus, Domine Iesu.*

Deacon's admonition
Blessing
Diaconal admonition for the order of Communion
*Ad accedentes* (Communion song)
Antiphon after Communion
Announcement of feasts
Dismissal by the deacon[42]

Several points must be noted about the *Ordo Missae* reproduced together with the formulary of the Mass of St. James after the Saturday of the octave of Easter: the Mass is preceded by the preparation of the priest in the sacristy, which consists of him washing his hands and reciting prayers while putting on his vestments; the paten and chalice are prepared when the priest reaches the altar, reciting a series of long prayers that ends with the recitation of the *Salve*. After the song of the *sacrificium*, he turns to offer the paten and chalice while reciting prayers; another prayer is recited before the *oratio admonitionis*. Even the narration of the institution is united to the prayer *Adesto*, in which Christ is asked to make himself present in order to bless the *offering*.

It is clear that all these prayers of apology by the priest are an integral part of the rite and that they have been a part of the rite since the Middle Ages, as has occurred in the Roman liturgy.

3. *The* Ordo Missae *in the* Missale Hispanico-Mozarabicum
The Hispanic rite also has gone through the reformation of the Mass, as did the Ambrosian, according to the norms and directives of Vatican Council II, under the auspices of the cardinal archbishop of Toledo, Marcelo González Martin.

The following is the *Ordo Missae* of the new Hispanic-Mozarabic Missal.

Opening Rites
*Praelegendum*
*Gloria*

---

[42] Sources offer us the *Ordo Missae* in the *Missa Omnimoda* of the LOE 477–528; in the formulary of the first Sunday of Advent and in the formulary of the Mass after the Saturday of the octave of Easter, which is that of St. James in the Missal of Cisneros, in the *Missale Mixtum* and in the Missal of Lorenzana, and in one edition of 1885 for the Mozarabic chapel of the Cathedral of Toledo, which contains only the Ordinary of the *Expositio Missae*.

256

Trisagion
Prayer after the *Gloria*
(All these are omitted on weekdays of the entire year and on the
Sundays of Lent.)

Liturgy of the Word
Greeting: *Dominus sit semper vobiscum.*
Old Testament reading
*Psallendum*
Passion of the martyr
Blessings
Reading from the Apostle
Gospel
*Laudes*

Preparation of the Gifts
*Sacrificium* (offertory song)

Solemn Intercessions
Prayer of admonition
Prayer *Post nomina*

Sign of Peace
Prayer before the sign of peace
Song at the sign of peace
Sign of peace

Eucharistic Prayer
Introductory dialogue
*Illatio*
*Sanctus*
Post *Sanctus*
Narration of the institution
Prayer *Post pridie*
Concluding doxology

Communion Rite
Creed
Song at the breaking of the bread
Breaking of the bread into nine parts
Introduction to the Lord's Prayer
Lord's Prayer

*Sancta sanctis*
Commingling
Blessing
Song *ad accedentes*
Communion
Antiphon after Communion
*Completuria*[43]

## CELTIC LITURGY

The Stowe Missal presents us with an *Ordo Missae* of a very Roman-ized structure. Its features are the additions that were made to the Ordinary: the prayers in the first part of the Mass, those added to the Roman Canon, the breaking of the bread, with the canticle that takes place before the Our Father, and the structure of the rite of peace that resembles the Hispanic or Gallican structure.

(Litany) Prayer
*Gloria in excelsis*
Epistle, Prayer
Psalm, Prayer
Alleluia, Prayer
Litany of St. Martin,[44] Prayer, *Dirigatur*
Gospel, Prayer
Creed
Offertory song
Prayer over the gifts
Preface — *Sanctus*
Roman Canon (with many interpolations: litanies, list of saints,
    prayer of St. Ambrose)
Song at the breaking of the bread, the breaking of the bread
Lord's Prayer, embolism
Blessing at the sign of peace, song at the sign of peace
Song at the commingling, commingling
Song at Communion, Communion
Prayer of thanksgiving[45]

---

[43] *Missale Hispanico-Mozarabicum* (Spanish Episcopal Conference, Archbishopric of Toledo, 1991–1995) 61–88.

[44] This is the so-called *Deprecatio Sancti Martini*, consisting of some litanic prayers, similar to the prayer of the faithful.

[45] G-F. Wagner, ed., *The Stowe Missal*, HBS 32 (London, 1920) 3–19.

## CONCLUSION

From this close study of these Mass Ordinaries we are able to form the following conclusions:

1. There is a great similarity, or even identity, between the structure and content of the Ordinaries of the Gallican Mass and the Hispanic Mass, regardless of some elements introduced later in the Hispanic that were not of the same origin. In the Ordinary we should highlight the composition of the eucharistic anaphora, consisting of three variable pieces, in addition to the song of the *Sanctus* and the narration of the institution, which are invariable. The African anaphora probably had the same structure.

This leaves us with the problem of the origin of these two liturgies and their mutual relation. We believe that there is a primitive archetype in the development of both liturgies. The Ambrosian liturgy has followed another evolution, still having, nevertheless, many characteristics in common with the others.

2. All the Western liturgies share some characteristic and unique features:

a) Three readings in the celebration of the Mass: prophecy, or Old Testament reading; apostolic, or New Testament reading; and finally, the gospel reading.

b) The reading of the conclusion of the *passio* of the martyr whose feast is celebrated followed by the song of the *Benedictiones,* or song of the three youths. This reading was done after the first reading, the prophetic. In the *Ordo Missae* of Africa it is difficult to know the exact place of its proclamation.

c) The singing of the *Alleluia* after the gospel, not before, except in the Ambrosian liturgy.

d) The reciting of the diptychs before the eucharistic anaphora, without being a part of it, except in the Ambrosian liturgy.

e) The rite of peace before reciting the eucharistic anaphora.

In the Ambrosian liturgy, the rite of peace also takes place before the recitation of the eucharistic anaphora, although in the Missal of 1981 it is allowed to be celebrated after the anaphora but before communion.

In the African liturgy, the authors do not agree on the placement of this rite, although they tend to put it before the eucharistic anaphora.

3. The peculiar literary form and style of the formularies of the Masses, including the eucharistic anaphora in the Gallican and Hispanic liturgies.

The formularies of the Gallican and Hispanic Masses consist of nine forms for each Mass: one form for admonition, two for the diptychs, one for the rite of peace, three for the eucharistic anaphora, one for the introduction to the Our Father, and one form of blessing.

In addition, the style of these prayers should be noted. They employ a broad and exuberant style, usually using a theological and symbolical language, acquiring at times a lyrical tone. This style contrasts obviously with the style and structure of the Roman prayers.

The Ambrosian liturgy followed another evolution, one more similar to the Roman. The structure and style of the prayers are more like the Roman style and structure than like those of the Gallican or Hispanic.

## Bibliography

AFRICAN LITURGY

Casati, G. "La liturgia della messa al tempo di s. Agostino." *Augustinianum* 9 (1969) 484–514.

Dotta, C. "La sinassi eucaristica attraverso le opere di s. Agostino." *A* 6 (1930) 201–24.

Gamber, K. "Ordo Missae Africanae: Der nordafrikanische Messritus zur Zeit des Hl. Augustinus." *Römische Quartalschrift* 64 (1969) 139–53.

Marini, A. *La celebrazione eucaristica presieduta da sant' Agostino: La partecipazione dei fedeli alla liturgia della Parola e al Sacrificio Eucaristico.* Brescia, 1989.


AMBROSIAN LITURGY

Morin, G. "L'origine del canone ambrosiano a proposito di particolarità gallicane nel giovedì e sabato santo." *A* 3 (1927) 75–77.

_____. "Despuis quand un canon fixe a Milan? Restes de ce qu'il a remplacé." *A* 17 (1941) 89–93.

Paredi, A. *I prefazi ambrosiani: Contributo alla storia della liturgia latina.* Milan, 1937.

Triacca, A.-M. *I prefazi ambrosiani del ciclo "De tempore" secondo il "Sacramentarium Bergomense": Avviamento ad uno studio critico-teologico.* Rome, 1970.

____. "Per una migliore ambientazione delle fonti liturgiche ambrosiane-sinassico-eucaristiche (Note metodologiche)." *Fons vivus: Miscellanea liturgica in memoria di Don Eusebio-Maria Vismara*, 163–220. Bibliotheca Theologica Salesiana. Series 1. *Fontes* 6. Zürich, 1971.

____. "Le déroulement de la messe ambrosienne." *L'Eucharistie: Célébrations, rites, piétés*, 339–79. BELS 79. Rome, 1995.

Wilmart, A. "Une exposition de la messe ambrosienne." *JLw* 2 (1922) 47–67.


GALLICAN LITURGY

Frendo, J.-A. *The "post secreta" of the "Missale Gothicum" and the Eucharistic Theology of the Gallican Anaphora*. Rabat-Malta, 1977.

Germain of Paris. "Expositio brevis antiquae liturgiae gallicanae in duas epistolas digesta." PL 72:83–98.

Gros, M. Dels S. "Notes sobre les oractions 'post nomina' i 'collectio sequitur' del sacramentari gallicà München CLM 14429." *RCT* 9 (1984) 103–15.

Mone, F.-G. "Die gallicanische Messe." In *Lateinische und griechische Messe aus dem 2. bis 6. Jhr*, 1–72. Frankfurt am Main, 1850.

Pinell, J. "Legitima eucharistia: Cuestiones sobre la anámnesis y la epíclesis en el antiguo rito galicano." In *Mélanges liturgiques offerts au R. P. Dom Bernard Botte, O.S.B.* Louvain, 1972.


HISPANIC LITURGY

Bergh, T. "La messa mozarabica." *RL* 1–2 (1914–1915; 1915–1916) 14–24, 149–57, 23–26.

Cabrol, F. "Mozarabe (Messe)." *Dictionnaire de théologie catholique* 10:2518–2543. Paris, 1928.

Franquesa, A. "Die mozarabische Messe." *Liturgie und Mönchtum* 26 (1960) 58–70.

Gros, M. Dels S. "El 'ordo missae' de la tradición hispanica A." In *Liturgia y música mozárabes*, 1:45–64. Toledo, 1987.

Hernandez, F.-J. *Rúbricas generales de las misa gótico-mozárabe y el "Omnium offerentium."* Salamanca, 1772.

Pinell, J. "El problema de las dos tradiciones del antiguo rito hispánico: Valoración documental de la tradición B en vistas a una eventual revisión del Ordinario de la misa." *Liturgia y música mozárabes* 1:3–44. Toledo, 1978.

____. "Missale Hispanico-Mozarabicum." *Not* 24 (1988) 670–727.

Ramos, M. *La gran oración eucarística en la antigua misa española*. Granada, 1963.

CELTIC LITURGY

Gougaud, L. "Celtiques, liturgies." *DACL* II/2:2968–3032. Paris, 1910.

Pinell, J. "La liturgia celtica." *Anàmnesis* 2:67–70.

Sheppard, L. C. "Celtic Rite." *New Catholic Encyclopedia* 3:384–85. Washington, 1967.

Nathan D. Mitchell

# 11

# Worship of the Eucharist Outside Mass

Any discussion of the historical evolution of eucharistic worship outside Mass must address two independent — though closely related —
questions: (1) When, why and how did the celebration of the Eucharist emerge as a *distinctive* Christian ritual *detached from* a communal
meal? (2) When, why and how were the eucharistic *species* detached
from their essential connection with the eucharistic *action* of the
Christian assembly? A complete response to these questions would
fill a whole library; our chief concern here will be to sketch some of
the salient historical factors that contributed to the rise of a "cult" of
the Eucharist outside Mass.

## I. FOUNDATIONS

*1. Eucharist: From "Common Meal" to "Independent Rite"*
Virtually all modern New Testament scholars agree that eucharistic
origins are to be sought within the context of a complete communal
meal, one closely linked to Jesus' own historical ministry of table-
fellowship. As the late Norman Perrin argued, this meal provided
Christians with a firm (and renewable) bond between their Easter
faith and Jesus' own life:

"The central feature of the message of Jesus is . . . the challenge of the
forgiveness of sins and the offer of the possibility of a new kind of relationship with God and with one's fellow [men and women]. This
was symbolized by a table-fellowship which celebrated the present
joy and anticipated the future consummation; a table-fellowship of
such joy and gladness that it survived the crucifixion and provided
the focal point for the community life of the earliest Christians . . . ."[1]

[1] *Rediscovering the Teaching of Jesus.* New York, 1967, 107.

This idyllic picture must, however, be tempered by what we know about conflicts within the primitive Christian communities. The situation in Corinth, for example, was especially notorious [see 1 Cor 11:17-34]. There, socioeconomic disparity among the church's members caused disunity to erupt even at celebrations of the Lord's Supper.[2] Moreover, in the interracial communities of large urban centers — such as Antioch — the question of whether Jewish and Gentile Christians could dine together at the same table (eating the same foods off the same utensils) was a very sticky one.[3] There is, then, a decisive difference between the early Christian ideology of eucharistic *unity* (evident in texts such as 1 Cor 10:16) and the factual realities of social stratification and conflict (evident in 1 Cor 11:17-34).

Social pressures of the Corinthian kind may have helped to promote the ritual detachment of eucharistic rite from communal meal. It is even possible that such a movement had begun as early as the 50s, when Paul was writing his letters. In Corinthians, for instance, Paul (the earliest Christian writer to quote the tradition of Jesus' eucharistic words and deeds) tackled a pastoral problem that clearly arose from the "common meal" tradition. Astonishingly, however, the eucharistic theology he outlined in response *does not require* the continuance of that tradition for its logic, intelligibility, and coherence. Paul's argument is derived *not* from the ideology of meals in the late-antique world (an assumption many scholars make) but from distinctively Christian insights that are ecclesiological and christological, soteriological and sacramental. Thus, Paul argued that "the body of Christ" is not only *on* the table (identified with the bread and cup / christological), but also *at* the table (identified as the assembled church / ecclesiological). Moreover, he insisted that *eucharistic* dining embodies and enacts (*sacramental* emphasis) the central fact of Christian faith — the saving "death of the Lord until he comes" (1 Cor 11:26; *soteriological* emphasis).

[2] See G. Theissen, "Social Integration and Sacramental Activity: An Analysis of 1 Cor 11:17-34," *The Social Setting of Pauline Christianity*. Philadelphia, 1982, 145–74.

[3] On the complex question of table-fellowship among Christians in Antioch, see N. D. Mitchell, "Baptism in the *Didache*," *The* Didache *in Context: Essays on its Text, History and Transmission*, ed. C. Jefford, New York, 1995, 226–55; especially 238–40. See also, in the same volume, J. Riggs, "The Sacred Food of *Didache* 9–10 and Second-Century Ecclesiologies," 256–83.

Although other Christian leaders may have ignored or modified Paul's theology,[4] the symbolism of eucharistic dining was rich enough to stand on its own — even after the "meal" had been reduced to its simplest ritual elements (the blessing and consumption of "token" bits of bread and wine). For the principal outcome of this dining event was always κοινωνία, communion with God and others through the sharing of one bread, one cup. Thus, on the one hand, Eucharist was seen as an *eschatological sign* pointing to the joyful presence of God's kingdom, which begins its reign even before it fully arrives: "As this grain lay scattered upon the mountains, but was gathered to become one bread, so may your church be gathered into your reign, for glory and power are yours" [*Didache* 9.4]. On the other hand, Eucharist was perceived as a powerful *sign of reconciliation* signaling both the forgiveness of sins[5] and a new covenant between God and humanity: "Drink from [this cup], all of you; for this is my blood of the covenant which will be shed on behalf of the many for the forgiveness of sins" [Matt 26:27-28].

Such a dense, multivalent symbolism overwhelmed all the "ordinary" social meanings attached to the sharing of a meal (even when that meal was explicitly religious). So it is not surprising that what began *within* a meal (stage one) seems eventually to have been postponed to the *end* of a meal (stage two), and finally, to have become altogether *independent* of the meal (stage three).[6] This ritual independence may have been fully achieved before the end of the New Testament period. Willi Marxsen has argued, for example, that by the time Mark's Gospel was written (ca. 70 C.E.), the "common meal" setting had disappeared altogether.[7]

---

[4] See J. Riggs, "From Gracious Table to Sacramental Elements: The Tradition-History of Didache 9 and 10," *The Second Century* 4 (1984) 83–101, especially 93–100.

[5] On the meaning of forgiveness in the preaching of Jesus, see T. Sheehan, *The First Coming: How the Kingdom of God became Christianity*. New York, 1986, 66.

[6] On these three stages of development, see N. Mitchell, *Cult and Controversy*. New York, 1982, 19–27.

[7] See "The Lord's Supper as a Christological Problem," *The Beginnings of Christology*, Philadelphia, 1979, 88–122; here, 94–5. J. Crossan has argued that Mark's account reflects growing tensions in the Church between an *institutionalized Eucharist* (that does not even permit Jews and Gentiles to share the same table!) and the open, egalitarian, inclusive table-sharing that characterized Jesus' historical

At the risk of oversimplifying a complex history, it can be said that the gradual disappearance of the full formal meal made it possible for new eucharistic interests and emphases to emerge in later New Testament literature (the synoptics and John). Paul's theology, as noted above, was a delicate balance of ecclesiological, christological, sacramental and soteriological elements. The "apostle to the Gentiles" stressed God's free and gracious choice of a *new* community created through a *new* covenant sealed in Jesus' blood and ratified by the sharing of a ritual meal. Both bread and people may thus be rightly called "the body of Christ." Among later New Testament writers, however, the emphasis shifted — away from an "*ecclesiology of eucharistic action*" toward a "*christology of eucharistic presence.*" The "gracious table" of Jesus' ministry among the marginalized was receding from memory, replaced by a preoccupation with sacramental elements. The sacred ritual foods of bread and wine quickly became the chief source of the community's contact with the Crucified One. The *contents* of the bread and cup came to be understood in primarily christological rather than "covenantal" terms.[8] By the end of the New Testament period, then, covenant motifs (essentially *ecclesiological* in nature) had given way to christological ones (essentially *soteriological* in nature).

### 2. Two Patterns of Disengagement

a. *Disengaging eucharistic communion from its immediate liturgical context:* From the time of Justin Martyr (ca. A.D. 150), we have convincing evidence that these christological conclusions about the Eucharist had gained ground. For the faith that Jesus' presence in the bread and wine *endures* (even after the liturgy has ended) is implicit in Justin's account of Sunday worship in Rome. He reports that those who cannot attend the community's celebration (presumably the ill, the feeble, the dying) may still receive, through the ministry of deacons, the sacred food "hallowed by prayer and thanksgiving." This food, Justin

---

ministry. See *The Historical Jesus: The Life of a Mediterranean Jewish Peasant.* San Francisco, 1991, 360–7.

[8] Note how Paul quotes the tradition of Jesus' words over the cup: "This cup is *the new covenant* in my blood." In Mark and Matthew, this becomes: "This is my blood of the covenant . . ." (Mark 14:24; Matt 26:28). Luke reflects Paul's formula: "This cup is the new covenant in my blood . . ." (Luke 22:20).

informs us, is not "ordinary bread . . . or ordinary drink"; rather, it is "the flesh and blood of that Jesus who was made flesh."[9] Half a century later (if the *Apostolic Tradition* can be trusted as a reliable source), there is evidence for a Christian ritual of weekday Communion at home: "Let every one of the faithful take steps to receive the Eucharist before eating anything else. For if they receive in faith, even if some deadly thing is given them, after that it shall not overpower them." This eucharistic bread — obviously "reserved" at home — must be kept safely away from rodents and other pests, the *Apostolic Tradition* warns, and it must be consumed reverently for "it is the body of Christ, to be eaten by believers, and not to be dispised."[10]

By the beginning of the third century, then, pastoral priorities sometimes dictated that eucharistic *Communion* be disengaged from the assembly's act of eucharistic *celebration* — in order to accommodate persons absent from the Sunday synaxis (Justin), as well as Christians who wish to communicate at home during the week (*Apostolic Tradition*). In both cases, faith in Christ's continuing presence in the sacramental species is clearly expressed.

b. *Disengaging eucharistic celebration from Sunday*: Just as eucharistic *Communion* may be disengaged from eucharistic *liturgy,* so eucharistic *liturgy* may be disengaged from *Sunday* — the traditional day of Christian assembly. If a "weekly norm" for eucharistic celebration ("the Lord's Supper on the Lord's Day") was ever widespread, it receded rather quickly as celebrations multiplied on other days of the week. These Eucharists were "votive" in nature, attached to specific occasions of Christian life: e.g., days of communal fasting, prayer and penance (mentioned by North Africans like Tertullian and Cyprian); the cult of the saints and martyrs (with Eucharist celebrated to mark their *dies natalis*); and the inclusion of a eucharistic liturgy among the rites of Christian burial. Moreover, as Christian communities grew after the "peace of Constantine," bishops in large cities (like Leo in Rome, ca. 440–461) found that Masses sometimes had to be multiplied on a single day in order to accommodate the crowds of worshippers.[11]

---

[9] *First Apology,* 66; English translation in P. Palmer, *Sacraments and Worship* (= Sources of Christian Theology, vol. 1); London, 1954, 196–97.

[10] *Apostolic Tradition,* 36–37.

[11] For more detailed discussion of these items, see N. D. Mitchell, *Cult and Controversy,* 29–38.

Such historical developments are enormously important for understanding how a quasi-independent "cult" of the eucharistic species outside Mass could develop in later centuries. For the patterns that promoted the disengagement of *"celebration"* from *"species"* did not disappear; they intensified as the eucharistic elements came to be regarded as worthy of cultic distinction in their own right, independent of their originating source in the actions of the liturgical assembly. In sum, within a relatively short time *Eucharist* (as "action of the assembly") had become a *distinctive ritual independent of any meal.* Moreover, the *eucharistic species* had acquired *an independent value and significance that endured beyond the liturgical celebration.*

## II. THE RISE OF A CULT OF
## THE EUCHARIST OUTSIDE MASS

The principal features of the worship of the Eucharist outside Mass with which we are familiar today (e.g., eucharistic exposition and benediction; devotional "visits" and prayer in the presence of the reserved sacrament; the Forty Hours devotion; Corpus Christi processions; international congresses) developed rather slowly over several centuries. This development was fostered by changes that occurred both *within* the liturgy and *beyond* it. Here, only the most salient of these changes can be noted.

### 1. Liturgical Gestures

Augustine, in a famous commentary on Psalm 98 (99), reminded his people that "No one eats this flesh [of Christ] *unless he or she has first adored it.* . . . Not only do we not sin by adoring, but we would sin if we didn't!"[12] And in a celebrated passage from the mystagogical catecheses of Cyril of Jerusalem (+ ca. 386), we read:

"Make your left hand a throne for your right, because your right is about to receive the King; make a hollow of your palm and receive the body of Christ, saying after it: 'Amen!' . . . Then come forward to the chalice of his blood, not with outstretched hands, but bending forward *in the manner of one who worships and reverences.* . . ."[13]

---

[12] *Ennarationes in Psalmos* 98:9; Latin text edited by E. Dekkers and J. Fraipont in CCL 39; Turnholt, 1956, 1385–86.

[13] *Catecheses* V.21–2. Critical Greek text in A. Piédagnel and P. Paris, eds., *Cyrille de Jérusalem: Catéchèses Mystagogiques* (= SCh 126); Paris, 1966, 170, 172.

Both these texts indicate that by the late fourth century, in both East and West, the act of Holy Communion was accompanied by gestures of reverence and adoration. At the same time, sources from the sixth and seventh centuries, indicate that the custom of lifting ("elevating") the consecrated species (at the conclusion of the Eucharistic Prayer, for example, or when the people are invited to communion) had become a well-established custom in many places. The author of *Ordo Romanus I.* (ca. 700) thus notes: "When he [the pope] has said 'Through him, with him . . . ,' the archdeacon lifts the chalice, with its veil, by the handles and holds it, raising it toward the pope. The pope then touches the side of the chalice with the offerings. . . ."[14] This description — and others like it — show that *within the liturgy itself,* at critical points (the "Great Entrance" in the Byzantine tradition; the doxology of the anaphora; the invitation and approach to communion), ritual gestures of reverence toward the eucharistic species were proliferating. Moreover, ceremonial accretions had also begun to surround the *reserved* sacrament when it was brought into an actual celebration of the liturgy (as, e.g., the Western *Sancta* rite shows).[15]

*2. Eucharistic Liturgy Perceived as* History, *Rather Than* Mystery
During this same historical epoch, another trend emerged — viz., the custom of interpreting the liturgy as a series of ritual tableaux representing Jesus' life, passion and death. Such "allegorical" interpretations were already present in the work of Theodore of Mopsuestia (+ 428), who wrote:

"They bring up the bread and place it on the holy altar *to complete the representation of the passion. So from now on we should consider that Christ has already undergone the passion and is now placed on the altar as if in a tomb.* That is why some of the deacons spread cloths on the altar which remind us of [the] winding-sheets [used in burial] . . . ."[16]

---

[14] For the Latin text of OR I, see M. Andrieu, ed., *Les Ordines Romani du haut moyen âge,* vol. 2; Louvain, 1948, 74–108. English translation from R. C. D. Jasper and G. J. Cuming, eds., *Prayers of the Eucharist, Early and Reformed,* London, 1975, 113.

[15] On the *Sancta* and *fermentum* rites, see N. D. Mitchell, *Cult and Controversy,* 56–61.

[16] *Baptismal Homily* IV.26. For critical text see R. Tonneau and R. Devreesse, eds., *Les homélies catéchétiques de Théodore de Mopsueste* (= ST 145); Vatican City, 1949x.

As Theodore explains it, the eucharistic liturgy is a kind of ritual allegory reenacting the events of Jesus' suffering, death and burial. Similar interpretations appear in Western sources such as the *Expositio antiquae liturgiae gallicanae* (attributed to Germanus of Paris). In these texts, liturgy is seen as "history" rather than "mystery," as the rehearsal of *past* events rather than the celebration of *present* mystery. Perhaps the most extreme illustration of this tendency appeared in the work of Amalarius of Metz (+ 850), a liturgical commentator of the Carolingian era.[17] Though his interpretations seem fanciful (e.g., the subdeacon at a solemn Mass allegorically represents John the Baptist), it should be noted that Amalarius focused his attention *on the liturgical rites themselves,* rather than upon paraliturgical ceremonies (e.g., exposition, benediction) involving the Eucharist. His goal was a dramatic interpretation of the *liturgy* — rather than an extra-liturgical dramatization of the Eucharist.[18]

*3. Debates about the Real Presence*
A third factor contributing to the evolution of a cult of the Eucharist outside Mass can be found in the fractious doctrinal debates about the real presence that began during the Carolingian period, continued throughout the high Middle Ages, and were renewed during the Reformation.[19] *De corpore et sanguine domini,* published in 831 by Paschasius Radbertus (a Benedictine monk and later abbot of Corbie), represented a dramatic turning point in Western theology, for it was the first attempt to treat the Eucharist in a systematic doctrinal way (rather than as part of a mystagogical catechesis on the liturgy).[20] Paschasius emphasized the *realism* of Christ's presence: the *eucharistic* body and the *historical* body of Jesus are identical, for the sacrament contains the natural body that was born of a Virgin, crucified, and risen. Paschasius' discussion of the relation between *figura* (sign) and *veritas* (thing signified) in the sacrament was quite sophisticated, but his anecdotal examples often seemed crudely literal — as when he

---

[17] See J. M. Hanssens, ed., *Amalarii episcopi opera liturgica Omnia,* 3 vols. (= ST 138–40); Vatican City, 1948.

[18] See N. D. Mitchell, *Cult and Controversy,* 66.

[19] Detailed discussion may be found in N. D. Mitchell, *Cult and Controversy,* 73–86; 137–62;

[20] Critical text in B. Paulus, ed., *Paschasius Radbertus: De corpore et sanguine domini* (= CCCM 16); Turnhold, 1969.

cited (approvingly) the story of an old ascetic who discovers "a piece of flesh soaked in blood" in his hand at Communion time.

Against such crude exaggerations, Ratramnus, another monk of Corbie, sought to explain the real presence in a way that would compromise neither the integrity of the *sacramental* signs nor the necessity of *faith* for receiving them. Like Augustine before him, Ratramnus stressed the *real*, though *spiritual*, nature of eucharistic eating and drinking — actions that appeal to *faith* rather than to any sensate or materialistic perceptions of flesh and blood. "The body and blood of Christ which the faithful receive are signs, according to their visible appearance; but according to their invisible substance — that is, according to the power of the divine Word — the body and blood of Christ truly exist. As visible creatures [of bread and wine] they nourish the body; as the greater power of substance, they feed and sanctify the minds of the faithful."[21]

This argument between "realists" and "sacramentalists" dominated discussions of real presence in the Eucharist for centuries. Things came to a head in 1059, when Berengarius of Tours (whose eucharistic theology had been condemned as insufficiently "realist" by church leaders like Lanfranc) was required by a Roman synod to confess that after consecration Christ's body and blood "are *truly, physically* and *not merely sacramentally* touched and broken by the hands of the priests and crushed by the teeth of the faithful."[22]

While such hyper-realism may have preoccupied theologians, other factors were at work on the level of popular piety. As Miri Rubin has suggested, the medieval development of a eucharistic cult *outside* Mass is closely related to questions of social power, sacerdotal mediation, and the creation of a symbolic order in which people can "locate" themselves religiously and culturally. The Eucharist came to be seen as *the* most important object, *the* most critical "test" of one's status and identity in a power-system that made religious orthodoxy the *sine qua non* of social advancement. Rubin writes:

"The eucharist placed Christians within a symbolic system operating within a history of salvation, and it was lived as a drama reenacted at

---

[21] Ratramnus, *De corpore et sanguine domini*; Latin text in PL 121, cols. 125–70; here, *PL* 121:col. 147.

[22] A Latin text of the Berengarian confession may be found in DS 690.

every altar during every Mass. The God who was everywhere in every facet of nature, had to be domesticated, located, and his supernatural power had to be apportioned and routinized. It is this economy of the sacred, commuted into sacramental currency, that was being explored, and its most precious coin, the eucharist, evaluated and defined."[23]

### 4. The Rise of Eucharistic Devotions Outside Mass

The rise of eucharistic devotions outside Mass was not, however, simply the result of doctrinal debate or shifts in popular piety[24] (important as these may have been). It was also linked, as Rubin notes, to the larger history of medieval life and commerce, to the search for secure identity, status, and power in a social structure where modern institutions (like strong nation-states) did not yet exist. Here, however, attention will focus on four *liturgy-related* factors that helped shape eucharistic worship outside Mass: (a) piety linked to the reserved sacrament, (b) processions, (c) exposition of the consecrated species, and (d) benediction. For while theological controversy, sociopolitical conditions, and economic realities all contributed to this emerging cult, *the decisive factors appear to have come from evolution within the liturgy itself.*

### A. PRAYER IN THE PRESENCE OF THE RESERVED SACRAMENT

Although *reserving* the sacrament (especially for viaticum) was an ancient custom, "visiting" it as an act of devotion was not. In the late twelfth century, however, evidence for this practice emerges in documents like *The Ancrene Riwle,* a rule of life written for women living as solitaries near a church. Though secluded in her cell, the anchoress is encouraged to salute the Blessed Sacrament reserved on the church's altar: "Turn your thoughts to the body and precious blood of God on the high altar and fall on your knees toward him with these greetings: Hail, author of our creation! Hail, price of our redemption! Hail, viaticum of our journey! Hail, reward of our hope! . . . Be thou our joy . . . ."[25] The source of such salutations seems to

---

[23] M. Rubin, *Corpus Christi: The Eucharist in Late Medieval Culture.* Cambridge, UK, 1991, 14.

[24] On the earlier evolution of this piety, see N. D. Mitchell, *Cult and Controversy,* 86–96.

[25] M. B. Salu, ed., *The Ancrene Riwle;* London, 1955, 7.

have been the priest's private devotions *during* the eucharistic liturgy. Increasingly, however, from the thirteenth century onward, devout Christians were urged to pray in the presence of the reserved sacrament *outside* the times of liturgical celebration.[26]

## B. PROCESSIONS

In the late eleventh century, the *Monastic Constitutions* of Lanfranc (Berengarius's opponent) indicate that on Palm Sunday the sacrament was carried in solemn procession.[27] This custom was obviously a *eucharistic* variation on the much earlier *non-eucharistic* practice first reported in Egeria's famous fourth-century travel-diary. While Lanfranc's procession was still closely linked to the liturgy, it was obviously inspired by an attitude toward Eucharist quite different from the one implied in Egeria's narrative. After approval of the feast of Corpus Christi (in the papal bull *Transiturus*, 1264) eucharistic processions rapidly became common throughout Europe. Once again, changing patterns in medieval social and economic life helped create an atmosphere in which *the eucharistic species* were seen as channels of religious power, emblems of prestige, and "litmus tests" of orthodoxy. The upheaval created when large numbers of people began moving from manors to towns (in the twelfth and thirteenth centuries), the challenge of religious dissidents (e.g., heterodox movements like the Albigensians and the Cathari), the rise of lay-dominated "apostolic life" movements (e.g., the Beguines) — all these conditions reenforced the centrality of Eucharist as source and symbol of religious power.

## C. EXPOSITION

The *liturgical* roots of eucharistic "exposition" are ancient, rooted in the rite which took place immediately before Communion, when the gifts were lifted with the words "Holy things for the holy!" (or a similar formula). Until the beginning of the thirteenth century, this was the only point *within* the Western eucharistic liturgies at which believers were invited to gaze upon the species and reverence them. After the introduction of the "elevation" following the *verba Domini* (ca. 1200), an ever-greater emphasis was placed on "ocular" Communion —

---

[26] For more discussion, see N. D. Mitchell, *Cult and Controversy*, 164–70.

[27] See D. Knowles, ed., *The Monastic Constitutions of Lanfranc*; New York, 1951, 23–5.

on *seeing* the host and *receiving* the physical and spiritual benefits that were popularly believed to flow from this experience (e.g., restoration of health; long life; etc.).[28] Popular feasts like Corpus Christi helped highlight the (erroneous but popular) perception that *"seeing* the eucharistic species" has a value virtually equivalent to the actual reception of communion.

### D. BENEDICTION

The origins of this devotion are to be sought in two sources: the Liturgy of the Hours and the feast of Corpus Christi.[29] In Italy, during the thirteenth century, a popular evening devotion known as the *laude* arose. It consisted of Latin or vernacular songs (often addressed to the Virgin Mary) sung at the end of the canonical hours of vespers or compline. During the fourteenth century it became increasingly popular to perform the *laude* in the presence of the Blessed Sacrament (visible in a monstrance or other vessel). At the conclusion of the devotion, the people were blessed with the sacrament and dismissed. Another source of benediction was the liturgy for Corpus Christi. Evidence from the year 1301 shows that at the Benedictine monastery of Hildesheim, the Corpus Christi procession (still a recent innovation) included a "station" or pause during which the people sang an antiphon while the priest blessed them with the sacrament. It is thus plausible to suggest that benediction originated as a solemn "dismissal" or "stational rite" attached to some other liturgical service (the canonical hours, the Corpus Christi procession).

In time, of course, a veritable cornucopia of extra-liturgical devotions involving the eucharistic species developed. Some of these — like the Forty Hours devotion, which seems to have originated in Milan during the sixteenth century[30] — are still popular today. Until at least the fifteenth century, there was no thought that such practices might "rival" the eucharistic liturgy itself. Even the bull *Transiturus* (approving Corpus Christi) insisted that *participation in the liturgy* is the ordinary norm of eucharistic piety. During the Counter-Reformation, however, this theological principle was sometimes neglected in pastoral practice. Indeed, devotions like benediction (replete with music,

[28] See discussion in N. D. Mitchell, *Cult and Controversy,* 178–9. For details about the introduction of the elevation, see 151–7.

[29] For more detailed discussion of these sources, see ibid., 181–14.

[30] For the history of Forty Hours, see ibid., 311–18.

flowers, candles, and sumptuous vestments) sometimes rivaled — and even exceeded — the ritual impact of a "low Mass" (where there was no singing, preaching, or audible participation, and where there were few communicants).

Vatican Council II sought a eucharistic renewal in which full, conscious and active participation by the people would once again show that the liturgy is "source and summit" of the Church's life. While it did not reject worship of the Eucharist outside Mass, it sought to place it once more in an appropriate context. Such a cult, so *Sacrosanctum Concilium* 7 suggests, must be seen within the larger context of the many presences of Christ — in the celebrating people, in the Word, in the liturgy, in the ministers, in the eucharistic species. Within *this* context, it makes sense to celebrate that presence of the Lord which *begins* sacramentally during Mass and *remains* in the reserved Eucharist, where Christ is "in our midst day and night . . . full of grace and truth."[31]

---

[31] *Eucharistiae Sacramentum* ("On Holy Communion and Worship of the Eucharistic Mystery Outside of Mass," 23 June 1973) par. 2.

## Bibliography

Cooke, B. *Ministry to Word and Sacraments: History and Theology.* Philadelphia, 1976.

King, A. *Eucharistic Reservation in the Western Church.* New York, 1965.

Macy, G. *The Banquet's Wisdom: A Short History of the Theologies of the Lord's Supper.* Mahwah, N.J., 1992.

Mitchell, N. D. *Cult and Controversy: The Worship of the Eucharist Outside Mass.* Studies in the Reformed Rites of the Catholic Church, vol. 4. New York, 1982.

Power, D. *The Eucharistic Mystery: Revitalizing the Tradition.* New York, 1992.

Rubin, M. *Corpus Christi: The Eucharist in Late Medieval Culture.* Cambridge, 1991.

# 12

# The Liturgy of the Presanctified Gifts

## THE JERUSALEM LITURGY

The Liturgy of the Presanctified gifts refers to the liturgical act of Communion in which the eucharistic species consecrated at a previous Mass are consumed. It is foreshadowed in the primitive structure of the Lenten ferias and it develops within the Good Friday liturgy.

Egeria, in the second half of the fourth century, bears witness to the practice in the Constantinian basilica of the *Martyrion*, which was adjacent to the rotunda or *Anastasis*. The Mass *post crucem*, i.e., behind the rock of Golgotha on which stood the golden reliquary of the Cross, was celebrated but once a year: on Good Friday. She goes on to describe an exceptionally long synaxis of readings and prayers (ch. 27–8, pp. 79–80). This practice was approved by canon 52 of the Quinisext Council (the "Council in Trullo"). Egeria also tells us about the aliturgical services celebrated in Jerusalem every Wednesday and Friday of Lent at the "mother church" of Sion, where the people would assemble for the stational liturgy (ch. 27, 5f, p. 79). This was an application of canon 49 of the Council of Laodicea (314), which had decreed that the Liturgy of the Presanctified was to be celebrated only on Saturdays and Sundays of Lent: ὅτι οὐ δεῖ ἐν τῇ τεσσαρακοντῇ ἄρτον προφέρειν, εἰ μὴ ἂν σαββάτῳ καὶ κυριακῇ μόνον.

The history of this celebration can be followed in documents from the fifth to seventh centuries: the Armenian Lectionary published by Conybeare in the *Rituale Armenorum*, and the Georgian Canonarian published by Kekelidze,[1] which brings us to the first half of the

---

[1] K. Kekelidze, *Jerusalimskij Kanonar VII Veka*, Tiflis 1912. German translations: T. Kluge, "Quadragesima und Karwoche Jerusalems im siebten Jahrhundert," *Oriens*

seventh century. Finally, there is a lectionary belonging to a series of documents in the Syro-Palestianian dialect, most of which is very fragmentary. It was published by Lewis, who also published fragments of an older lectionary in the same dialect.[2] These latter tell about its liturgical development during the iconoclast period, the date of its final redaction.

A text attributed to St. Sophronius of Jerusalem (d. 638) speaks of it as an ancient institution dating back to St. James, brother of the Lord, or to Peter or other apostles.[3] We can imagine that Communion, although connected to the Sacrifice, was soon brought by volunteers to late-comers, the absent, and those imprisoned because of their faith who had a right to the body of Christ. This was the case during the persecutions. After 313, the practice of private Communion was maintained in monasteries without a priest, at least until the sixth century. On the other hand, Jacobite authors unanimously attribute the Liturgy of the Presanctified to Severus of Antioch (d. 538) between 511 and 518.[4]

Indirect evidence on the apostolic origin of this rite comes from the letter of Innocent I (401–417) to Decentius, bishop of Gubbio. The Pope emphasizes that there is no eucharistic celebration during the last two days of Holy Week.[5]

Although Renaudot rightly says that no presanctified exists in the Coptic liturgy (Rahmani mentions sources but does not give them), the Egyptian Church had this rite at one time.[6] Socrates of Alexandria

---

Christianus, 2 s., V (1915) 201–33; "Oster und Pfingstfeier Jerusalems in siebten Jahrhundert," ibid., VI, (1916) 223–39, and Peradze, "Die Weinachtsfeier Jerusalems in siebten Jahrhundert," ibid., S. 3, I (1927) 310–18.

[2] A Palestinian Syrian Lectionary, Studia Sinaitica vol. VI, Londen 1897; Codex Climaci Rescriptus, Horae Semiticae, VIII, Cambridge 1912; see also F. C. Burkitt, "The Old Lectionary of Jerusalem," Journal of Theological Studies, XXIV (1923) 415–24.

[3] Commentarius liturgicus, n. 1, PG 87, c. 3981. Leo Allatius attributes this opinion to Michael Cerularius (1043–59) in De Missa praesanctificatorum, c. 1582. See also Simeon of Thessalonica, Responsiones, q. LV, PG, 155, 904. An analogy with the Presanctified is seen by Thibaut, Origine, 43–44, in chap. IX of the Didache, by reason of the attribute of the broken bread: περὶ τοῦ κλάσματος.

[4] It is first attested in the Nomocanon of Bar Hebreus, chap. IV, sect. VIII: Codrington, The Syrian, t. V, 370. This also included the signing of the particle within the chalice that had been consecrated the previous Sunday. See also 373–75.

[5] Ut traditio Ecclesiae habeat isto biduo sacramenta penitus non celebrari: Ep. XXXV, c. IV, 4.7. PL 20, 555–56.

[6] Renaudot, II, 85.

says that since the time of Origen (185–254) a synaxis was held each Friday in Alexandria. The Scriptures were read and explained, and everything was done as at Mass except for the consecration of the Mysteries.[7]

There is also said to be another prayer in the Liturgy of St. Basil, after the reception of the Holy Mysteries, taken from the Liturgy of the Presanctified of the apostle Mark.[8] Following the *Constitution of Christodoulos* (1047–77) this liturgy was celebrated on Holy Thursday.[9]

Thibaut maintains that the presanctified derives from a special modification of the evening Mass for Holy Thursday in Jerusalem and became an institution with Chalcedon. It is certain that since the fourth century in Jerusalem, as Egeria attests, a second Mass was celebrated that day to commemorate the Last Supper. It is also mentioned by the Council of Carthage (397) in canons 28–29, and by St. Augustine in letter 14 *ad Januarium*. This rite was apparently modified in the sixth century, when general Communion was transferred to the next day, on which there was no liturgy, and the Holy Thursday evening Mass was abolished.[10]

In any case, we come to a point where the Liturgy of the Presanctified is simply a solemn reception of Communion on fast days, perhaps preceded by the Our Father, for as the *Didache* points out, there is no better preparation for Communion. Since Mass is a joyful celebration, it would have conflicted with days of fasting, stational days, and Holy Thursday.

## FROM ANTIOCH TO BYZANTIUM

It may have been Severus of Antioch who publicized and spread the Liturgy of the Presanctified. Then it apparently moved from Syria to Constantinople where it developed and assumed its Byzantine character. This took place during the time of the patriarch Sergius (617), who says it was used beginning with the first week of the Lenten fast.[11]

During Lent, from Monday to Friday of each week, the Byzantine rite offers us one reading for the morning service of τροθέχτι and two readings for Vespers and the Liturgy of the Presanctified that follows

[7] *Historia Ecclesiastica*, l. V, c. XXII, PG 77, 636–37.

[8] Redaudot, I, 76.

[9] Renaudot, *Historia patriarcharum alexandrinorum*, Paris 1713, 422.

[10] *Monuments*, 23, 44; *Origine*, 39–40. Andrieu, on the other hand, maintains it was a creation *ex nihilo* from the Byzantine liturgy: *Immixtio*, 196.

[11] *Chronicon Paschale*, PG 92, 989.

(ἡ θεία λειτουργία τῶν πρηγιασμένων or ἡ προηγιασμένη). All three are taken from the Old Testament. The entire development of the Byzantine liturgy for Good Friday is especially important. Its richness is in striking contrast to the austere Roman simplicity of the office for that day — especially if we disregard any Oriental influence it contains, including the Mass of the Presanctified, which is not mentioned at all in the oldest *Ordines Romani*. The absence of an entrance rite in today's Roman liturgy for Good Friday is another sign of its antiquity.

Originally it must have been an aliturgical synaxis with a very primitive structure: a Mass of the Catechumens without an entrance rite. On the other hand, the Byzantine liturgy for Good Friday presents a majestic and commemorative ritual, which probably originated in Palestine. Besides the reading of the Passion, the ancient office is marked by two important features: the second reading, which refers to the Jewish passover, and the first, which proclaims the resurrection in the words of the prophet Hosea: "On the third day he will raise us up." At the time of Heraclius the Presanctified was already celebrated on Wednesday and Friday of Cheese-fare Week (προγήστιμος or τυροφάγος ἑβδομάς). This compromise is meant to mitigate the austerity of Palestinian monastic usage, where neither the complete liturgy nor the Liturgy of the Presanctified was celebrated.[12] The Oriental discipline, then, does not envision the eucharistic liturgy on fast days, only a simple Communion service, which is the essential part of today's Liturgy of the προηγιασμένα. In the East, except for the Nestorians, the eucharistic liturgy is celebrated only on Saturdays and Sundays of Lent. The early Ambrosian liturgy had a similar practice.[13]

Whereas the Jacobite, Assyrian, and Maronite Churches have the rite of the signing of the chalice, in the East only the Byzantine Church has the rite of the presanctified.

The oldest manuscript is Barberini 77 (eighth–ninth centuries), which contains only the priest's part.[14] There are also two Syriac manuscripts: Vat. Syr. 40 (1553) and 41 (fourteenth century). The first, which is anonymous, contains three liturgies in Syriac for the use of

---

[12] See the τριώδιον, ed. Rom., 54. For the opposite use, 81.
[13] Baumstark, 213.
[14] It was published by Brightman, 345–52.

the Byzantines in Syria; the second attributes the Liturgy of the Presanctified to St. Basil.[15]

## THE BYZANTINE LITURGY

The Liturgy of the Presanctified is not a sacrifice since it lacks the offering and consecration. Canon 52 of the Council in Trullo (692) prescribes it for every day of Lent except Saturdays, Sundays, and the feast of the Annunciation, 25 March.[16] Nicephorus, patriarch of Constantinople (815–816), prescribes the presanctified three times a week during Lent — besides Wednesdays and Fridays during the year and the feast of the Holy Cross, September 14.[17] Nowadays it is celebrated only on Wednesdays and Fridays of Lent, the first three days of Holy Week, and certain saints' feasts. In his fifth treatise on fasting, St. John Damascene prescribes it for all of Holy Week. Its use on Good Friday was abandoned by the Slavs in the thirteenth century and by the Byzantines in the fourteenth.

The structure of the presanctified imitates that of Vespers and commemorates in some way the burial of Christ. Here we might recall the terminology and devotional practice of the Holy Thursday-Good Friday "sepulchers" seen in Latin countries around the Mediterranean.

It is celebrated between ten and eleven o'clock in the morning and is followed by Vespers. In the East, strict fasting was observed until three in the afternoon and ended with Communion. For this reason, until the last century the Liturgy of the Presanctified was celebrated in the afternoon.[18]

At the Sunday Divine Liturgy, the celebrant prepares the "Lambs" (ἀμνοί) for the presanctified the following week, cutting them from the bread prepared for the offering (πρόσφορα) and using for each the same gestures and the same prayers of the day. He raises them at the elevation and makes the Sign of the Cross on them with a spoonful of the precious blood from the chalice. Then he places them in the *artophorion* or tabernacle.

---

[15] Assemani, 280f; Goar, 177f. Some Byzantine missals, because of the word *Pater*, attribute it to St. Gregory the Great (see *Ep.* IX, 12). See also Thibaut, *Origine*, 42 and *Monuments*, 2.

[16] Mansi, XI, 697f.

[17] Pitra, 311.

[18] O. Nilles, *Calendarium manuale utriusque Ecclesiae orientalis et occidentalis*, Innsbruck 1896–1897, t. II, 252.

At the Great Entrance, the celebrant goes to the *prothesis* and takes one of the hosts, together with the chalice which has been prepared in the usual way with wine and water. Formerly the consecrated chalice was reserved with the "Lambs," as witnessed by the prayer that still accompanies the entrance: "Behold, the body and blood of the Savior are coming to the altar, escorted by invisible angelic hosts."

Before the breaking of the bread, he says: "Deem it proper to impart to us, with your mighty hand, your most pure body and precious blood, and through us, to all the people."[19] Thus the texts mention the precious blood, even though intinction of the presanctified and reservation of the consecrated chalice are no longer practiced.

## THE RITE

### 1. *Vespers, Litany,* Prothesis

We have said that in the Byzantine rite the Liturgy of the Presanctified forms part of Vespers. After the psalms and hymns, the deacon says the Great Litany as at the Divine Liturgy. The celebrant goes to prepare the gifts, making the *prothesis* with almost no prayers since the Sacrifice has already been completed. He prepares the chalice as usual with wine and a little water. The deacon then says the Little Litany, and the recitation of Vespers begins.[20]

### 2. *Little Entrance, Readings*

The deacon carries the censer and the priest the book of the Gospels, if there is to be a gospel reading (February 10, St. Charalampos; February 24, the Finding of the Head of the Baptist; March 9, the Forty Holy Martyrs). The Old Testament readings are taken from Genesis, Exodus, Proverbs or Job (usually Gen 7:6-9; Prov 9:12ff). Then the celebrant incenses the altar on all sides, intoning Psalm 140 with the refrain taken from verse 2: "Let my prayer rise like incense. . . ." At this point, when called for, the Epistle and Gospel are read as in the Liturgy of St. John Chrysostom.[21] The gospel was not read until the time of Simeon of Thessalonica.[22]

---

[19] Andrieu, 197f.
[20] Charon, 103, 113, 117; Goar, 160.
[21] Charon, 132f.
[22] *PG* 155, 905.

### 3. Litany, Prayers for the Catechumens, Prayers for the Faithful
Everything is as in an ordinary liturgy. On Wednesday of mid-Lent the catechumens who are to be baptized at Easter are dismissed, and the faithful are asked to pray for them.

### 4. Great Entrance
Introduced perhaps in Antioch along with the Creed by Peter the Fuller in 471 to protest against the Arian and Macedonian heresies, it entered the ordinary liturgy in Byzantium under Justin II (565–578). The prayers preserved in the ordinary liturgy seem to attest that they once accompanied the transfer of the presanctified gifts.[23]

### 5. Our Father
The deacon introduces the Lord's Prayer with a long litany, which joins that of the Great Entrance with that which precedes the Our Father. The prayers that occur between these two rites, namely the anaphora, are omitted, and everything continues as usual. The Our Father is at the center of the Liturgy of the Presanctified; perhaps originally it was its only prayer formula.

### 6. Elevation, Fraction, Communion
At one time the elevation took place during the recitation of the Our Father; later it was separated. Nowadays the celebrant touches the gifts under the veil, saying: "Holy presanctified things for the holy."[24] The Barberini and Grottaferrata manuscripts attest the opposite. Then the bread is broken, and a portion is dropped into the chalice while the choir sings the κοινωνικόν from Psalm 33: *Taste and see*. The assembly receives Communion, which is the object of the presanctified. The deacon receives the chalice, saying nothing. In reality, he should not do this, seeing that the chalice with consecrated wine is not reserved. Sometimes the bread is distributed to the faithful with a spoonful of the wine, an expression of the belief in consecration by contact, which is held by some.[25] After Communion, there is a thanksgiving for the heavenly bread and lifegiving cup and for having partaken of the body and blood of Christ. This final mention presupposes a time when the consecrated chalice was reserved. Finally, the celebrant distributes the pieces of "eulogy" or blessed bread.

[23] Thibaut, *Origene*, 44.
[24] Goar, 172.
[25] Andrieu, 206; for testimonies such as that of Michael Cerularius, 201–4.

# Bibliography

## a) Texts and Translations

Assemani, S. E., and J. S. *Bibliothecae Apostolicae Vaticanae codicum manuscriptorum catalogus.* 3 vols. Paris, 1926; originally Rome, 1758.

Brightman, F. E. *Liturgies Eastern and Western.* Vol. 1:494–501. Oxford, 1965.

Charon (Korolevsky), E. *Les saints et divines liturgies, en usages dans lÉglise grecque catholique orientale.* Beirut, 1904.

Codrington, W. H. "Liturgia praesanctificatorum syriaca Sancti Joannis Chrisostomi (testo siriaco e versione latina." In *Studi e ricerche intorno a S. Giovanni Crisostomo,* 719–29. Rome, 1908.

Conybeare, F. C. *Rituale armenorum.* Oxford, 1905.

Egeria. *Peregrinatio ad Loca Sancta.* Ed. P. Geyer, 35–101. CSEL 39. Vienna, 1898.

Goar, J. Εὐχολόγιον, *sive Rituale Graecorum.* Venice, 1730.

*Missale Syriacum iuxta ritum Ecclesiae Antiochenae Syrorum.* Rome, 1843.

Renaudot, E. *Liturgiarum orientalium collectio.* 2 vols. Westmead, 1970.

## b) Historical Sources

Mansi, J. D. *Sacrorum conciliorum nova et amplissima collectio.* 31 vols. Florence-Venice, 1757–1798. Reprinted and continued by L. Petit and J. B. Martin, 53 vols. in 60. Paris 1889–1927; repr. Graz, 1960–.

Pitra, J. B. *Juris ecclesiastici graecorum historia et monumenta.* Vol. 2. Rome, 1968.

## c) Special Studies on the Liturgy of the Presanctified

Allatius, Leo. *De missa prae-sanctificatorum, a seguito del trattato De Ecclesiae Occidentalis atque Orientalis perpetua consensione.* Colonia, 1648.

Andrieu. M. *Immixtio et consecratio: La consécration par contact dans les documents liturgiques du Moyen Âge.* Paris, 1924.

Codrington, W. H. "The Syrian Liturgies of the Pre-sanctified." *JThS* 4 (1903) 69–82; 5 (1904) 369–77, 537–45.

Moraitis, D. "La Messe des Présanctifiés." *Ellenika Parartema* 9 (1956) 220–28.

Raes, A. "La communion al calice dans l'office byzantine des Présanctifiés." *OCP* 20 (1954) 166–74.

Theodore the Studite. *Explicatio Divinae Liturgiae Praesanctificatorum.* PL 99:1687ff.

Thibaut, J. B. *Monuments de la notation ekphonétique et hagiopolite de l'fglise grecque.* St. Petersburg, 1913.

____. "Origine de la Messe des présanctifiés." *Les Echos d'Orient* 19 (1920) 36–49.

Vagaggini, C. "La liturgie des Présanctifiés." *Roma e* l'Oriente 1 (1910) 297–307.

____. "La liturgia dei presantificati nel rito bizantino." *RL* 26 (1939) 87–92.

Philippe Rouillard, O.S.B.

**13**

# The Viaticum

Most religions have rites destined to assist the dying by helping and protecting them in the mysterious and fearful journey from this present world to the world beyond. In some African tribes, the chief could not depart alone for the land of the dead: he had to be accompanied by his wives, and escorted by servants or warriors, who therefore were immolated. In a different mode, the Greeks and the Romans often placed a coin in the dead persons' mouths, to allow them to pay Charon who ferried the deceased over the river Styx to bring them to Hades. This costly crossing remains present to the Church's memory; it is depicted, among other places, in Michelangelo's fresco of the Last Judgment in the Sistine Chapel.

Christians too have wished to accompany their dead in their migration toward the kingdom of heaven. Their faith led them to offer to the dying Communion in the body (and blood) of Christ so that they might end their lives with this pledge of resurrection and that their own *transitus* might be closely associated with the paschal mystery of Christ. The name "viaticum" was given to this ultimate Communion (*viaticum* in Latin from "way," "route"), since it is food for the journey.

In this chapter we shall study the history of this rite, its celebration (with or without Mass), according to present day liturgical books, and, finally, its theology and pastoral utilization.

HISTORY OF THE VIATICUM
The word "viaticum" is not specifically Christian. The Romans used it to designate the meal offered to those about to undertake a journey, or else the provisions taken along on the road. The Latin-speaking Christians

applied this word to the eucharistic Communion given in view of this last voyage. In the second and third centuries, there is not any text that explicitly mentions the viaticum brought to the dying. It is true that Justin of Rome (d. ca. 165) says that at the end of the Sunday Eucharist, the deacons carry Communion to the absent members of the congregation.[1] About the year 200, Tertullian of Carthage writes that Christians take home the consecrated bread to give Communion to themselves during the week.[2] Neither of these texts has any explicit mention of the dying.

The earliest reliable document emanates from the Council of Nicaea (325) which, in canon 13, states: "Concerning those who are about to depart for their exodus, the ancient and canonical law will be observed, so that those about to set out on their exodus be not deprived of this last and most necessary viaticum." It is significant that the first general council held after the end of the persecutions should treat of the administration of the viaticum; this an obvious proof of the importance of this custom. Besides, the council does not initiate any new discipline but prescribes that "the ancient law" of the Church — whose origins are unknown to us — continue to be observed. The question under discussion is that of the apostate Christians, not fully reconciled, from whom one must not withhold the viaticum.

From the fourth to the eighth centuries, many hagiographic stories report that, at the moment of death, Christians receive Communion from the hands of a priest, or of a layperson, or from their own hands. Thus, St. Gregory the Great reports that St. Benedict, at the point of death (ca. 547), asked his disciples to carry him to the oratory *ibique exitum suum dominici corporis et sanguinis perceptione munivit*[3] "and there strengthened his dying moments by receiving the body and blood of Christ." St. Benedict is intent on receiving the viaticum, but the text does not clearly specify whether he receives it from someone else or takes it himself. In most accounts Christians receive Communion under both species, bread and wine; sometimes they receive only "the body of Christ," but this expression can mean both the bread and the wine. In certain cases they receive the bread dipped in the wine, which makes it easier for them to consume. A council of Toledo in 675

---

[1] *I Apologia* 67, 5.
[2] *De oratione*, 19.
[3] *Dialogues* II, 37, 23.

recommends this practice which enables the faithful to more easily swallow the eucharistic bread (canon 11).

The first liturgical books that treat of the viaticum are the Roman *Ordines* going back to the seventh and eighth centuries. A ritual for funerals entitled *Ordo qualiter agatur in obsequium defunctorum* ("How the funerals of the dead are to be conducted") describes in full detail the Christians' death, celebrated as a liturgy: "As soon as you see the dying persons near their end *(exitum)*, they must receive Communion from the holy sacrifice, even though they have eaten on that very day, because Communion will be a defense and a help for the resurrection of the just. Indeed, Communion itself will raise them up. After Communion, the Passion of the Lord will be read before the sick persons, by a priest or a deacon, up to the moment when the soul leaves the body."[4] A ritual from the same period beautifully entitled *Incipit de migratione animae* ("Here begins the treatise on the migration of the soul") follows a slightly different order for the performance of this liturgy: "As soon as the hour of the *exitus* approaches, they begin to read the Gospel of John concerning the passion of the Lord (followed by the singing of Psalm 41 and a litany). When this is over, the priest recites the oration of the commemoration (or of the recommendation) of the soul. Then, before it leaves the body, the priest gives it Communion with the body and the blood, lest the soul should come out *(non exeat)* without viaticum; it is the body of the Lord."[5]

The liturgy presented in this second ritual is better structured; it begins with a reading of God's word (the account of the passion), continues with a psalm, an intercession, and an oration, and ends with the Communion to the body and blood of Christ. For its part, the *Ordo* 49 gives a rule that will continue to be maintained in the Church: the viaticum dispenses from the law of eucharistic fast; besides, the *Ordo* incorporates into its ritual this fine theological affirmation: the Communion given in viaticum is for the dying person the assurance and even the sacrament of resurrection.

The medieval councils prescribe that only priests or deacons should bring the viaticum to the dying, while allowing that, in case of necessity, acolytes or even lay persons might exercise this ministry.

---

[4] *Ordo* 49, 1–2; M. Andrieu, ed., *Les "Ordines romani" du haut moyen âge*, IV, 529.
[5] *Ordo Phillips* 1667, H. Franck ed., *A. L. W.* Vi, 2 (1962) 363–64.

In the *Rituale Romanum* of 1614, the viaticum is treated as a particular form of the Communion of the sick (IV, 4), preceding the sacrament of extreme-unction. It is stated that the faithful in danger of death are obliged to receive the viaticum; should the danger of death continue for any length of time, the viaticum can be received several times, on distinct days. The priest bringing the viaticum, accompanied by several clerics, sprinkles the place with holy water, hears the sick person's confession if need be, and gives him or her the viaticum, saying, *Accipe, frater viaticum corporis Domini nostri Jesu Christi, qui te custodiat ab hoste maligno, et perducat te in vitam aeternam* ("Receive, my brother [or sister] the viaticum of the body of our Lord Jesus Christ, who may preserve you from the wicked enemy and lead you to eternal life"). But, as the unction of the sick was administered after the viaticum, the latter is no longer the sacrament of the dying as it had been since the beginning.

### THE CELEBRATION OF THE VIATICUM TODAY

Vatican II wished to restore the viaticum to its original place, so that it might again be the sacrament of Christian death: "In addition to the separate rite for Anointing of the Sick and for Viaticum, a continuous rite shall be prepared in which the sick [person] is anointed after he [or she] has made his [or her] confession, and before he [or she] receives Viaticum" (*SC* 74). We find descriptions of the viaticum in different liturgical books. On the one hand, the *Ordo unctionis infirmorum* from 1972 foresees the administration of the viaticum during Mass or outside Mass (ch. 3), but also the continuous rite comprising penance, unction, and viaticum (ch. 4). On the other hand, the Ritual *De sacra communione . . . extra missam* from 1973, treats of the Communion in general and the viaticum in particular (ch. 2). Finally, the *Missale Romanum* offers a formulary *Ad ministrandum viaticum* among its ritual Masses.

The *Ordo unctionis infirmorum,* either in the *Praenotanda* (nos. 16–31), or in the body of the ritual, recommends that the viaticum be given during a Mass celebrated in the sick person's room. In the beginning of the liturgical celebration, the officiant is invited to state — in a surprising manner — that Christ left us the sacrament of his body and blood in order that at the hour of death, we may be strengthened by the viaticum and provided with this pledge of resurrection (no. 103). Such a presentation of the Eucharist is obviously too limited, and most translations into vernacular languages have corrected it, by saying that Christ entrusted to us the sacrament of his body and blood, and that it is fitting that we should receive this sacrament in viaticum at the moment of our going to the Father.

At the end of the Liturgy of the Word, a profession of faith has been introduced, under the form of questions and answers; this links the final communion of the sick person to his or her baptismal birth. When giving Communion to the sick person, the priest says, "*Corpus Christi*" (or *Sanguis Christi*). *Ipse te custodiat et perducat in vitam aeternam.* The mention of the "wicked enemy" that appears in the tridentine formulary has been removed. At the end of Mass, after the blessing, the priest may give the plenary indulgence *in articulo mortis* ("at the moment of death") which, when the viaticum is administered without a Mass, finds a more normal place at the end of the penitential act.

Let us also note that, in the absence of any priest or deacon, the viaticum may be brought to the dying person by any faithful who is a eucharistic minister. As far as possible the sick will receive Communion with both bread and wine; depending on circumstances and their physical state, they may be given only the bread or only the wine.

A felicitous effort has therefore been made on the liturgical plane to give back to the final Communion its place and its function of last sacrament, that of the effective participation in the death and the resurrection of Christ. The continuous rite comprising penance, unction, and viaticum, emphasizes the complementary relationship between the first Christian initiation with its three steps, and the fulfillment of this initiation. Obviously, the three sacraments given to the dying correspond to baptism for the remission of sin, to the unction of confirmation, and to the first eucharistic Communion. However, experience shows that it may prove difficult for the sick to receive and really live three sacraments in such a short time.

THEOLOGY AND PASTORAL CONCERN
It is striking to see with what insistence the Church has, through the centuries, commanded or recommended the viaticum as death nears. At least since the ritual of 1614, the reception of the viaticum is presented as coming under a divine command, based on Jesus's word. "Those who eat my flesh and drink my blood have eternal life, and I

will raise them on the last day" (John 6:54). This argumentation fails to be convincing because Jesus's word applies to every Communion and not only to the viaticum. Whereas the *Ordo unctionis infirmorum* of 1972 still retains the mention of precept and quotes the gospel text (nos. 26 and 27), the *CIC* of 1983 is far less binding (canon 921); it only advises the faithful in danger of death to be fortified *(reficiantur)* by the viaticum, but does not spell out any obligation. The traditional insistence on the "precept" of the viaticum may be explained by the fact that, for many centuries, most Christians received Communion only very rarely.

Anyhow, in practice, will the precept be observed? We must recognize that in many countries, few Christians receive the viaticum before dying, and that the pastors do not seem to be troubled by this state of affairs. In rich nations, 75 percent of the population die not at home but in hospitals or clinics. Now, it is not easy to celebrate Mass in a hospital ward or room, and it is not always feasible to bring communion to a dying person. Besides, in many regions, the anointing of the sick is still regarded as the last sacrament.

Concretely, because of the progress of medical care, it happens often enough that the sick remain critically ill for days or weeks. When should the viaticum be brought to them? The *Ordo unctionis infirmorum* (no. 27) stresses that the sick person should receive the viaticum when he or she is still fully conscious. No one knows how long this full consciousness will last. The French ritual of the *Sacraments pour les malades* from 1977 suggests a good pastoral solution: "To the sick persons aware of their approaching death, and able to receive Communion, it will be possible to propose, if expedient, that a special significance be given to one of their Communions, not necessarily the last one. In this Communion under the mode of viaticum, the readings, the orations, and if possible the Communion under both species and the Mass will make manifest the paschal dimension of the Eucharist; they will strengthen in the sick Christians the certitude of being accompanied by Christ at the moment of the point of going to the Father with him" (no. 145). Such a suggestion is well within the range of the adaptations of which the Roman *Ordo* entrusts the decision to episcopal conferences (nos. 38–9).

The effort realized on the liturgical plane by the new ritual of the viaticum has not yet produced all its good results in practice. However, it is fruitful, by urging theologians to a deeper reflection on the

Eucharist as a sacrament of the resurrection. It also encourages ministers to help sick persons in danger of death understand all the richness that the eucharistic presence of the risen Christ is for them in their solitude and anguish.

## Bibliography

Beauduin, L. M. "Le Viatique." *MD* 15 (1948) 117–29.

Bride, A. "Viatique." *Dictionnaire de théoloqie catholique* 15 (1950) 2842–58.

Browe, P. "Die Sterbekommunion in Altertum und Mittelalter." *ZKTh* 60 (1936) 1–54; 211–40.

Falsini, R. "Il senso del Viatico, ieri e oggi." In *Il sacramento dei malati*, 191–208. Turin, 1975.

Grabka, G. "The Viaticum: A Study of Its Cultural Background." *Traditio* 9 (1953) 1–43.

Hannon, J. J. *Holy Viaticum: A Historical Synopsis and a Commentary*. Washington, 1951.

Ramos, M. "La eucaristia come viatico: El sacramento del transito de esta vida." *Ph* 19 (1979) 43–48.

Sicard, D. "Le viatique: Perspectives nouvelles." *MD* 113 (1973) 103–14.

_____. "La celebrazione pasquale del viatico." In J. Gelineau, ed., *Assemblea santa*. 569–73. Bologna, 1991.

Adrien Nocent, O.S.B.

# 14

# Questions about Specific Points

## CONCELEBRATION

*1. Preliminary Approach to the Question*
The meaning of "concelebration" is more complex than it first appears; it depends on several elements, and especially on what is understood by "celebration" and "priesthood." If, by "celebration" one means the activity of the assembly of the baptized, this presupposes that a "genuine priesthood" is attributed to the faithful, although this priesthood differs in degree from that of bishops and priests. This is the thinking of *Lumen gentium.* In this case, it is legitimate to say that the entire assembly concelebrates, because as a whole, it offers the sacrifice of praise to the Father with Christ, its head. But, most often, the term is used in a restrictive way. It applies to those who have received the sacrament of holy orders and in virtue of it, together, actualize in the present moment the unique sacrifice of Christ; thus they serve the faithful by enabling them in their priestly function to join in the offering of the sacrifice. It is with this latter understanding that we shall briefly study concelebration, while avoiding to "clericalize" the celebration as though it excluded the non-ordained.

When examining the historical development of concelebration, we must be careful not to apply to the past what a subsequent period may have understood by priesthood and priestly function. It is obvious that the desire to see the possibility of concelebration becoming more prevalent in the Roman Church was aroused for a large part by a conception — not necessarily primitive, or even ancient — of the role of the priesthood and the "eucharistic frequency." We no longer need to demonstrate that in the first centuries, and probably later on, the priest does not celebrate the Eucharist out of devotion but as a service to the community. Similarly, the Eucharist is celebrated on Sundays and feastdays, then progressively on certain other feasts, but it is known that only in the eighth century did Mass begin to be celebrated on Thursdays in Lent besides the other weekdays.

In our own time it is taken for granted — although it is not an imperious obligation — that priests should celebrate the Eucharist every day even though there is no service to be rendered to any community. This is part of the contemporary spirituality of the priesthood.[1] Vatican II stated that the chief reasons for concelebration were the manifestation of the Church and the unity of the priesthood, and it was easy for the council to invoke the earliest custom of the Roman Church which knew only the concelebration of the priests with their bishop.

The majority of priests, however, wished to concelebrate in order not to have to celebrate in isolation, and this is why concelebration among priests without the bishop was introduced, a practice foreign to the Roman tradition. Some may say that the presiding priest is a sort of delegate of the bishop, but this is a rather unsatisfying fiction. It is interesting to read in the documents of Vatican II, the participants' contributions and discussions on the topic of concelebration. On the one hand, such reading shows a multiplicity of viewpoints, and, on the other, the overall lack of theological content of the arguments. Be that as it may, the ritual of concelebration published in 1965 gives the following definition, "In this form of celebration, several priests, by virtue of the same priesthood and in the person of the Sovereign Priest, act together with one single will, one single voice, and, in one single sacramental action, accomplish and offer together the unique sacrifice and together participate in it."[2]

---

[1] In 1958 the Congregation for Religious reprimanded a monastery where priest-monks received Communion at the conventual Mass; they were reminded of their obligation to celebrate the Eucharist and told that to refrain from doing so was regarded as a grave abuse.

[2] *Ecclesia semper, AAS* 57, 1965, 411. Trad. fr. C.N.P.L. in: *La liturgie.* Documents conciliaires 5, Paris 1965, 161. It uses the Latin text for preciseness: *In hac ratione Missam celebrandi plures sacerdotes, in virtute eiusdem Sacerdotii et in persona Summi Sacerdotis simul una voluntate et una voce agunt, atque unicum Sacrificium unico actu sacramentali simul conficiunt et offerunt, idem simul participant.*

The expression *una voce agunt* ("they act with one voice") is noteworthy. In the first centuries only the principal celebrant said the Eucharistic Prayer, which he himself composed. Our theology of the sacramental matter and form does not recognize form as a gesture, for instance, the laying on of hands by all concelebrate during the Eucharistic Prayer, according to *The Apostolic Tradition*.[3] This does not authorize us to project our modern way of seeing into the past or even the future, since the Church has the power to determine the conditions under which a sacrament is to be performed, and since these can be modified as was the case of holy orders for example. However, today, one must strictly adhere to the declarations made by the Holy Office in 1957, *Ex institutione Christi ille solus valide celebrat qui verba consecrationis pronunciat* ("As instituted by Christ, only the person who pronounces the words of consecration celebrates in a valid manner").[4]

## 2. The Stages of the History of Concelebration, Theology and Pastoral Practice

### A. THE FIRST THREE CENTURIES

From the study of the documents of this period, one learns that the Eucharist was understood as one celebration presided by the bishop surrounded by his *presbyterium* ("clergy") and the whole community of the faithful. The Eucharist is not an individual and devotional act, but an action of the whole Church.

On this point, the celebrated text of Ignatius of Antioch is well known: *"Take care to participate only in one Eucharist, because there is one single flesh of our Lord Jesus Christ and one single chalice to unite us in his blood, one single altar, as well as one single bishop with the priests and the deacons, my fellow servants; thus, all you will do, you will do according to God."*[5]

But, more explicitly, *The Apostolic Tradition*, written in the beginning of the third century, describes in chapter 4 the celebration of the Eucharist on the day of the consecration of the bishop. The gifts are brought and the bishop recites the Eucharistic Prayer alone, while the priests extend their hands in silence. At that time, the Eucharistic

---

[3] *The Apostolic Tradition*. Geoffrey J. Duming, ed. *Hippolytus: A Text for Students*, with Introduction, Translation and Notes (Bramcote Nottingham, 1976, 10.

[4] *AAS* 49, 1957, 370.

[5] Ignace d'Antioche, *Lettre aux Philadelphiens* 4, SChr 10, 143–5.

Prayer did not have a fixed text and Hippolytus himself takes care of telling us that the formulary he proposes is only one example and that it must not be said as if by memory.[6]

The *Didascalia Apostolorum*, a Syriac document, speaks of a local bishop receiving another bishop and inviting him not only to concelebrate but even to consecrate the wine when himself will have consecrated the bread. Even if the fact is not authentic, it would show that only the bishop pronounces the words but that the two bishops offer one single sacrifice.[7]

## B. FROM THE FIFTH TO THE EIGHTH CENTURIES

At the end of the fourth century, it seems that the Eucharistic Prayer became more or less fixed. We find in the *De Sacramentis* of Ambrose, the very formulation — practically verbatim — of what would become the future Roman canon.[8]

It appears that concelebration continued in existence until the sixth century, at least for the major feasts and the stational celebrations. The *Liber Pontificalis* describes the custom in force during the fifth and sixth centuries. In Rome, the ministers lift the patens while the priests in front of the bishop, celebrate the Eucharist with him. And at the end, they receive the Eucharist from the bishop's hand in order to distribute it to the people.[9] The text does not say whether the priests pronounce the words of consecration with the bishop. However, as the churches increase in number in the service of the communities, concelebration grows rarer, but in Rome, it was felt important to keep alive the ideal of celebrations by the bishop surrounded by priests and faithful. Consequently, the rite of the *fermentum* continued to be a reminder of this ideal, and the priests unable to join the bishop received from him, at the time of Communion, a fragment of the bread consecrated by the bishop, in order to stress their communion with him.[10]

---

[6] *La Tradition Apostolique*, op. cit. c.4, 10–1 and following - c. 29, .28–9.

[7] *Didascalia et Constitutiones Apostolorum*, II, 58. Ed. F. X. Funk, vol. I, Paderborn, 1945, 168.

[8] Ambroise de Milan, *De sacramentis, de mysteriis*, IV, V, 21–25, VI, 26–27 Ed. B. Botte, SCh 25 bis *Des sacrements, des mystères*, 114–17.

[9] L. Duchesne, *Liber Pontificalis, Texte, introduction, commentaire*, I, Paris 1945, 139.

[10] Innocent I, *Epist. 23 ad Decentium* 5, PL 20, 556–57.

## C. FROM THE EIGHTH TO THE THIRTEENTH CENTURIES

Although the rite of concelebration is still in use at this time, it has nevertheless undergone rather profound transformations which the *Ordo romanus* III demonstrates, transformations affecting both the rite itself and the frequency of its use. Here we hear of cardinal-priests. They stand near the altar and hold three gifts in their hands. They join the pope in reciting the Eucharistic Prayer and the words of consecration, but only the pope does the movements; this sort of concelebration takes place only at Easter, Pentecost, the feast of St. Peter, and Christmas.[11]

The above modifications are important ones. Of course, the point is still to manifest the unity of the Eucharist and that of the priesthood, but the sign has been altered. First, only the cardinal-priests are admitted to the concelebration and no longer the whole *presbyterium* around the bishop. True, the bishop of Rome has cardinal-priests in his *presbyterium*, but now this is represented only by the cardinals, which divides the *presbyterium* and makes for a more spectacular but less significant concelebration. Second, the concelebration has now become "spoken." This accords with the theological thinking of the time, prone to conceive of the sacraments in terms of matter and form. As for the frequency of the concelebration, it was bound to diminish because of the increase of the parish communities, and it is understandable that, especially on Sundays and feastdays, the priests, busy with their ministry to the community, were unable to concelebrate; the exception was that of the cardinal-priests whose administrative tasks did not prevent them from being free on those days.

## D. FROM THE THIRTEENTH CENTURY TO VATICAN II

Even the concelebration reserved for great solemnities falls into disuse and is preserved — under a seriously mutilated form — at the consecration of bishops and the ordination of priests.[12] The Roman Pontifical, whether that of the twelfth century, or that of the Roman Curia in the thirteenth century, as well as the compilation of William Durandus at the end of the thirteenth century give us this information and reveal to us the decline of the concelebration with the rejection of its

[11] *Ordo III*, Ed. M. Andrieu, *Les Ordines romani du haut moyen âge*, II, Louvain 1960, 131.

[12] M. Andrieu, *Le Pontifical romain au moyen âge*, I. Vatican City 1938, ST 150–1, Idem, op. cit. II, Vatican City 1940, ST 87, 349–50 - Idem, op. cit. III, Vatican City 1940, ST 88, 370–71.

earliest form in the Roman Church. Other factors in this process were the increasingly preponderant influence of an excessively scholastic theology and the tendency to consider sacraments too exclusively from the point of view of their individual efficacy, at the expense of their ecclesial aspect that became obfuscated. When it was elaborated, the theology of the High Middle Ages had at its disposal only these impoverished rites of concelebration. Many among us still knew the ritual in use until 1964 as found in the *Pontificale romanum* of Clement VIII. According to it, the recently ordained priests were concelebrating at the foot of the altar, on bent knees, pronouncing all words under the bishop's guidance, but not receiving the holy blood. In fact, they were not celebrating their first Mass, because a Mass validly celebrated requires that the priest receives Communion under both species consecrated by him.

### 3. The Liturgical Renewal of Vatican II

a. The restoration of the custom of concelebration at the time of the liturgical renewal has various points of departure. In the first place, there was a rediscovery — begun long ago — of the community aspect of the Eucharist. It is beyond doubt that the individualistic and devotional way of regarding the celebration of the Mass was increasingly felt by many people to be a deviation. It was not rare to see three Masses celebrated at the same time; the custom books of some religious congregations even provided for three Masses to be read simultaneously at the funeral of one of their members. Besides, the multiplication of congresses, conventions, and spiritual exercises attended by many priests caused among them a certain uneasiness about having to multiply the celebrations or even having to abstain from celebrating when circumstances made it impossible. Communities with many members came to reflect on the strangeness of all these individual celebrations, not primarily because the sacristans' workload was heavy but because people began to increasingly feel that a fragmentation of the Eucharist had been occurring which obscured the sign of the one bread and the one cup. The result was that the conciliar discussions at Vatican II were a medley of pastoral as well as theological motivations.

Finally, the council produced three documents treating of concelebration, either explicitly or casually. The Constitution on the Sacred Liturgy emphasizes concelebration in three places. First, it is stated that, in any case, communal celebration is to be preferred to individual and quasi-private celebration, and that this principle applies to Mass (*SC* 27 and 41). But, in a positive way, *SC* declares that the custom of concelebrating should be reestablished and spread, neither for archeological nor contingent and particular motives but for theological and pastoral reasons (*SC* 57 and 58). And the council gives norms which will serve to create a ritual for concelebration. In the Decree on Ecumenism (*Unitatis redintegratio* 15) and in the Decree on the Ministry and Life of Priests (*Presbyterorum ordinis* 8), the council returns to the topic of concelebration, but briefly.

b. The council wished to insist on the theological value of eucharistic concelebration by underlining how it shows the threefold unity deriving from what the eucharistic celebration is in itself. This threefold unity is (1) the unity of the priesthood, which is thus rendered most visible, (2) the unity of the sacrifice, in accordance with New Testament theology: one sacrifice, that of Christ who, once for all offered himself to the Father as a spotless victim (Heb 9:11-28), and (3) the unity of the people of God because concelebration cannot be viewed as expressing only the unity of the ordained priesthood — it would thus be clericalized — but it signifies and realizes the unity of the whole people of God.

c. At the time the ritual for concelebration was in the making, it was unthinkable to foresee a ruling that would mandate the silence of the concelebrants and reduce the sign of their celebration to gestures such as the laying on of hands. The long-held position of the Holy Office, which we have recalled, that of Pope Pius XII, and that of many other documents showed the line to follow. The rite demands that all the concelebrants pronounce the central part of the Eucharistic Prayer, which can also be sung by all. However the proclamation of the text in a loud voice produces a less than edifying result. The difficulty was resolved by prescribing that the voice of the principal celebrant be clearly heard and distinct and that the concelebrants recite the text attributed to them *submissa voce* ("in a low voice"). One must recognize that this rubric is rarely observed to the detriment of the dignity of the celebration.

A series of official documents has been published after the promulgation of the rite of concelebration.[13] We must note that *Eucharisticum*

---

[13] *Inter Oecumenici* (1964) 15 – *Variationes in Ordine Hebdomadae Sanctae* (1965), – *Ecclesiae semper* (1965), – *Eucharisticum Mysterium* (1967) 8, 47 – *Pontificales Ritus*

*Mysterium* dating from 1967, does not hesitate to state that concelebration is an excellent form of celebration and it urges priests to prefer it to individual celebration. However the right to individually celebrate is not restricted. In our day the right to concelebrate is widespread, and even a large priestly community is allowed to concelebrate several times a day in order to avoid too great a number of concelebrants at any one Mass.

d. The ritual does not take into account the ancient tradition of the Roman Church according to which priests concelebrate around their bishop and do not concelebrate among themselves. The principal celebrant is considered the bishop's delegate; however, this fictional explanation does not satisfy certain priests who do not concelebrate without the bishop. Despite discussions on this subject, there has been no attempt to limit the number of concelebrants. One must admire this generosity, but one cannot help recognizing that massive concelebration — as it happens on certain occasions — does not go without surprising and even scandalizing the faithful by its enormity that distorts the nature of the Eucharist. It is imperative that the concelebrants' number does not exceed the lay participants', for fear of making the celebration of the Eucharist a clerical affair instead of a sign of the unique priesthood of Christ.

e. The ritual of concelebration is rather lenient about the places occupied by the concelebrants and their gestures. It is preferable that they stand around the altar, but it is not obligatory. It is highly desirable that they be in the space of the presbyterium and not just anywhere, and certainly not among the faithful. Only one gesture is mandatory, that of extending both hands when the first *epiclesis* is recited. For the consecration, if desired — but it is not obligatory — the concelebrants extend their right hands in the direction of the gifts being consecrated. An interminable discussion took place on the way of holding the hand: should it be a laying on of the hand, or should the palm be turned to the side and not to the ground, as if to point to the eucharistic species? This is the way the matter is understood in the ceremonial of bishops and in an answer given by the Congrega-

---

(1968) – *Institutio Generalis Missalis Romani* (1969) 153–208 – *Ordo Benedictionis Abbatis et Abbatissae* (1970) Praenotanda 4.5, 8, – *Ordo confirmationis* (1971) Praenotanda 13, 19 – *Declaratio de concelebratione* (1972), document of the Congregation for Divine Worship.

tion for the Sacraments and Divine Worship to a question put to it, a non-official answer, however.[14] One must recognize that such a gesture has neither precedent nor equivalent in the whole history of the Roman liturgy, in which on the contrary the laying on of hands is frequent. The recommended gesture belongs rather to the Byzantine liturgy into which it seems to have been introduced at the time of the controversies about the *epiclesis* following the consecration, to signify faith in the efficacy of the consecratory words.

As for the manner of receiving Communion under both species, the ritual leaves the utmost freedom. However, if the bishop presides, it is appropriate that the concelebrants receive the consecrated bread from his hand. In other cases, the concelebrants take themselves the bread and the cup at the altar, or else they pass to one another the paten and also the chalice.

f. The vestments for the concelebrations are the same as those used for a non-concelebrated Mass. For a reasonable motive, the concelebrants can put on only the alb and the stole.[15]

COMMUNION UNDER BOTH SPECIES

*1. A Nearly Fifteen-Century-Old Custom*
Such a title as "Communion under Both Species" would have surprised the early Christians and even more the disciples who were contemporaries with Christ and the apostles, to whom the possibility of receiving the Eucharist under one species would never have occurred. Had not Jesus said, "Take and eat, all of you . . . take and drink, all of you. This is my body, this is my blood?" Prior to the tenth, or even the twelfth century, such an approach would have been scandalous. It is interesting to consider how St. Leo the Great disapproved of the Manicheans of his time who received only the bread, a practice the pope regarded as sacrilegious.[16]

In fact, throughout the centuries, the Church always recognized that the eucharistic sacrifice is not complete unless the priest at least

---

[14] *Not* 1, 1965, 143, qui précise *IGMR* 174 c, 180 c, 184c, 188c. *Caeremoniale Episcoporum* n.106, nota 79, Vat. Typis Polyglottis 1984, 15- I. Fossas, *Manu dextera ad panem et ad calicem extensa. Historia di una controversia, EO* 9, 1992, 201–16.

[15] Instruction of the Council and of the Congregation of Rites *Eucharisticum Mysterium,* 25 May 1967, n.47. *Enchiridium documentorum instaurationis liturgiae,* I, 1963–1973, Torino, 1976.

[16] Sermo 42, De quadragesima 4. *CCL* 138 A, 267.

receives Communion under both species in order to obey the Lord's command. In the *De defectibus circa Missam occurrentibus*, the Missal of Pius V goes so far as to say that should a priest die after having received the bread, another priest should consecrate some bread and receive the consecrated wine; only then would the Mass be a real Mass. This measure concerned the integrity of a celebration.

It is true that the Church had known a time when the faithful carried home some consecrated bread in order to receive Communion when there was no eucharistic celebration. However, even then, the preferred usage was to also keep in the church some consecrated wine for Communion if there was no eucharistic celebration. This gave rise to a strange custom when, in the *tituli* people wanted to receive Communion on Good Friday. To reserve wine is no easy thing. So there arose the practice of dipping into wine the bread consecrated on Holy Thursday, in the belief that the wine would be consecrated through mere contact.[17] This usage shows how deeply Christians felt it necessary in an assembly to receive Communion under both species. Until Vatican II, the Roman Church kept the custom of bringing to the celebrant a chalice of wine into which he deposited a small piece of the bread consecrated at the Mass of Holy Thursday, but then no one believed in the consecration of the wine by contact. This rite was eliminated at the time of the reform of Holy Week. The Byzantine rite of the presanctified continues to observe the custom of dipping into the wine the bread consecrated at the Mass of the preceding Sunday before consuming it; this custom is familiar to faithful of this rite on Wednesdays and Fridays in Lent.

### 2. A Progressive Lessening of the Sense of Sign

Once more, we must underline the fact that, among Western Christians, the concern for the practical and the quasi-exclusive attention to the conditions of validity have the result of altering the authenticity of certain rites to the point of causing their abandonment. The examples are many. Let it suffice to cite the baptismal immersion, impractical and, as a consequence rarely practiced, but fortunately, undergoing a partial recovery; the fraction of the bread, most often reduced to a rite which is little more than a vestige, because it is easier to use small hosts; the Communion given with hosts conse-

---

[17] M. Andrieu, *Immixtio et consecratio*, Paris 1924 - *OR* II 56–64.

304

crated at previous Masses, although the *Ritus servandus* in the Missal of Pope Pius V legislates that Communion be given with pieces of bread consecrated at that Mass itself.[18] So many rites have been distorted by the search for what is practical and are often presented today as due to pastoral concern! This is a conception of law gone awry and a stubborn attachment to a dogmatic definition which, in the mind of some, dispenses from respecting in practice the integrity and scriptural foundations of a sacramental sign.

This was the case for Communion under both species. It is obvious that the communion from the cup is not practical; besides, for certain people — according to the degree in which they submit to what is called civilization — it causes repulsion. Grievous and frequent epidemics were not conducive to favoring the practice of having large numbers of people drinking from the same cup. People looked for remedies; to receive Communion through a straw *(fistula, calamus, pugillaris),* as was done for several beverages, seemed appropriate enough. This custom was observed at the papal Mass as recorded in *OR* I, III. Several other documents mention it, for instance, the *Consuetudines cluniacenses* ("Customs of Cluny").[19] However Bernold of Constance disapproves of this usage.[20] Hugh of St. Victor rejects it for a reason which must have impressed his contemporaries: Only to Judas did Jesus give bread dipped in wine.[21]

In the beginning of the twelfth century, about 1110, basing himself on dogmatic reasons, Rudolf of Liège sadly exemplifies the loss of the sense of the scriptural sign and the exclusive concern for validity. The whole of Jesus Christ is present in the consecrated bread; this is cited by Cardinal Bona in his work *Rerum Liturgicarum.* St. Thomas himself advises not to give the holy blood to the faithful out of prudence.[22] The Dominican and the Franciscan Orders had ceased giving Communion under both species and they contributed for a large part to the abolition of the rite. However, here and there, until the fifteenth century, one finds instances of Communion under both species.

---

[18] *Ritus servandus* X,8.
[19] K. Hallinger, *Consuetudines monasticae,* 10, Siegburg 1983.
[20] *Micrologus, PL* 148, 1458.
[21] *Summa Sententiae,* VI, 9. *PL* 176, 145.
[22] *Summa Th.* P.III. q 80, art. 12.

## 3. Local, then General Abolition of the Rite

Communion under both species became the battle cry in the revindication of dissidents such as John Huss who thus provoked the repudiation of Communion under both species at the thirteenth session of the Council of Constance in 1415. As for the Protestants who argued that Communion under one species did not constitute a complete Eucharist, they caused Pope Martin VI to confirm in 1418 the decision taken previously in Constance. The Council of Trent was strong in affirming the complete presence of Christ under either species, but did not decide anything concerning the custom of receiving Communion under both species.[23] Still in 1564, Pope Pius IV allowed German bishops to grant Communion under both species in their dioceses, but because of serious difficulties, this privilege was revoked in 1565.[24]

## 4. The Progressive and Measured Restoration of Communion under Both Species

In our time at the close of our century, there is a great desire for authenticity in the signs; this was clearly manifested at Vatican II, independently from any dogmatic crusade or any partisan bias. Strangely, it is more on the part of the traditionalists that the refusal to accept this restoration appears as a sort of flag for revindication.

Vatican II decided to restore Communion under both species out of respect for the sign instituted by Christ. Not for a moment was this decision meant to invalidate what the Council of Trent had proclaimed. The explanation of the theologians at Trent cannot be contradicted: the grace of the sacrament is not conferred *ratione specierum sacramentalium, sed ratione ipsius rei quae sub specie sacramentali continetur*[25] ("in virtue of the sacramental species, but in virtue of the very thing which is contained under the sacramental species"). We have here a proposition of faith that cannot be contradicted. "The dogmatic principles established by the Council of Trent being main-

---

[23] Sess. XIII, De eucharistia. Cf. S. Frankl, *Decretum Tridentinum de communione sub utraque Specie*, Collectanea theologica, 1937, 256. See also several earlier references: M. Righetti, *Storia liturgica*, Vol. III, p. 507 and following.

[24] G. Constant, *La concesssion à l'Allemagne de la communion sous les deux Espèces*. Library of the French School of Athens and of Rome, Paris 1923.

[25] Cf. note 2.

306

tained," SC restores this practice in certain circumstances.[26] In 1967 the Instruction *Eucharisticum Mysterium* declares that "Holy Communion, inasmuch as it is a sign has a more perfect form when it is given under both species. . . . Under this form, the sign of the eucharistic banquet is more thoroughly illuminated and thus the commandment according to which the new and eternal covenant is sealed in the blood of Christ, as well as the relationship between eucharistic banquet and eschatological banquet in the Father's kingdom are more clearly expressed."[27]

Such a statement unavoidably provoked the remark: If this mode is more perfect, why is it conceded so parsimoniously? Effectively, in 1970, this concession was made much less restrictive.[28]

Nowadays, the practice of giving Communion under both species has become general enough and in certain places occurs at all eucharistic celebrations. It seems that this restoration has not given rise to abuses; besides it does not conceal any special agenda but has given back to the sign its complete authenticity, and we must be thankful to the magisterium. It is up to each diocese and each liturgical commission to see what is the most appropriate manner of realizing the "Eat and drink, all of you."

## COMMUNION IN THE HAND

It is strange that the possibility of receiving Communion in the hand caused a number of persons to be astonished, even sometimes scandalized. What we deal with here are different sensibilities and a lack of historical knowledge: the custom of receiving Communion on the tongue is thought to be an ancient tradition whereas it came into existence in the Middle Ages and more precisely in the ninth century. J. Jungmann thinks that the change from hand to mouth coincides with the replacement of leavened bread by unleavened. A synod in Rouen in 878 promulgates this general rule: *nulli autem laico aut feminae eucharistiam in manibus ponat, sed tantum in os eius* [29] ("that the Eucharist never be given to a layman or woman in the hands but only in the mouth").

---

[26] *SC* 55.
[27] Instruction of the Congregation of Worship of 25 May 1967 n.32. *EDIL1*, 930.
[28] Ibid. 29 June 1970, nn. 2144–53.
[29] Can. 2, Mansi, X, 1199 s.

However, even into the eleventh century, there are allusions to laypeople receiving the host in their hands.[30] It seems that various motives underlie this change. For instance the cleanliness of hands, although most often there was near the entrance to the church a fountain where people could wash their hands. But, more powerful than other motives, a new sensibility arose, very lofty no doubt, that stressed what will be called the *mysterium tremendum* [31] ("the awesome mystery"). As a consequence, prescriptions aiming at insuring respect for the Eucharist were multiplied, in accordance with the mentality of the time, between the ninth to the eleventh centuries. However, the testimonies dating back to Christian antiquity prove that Communion in the hand was normally accepted and preferred.

One knows the catechesis in which St. Cyril of Jerusalem gives a precise description of the way the faithful received the eucharistic bread in the hand with utmost respect and attention to avoid any carelessness: "When you approach, do not advance with open palms and fingers apart, but make your left hand like a throne for your right, which is about to receive the King. And having cupped your palm, receive the Body of Christ, saying, 'Amen.' Then after you have with care hallowed your eyes by touching them with the Holy Body, partake thereof, taking heed lest you lose any of it."[32] But it is easy to understand that what was in Cyril's time the greatest mark of respect, to make one's hand into a throne to receive the King, could little by little appear disrespectful, because to touch with the hand connotes a certain intimacy which our sinful nature is not worthy of achieving; to touch with one's hand is a privilege; therefore people preferred to receive the bread in the mouth and, later on, especially from the fourteenth century on, while kneeling.

Today, for many people, to open one's mouth and stick out one's tongue to receive the bread seems on the contrary a lack of respect and nobody would think of doing this to manifest one's unworthiness and one's desire to receive the Lord who is coming. For a large number of persons in our day this gesture does not correspond to

[30] See also J. Jungmann, *Missarum Solemnia*, op.cit. 306 and following.

[31] J. Jungmann, *Die Stellung Christi im liturgischen Gebet*, LQF 7 / 8, Münster 1925, 217.

[32] *St. Cyril of Jerusalem's Lectures on the Christian Sacraments: The Protocatechesis and the Five Mystagogical Catecheses*, Frank. L. Cross, ed. (Crestwood, N.Y., 1977).

what they instinctively feel, but to extend one's hands with respect and place the bread immediately into the mouth after receiving it is the maximum reverence that can be shown.

Taking account of all these divergent sensibilities, the option of receiving the bread in one's hand has been granted, depending on the dioceses and the thinking of the faithful. Even when the option of receiving Communion in the hand has been given, respect is shown to the sensibility of each individual believer who makes it clear how he or she desires to receive the Eucharist, either on the tongue or in the hand; the celebrant cannot in any way impose either way of receiving Communion; each person is at liberty to choose one or the other way of receiving the eucharistic bread.

Of course, it is good to teach the faithful who receive the bread in the hand to consume it immediately and not to circulate in the church while holding it in hand. In certain dioceses, it is still feared — and not always wrongly, as rather recent experience proves — that Communion in the hand may be the willful occasion of sacrilegious profanations afterwards. This danger can be lessened if the people are taught to place the bread in the mouth in front of or beside the person who distributes the eucharistic bread. In any case, this danger is not totally avoided even in the case of Communion in the mouth.

We should come to this point where no one despises others for their choices, avoiding accusations of either narrowness of view or lack of reverence; each one is entitled to his or her own sensibility and this requires mutual respect.


FREQUENCY OF COMMUNION

*1. The Problem Concretely Encountered Today*
Two opposite tendencies are discernible today. On the one hand, certain persons are not favorable to daily Masses, and this for a variety of reasons. They often invoke the custom of the early centuries, but they add specific psychological arguments: the frequency of the celebration robs it of its impact, generates a weary feeling, and flattens the relief it could give to ordinary life. The eucharistic "rhythm" cannot run counter to the human rhythm of the great moments of encounter. They also adduce theological reasons: Is the Eucharist intended to be thus repeated as though its quality were not exceptional and required continual repetitions?

On the other hand, some persons desire that celebrations be multiplied in the same day. For certain, this tendency is merely devotional and therefore subject to critical examination. But others feel that, to prove the reality of their participation in the celebration, they must receive Communion, for example at the community Mass in the morning, but also at the funeral Mass they are obliged to attend, or at a wedding Mass. In this wish for the multiplication of Masses and Communions, we must make a distinction between what is pure devotion and what is desire for full participation in the various celebrations in which one is obliged to take part.[33]

## 2. Evolution of the Frequency of Eucharistic Celebrations in the Course of History

Although it is indisputable that the early Church preferred Sunday as the day to celebrate the Eucharist precisely because of the resurrection, it would no doubt be exaggerated and imprudent to affirm that the Eucharist was celebrated only on Sunday. The mere reading of the Acts of the Apostles 2:42, 46 invites us to prudence. However, one cannot interpret the "day by day" literally — Paul writes that he dies everyday (1 Cor 15:31) for his disciples — but it suggests a frequency exceeding the exclusive Sunday celebration. One could imagine a scenario, which has no proof whatsoever: After taking part in the prayer in the Temple, Christians come back home and consume the bread that they have brought back from the Sunday celebration. Such a hypothesis would suppose a Communion with the presanctified and therefore a Communion more frequent than that on Sunday. Nevertheless, the preference granted to the Sunday celebration is obvious: the *Didache*,[34] and, a little later, in 150, Justin[35] in his *Apology*, show it abundantly. At the same time, there is no lack of documents attesting to some celebrations during the week. One knows Tertullian's difficulties with the synaxes of the Wednesdays and Thursdays which were

---

[33] It seems impossible to endorse the criteria proposed by K. Rahner and A. Häussling: One may celebrate the Eucharist whenever the frequency of its celebration increases the faith and devotion of those who celebrate it and when the celebrants can lend themselves to be edified as "Church." These criteria seem fuzzy and difficult to be objectively delineated. We shall come back to this topic a little later.

[34] *Didachè* 14,1. Ed. J. P. Audet, Paris 1958, 240–1.

[35] *Apologie* 1,67. Ed. L. Pautigny, 1904, Texts and documents 1,143.

fast days, because the Eucharist — of which people at that time had a very realistic conception — being the supreme food, broke the fast.[36]

We must remember that on Sundays, it was allowed to take, besides the consecrated bread to be consumed immediately, some consecrated bread to be kept at home and eaten before any other food; on fast days it was eaten in the evening.[37] This custom continued to be observed for a long time among the Egyptian monks; St. Basil alludes to it.[38] Although we have no knowledge of the criteria in this matter, we can recognize that Communions were frequent enough, far more frequent than the eucharistic celebrations.

However, this frequency diminished in certain regions. The Synod of Agde, in 506, enjoins three Communions during the year, at Christmas, Easter, and Pentecost.[39] From the ninth century on, the number of Communions clearly decreases, even in religious Orders. P. Browe cites the case of Benedictine monasteries where monastics received Communion three times a year. Among Poor Clares, confession was monthly and so was Communion.[40]

It is plausible that as it was getting farther away from its origin, the Church experienced a normal lessening of fervor. But this is far from being the only or the principal reason for the decline in the frequency of Communion. One may wonder whether the fight against Arianism and the stress placed on the divinity of the person of the Son, of Christ, have not contributed in part to overemphasize the divine and royal dignity and caused a sort of fear of approaching so great a sacrament. One also must take into account the very severe penitential discipline that kept the sinners away from the Eucharist until the time when, after a lengthy period of penance, they had found reconciliation with God and the Church. Such a penitential discipline had a twofold effect on eucharistic frequency. In the tenth century, the discipline of the commutation gives momentum to this twofold effect. Although the sinners were kept away from the altar, their penance can be considerably shortened and lightened if they can have a series of Masses celebrated in exchange for their penalties.

[36] Tertullian, *De oratione* 19, 1.3-4. CCL 1,267 and following.
[37] Ibid.
[38] Basile, *Ep. XCIII: PG* 32. 485.
[39] Mansi, VIII, 327.
[40] P. Browe, "Die häufige Kommunion im Mittelalalter," op. cit. 89–97.

On the one hand, the sinners remain away from the Eucharist; on the other, the priests are called upon to multiply Masses for the sinners' salvation.[41]

During the same period, "Apologies" are introduced into the Mass formulary; they are prayers asking for the forgiveness of sin. The Missal of Pius V, published in 1570, carries numerous traces of these apologies, which were part of the Missal of the Roman Curia published in 1474.[42] All this resulted in this paradoxical situation: as the Communions diminished, because many sinners were kept away from the altar, the number of Masses asking for the pardon of sin increased to such a degree that the Abbey in Florence, for instance, received the order not to celebrate more than thirty Masses for the same sinner.

Another example is found in the penitential of Vienna: a priest will not be allowed to celebrate more than seven Masses per day for his own intentions, but if a penitent asks him to celebrate, he is free to offer Mass as often as he wants, even more than twenty times on the same day.[43]

In the Roman liturgy the custom of celebrating three Masses at Christmas has persisted, a usage that can be understood when the bishop of Rome was obliged to celebrate Mass in three important sectors of his city. But this became a personal devotion when every priest was allowed three Masses one after the other at the same altar, and most often without any participation by the faithful. The custom of the three Masses on November 2 said by the same priest and in the same conditions as at Christmas arose in the fifteenth century; in 1919, Benedict XV extended to the whole world the privilege of the three Masses.

### 3. Today's Frequency of Eucharistic Celebration and Communion
The decree *Presbyterorum Ordinis* recommends that the priests celebrate the Eucharist every day even in the absence of participants (*PO* 13). In our own day, although it is less scrupulously observed than in the past, the daily celebration is still part and parcel of priestly spir-

[41] C. Vogel, "Le péché et la pénitence. Evolution historique de la discipline dans l'Eglise latine," AA.VV., *Pastorale du péché*, Paris-Tournai 1961, 147–234.

[42] A. Nocent, "Les apologies dans la célébration eucharistique," *Liturgie et rèmission des péchés*, Rome 1975, 179–96.

[43] *Paenitentiale Vindobonense* A, c.45. Ed. Wasserschleben, 420.

ituality. The law requires that priests celebrate the Eucharist frequently and even everyday (*CIC* 904) as is recommended in the Decree *Presbyterorum Ordinis*. For seminarians, the law sees their participation in the daily eucharistic celebration as a source of energy for their spiritual life and their apostolate (*CIC* 246, par. 1). The same demand is imposed on religious (*CIC* 663, par. 2). As for the faithful, the Code of Canon law specifies that they must receive Communion at least once a year, and, barring a real impediment during paschal time (*CIC* 920). But today the law permits the faithful who already have received communion that day to receive it a second time, provided it is during the eucharistic celebration (*CIC* 917).

One would like to know the mind of the lawgiver. It is difficult to suppose that these rulings were made only to foster what is merely devotional. But, on the contrary, one should be grateful that Christians who are bound to attend two celebrations on the same day are allowed to participate in a complete way to the sacrifice they offer. Such would be the case, for example, for a religious woman who takes part in the community Mass but who must also attend a funeral Mass. But would it be in accordance with the mind of the lawgiver that a community which has a chaplain and receives another priest for a few days, arrange for having two separate Masses during the day and thus receive Communion twice?

Let us observe that the law nips in the bud the possibility of a priest's yielding to love of money brought by the multiplication of daily celebrations. First, barring exceptions granted or even requested by the Ordinary, for instance because of lack of priests, a priest cannot celebrate more than two or three Masses on the same day (*CIC* 905, par. 1 and par. 2). Except for the three Christmas Masses, he can keep for himself only the stipend received for one Mass, the other stipends are given to the diocese, according to the bishop's rulings (*CIC* 951, par. 1).

*4. Establishing Criteria, for the Frequency of Celebration
and Communion, a Difficult Task*
The increase of faith and devotion is a criterion difficult to verify, whether by the person involved or by other persons. Subjectivity in judgments is a risk. In any case, it seems that two criteria of legitimate frequency are reliable. Regarding the celebration of Mass, there must be a need and the service to render to the faithful hard put to

find a celebrant. Regarding Communion, there must be the moral obligation to participate on the same day in two different celebrations in two different places. As for the rest, the criteria are blurred and one could think that there is no reason why the "eucharistic rhythm" should conflict with the normal human rhythm of the desire for important and profound encounters. In no way should the Eucharist be likened to the devotion toward a saint whom one wants to pray to. The multiplication of Masses and Communions should not become a risk for the "devotion" to Mass to be merely a sort of infallible means of satisfying one's own desires instead of, first of all, a means of communication with Christ for one's sanctification.

## THE SUNDAY CELEBRATION
## IN THE ABSENCE OF A PRIEST

*1. Rise and Progressive Development of These Assemblies*
As can be noticed, the bibliography is mainly German, and that is normal enough because it is in Germany that the theological and pastoral problem has been discussed for the first time in Europe, especially by H. Aufderbeck. To tell the truth, the same problem had occurred much earlier, in Africa. In 1893, in Burundi Sunday assemblies were presided over by catechists, and in 1943 this type of assembly became mandatory in places where missionaries could not come. In 1930, Togo followed the example of Burundi and little by little the custom spread to the rest of Africa, then to Asia, then to South America.[44]

Vatican II did not overlook such initiatives and encouraged a Liturgy of the Word on Sundays and feastdays (*SC* 35). Shortly afterwards, the Instruction *Inter Oecumenici*, in 1964, also supported a Liturgy of the Word, presided by a deacon if available, or by a layperson designated to lead the service. [45] Besides, in 1967, the Instruction *Eucharisticum Mysterium* directed that, if no priest was present, a minister who had received the faculty might distribute the Eucharist.[46] Less than ten years later, the Instruction *Immensae Caritatis*, dating from 1973, gave permission to designated laypersons to give Communion.[47] As for the structure of the service, the Instruction *Inter*

[44] A. J. Chupungco, *Liturgies of the Future*, op. cit., 192 and following.
[45] *Inter Oecumenici*, 37.
[46] *Eucharisticum Mysterium*, 33 c.
[47] *Immensae Caritatis*, 1.

*Oecumenici,* in 1964, saw it as identical to the Liturgy of the Word at Mass.[48] As we have said, Germany was the first country in Europe to engage in this experience, which had not been left to improvisation but had been carefully studied and implemented under the name of "Stational Celebrations." In 1979, two thousand parishes already practiced this "stational liturgy." In France, there were eleven hundred in 1977.

*2. Basis for These Assemblies in an Old Tradition with Its Survivals.*
This sort of celebration could cause problems, especially in Germany, because it bore a close similarity to Protestant services, and also because it presented a danger of leading to exaggeration and of possibly obfuscating the primacy of the celebration of the eucharistic sacrifice, especially on Sunday, the weekly commemoration of the Lord's resurrection. Despite the problems it could pose, this sort of celebration of the word followed by Communion was not a novelty in the Latin Church. It existed in Tertullian's time, and in the *Apostolic Tradition,* attributed to Hippolytus of Rome, it was regarded as very important: it is mentioned twice: the faithful must give preference to joining the assembly in order to listen to the word proclaimed for the comfort of their souls and they should be eager to go to church where the Spirit flourishes.[49] The Latin Church had kept the custom of having a Liturgy of the Word followed by Communion on Holy Wednesday and Good Friday; later on, it only continued to have it on Good Friday.

*3. Success and Spreading of These Experiences*
*Until Their Official Recognition*
The usage of these liturgies had also developed in France under the name of *Assemblies dominicales en l'absence de prêtre* ADAP, ("Sunday Assemblies in the Absence of a Priest"). In 1977, more than 1,100 parishes located in 67 dioceses, celebrated these liturgies.

   In 1988, these liturgies of the word with Communion distributed by a delegated minister were officially recognized. By that time the period of experimentation was left behind. Indeed, on June 2, 1988, the Congregation for the Sacraments and Divine Worship promulgated a *Directoire pour les assemblées dominicales en l'absence du prêtre* ("Directory

---

[48] *Inter Oecumenici,* 37.
[49] *Tradition Apostolique,* op. cit. c.35, p. 82–3; c. 41, p. 88–9.

for the Sunday Assemblies in the Absence of a Priest").[50] The presentation of the document by P. Tena specifies that, the homily being reserved for the priest or deacon, it is desirable that the pastor prepare the sermon and have it read by the person presiding the assembly in his name. For other things, the rulings given by episcopal conference must be observed.[51]

### 4. Detailed Organization of these Assemblies

One must admire how from the start, these assemblies were theologically and liturgically well prepared. This was the case for Germany where the Synod of Dresden gives excellent indications on the theology of these assemblies and the way in which they are conducted. Their goal is clearly outlined: to give to the faithful the opportunity to gather around a delegate of the bishop in order to listen to the word of God, receive the bread of life, concentrate on praying for all, and give a witness of God's love. The ministers who preside over these stational liturgies and are called "auxiliary deacons" are to be presented by the pastor and the parish council and to be delegated by the bishop after an appropriate formation.

The order of the celebration is established as follows: Greeting, penitential act, proclamation of the word of God with homily, general intercessions, distribution of Communion, blessing, and dismissal. The document strongly stresses the profound difference between these celebrations and the sacrifice of the Mass, which remains at the apex, although, of necessity, it is celebrated more rarely. This stational liturgy must emphasize the connection of this assembly with the parish, the diocese, the universal Church.[52]

The preliminary studies done by the French churches in view of these ADAP are no less admirable. Of course, the lack of priests has rendered these assemblies necessary as has also the will to maintain and manifest the Christian community. In 1977, Pope Paul VI had given specific guidelines to the French bishops concerning these assemblies. He observed that our contemporaries prefer human size communities, provided they avoid the ghetto mentality. He warns

---

[50] "De Celebrationibus dominicalibus absente Presbytero," *Not* 263, 1988, 366–78. Found in the French translation of the document published by Cerf, Paris 1988, with a presentation of the bishops' commission of the liturgy.

[51] *Not* 263, 1988, n.43, p. 376.

[52] H. Aufderbeck, *Sonntagsgottesdienst ohne Priester,* cit. p. 95 and following.

about what would be excessive and could lead people to believe this is at last the best solution. He insists on the fact that the celebration of the Mass is the primary objective.[53]

*5. Some Reflections*

a. It seems that these assemblies are becoming more numerous everywhere. One would wish that this be only a momentary development and that again priestly vocations be numerous. These assemblies offer a significant advantage but they also entail a true danger. An advantage: in our Latin Church, they underline the importance of the proclamation of the word as a mode of presence of the Lord among us, as *SC* 7 states. They offer the opportunity for giving the readers a good biblical-liturgical understanding of what they must proclaim, to teach them the style of proclamation, to instill the importance of the ambo, of the book of readings, of the evangelary and its dignity, of the gospel procession, of the homily, of well-structured general intercessions pertaining to the concrete assembly while remaining open to the universal Church, its hierarchy, the world. A danger: the most serious would be to lead participants to think that they are a substitute for the Mass. We must not minimize their importance, but they must remain at their proper place; Communion outside Mass in particular must be explained and shown to be in reference to the eucharistic sacrifice itself which is the summit of the life of the Church, an affirmation that cannot apply in the same way to Communion.

b. These assemblies offer a good opportunity for training some of the faithful for a special participation in the action of divine worship, for giving them a deeper understanding of what they perform. But there is also the possible danger — by no means merely hypothetical — of fostering in them a new form of clericalism and an overemphasis on their role.

c. However, one should not focus on the negative or the less fortunate aspects of these new forms of Christian assemblies. They came to be only recently, and it is legitimate to say that, provided they are implemented with in-depth preparation and with prudence, they are fruitful.

[53] Text given in *Documentation catholique* 74, 1977, 351 and following. For the experience of Germany and France, see *DEL* 92–4, an excellent presentation which we use here.

# Bibliography

CONCELEBRATION

AA.VV. "In ritum concelebrationis commentarius." *EphLit* 79 (1965) 219–35.

AA.VV. *Théologie et pratique de la concélébration.* Tours, 1967.

Augé, M. "Concelebrazione eucaristica." *NDL* 259–69.

Danneels, G. *Collationes Brugenses et Gandavenses* 9 (1963) 160. Completed by
P. Thion in *NRT* 86 (1964) 579–607.

Jounel, P. "La célébration et la concélébration de la messe." *MD* 83 (1965)
168–82.

_____. *La concélébration.* Tournai, 1966.

Schmidt, H. A. P. *Introductio in liturgiam occidentalem,* 406–10. Rome, 1960.

Zitnik, M. *Sacramenta: Bibliographia Internationalis.* s.v. "Concélébration."
Rome, 1992.


COMMUNION UNDER BOTH SPECIES

Augé, M. "La comunione sotto le due specie." *Anàmnesis* 3/2:278–80.

Danneels, G. "Communion under Both Kinds." In *The Church and the Liturgy,*
153–8. Concilium 2. Glen Rock, N.J., 1964.

Fischer, B. "Die Kelchkommunion im Abendland: Eine historische Skizze." *LJ*
17 (1967) 18–32.

Lopez, J. "La comunión bajo las dos especies." *Ph* 28 (1989) 296–305.

Roguet, A. M. "La communion au calice." *ViSpi* 112 (1965) 725–35.


COMMUNION IN THE HAND

Composta, D. "La comunione sulla mano: Storia, rito, catechesi." *RPL* 156
(1989).

Dölger, F. J. ΙΞΤΥΣ: Das Fisch-Symbol in frühchristlicher Zeit. 2nd ed. Münster, 1928– .

_____. *Antike und Christentum: Kultur und religionsgeschichtliche Studien.* 2nd ed.
Vol. 3 (1932) 231ff.; Vol. 5 (1936) 232ff. Münster, 1929–1950.

Jungmann, J. *The Mass of the Roman Rite: Its Origins and Development,*
2:374–91. Trans. F. Brunner. Christian Classics. Westminster, Md., 1986.
Reprint 1992. Originally published New York, 1951–1955.

"Modalità per la distribuzione della santa communione." *RL* 76 (1989) 555–
64. See also "Istruzione sulla comunione eucaristica." *Not* 25, no. 11
(Nov. 1989) 825–32.

Nussbaum, O. *Die Handkommunion.* Cologne, 1969.

Oury, G. "La communion dans la main." *Esprit et Vie* 79 (1969) 201–8.

Verheul, A. "La communion dans la main." *Questions liturgiques et paroissiales* 50 (1969) 115–22.

## FREQUENCY OF COMMUNION

Baldovin, J. "Reflections on the Frequency of Eucharistic Celebration." *Wor* 61 (1987) 2–15.

Browe, P. "De frequenti communione in Ecclesia occidentali usque ad annum c. 1000, documenta varia." *Gregoriana* (1932) 82.

DeClerck, P. "La fréquence des messes: Réalités économiques et théologiques." *MD* 121 (1975) 151–8.

Didier, J.-C. "La communion bis in die." *Esprit et Vie* 86 (1976) 564–65.

Dublanchy, E. *Communion fréquente. DThC* 3 (1908) cols. 515–52.

Häussling, A. "Motives for Frequency of the Eucharist." In *Can We Always Celebrate the Eucharist?* Ed. M. Collins and D. Power, 25–30. Concilium 152. New York, 1982.

Jungmann, J. *The Mass of the Roman Rite: Its Origins and Development,* 2:359–67. Trans. F. Brunner. Christian Classics. Westminster, Md., 1986. Reprint 1992. Originally published New York, 1951–1955.

Rahner, K., and A. Häussling. *Die vielen Messen und das eine Opfer.* Freiburg-Basel-Vienna, 1966.

Taft, R. "The Frequency of the Eucharist Throughout History." *Can We Always Celebrate the Eucharist.* Ed. M. Collins and D. Power, 13–24. Concilium 152. New York, 1982.

## THE SUNDAY CELEBRATION IN THE ABSENCE OF A PRIEST

Certain periodicals have devoted an entire issue to this problem. We mention a few of them, referring the reader to either *NDL* (1984) and other sources for the rest:

"Assemblea senza presbitero." *NDL* 132–7. French translation: "Assemblées en l'absence de prêtre." *Dictionnaire encyclopédique de la liturgie,* 91–97. Turnhout, 1992.

Aufderbeck, H. *Stationsgottesdienst.* Leipzig, 1972.

\_\_\_\_. *Sonntagsgottesdienst ohne Priester.* In Th. Maas-Ewerd and Kl. Richter, *Gemeinde im Herrenmahl: Zur Praxis des Messfeier,* 95–6. Freiburg i. Br., 1976.

Brulin, M. "Assemblées dominicales en l'absence de prêtre." *MD* 130 (1977) 80–113.

Chupungco, A. *Liturgies of the Future*. New York, 1989.

Hofinger, J., and others. *Pastorale liturgique en chrétienté missionaire*. Part 3: Les célébrations en l'absence du prêtre. Lumen Vitae 14. Brussels, 1959.

Kaczynski, R. "De liturgia dominicali sacerdotibus deficientibus celebrata." *Not* 8 (1972) 375–83.

Liégé, P.-A. "Accompagnement écclésiologique en l'absence de prêtre." *MD* 130 (1977) 114–28.

*LJ* 4 (1979).

*MD* 130 (1977); 175 (1978).

Nussbaum, O. *Sonntäglicher Gemeindegottesdienst ohne Priester*. Würzburg, 1985.

Ruh, U. "Priesterlose Sonntagsgottesdienste." *Herder-Korrespondenz* 34 (1980) 203–6.

Schillebeeckx, E., and J.-B. Metz, eds. *The Right of the Community to a Priest*. Concilium 133. New York, 1980.

David N. Power, O.M.I.

# 15

# Theology of Eucharistic Celebration

PROLEGOMENA AND METHODOLOGICAL PRINCIPLES
Ecumenical accords between Churches that have been forged in the
last thirty years attend to the convergence of liturgical forms as a key
expression of convergence in eucharistic faith. In this, they implicitly
point to the eucharistic celebration as itself a theology. The document
of the Faith and Order Commission of the World Council of
Churches on *Baptism, Eucharist and Ministry,* commonly referred to as
*BEM,*[1] while giving a list of elements to be found in celebration, more
or less common among churches, also notes the diversities in liturgy
and practice. Being itself a theology, eucharistic liturgy is indicative
in an ecumenical context both of convergences and of divergences.

In his monumental work on the Eucharist, in the handbook named
*Gottesdienst der Kirche,*[2] Hans Bernard Meyer first offers the history of
the eucharistic liturgy, and then turns to its liturgical theology. As
methodological principle in this latter task he proposes to consider
the conjunction between the liturgies of the Last Supper, of the Lord's
Supper of the primitive Christian communities, and of the eucharistic
celebration of the following centuries. Eucharistic dogmas or doc-
trines, he states, have to be understood by way of their relation to
liturgical action.[3] What is of interest in this proposal is the theological
priority given to liturgical celebration, both as theological source and
as objective of magisterial or theological teaching. Though differing

---

[1] *Baptism, Eucharist and Ministry.* FOP no. 111 (Geneva, 1982).

[2] H. B. Meyer, *Eucharistie,* mit einem Beitrag von I. Pahl, *Gottesdienst der Kirche.*
*Handbuch für Liturgiewissenschaft,* Teil 4 (Regensburg, 1989).

[3] Ibid. 446.

somewhat from it, like the theological part of Meyer's volume, this present essay supposes the history offered in the foregoing chapters, and refers to what history unfolds by way of reflection upon it. Rather however than review theologies of celebration in different epochs, as done by Salvatore Marsili in *Anàmnesis*,[4] the choice is to develop a reflection on eucharistic celebration, relating it to larger realities, addressing the elements of celebration and using historical data in the process.

While a theology of celebration is not equivalent to a doctrinal theology that is mainly interested in studying magisterial and confessional formulations of eucharistic belief, it is not inseparable from it. In fact, the forms of liturgical celebration in which faith is expressed have been diversely influenced through time by doctrinal debates and confessions. One need only think, by way of example, of the importance of Berengarian debates in the eleventh century, and of the practical response of Lanfranc in organizing the Palm Sunday procession with the reserved Sacrament on Palm Sunday.[5] In East-West controversy, differences on the doctrine and liturgical role of the Holy Spirit, and on the relation of Old and New Testaments, were closely allied to differences on the form of bread to be used in eucharistic celebration.[6] At the time of the Protestant and Catholic Reformations, practice was key to doctrine, as witnessed by Luther's condemnation of the Roman Canon[7] on the one side and the tridentine decisions on such things as the Canon of the Mass, Communion under two kinds, and solitary celebrations by priests, on the other.[8] The relation between liturgical practice and belief is inescapable in the light of history.

In short, in attending to celebration as theology, or to what some call *liturgia prima* or *orthodoxia prima*, one looks for the pattern of belief expressed in the forms, that is in rites and texts, and in the man-

---

[4] S. Marsili, "Teologia della celebrazione dell'eucaristia." *La Liturgia eucaristica. Anàmnesis,* 3/2, 9–186.

[5] See N. D. Mitchell, *Cult and Controversy: The Worship of the Eucharist Outside Mass* (New York, 1982, Collegeville, 1990) 170f.

[6] See M. Smith, *And Taking Bread. Cerularius and the Azyme Controversies of 1054, Théologie et Histoire* 47 (Paris, 1978).

[7] See Martin Luther, "Abomination of the Secret Mass," *Luther's Works* (Philadelphia: Fortress, 1955) 36, 314–23.

[8] *Concilium Tridentinum,* Doctrina et Canones de Ss. Missae Sacrificio, DS 1738–59.

ner of its celebration, but without neglecting how this relates to doctrinal disputes and developments. One is aware that there is a connection between the traditional forms as they are acknowledged and appropriated, and the thought brought to the eucharistic action that serves to give it shape, within different contexts and cultures. Such a context must not ignore the relation to christian ethics of eucharistic celebration.

## 1. Process of Adaptation

The need for hermeneutical art[9] in interpreting tradition has come to clearer light today because of the acknowledged attention to the place of culture in celebrating liturgy, and because of the part that the Gospel and sacrament may be seen to play in going to the roots of culture.[10] Eucharistic celebration is an action of a people in a given place and time, within a particular culture. While theology reflects on the past, it also has to reflect on how the process of inculturation is inbuilt to the nature of the Eucharist as Christ's memorial and his present action in the Spirit. In considering the past, theology has to attempt to differentiate between what is of the very nature of Eucharist and what is determined by cultural reality and perspectives. This has to do not only with the form of rites or the language used in prayer, but with the prevailing creedal and theological affirmations about the mystery.

## 2. Critique and Retrieval

The purpose of a theology of eucharistic celebration is certainly to probe and bring to life the great gift of the Eucharist given by Christ to the Church, to be kept and celebrated in the communion of the Spirit. Careful understanding of tradition, and its pertinence to conditions of celebration, is primary. However, in hermeneutical procedure and in looking at the relation between the apostolic tradition and culture, reflection on tradition has to include some critical comment, in the very name of fidelity to what has been passed on. Particular cultural perspectives may all too easily appear to be an integral part of the tradition until they are questioned. The human reality of

---

[9] Semiotics and hermeneutics both influence the study of the eucharistic celebration, but space does not allow a methodological elaboration on this.

[10] Joannes Paulus II, "Litterae Encyclicae de perenni vi mandati missionalis," no. 52, *AAS* LXXXIII (1990) 300.

Church and celebration can also mean that particular interests or passing concerns can take on too much importance. One therefore brings to tradition not only an effort to penetrate the significations inherent to celebration, but also a mind ready to ask questions about that signification. The more attention is given to the diversity of tradition, the more such questions will arise. These questions need to sort out what is essential from forms and meanings that can change and shift, and indeed may need to change in order that the Eucharist may be the gift and memory that the gospel proclamation intends.

### 3. *What is Considered*
In developing a theology of eucharistic celebration, this essay begins with some consideration given to liturgical directives in today's Churches, since these reflect what accent is today brought to celebration, as distinct from what an actual study of texts may reveal. It then looks at the New Testament sources of the eucharistic tradition, keeping in mind that the interpretation of the supper narrative in particular is much influenced by developments in liturgical form and in eucharistic theology. It then offers reflections on the components of liturgical celebration as these are known from history, linking this where helpful to theologies of Eucharist in different epochs. In the entire process, interpretation, critique and retrieval work together, seeking to find the ways for the continued renewal of the celebration in the Church of the Lord's Supper.

### LITURGICAL DIRECTIVES IN TODAY'S CHURCHES
Before looking theologically at the historical texts and rites themselves, we can consider how official directives play their part on the contemporary scene. Since the essay is written for a Roman Catholic compendium, most attention is given to Roman Catholic directives, but a look at ecumenical accords can give a sense of how this relates to positions of other Churches.

### 1. *The Roman Missal*
The General Instruction on the Mass in the *Missal of Paul VI* (1975) spells out the theology of the Eucharist that is to govern the celebration enacted.[11] An opening section on the unchanging faith and tradi-

---

[11] *Missale Romanum ex Decreto Sacrosancti Oecumenici Concilii Vaticani II Instauratum Auctoritate Pauli PP. VI Promulgatum*, editio altera typica (Roma, 1975).

tion places the foundation of the Eucharist at the paschal supper, in which Christ instituted the *sacrifice* of his body and blood, to be celebrated in *memorial*. From this premise, the introduction develops both the sacrificial character of the Mass, in which the priest acts *in persona Christi* and *nomine totius ecclesiae*, and the mystery of the real presence, placing some accent on adoration. It allies the nature of sacerdotal ministry with the power to act in the person of Christ and perfect the sacrifice. It then allows for the participation of the royal priesthood of the faithful through spiritual sacrifice. Communion in the body and blood of Christ is mentioned in the last place, it being seen as the means of bringing the faithful together as one.

Chapter 1 of this instruction is devoted to the celebration of the Eucharist. It recalls the centrality of the Eucharist to the life of the Church, the role it plays in human sanctification and in divine cult, and the commemoration of the mysteries of Christ within the eucharistic celebration through the course of the year. It goes on to stress participation in the sacrifice, memorial of the passion and resurrection, reiterates the role of the priest, and asks for attention to forms that generate the greatest participation. In chapter 2, on the structure of the Mass or Lord's Supper, the first article stresses the sacrifice to be offered, the presence of Christ in the congregation, in the person of the minister, in the word, and in the eucharistic species. In the second article, the two parts of the Mass are noted, namely, the preparation of the table of the Word which leads to the table of the body and blood of Christ, by which the faithful are nourished.

On the parts of the Mass, the eucharistic prayer *(Prex eucharistica)* is called the *centrum et culmen totius celebrationis* (IGMR, Cap. II, 54), calling forth the participation of all through joining with the priest in the confession of God's great deeds and in the offering of the sacrifice. The sacrifice itself is said to be performed through the repetition of the words of Christ at the Supper. Mention of the rite of communion is introduced with the word *expedit,* saying that it is a fitting way to share in the mystery. This is based on the nature of the eucharistic celebration as a *convivium paschale.*

In these directives, it is clearly participation in the eucharistic prayer, which is interpreted as the offering of sacrifice through the power of Christ, that is given primary importance. Communion appears to be secondary, something which is suitable but not necessary to participation in the celebration of the eucharistic mystery. While this is offered as an interpretation of tradition, the particular focus now given to celebration is clear.

## 2. Faith and Order Paper No. 111

The ecumenically prepared paper, called *BEM* for shorthand, gives its own primary understanding in spelling out the "Meaning of the Eucharist," after it has referred to its institution at the supper:

"The eucharist is essentially the sacrament of the gift which God makes to us in Christ through the power of the Holy Spirit. Every Christian receives this gift of salvation through communion in the body and blood of Christ. In the eucharistic meal, in the eating and drinking of the bread and wine, Christ grants communion with himself. God himself acts, giving life to the body of Christ and renewing each member. . . ." (*BEM* 2).

Having thus emphasized the table and the sacramental gift, *BEM* later lists the following aspects of the essentially one complete act: thanksgiving to the Father, memorial of Christ, invocation of the Spirit, communion of the faithful, meal of the Kingdom. Oddly enough, it says little about the proclamation of the word in the eucharistic liturgy.

## 3. Lutheran/Roman Catholic Accords

The 1978 statement of the International Commission appointed by the Lutheran World Federation and the Roman Catholic Church lists much the same elements as appear in *BEM*,[12] but it is helpful to note what Catholics and Lutherans then ask to be considered by the other Church in terms of liturgical form. Lutherans would expect avoidance of Masses without congregation, better use of the possibilities of proclamation within each celebration, and Communion under both species. Catholics express the desire to see more frequent celebration of Holy Communion, greater participation by the congregation as a whole, and a closer link between the liturgy of the word and the liturgy of the sacrament.[13]

## 4. Anglican/Roman Catholic Accords

While ARCIC does not treat of the actual celebration, in addressing reservation of the sacrament it has this to say: "The whole eucharistic

[12] Lutheran/Roman Catholic Joint Commission, *The Eucharist* (Geneva, 1980) no. 76.

[13] Ibid.

action is a continuous movement in which Christ offers himself in his sacramental body and blood to his people and in which they receive him in faith and thanksgiving" (Final Report, Elucidations 8).[14] This is one way in which to express the relation between the Eucharistic Prayer and the Communion rite, pointing to the prayer as a movement which is incomplete without the Communion of the congregation.

### 5. Roman Catholic/Orthodox Statement

In all their conversations with other Churches on celebration the Orthodox accentuate the *epiclesis,* and the manifestation of the mystery of the Trinity in the celebration. In the common statement of the International Commission for Theological Dialogue between the Roman Catholic Church and the Orthodox Church on the Mystery of Church, Eucharist and Holy Trinity,[15] the Orthodox influence is evident in the accent put on the *epiclesis.*

Affirming that the entire celebration is an *epiclesis,* made more explicit at certain moments, and making present the mystery of the Trinity, the statement goes on to say:

"In it one passes from hearing the word, culminating in the proclamation of the Gospel — the apostolic announcing of the Word made flesh — to the thanksgiving offered to the Father and to the memorial of the sacrifice and to communion in it thanks to the prayer of *epiclesis* uttered in faith. For the *epiclesis* is not merely an invocation for the sacramental transforming of the bread and cup. It is also a prayer for the full effect of the communion of all in the mystery revealed by the Son."[16]

Communion is then presented as the extension through the presence of the Spirit of the sacrament of the Word made flesh to all the body of the Church. The prayer and sacramental Communion together are the form of communion in Christ's self-offering to the Father.

---

[14] *Anglicans and Roman Catholics: The Search for Unity,* The ARCIC documents and their reception, edited by Christopher Hill and Edward Yarnold (London, 1994) 27.

[15] Orthodox/Roman Catholic Theological Commission, "The Church, the Eucharist and the Trinity," *Origins* 12 (1982) 157–60.

[16] Ibid., no. 6.

## 6. Issues

A number of theological issues arise from these directives and discussions, affecting the reality and understanding of eucharistic celebration. The principal question has to do with the theological relation between communion and sacrifice, and the practical relation of the eucharistic prayer to the communion meal and ritual. The connection between word and sacrament is also at stake, as is the communal and relative participation of community and priest in the sacrifice. Especially in light of the Eastern theology of *epiclesis*, western theology has to give more attention to the relation between the action of the Eucharist as the memorial of Christ, done in his name, and the action of the Spirit.

## NEW TESTAMENT SOURCES[17]

From these opening questions, we turn to pertinent New Testament texts, keeping in mind that beyond strict New Testament exegesis these considerations are shaped by the later tradition of eucharistic celebration. What counts here is not a historical reconstruction, but the appeal to the New Testament texts, especially the supper narratives, which underpin a theology of celebration, influencing its forms and its understanding.

When the Church looks back to the supper as the act of the institution of the Eucharist, relating it to the way in which early christians celebrated the Lord's Supper, many exegetical problems affect its interpretation. On the part of scholars, there have been many different approaches to this. Some are here mentioned for their current importance in regard to ritual and its interpretation. They have to do especially with the relation of the supper to the pasch.

## 1. Supper and Eucharist

While the Supper Narrative plays the role of a foundational narrative in relation to the Eucharist, especially because of the memorial command, it cannot be taken as the sole indication of the actual origins or rites of the Eucharist in the early Church. We need to attend to a more general setting in the life of the Church as a community and

---

[17] For a brief review of the material, with pertinent literature, followed by a theological reflection, see Meyer, op. cit. 61–86. See also X. Léon-Dufour, *Le partage du pain eucharistique. Selon le Nouveau Testament* (Paris, 1982). English translation, *Sharing the Eucharistic Bread. The Witness of the New Testament* (New York, 1987).

look at the relation of the Eucharist to Jesus's meals, including post-resurrection meals. This setting points to the context of common life, to the sharing of communities in apostolic teaching and in love, and to the different ways in which Jewish forms of meal and prayer could have influenced the early Christian Eucharist.

The Jewish or hebrew roots of the Eucharist are to be found primarily in meal, in meal blessing prayer, in memorial command, and in the symbolism of bread and wine. They are also found in practices of sacrifice, especially communion sacrifice, and in the joining of prayers of praise with it. These considerations bring us beyond the immediate context of the paschal seder, as well as of the actions of Jesus at the supper, relating them to a larger picture.

### 2. Eucharist and Pasch

Efforts to show that the meal shared by Jesus with his disciples was a paschal seder are many, just as are the counterefforts.[18] While paschal images abound in the account of its preparation and partaking, some exegetes think that this is not enough to prove that it was a seder. The Supper therefore may not have been a pasch. If it is narrated in this way, this may have been more to give typological meaning to the death of Jesus than to establish anything about the basic rite for the Eucharist. Thus comparisons with the Jewish paschal seder are not to be pushed very far.

For others, however, it is equally important to show that the Supper was a pasch and that the Christian Eucharist has affinities with this. Something can be known about both rite and meaning of eucharistic celebration by relation to the paschal seder, in as far as its ritual can be reconstructed. Joachim Jeremias was strong on this point, but the one who has again brought the matter into prominence is Cesare Giraudo.[19] He presses the connection very strongly because of the connection which he makes with the history and notion of reconciliation, as well as with a particular understanding of keeping memorial.

He thinks that if Jesus instituted the Christian ritual during a paschal seder, he related his death and its commemoration to the

---

[18] The discussion surrounding the book of J. Jeremias, *Die Abendmahlsworte Jesu* (Göttingen, 3rd ed., 1960) has acquired almost classical status.

[19] Cesare Giraudo, *Eucaristia per la Chiesa. Prospettive teologiche sull'eucaristia a partire dalla "lex orandi,"* Aloisiana 22 (Brescia and Rome, 1989).

dynamic of reconciliation present in God's successive covenants with humanity. Starting with the Genesis story, God's action is always destined to reconcile humanity with God and to reconcile the human race within itself, by restoring its original unity. This covenant reconciliation is present in the promise made to the first couple, in the covenant with Abraham, and in the Exodus covenant. It is always associated with blood, with an immediate historical future of liberation, and with an eschatological prospective of ultimate and complete reconciliation. Giraudo sees all of this kept alive by the pasch, with its rites of commemoration and future anticipation. In his celebration of the pasch, Jesus assumes this covenantal history and carries it forward to a new and decisive moment. The immediate future of his pasch is his saving death, through which humanity is reconciled. The long-term, eschatological future is found in the promise of his resurrection and embraces the whole future of the life of the Church, until the moment of final reconciliation at the end of time.

In his interpretation of ritual acts of memorial, Giraudo underlines the prime role of the narrative that underlies the blessing. He suggests that the Jewish people in keeping the memorial of the pasch did not so much actualize the original paschal and Exodus events commemorated, as go back themselves to be present to these events as saving and eschatological. As the rites have it, Jews were to celebrate "as though" they themselves crossed over the Red Sea and entered the promised land. In inviting the disciples to keep memorial of him in narrative and in the rites of bread and wine, Jesus invited them to return in Eucharist to the saving moment of his own pasch. In it his followers would continue to find the promise of an immediate reconciliation, fitting into their own history, and the long-term eschatological promise of a final reconciliation yet to come.

These diverse opinions are a reminder that while the importance of the supper narrative to the origins and celebration of the Eucharist is certain, there is some ambiguity about the exact relation of Eucharist to supper and of supper to pasch. This affects approaches to both ritual and meaning of the Eucharist. The looser the connection with the Supper in ritual, the more is the inclination to look at the practices of the early communities for a matrix of celebration. The firmer the connection, the stronger the matrix provided by the Last Supper itself.

### 3. *Eucharist and Sacrifice*

Since traditionally the eucharistic mandate of Christ is located at the Last Supper, attention is given to the gospel narratives for what they may teach about the proper forms of celebration. An aspect of the supper narratives that is an important background to eucharistic prayer and celebration on the one hand, and has caused much controversy on the other, is their use of sacrificial language. In giving the gift of the bread and the cup, the words of Jesus reported in the supper narratives use abundant sacrificial imagery, evoking many strands in the cultic and historical past of Israel. The imagery that comes to the fore by very reason of the fact of sharing bread and cup is that of communion and covenant sacrifice. Jesus invites his disciples to a communion with him in the fruits of his self-giving, through communion in the death by which God makes covenant with humanity. That points to the primacy of the language of communion in the sacrificial interpretation of the Eucharist. Some expiatory images also occur in Jesus's words when he refers to the death that seals the covenant in whose benefits the disciples are to share. These bring out the point that his death is to bring about the forgiveness of sins. This, however, is given a very personal rather than cultic tone by way of the analogy with the Suffering Servant of the Servant Songs in Isaiah. In those songs, the language of expiatory sacrifice is used metaphorically, to show how in the devotion of a life of service and witness, even unto death, God's servant is to bring salvation to the people.

Insight into this meaning given to the Eucharist by this narrative of institution must come from within the action and words of Jesus. His is an action of self-gift. He gives himself over, pours himself out, to and for his disciples, anticipating that his death will be suffered for the forgiveness of sins, for reconciliation with God. He makes this gift with *eucharistia*, with thanksgiving, according to the ritual of Jewish meals. In this, his own self-gift, both in death and in the sacramental bread and wine, is presented as God's gift, as the gift of the one sent by God to give life to the world. It is also his own acknowledgment that all comes from God, and that his gift to his disciples is a dedication, and in this sense an offering, to the One who sent him. It is to explain this double giving, to God and to humankind, that the New Testament narratives make use of the Old Testament paradigms and language of sacrifice. If theology takes a point of departure from the supper narrative by way of pointing out its character as sacrifice or offering, it is in this sense that it must be done.

### 4. Memorial

The meaning and form of keeping memorial is much affected by these discussions of pasch and sacrifice. Some insights into this can first be culled from giving attention to the Jewish matrix. Others, with a more ethical implication, flow from the context of early Christian discipleship, which then bring the Johannine story of the supper into greater focus. Much depends on how commemoration relates to history, and on how narrative and blessing converge.

Relating the supper narrative to ways of keeping memorial in Jewish custom is helpful to an understanding of the role which it plays in celebration and theology. To see the supper narrative as an embolism in the Eucharistic Prayer, as will be explained further down, is already a reminder that for the Jews all memorial is done in obedience to God's command. Second, within Jewish tradition this commemoration is inherent to the covenant between God and the people. Third, it means that God continues to remember the people, as the people vow to keep memory of God's saving deed and their own covenantal promises. Fourth, narrative, blessing and ritual actions combine to mark a commemorative celebration.

These are all factors which serve to understand the form and the meaning of Christian memorial. When they are seen to be taken over in some way into the celebration of Christ's memorial, this enriches the appreciation of the context of community and the relation to ethical orientations. What became the weekly didactic and ritual gathering was the occasion to bring to the fore the common sharing of a life in Christ, and especially the care of the poor. When this sense of oneness was transgressed by the Corinthians in both life and ritual, it brought forth Paul's strong reproof. Collating this with the Johannine account of how Jesus washed the feet of the disciples, and gave the memorial ordinance to do as he had done, in obedience to his love commandment,[20] is a reminder that the memorial celebration must fit into a life of obedience to the Gospel, and that in this context it fosters such a life.

---

[20] Attention to this narrative, which he calls the testamentary tradition, is one of the great contributions of Léon-Dufour's study, *Sharing of the Eucharistic Bread.*

In explaining the exact relation to Christ's death, both Odo Casel and Cesare Giraudo appeal to the transhistorical character of Christ's act.[21] This seems too abstract and may be avoided by a better sense of history, and of how ritual commemoration affects historical links.[22] In writing of remembrance, historical representation, and the psalms, Claus Westermann avoided this dilemma by pointing to how the course of history is affected by remembrance, and to how it takes shape in face of immediate events or reality.[23]

The Israelites were forced to ask the meaning and effect of God's past action in history when they were faced with tribulations that called their status as chosen people into question. Their basic conviction was that the God who once acted in their behalf and made covenant with them continued to be their God and continued to be present among them. It was necessary then to tell the narrative in such a way that the link between the past and present distress would emerge, and the future faced in hope. What dominates this understanding of memorial is not the idea of a transhistorical act, but of a force present in history as a result of historical interventions, that continue to be remembered with praise and proclamation, even in times of great communal suffering.

This could be a better model for understanding the nature of the Eucharist as memorial. It seems especially apt when memorial is related to the gift of the Spirit, given to the Church at Pentecost and promised by Christ at the Supper according to the Johannine account of that evening. The pasch of Jesus with its Pentecostal fulfillment is the entrance into history of the divine Spirit, which, as God's gift given in the name of Jesus and through the gift of his body and blood, continues to operate in the Church and in the world. This model also compels us to be attentive to the language which is used,

---

[21] Giraudo, *Eucaristia*, 577–79, suggests that his theory is opposed to that of Odo Casel, who through a reading of patristic and liturgical texts wrote of bringing the past events forward into the present. The theories are however similar in their appeal to something transhistorical in the events narrated.

[22] This fits with the protest of E. Kilmartin that it is better to return to a Thomistic metaphysics of causality than to give a nebulous transhistorical character to Christ's saving deeds. See E. Kilmartin, "The Catholic Tradition of Eucharistic Theology: Towards the Third Millennium." *ThS* 55 (1994) 449–54.

[23] Claus Westermann, *Praise and Lament in the Psalms*, trans. from German (Atlanta, 1981) 214–49.

to the force of story and image in recalling the deeds of Christ, since it is through proclamation that the pasch continues to be present and active in the life of Christian communities.

## 5. Summary

When the supper narrative is taken in relation to the celebration of the Lord's Supper in early Christian communities, the context is broadened. We can see from the evidence how these Christians enacted both the mandate to remember Christ in loving one another, given in the washing of the feet, and the mandate to keep memorial in the celebration of the gift of his body and blood. Christ expressed the intention of that gift in anticipating his death even as he gave thanks to the Father. To give voice to what he was doing for the world in being handed over to death, he recalled the pasch, the sacrifice of the covenant, and the self-giving of the Suffering Servant, so that the evangelists indeed could present his death as his own passover. The ritual relation of the Last Supper to the paschal seder is still controverted, but nonetheless it is in relation to it, and to other Jewish ways of remembering, that the meaning of the Eucharist as a memorial is explored.

These considerations serve as prelude to reflection on the eucharistic celebration itself as it took shape, especially on Communion, the Eucharistic Prayer, the relation between word and sacrament, rites of offering, and community ministries.

## COMMUNION IN THE BODY AND BLOOD OF CHRIST

The Eucharist is the sacrament of Communion in the body and blood of Christ. It is as such that it is the sacrament of the Church and the sacrament of communion in his paschal mystery. Justin Martyr caught the sense of this table, when after describing the eucharistic rite which follows baptism, he affirmed:

"We call this food the Eucharist . . . Not as common bread or as common drink do we receive these, but just as through the word of God, Jesus Christ, our Saviour, became incarnate and took on flesh and blood for our salvation, so . . . the food over which we give thanks has been given by the prayer of His word, and which nourishes our flesh and blood by assimilation, is both the flesh and blood of that incarnate Jesus."[24]

[24] *Apologia* I.66.2. The original text is given in *Prex eucharistica: Textus e variis liturgiis antiquioribus selecti,* edited by A. Hänggi and I. Pahl. *SF* 12 (Fribourg,

Irenaeus caught the sense of this table also, when even after he had spoken much of oblation, he protested against the Gnostics that nourishment with the blessed bread and wine assured the resurrection of human flesh:

"Since both the mixed cup and the prepared bread receive the word of God and become the eucharist of Christ's body and blood, from which the substance of the flesh is strengthened and established, how can they say that the flesh which is fed on the body and blood of the Lord, and is one of his members, is incapable of receiving the gift of God which is eternal life?"[25]

Such citations could be multiplied. These few are given here as simple reminders that the sacrament of the Eucharist is the communion in Christ's body and blood, in the gift given, sanctified, and received with thanksgiving. They are gifts given in the power of the Spirit, to make of the Church one in Christ and in the reality of his paschal mystery.

In celebration this calls for concentration on the gift which Christ makes, which God makes in Christ and in the Spirit. Human giving is only a response to this, made in different ways. The sacrament is a table action, with blessing and communion in what is blessed.

The anthropological grounding for eucharistic celebration is to be found primarily in the Communion rite. This is actually implicit in the *IGMR* Cap. VI.283, when it says that to be a true sign the bread is to look indeed like bread, even though it is to retain the form of unleavened wheaten bread. This is followed up by a recommendation that the fraction be a visible breaking of the one bread, to be shared among the many in sign of the charity that binds them as one body.

Some provision has been made for a wider extension of Communion in the cup of Christ's blood (*IGMR* III.240). This is also intended to realize the sign value of the sacrament more fully, especially to show forth its character as a eucharistic and eschatological table fellowship in the kingdom of the Father.[26]

---

1968) 70f. The English translation is taken from *The Eucharist,* edited by D. Sheerin, *Message of the Fathers* 7 (Wilmington, 1986, Collegeville, 1990) 34.

[25] Irenaeus, *Adversus Haereses* V, 2.3. *SCh* 153 (Paris, 1969). English translation from *Eucharist* 252.

[26] According to all prescriptions so far, however, the cup is to remain everywhere fruit of the vine, as the bread is to be wheaten, since this is deemed to

The symbolism of bread and wine brings many realities together to relate them to Christ's memorial and presence. They bring to thanksgiving the gift of creation. They bring the struggles of human history, where the provision of bread is caught up in the effort to bring forth fruit from the earth in peace. They bring to the table the lives and work of the faithful gathered together. As common food and drink, shared in common when blessed, they bring the community together as one at Christ's table, to receive Christ's gift. At this table, the community itself assumes the identity of being one social body, united by the bonds of charity and mercy, being in the Spirit itself the body of Christ by which it is nourished, Christ in his members taking a part in earthly dwelling and human living.

In the past, these meanings were served by a diversity of ritual actions which gave form and shape to Communion at Christ's table and altar. In the period of domestic liturgy, the provision of the elements and the reality of sharing at one table could be more readily expressed in the Communion from the table. In the development of the liturgy of the basilica, the singing of a Communion antiphon accompanying a procession to the table expressed the joy of access to the gift, as well as the harmonious unison of voices lifted up in chant. For whatever reason, christians became reluctant to receive Communion and participated in other ways, so that the very sense of the sacramental celebration was affected. When the Eucharist can be celebrated as a share in Christ's altar and offering, without a share at his table, the very meaning of the sacrifice is itself changed.

Ancient and medieval theologies were, in keeping with earlier liturgies, theologies of eucharistic communion, even though in time they were inclined to stress the words of Jesus rather than the blessing prayer. This theology of Communion relates the Eucharist to the movement of the incarnation, in which God comes towards us in the gift of Jesus Christ and the Spirit, to transform life on earth and to bring us in them to glory, evoking a movement on the Church's part to enter into this trinitarian relation.

---

belong to Christ's institution and to lie outside the Church's power of legislation. Some argue that this violates the sign value for many cultures and regions of the world. For a full discussion of the relation between eucharistic elements and culture, see R. Jaouen, *L'Eucharistie du mil. Langages d'un peuple, expressions de la foi* (Paris, 1995).

While this understanding of the Eucharist is currently supported by appeal to ancient theologies, it is not adverted to enough in medieval writers. For Thomas Aquinas,[27] for example, the sacrifice is completed in the consecration of the people's gifts by Christ, so that he gives himself immediately to them in his body and blood and in the nourishing, inebriating and unifying power of his passion which is remembered and represented in the signs and words of consecration.[28] While Bonaventure attended rather more to the offering of Christ as sacrifice, he too kept the balance between communion and sacrifice, asserting the reason for the presence of the body and blood of Christ to be found in the need for "the sacrifice to be perfectly propitiative, the sacrament perfectly unitive, and the food perfectly reflective."[29]

The sixteenth-century Reformers, therefore, in their efforts to allow the gift of the sacrament to prevail over practices of sacrifice were in line with ancient and high medieval tradition, though like the members of the Roman Church themselves they had lost touch with the blessing prayer and its significance. It is the unity between blessing and communion as one integral action which needs to be respected in a liturgical theology, sensitive to form and rite.

## THE EUCHARISTIC PRAYER

In looking back to the Lord's Supper and to early tradition, eucharistic theology has been influenced since 1945 by Gregory Dix's delineation of the eightfold elements of the celebration and the fourfold shape of the eucharistic rite, which he divided into offertory, prayer, fraction, and Communion.[30] This has been helpful up to a point, but Dix was too restrictive in his reading of the tradition, because he wanted to find one common origin of eucharistic form which continues to be verified in different traditions. That is why he based his analysis on a reading of the

---

[27] Thomas Aquinas, *Summa Theologiae* III, Q. 83, art. 4. For a discussion of Aquinas on the Eucharist, see D. Power, *The Eucharistic Mystery: Revitalizing the Tradition* (New York, 1992) 208–40.

[28] *STh* III, q. 83, art. 1. Marsili, *Liturgia eucaristica*, 99–107, gives a rather narrow reading of the *STh*, where he seems to miss the integral part of Communion in the representation and efficacy of Christ's passion, and the objectivity inherent to the notion of instrumental causality.

[29] *Breviloquium* VI, IX, 3.

[30] G. Dix, *The Shape of the Liturgy*. Additional notes by P. Marshall (New York, 1982).

New Testament supper narrative. Eucharistic tradition is rather more diverse than he accounted for, and more is now gained by comparing different early traditions and practices, finding whatever unity in diversity is found therein. While some still stress the origins of the Eucharist at the supper in their theologies,[31] it is becoming more acceptable to look back at how these narratives were integrated into Eucharist, rather than working forward from them. In studying liturgical components, not only different ritual patterns but more importantly the signification thus expressed is brought to the fore. This in itself opens the way to a grasp of the role of culture and cultural forms, and of future possibilities.

Since the blessing prayer is key to understanding the signification of Communion in the sacrament of Christ's body and blood, much contemporary liturgical theology centers on its explanation.[32] This is in contrast with the theologies that related to Reformation controversies, largely ignoring the prayers and forms of celebration.

There have been different theories about the origins of the prayer, affecting the meaning that is given to it.[33] While for some time, efforts were made to retrieve an *Uranaphora*, a common primitive form if not necessarily one fixed text, this has given way to a comparison between a variety of texts, from which a kind of unity in diversity emerges. They are looked at here for the sake of their theological implications.

*1. Different Theories About the Prayer's Development*
Jean-Paul Audet[34] was one of those who drew sharp attention to Jewish origins of the eucharistic prayer. From biblical readings, he forged

[31] For example, Giraudo, *Eucaristia*.

[32] The most useful collection of prayers is *Prex Eucharistica*, edited by Hänggi and Pahl, henceforth cited as *Prex*. English translations are collected in *Prayers of the Eucharist: Early and Reformed*, edited by R.C.D. Jasper and G. J. Cuming (New York, 1987). Meyer surveys the principal early prayers in different liturgical families, *Eucharistie*, 87–110. For the text and a longer analysis of a number of texts, see C. Giraudo, *La Struttura letteraria*.

[33] For a summary, see P. Bradshaw, *The Search for the Origins of Christian Worship* (Oxford and New York, 1992) 131–60, and for literature, Meyer, *Eucharistie*, 87–89, followed by an overview of different traditions. For a complete study of origins and texts, see C. Giraudo, *La struttura letteraria della preghiera eucaristica. Saggio sulla genesi letteraria di una forma: tôdâ veterotestamentaria,beràkâ giudaica, anafora cristiana*. AB 92 (Roma, 1981). See also E. Mazza, *Alle origini dell'anafora eucaristica* (Roma, 1992). *The Origins of the Eucharistic Prayer* (Collegeville, 1995).

[34] J-P. Audet, "Esquisse historique du genre littéraire de la 'bénédiction' juive et de 'l'eucharistie' chrétienne." *RB* 65 (1958) 371–99.

a theory about the nature and structure of the *berakah,* inviting eucharistic theologians to consider this as the foundation for the early Christian prayers. While his analysis of the structure of the *berakah* has been long since questioned, he has the merit of having drawn attention to the importance for eucharistic history and theology of such a study. Louis Bouyer[35] extended the study of a possible Jewish matrix for the Eucharist to meal prayers and synagogue prayer. He included the latter because of the *Qedushah* which could be seen as source of the *Sanctus* in Christian blessing. Bouyer pointed to the blessing for creation, the blessing for redemption, and the eschatological motif, which in his opinion formed the basic structure of these prayers. The inclusion of a sacrificial motif in the christian Eucharist was clear quite early on, at least by the time of the prayer in the *Apostolic Tradition.* At the same time, for Bouyer the form of sacrifice in Jewish practice which serves as the model for the Eucharistic Prayer is the Communion sacrifice. In this, the participants received life through eating of the victim. For Bouyer, the prayer and the table are inseparable elements of the one sacrificial meal.

Without analyzing prayers in the same way as other authors, Henri Cazelles[36] suggested a way of relating sacrifice, meal and prayer to one another. He did this by connecting the memorial of Christ's death with levitical blood-offerings (Lev 17:1) and by that route connecting the prayer with the *todah,* or praise of God's salvific deeds by the people, which accompanied temple offerings. This contribution served to underline the fact that offering and communion go together, or in other words that offering and meal cannot be considered apart in explaining the Eucharist.[37] It also drew the attention of others[38] to the genre of *todah* or proclamation of praise in remembrance of God's great deeds that not only accompanied sacrifice but belonged as well in other settings of Jewish life. Studies bring out its commemorative

---

[35] L. Bouyer, *Eucharistie: théologie et spiritualité de la prière eucharistique* (Paris, 1966). *Eucharist. Theology and Spirituality of the Eucharistic Prayer* (Notre Dame, 1968).

[36] H. Cazelles, "L'Anaphore et l'Ancien Testament." In *Eucharisties d'Orient et d'Occident,* vol. 1 (Paris, 1970) 11–21.

[37] Cazelle's position is corroborated by the study of Jean Laporte, *La doctrine eucharistique chez Philon d'Alexandrie* (Paris, 1972). For the importance of these perspectives to a liturgical theology of the Eucharist, see Meyer, *Eucharistie,* 449–52.

[38] Especially C. Giraudo, *Struttura letteraria della preghiera eucaristica* (Rome 1981).

and its spiritual, rather than its purely ritual or propitiatory character, while at the same time leaving room for the connection with the sacrifice of Christ's death that in self-offering surpassed ritual offerings.

There are indications that the early form of Christian eucharistic prayer may not have included the supper narrative, and that on the basis of the Jewish models the prayer is quite complete in structure without it.[39] Its inclusion as a standard part of the prayer therefore needs explanation. Louis Ligier,[40] working from the table *birkat ha-mazon*[41] and Cesare Giraudo[42] from the larger genre of *todah,* both offer explanations of this inclusion by looking at the introduction of an *embolism* in various Jewish blessings. This is a verse or verses introduced into an already complete structure, in order to give a foundation and a motive for continuing the memorial and the praise expressed in the prayer. Ligier points out that the final blessing, or *birkat ha-mazon,* of the Jewish meal had a fixed structure, but that it included an addition for great feasts, such as the pasch. This related both to the significance of such an event in itself and to the significance of its constant memorial. It also referred to the divine command to keep memory. Cesare Giraudo in looking at psalms and other Old Testament prayers points to embolisms which also command the repetition of the praise for specific events, because of their significance in salvation history.

By such parallels, light is cast on the inclusion of the supper narrative and especially on the significance of the memorial command in the christian eucharistic prayer. This inclusion relates the origins of Christian Eucharist to the Last Supper when Jesus anticipated his death in prayer and in offering the gift of his body and blood to his disciples. In doing so, he spelled out the significance of his death in

---

[39] This depends on whether the prayers in *Didache* 9 and 10 are accepted as a Eucharist, and on the absence or inclusion of a Supper Narrative in Addai and Mari. On this latter, see the edition by A. Gelston, *The Eucharistic Prayer of Addai and Mari* (Oxford, 1992).

[40] Among his various articles, see L. Ligier, "Les origines de la prière eucharistique." *Questions Liturgiques* 53 (1972) 181–202. "The Origins of the Eucharistic Prayer: From the Last Supper to Eucharist." *SL* 9 (1973) 161–85.

[41] In his studies of what he calls paleoanaphoras, or earliest eucharistic texts which it is possible to reconstruct, E. Mazza offers arguments to show the connection of christian Eucharist with the Jewish table ritual, and particularly with the *birkat ha-mazon.* E. Mazza, *Alle origini dell'anafora eucaristica.*

[42] C. Giraudo, *La Struttura letteraria della preghiera eucaristica* (Rome, 1981).

salvation history by drawing on the memory of pasch, Exodus, and Suffering Servant, and he gave the command to keep memorial of him in the sharing of his gift, with blessing.

For a theology of eucharistic celebration, such studies of early prayers allow attention to its character as memorial prayer, and to the theological significance of its basic structures, while still allowing room for dispute over certain points and especially room for a greater diversity in the historical compendium of prayers. Tracing the history of the prayer remains enigmatic. Theological reflection, however, while it benefits from these endeavors is not dependent on exact historical reconstruction. It can choose to consider the interplay between different texts, and working from form, genre, image and metaphor, recognize the possibility of different theologies within one common desire to observe the supper command to keep memory.

A. A PRAYER OF BLESSING

The Eucharistic Prayer is a blessing prayer. God is blessed and thanked, and it is this which transforms the gifts over which the prayer is made. The prayer is a prayer of the gathered community, its purpose is to bless the bread and wine so that in a communion with thanksgiving memorial may be kept of Jesus, in obedience to the memorial command.

Even the discussion of origins reflects the fact that among the prayers, there is some diversity in basic structure, rooted seemingly in a diversity in Jewish prayer. To notice this is important because the structure affects the meaning of the celebration and the form of keeping memorial. Following the pattern of Jewish meal prayer, in all probability the earliest Christian prayers included a blessing for creation, a blessing for redemption, and a blessing for the Church. This last, on the basis of the blessing for Jerusalem in the *birkat ha-mazon*, was in the form of a petition, but in Jewish fashion a petition followed by a phrase blessing God's Name was itself a *berakah*.

Some scholars uphold a basic structure of praise/thanksgiving/petition, others one of thanksgiving/petition. Thomas Talley[43] in his work has concentrated on the shift from praise to thanksgiving in the

---

[43] Among his contributions, see Thomas Talley, "Sources and Structures of the Eucharistic Prayer." In T. Talley, *Worship: Reforming Tradition* (Washington, D.C., 1990) 11–34.

Christian tradition, upholding a move from a threefold to a twofold schema for the Christian prayer, finding considerable significance in that. For him this marks the specifically Christian character of Eucharist and its theological departure from its Jewish matrix. In his work on paleoanaphoras, Enrico Mazza supports a threefold structure, rooted in the Jewish table prayer, but he calls the first two sections eucharists, and the third petition.

While the inclusion of creation within thanksgiving is not a problem for Mazza, for others the distinction of praise from thanksgiving pertains to a distinction between the works of creation and the works of salvation history. The possibility of this pattern of praise, thanksgiving and petition, alongside one of twofold thanksgiving and petition, is supported by the structure of the prayers in the *Didaché*, the prayer of *Addai and Mari*, and the prayer of Book VIII of the *Apostolic Constitutions*. It is a theological option to make some distinction between the praise of God in creation and thanksgiving for the history of the works of redemption.

Giraudo[44] in his studies has averted to the division between prayers whose major focus is on the remembrance of thanksgiving, and those whose focus is on the petition for present help and for an eschatological future. He refers thereby to prayers which have an anamnetic structure and those which have an epicletic (meaning intercessory) character. Their difference is marked by the inclusion of the embolism of the supper narrative and memorial command either within thanksgiving, as in the West Syrian type of prayer, or within the petition, as in the Roman canon.[45] The prayers that amplify the thanksgiving include diverse paradigms for understanding Christ's pasch, and also more readily include the remembrance of creation. Emphasis on petition on the other hand is more prone to underline the sacrificial and expiatory interpretation of Christ's death, and of the Church's action. Making sacrifice expresses true devotion and founds the petition that gains God's favor.

## B. Keeping Memory

There is difference in what is remembered and in how events are remembered. This means diversity in the theological significance given

---

[44] As well as *La Struttura* see C. Giraudo, *Eucaristia*, 382–506.
[45] See the listings in both *Struttura* and *Eucaristia*.

to the mystery of Jesus Christ, and to what is being done in keeping memorial.

The earliest images for remembering Christ center on his teaching, the revelation given in him, and on the self-abasement of his death. It may have been the influence of paschal homilies that led the Anaphora of the *Apostolic Tradition* to use paschal imagery that portrays the descent into hell by voluntary death as the conquest of the powers of the underworld, death and sin.[46] While the death anticipates the resurrection, the image of voluntary descent gives primacy to the significance of Christ's death in the work of redemption. Paschal imagery occurs in some early Roman prefaces, for example for Christmas and Easter,[47] but in this case it is the type of the Paschal Lamb that serves in remembering Christ, our Paschal Sacrifice. This lends to the use of the sacrificial types of Abel, Melchisedech and Abraham to depict the meaning of Christ's death.

In some cases it is the self-abasement of the Word in taking on the flesh of a sin-laden humanity which is most to the fore. This happens in the prayer of *Addai and Mari*.[48] The same is found in the outline of a eucharistic prayer found in the catechesis of Theodore of Mopsuestia, where however it leads to attention to the passion, in which this is consummated.[49]

In this catechesis of Theodore, the resurrection of Christ is associated with the descent of the Spirit upon the offerings and the people, rather than worked into the thanksgiving remembrance.[50] On the other hand, the thanksgiving section of some prayers does bring death and resurrection more closely together. The prayer referred to as the Egyptian Anaphora of Basil[51] follows an almost creedal formula in proclaiming the incarnation, baptism in the Jordan,[52] death on the Cross, descent into hell, resurrection from the dead, ascent into heaven, seating at the right hand of the Father, and the coming judgment, before moving into the Supper.

[46] Mazza, *Origins* 102–6.
[47] *Liber Sacramentorum Romanae Aeclesiae Ordinis Anni Circuli*, edited by L. Mohlberg (Rome, 1960) no. 20, 466.
[48] *Prex* 377.
[49] *Prex* 214.
[50] *Prex* 217.
[51] *Prex* 350f.
[52] This is by implication. The thought is further elaborated in the Byzantine Basil.

The Byzantine Anaphora of Basil of Caeserea amplifies upon this with considerable imagery.[53] In reference to the Incarnation, Basil employs the image of κένωσις from Philippians 2. He commemorates Jesus's baptism in the Jordan, where he locates the origins of Christian baptism and the gift of the Spirit that makes of the disciples a royal and holy people. The cross is the means of Christ's descent into hell, where he loosed the pains of death, as it is also a condemnation of sin in the flesh. The resurrection is the resurrection of the first-born from the dead, as the ascension into heaven is the preparation of the final coming. Rather than concentrate uniquely on "the voluntary and life-giving death" presaged at the supper, or on a single image such as that of sacrifice, Basil sets up an interplay of events and images which together form the significance of the works of the word made flesh.

A varied consideration of the prayers also allows us to see how change can take place within the one ecclesial tradition, or even through changes introduced into the same prayer. Comparing the Egyptian Basil with the Byzantine shows how a prayer can be amplified. It is also instructive to see the move from the prayer of *Addai and Mari* with its focus on the redeeming power of the incarnation to the *Sharar,* with the strong accentuation of sacrificial blood offered in the death on the cross and on the victim present in the Church's eucharistic sacrifice.[54]

Not only do the differences emerge in what is remembered. They show up also in what the genres of prayer suggest to be the act of remembering. The continuity both past and future of the history of salvation is underlined in the long prayer of Book VIII of the *Apostolic Constitutions.*[55] The death of Jesus Christ, remembered here as sacrifice and also as a freeing of humanity from the powers of death, is a turning-point in history, but this is penetrable only in going back to creation, to protohistory, and to Old Testament history, and in looking forward to the history yet to unfold.

This is in nice contrast with the prayer in Book VII[56] of the same collection which keeps memory of Christ in a short creedal formula,

---

[53] *Prex* 231–35.

[54] *Prex* 413.

[55] *Prex* 83–92.

[56] *Les Constitutions apostoliques,* Livres VII et VIII, edited by M. Metzger. *SCh* 336 (Paris, 1987).

professing faith in the incarnation, the suffering, the death, the resurrection and the ascension to God's right hand. With this profession or proclamation, the accent of the prayer is on nourishment through the life-giving body and blood of the word made flesh. Yet another sense of keeping memorial is found in the Anaphora (and indeed the theology of the homilies and catechesis) of John Chrysostom.[57] For this prayer, the Church praying on earth is above all caught up in the here and now presence and action of Christ, united with the heavenly liturgy where he is High Priest. On the other hand in the remainders of the prayer traced from the mystagogy of Theodore of Mopsuestia, commemoration and present prayer in Christ's Spirit is but a prolepsis of participation in the glorious heavenly liturgy to come.

## C. Expanding the Elements of Prayer

There is fitting discussion about the history, form and meaning of certain parts of the prayer, especially the anamnesis, the epiclesis and the *Sanctus*. As with the inclusion of the supper narrative and memorial command, light is shown on their inclusion by way of reference to the basic structure of a prayer keeping memory of Christ and of God's works in thanksgiving and intercession. The prayer is always to be seen as a whole or as a unit. Everything in it, whether the words of Jesus, or the epiclesis, or the anamnesis, has meaning and effectiveness, because it belongs within this unit of blessing. Thus, stylistically, the narrative and memorial command, the anamnesis, epiclesis, and *Sanctus,* were all insertions into an already literary complete prayer of blessing. They took meaning from it, and they added meaning to it, in this way construing the sacramental reality of eucharistic remembrance.

## D. *Anamnesis*

The addition of the anamnesis goes with the inclusion of the memorial command. It is an avowal of what is being done in giving thanks, in obedience to Christ's word. It relates the eucharistic action in prayer, and in bread and wine, to the Supper and to the great events of Christ's salvific work, as a summary of the whole meaning and purpose of the entire thanksgiving. In fact, the insertion of the anamnesis formula had considerable effect on the overall meaning of the

[57] E. Mazza, *Mystagogy. A Theology of Liturgy in the Patristic Age* (New York, 1989) 105–40.

prayer. While it is introduced to express obedience to the memorial command, it serves to bolster an imagery of Christ's mystery where death, resurrection and ascension are presented as one complex act, thus prevailing over the accent upon the death of the thanksgiving section of some prayers. This form of paschal imagery coincides very well with the image of pasch as transition or initiation, whose influence on christian belief and liturgy owes so much to the paschal interpretation of Origen.

It is in connection with this formula of the *anamnesis* that we can also consider how the Church's prayer and memorial action relates to the present action of Christ. Early theologies certainly proclaimed the resurrection of Christ in conjunction with his death, but they were content to see the Eucharist as a memorial of the Passion, done in the power of the Spirit, in some way joining with and imitating what Christ did.[58] For Irenaeus it was to invoke the Name of Christ, creating and redeeming word, over the bread and wine offered by the Church, and to see the bread and wine transformed, like Christ's own flesh, into the nourishment that leads to the resurrection of the body. For Origen and Clement, it was to receive the Eucharist with the word as the gnosis that leads to contemplation of God's infinite mystery. For Cyprian, it meant that in the Church the bishop offered "according to what Christ offered" in the passion, acting in the place of Christ himself.

It is in the fifth century mystagogy that the eucharistic action is related more directly to Christ's heavenly action.[59] This may be associated with the common presence of a succinct *anamnesis* formula in the composition of prayers, which seems to encourage a relation to the action of Christ, where he is now seated at God's right hand. The Letter to the Hebrews provides a new paradigm for understanding the death of Christ and for eucharistic memorial. The association is not however done in entirely the same way. Both John Chrysostom and Theodore of Mopsuestia relate the death of Christ to his entry into the heavenly sanctuary and the eucharistic liturgy to the heavenly liturgy of Christ the High-Priest. While Theodore, however, sees the Eucharist largely as anticipation of full communion in this liturgy, John Chrysostom sees it as a present participation, thus accentuating the role of the bishop as Christ's visible representative. On the other

[58] Following is a summary of D. Power, *Eucharistic Mystery*, 114–16.
[59] See E. Mazza, *Mystagogy*.

hand, Augustine's view[60] of the Eucharist that continued to underline the representation of Christ's death, by which he threw himself into the embrace of the Father, and as the offering of the *totus Christus*, head and members, fits with the Roman inclusion of the anamnesis formula in the intercessory part of the prayer, where it coincides with the petition for the acceptance of the sacrifice.

## E. *EPICLESIS*

The *epiclesis*[61] has far more importance than the west has ever granted it. It does not enter the Eucharistic Prayer in the same way or with an identical format in all traditions. In *Addai and Mari* (or in some later version of the original), while it is said over the offering made by the people, it is distinctly eschatological in tone. That befits the East Syrian accent on receiving the food of immortality at Christ's table. In the Sharar, however, which has reworked *Addai and Mari*, or some kindred text, the *epiclesis* is separated from the Supper Narrative by the heavily sacrificial prayers that follow on this latter. In the Antiochene tradition, the invocation is addressed more closely to the transformation of the gifts and to present ecclesial communion in the one body. In the Alexandrian tradition the early evidence of the *Strasbourg Papyrus* does not have an *epiclesis*, but the Holy Spirit is directly associated with the power of the Church to offer the sacrifice of thanksgiving.[62] The Liturgy of Mark[63] retains this formula, but then places an invocation for the descent of the Spirit upon the sacrifice, which now includes the gifts of the faithful, before the supper narrative. The *epiclesis* is repeated when the *anamnesis* is said, invoking the action of the Spirit over the loaves and the cup.[64]

---

[60] D. Power, *Eucharistic Mystery* 151–6, drawing largely on *De Civititate Dei* X, 6.18.20.24 (*CCSL* 47). Note how Augustine places thanksgiving at the *end* of the liturgy, after Communion, in the *Epistula 149 ad Paulinum*, CSEL 34, 359–64.

[61] On the Holy Spirit in the Byzantine Liturgy, as interpreted by the Fathers, see F. R. Gahbauer, "Der Hl. Geist in der Byzantinischen Liturgie nach der Überlieferung der Kirchenväter." *EO* 12 (1995) 71–101.

[62] *Prex* 116f.

[63] *Prex* 101–15.

[64] With the addition of an *epiclesis* of the Spirit into the new prayers of the Roman Missal, there is preoccupation with the dispute over whether the power to consecrate is to be attributed to the words of Jesus or to the invocation of the Spirit. In older prayers, there was no such problem because the meaning and power of the prayer was located in its total proclamation.

The *epiclesis* has ecclesiological and sacramental significance. The Church gathers in the name of Christ only through the gift and power of the Holy Spirit. The Spirit brings the people together, inspires their prayer, sanctifies them and their bread and wine, so that as a holy Church they may participate in the sacrament of Christ's body and blood. The ecclesiological and pneumatological significance of the Eucharistic Prayer belong together. In its own way, Basil's Anaphora brings this out by relating the creation of the holy people to the outpouring of the Spirit in the baptism of Jesus at the Jordan. The entire salvific work of Jesus, and the gathering of the Church called together by him, are thus put under the seal of the Spirit. The *epiclesis* of the Liturgy of Mark is also ample in relating the work of the Spirit to the Eucharist by relating the power of the Spirit to the preaching of law, prophets, and apostles, and to the entire work of sanctification, in which the Spirit is operative as the "fountain of divine endowments, consubstantial" with the Father and "sharing the throne of the kingdom with the Father and the only-begotten Son," Jesus Christ. This is a reminder that though the risen Christ sends the fullness of the Spirit, it has been at work in the world since the beginning.

### F. SANCTUS

The *Sanctus*[65] has entered the prayer in different ways and at different junctures of the prayer. Its meaning may be most apparent in the Anaphoras of Basil and John Chrysostom, where it is introduced after the thanksgiving for God's awesome mystery and clearly joins the praise of the Church with the praise of the angels. With them the Church lauds the manifestation of the great and ineffable mystery of the Trinity of divine persons, and their work of creation and sanctification, whereby they bring creatures into the enjoyment of this divine life. This meaning is not as apparent when the *Sanctus* comes after the christological section of the thanksgiving, but it is still the way of joining heaven and earth in God's praise through Christ.

### G. A PROPHETIC AND ESCHATOLOGICAL PRAYER

When Paul addressed the Church of Corinth on its celebration of the Lord's Supper, he told them that in it they proclaimed the death of the Lord until he comes. The sense of proclaiming on the one hand, and

---

[65] B. D. Spinks, *The Sanctus in the Eucharistic Prayer* (Cambridge, 1991).

of anticipation and expectation on the other, is certainly picked up by the various Eucharistic Prayers. We have seen how the Liturgy of Mark relates the work of the Spirit to the Eucharist by relating it to the proclamation of law, prophet, and gospel. It may be more difficult for us today to appreciate that song and praise are a fine form of proclamation, or of announcing and divulging the news of salvation. Relating the Eucharistic Prayer to the matrix of Hebrew psalms helps us to grow in this appreciation. Psalms 105 and 106 for example rehearse and proclaim the great deeds of salvation in some detail, but they do so in a setting of thankful remembrance and of hope for God's continuing rule. The anaphora which most clearly resembles this proclamatory style is that of Book VIII of the *Apostolic Constitutions*.

Other prayers give an eschatological tenor to the prayer and thus to the sacrament in variant ways. As seen above, the Anaphora of Chrysostom sees in the Church's memorial a sort of present eschatological fulfillment in as much as the Church's liturgy is already a participation in the heavenly, whereas Theodore is more geared to what is to come in the future. For its part, the Roman Canon by its accent on offering sacrifice and its prayer for the angel unites the Church's Eucharist with the heavenly altar and offering of Jesus Christ.

## H. OFFERING AND SACRIFICE

Sacrifice is what the Roman Church has always underpinned in teaching about the Eucharist, but the senses in which the Eucharistic Prayers use the language of sacrifice need careful attention.

There seems little doubt that when eucharistic prayer, as in the Alexandrian text found in the *Strasbourg Papyrus*, began to speak of the prayer itself as sacrifice, this was by way of reference to Mal 1.11 and meant sacrifice of praise.[66] After that, the euchology went in different directions, assuming different things under the nomenclature of sacrifice. The gifts of bread and wine brought by the Church are certainly seen as offerings, offerings to express dedication and offerings which are to be taken up by the Spirit to be sanctified through the prayer in the name of Christ. The Liturgy of Mark is the most ample in taking note of the many ways in which Christians practiced sacrifice, joining this with the eucharistic offering. It refers to the gifts which the faithful

---

[66] This text was applied to the Eucharist, but not in prayer, by the *Didache*, Justin Martyr and Irenaeus.

bring for the service of the Church, for the giving out of their want or out of their plenty. The offering of lives in obedience to the Gospel, expressed in liturgical prayer, recalls the command of Paul in Rom 12:1.

It is often in the introductory part of the prayer, or in the *anamnesis*, that the prayer itself is portrayed as a sacrifice, in the sense that it is a sacrifice of thanksgiving. There is no good reason, however, to separate the sacrifice of praise from the expiatory and sin-forgiving power of Christian prayer when it is united with the reception of the gift of Christ's body and blood. The blessing of the gifts in the power of the Spirit needs to be considered at one with the table at which Christians eat and drink unto the forgiveness of sins and immortality. When the Eucharistic Prayer and Communion table are seen together to constitute one sacrifice, thanksgiving and expiation go readily together, with elements of both expressed both in prayer and in sharing of the body and blood. It is as a gift received with thanksgiving, that is, taken as gift in an action in which thanksgiving is offered for what has been wrought in Christ, that the Eucharist unites the Church with the sacrifice of Christ.[67]

A full appreciation of the community action in sharing in Christ's sacrifice raises questions about the distinction made in the Roman Missal between the sacramental sacrifice offered by the priest and the spiritual sacrifice offered by the baptized. The best way to consider the sacrificial nature of the Eucharist, and the sacrificial tone of the prayer, is to follow the line of thought opened by Cazelles and Bouyer. This is to underline the inseparability of meal and sacrifice, to recognize that it is in eating and drinking of what is blessed in thanksgiving to God that the sacramental sacrifice is perfected. This movement in effect relates well to the action of the Last Supper. Jesus offered himself to the Father in offering himself to his disciples as their nourishment. He did this in thanking God for sending him to give his life for the forgiveness of sins and the reconciliation of humankind, willingly anticipating thereby the act of his death by which, in giving himself for the many, he dedicated

---

[67] Separation of sacramental thanksgiving and expiation was a peculiarly sixteenth century polemic, resulting from late medieval Mass customs and in large part from an under-appreciation on all sides of the eucharistic prayer tradition. On the position of the Council of Trent, see D. Power, *The Sacrifice We Offer. The Tridentine Dogma and Its Reinterpretation* (New York, 1987). On the Reformers, for an overview see K. Stevenson, *Eucharist and Offering* (New York, 1986) 130–48.

or gave himself to the Father. In Eucharist, the Church receives communion in this death at the table, where it joins in thanksgiving to God in memory of Christ, and nourished by his gift unites itself with him in the dedication of life to God's service on behalf of the world. The distinction of the Missal does not seem to do justice to this.[68]

## I. Remembrance of the Dead

One of the reasons why the Roman Church and western medieval theology gave such prominence to sacrifice was the growth in the practice of making Mass offerings, so that priests might offer it for the dead.[69] This was however a departure from the early Church's way of commemorating the dead.

A quite early christian custom was to celebrate the Eucharist over or near the tombs of martyrs, whose witness in death drew them more fully into the pasch of Christ. It was also customary to remember all the dead on their anniversaries, and to celebrate in cemeteries during the week, adding thus to the weekly Sunday gathering. It is this strong sense of communion between those who live in Christ and those who have died in Christ, expressed in the act of commemorating Christ's pasch, that is the basis for reciting the names of the saints and of other deceased in the Eucharistic Prayer. With this, even from the time of Tertullian,[70] there went the idea that while those honored and commemorated as saints could be of assistance to the living in joining them more closely with Christ, the living could be of assistance to those dead needing purification in order to enter into God's glory with Christ. Thus prayers were extended to name the honored dead, and to make intercession for those whom it wished to commend in Christ and the Spirit to God.

Remembering the dead has taken on new significance in our time, in face of atrocities such as the Shoah, Hiroshima, famine, ethnic

---

[68] This study does not, however, resolve the question as to whether it can be said that the Church offers the body and blood of Christ, a formula still controverted in the midst of increased ecumenical convergence. See Lutheran/Roman Catholic Joint Commission, *The Eucharist*, 58–60.

[69] See especially the articles, A. Angenendt, "Missa Specialis: Zugleich ein Beitrag zur Entstehung der Privatmessen," *Frühmittelalterliche Studien* 17 (1983) 153–221; C. Vogel, "Une mutation cultuelle inexpliquée: le passage de l'eucharistie communautaire à la messe privée," *RSR* 54 (1980) 231–50.

[70] Tertullian, *De Corona* 3,3 (CCSL 2, 1043).

wars, and large-scale urban violence, in which so many persons have died at the hands of human agents and in such gruesome ways. These are dangerous memories, threatening to our belief in humanity, and indeed to faith in God. For that very reason, the memory of victims needs to be taken up in the eucharistic action in which memory is kept of the death of Christ, with the constant hope that his voluntary death may undo the powers of death, as they lay claim to the victims of violence and to the world.

J. SUMMARY

In the traditional prayers which have been studied for their theological import, the controlling image is that of keeping memorial of Christ's saving action. This either accentuates the death, or it offers a more expansive image of pasch, inclusive of the incarnation, the resurrection and ascension, adding the hope of the eschaton. When memory of creation and of God's action in saving history is included, this proclaims more powerfully that Christ's mystery belongs to history and transforms history.

Different images are used to express what is remembered, thus proffering variant meanings of the memorial action. Christ's death is sometimes proclaimed as the voluntary descent into hell, there to vanquish the powers of death. Sometimes it is proclaimed as the sacrifice of expiation, in which sins were forgiven and reconciliation effected. When the mystery is proclaimed in greater fullness, the paschal and sacrificial imagery are used to relate the Church's action to Christ's heavenly and priestly liturgy.

The memorial is kept in blessing and table, as one action. It is done in the power of the Spirit, now active in the life of the Church and in its liturgy. It anticipates the fullness of what is to come. The sacrificial imagery is extended to include the thanksgiving of the Church, the self-offering of the faithful, and the offering of gifts, all these being ways in which through the power of the Spirit communion in Christ's saving act shows forth at the blessing table of his body and blood.

2. *New Eucharistic Prayers*[71]

The Roman Missal of 1975 added several new prayers for use in the eucharistic liturgy, and others have been adopted and permitted for

[71] For a useful study of the new prayers for the Roman Missal, see E. Mazza, *Le odierne preghiere eucaristiche* (Bologna, 1984), with English translation, *The Eucharistic*

use in various parts of the world since then. Other western churches too have considerably added to the repertory of Eucharistic Prayers in the last twenty-five years. Indeed, the number of new prayers is so great that comment on them all is impossible. A few general remarks, made from a theological perspective, suffice here.

Many of these new prayers are a retrieval from the resources of eastern liturgies. However, their composition often marks a change from the format of the original source, and is affected by doctrinal concerns that remain from sixteenth-century controversies. It is a good instance of how doctrinal concern and liturgical formula interact, so that neither can be understood without reference to the other. Some examples will suffice to show how prayer formulas intertwine with a theology of eucharistic celebration.

The first example has to do with how churches have dealt with the prayer taken from the *Apostolic Tradition*. Eucharistic Prayer II of the Roman Missal drew heavily on it. However, because it wished to include an invocation of the Spirit that would not take from the theological persuasion of the consecratory power of Christ's words, it added an *epiclesis* to the one already present in the original anaphora, placing it before the supper narrative. The effect is twofold. First, there is a double *epiclesis*, which somehow separates the sanctification of the gifts from the sanctification of those who receive them. The second is that structurally the prayer is now arraigned among those which place the embolism in the intercessory section rather than in the anamnetic.

On the question of eucharistic sacrifice, the Roman prayer can be compared with the adaptation of this anaphora by other Churches. The Roman composition had changed the offering formula within the *anamnesis* from "we offer you this bread and cup" to "we offer you this life-giving bread, this saving cup," to assure that it be clear that it is not bread and wine, but consecrated bread and wine, which are offered. The *Alternative Service Book 1980* of the Church of England[72] has

---

Prayers of the Roman Rite (New York, 1986, Collegeville, 1990). For a comment on the so-called Swiss-Roman Canon, now adopted into the Roman liturgy in many countries and languages, see C. Giraudo, *Preghiere eucaristiche per la chiesa di oggi*, Aloisiana 23 (Brescia, 1993) 19–161.

[72] *The Alternative Service Book 1980. Services authorized for use in the Church of England in conjunction with the Book of Common Prayer* (Clowes, 1980) 136–38.

also drawn on the *Apostolic Tradition*. Within the *anamnesis*, the prayer recalls the "perfect sacrifice" made once for all upon the Cross, and of the gifts it simply says that "we bring before you this bread and this cup," finding in this act an expression of duty and service and a spiritual sacrifice of praise and thanksgiving. The adaptation of the same prayer in the *Lutheran Book of Worship* (USA)[73] omits any mention of offering, but in the *anamnesis* it says "we lift this bread and cup before you, giving you thanks," referring to them at the *epiclesis* as "the gifts of your Church."

All of these usages of a common traditional source may be doctrinally reconcilable within an understanding that the Eucharist is the sacramental or representational memorial of Christ's sacrifice. They do however reflect different theologies of celebration, with differing perceptions of how the Church participates by thanksgiving and table in this sacrifice and sacrament. While the relation of this to all agreed ecumenical statements on this score is not possible to make here, *BEM* may be said to mirror the efforts of these dialogues when it says: "The eucharist is the memorial of the crucified and risen Christ, i.e., the living and effective sign of his sacrifice, accomplished once and for all on the cross and still operative on behalf of humankind" (*BEM* 5). It then states: "The anamnesis in which Christ acts through the joyful celebration of his Church is both representation and anticipation" (*BEM* 7), following this by stating: "Representation and anticipation are expressed in thanksgiving and intercession" (*BEM* 8). Apart from a more general allusion to the sacrifice of praise, language of offering is reserved for the offering of self by the faithful (*BEM* 10).[74]

Some local churches have composed new prayers that have accommodation to cultural rhythms and perspectives in mind. This is a theological as well as an artistic process. It involves an interpretation of eucharistic tradition, not only a linguistic feat. It is appropriate to note that the process can raise new theological questions, beyond any effort to work with standard theological explanations, but the study of such questions is not here possible.

---

[73] *Lutheran Book of Worship*, prepared by the churches participating in the Inter-Lutheran Commission on Worship. Ministers Desk Edition (Minneapolis, 1978) 226.

[74] In the marginal commentary, rather than in the body of the text, *BEM* relates disputes about the propitiatory offering to the power of Christ's intercession, effectively present in the intercession of the Church (*BEM*, Commentary [8]).

### 3. The Performative and the Prayer

Performance, or the way of proclaiming the prayer in tone, body and gesture, affects and even changes the meaning of the written text. In other words, the code of meaning is related to factors external to the text, which appear first in performance and actually get written into the code as rubrics or directives. This is found to have happened, e.g., when Roman *Ordines* prescribe that the bishop enter alone and silently into the canon, or when they add supplementary ritual actions surrounding first the doxology,[75] and then the recitation of the words of Jesus handed down in the supper narrative. In this the East contrasts with the West, since it first introduced supplementary ritual actions to enhance the significance of the *epiclesis*, while later adding some to the proclamation of the words of Jesus. In today's Roman liturgy there is a plurality of actions asked of the presider or of concelebrating clergy to bring out specific points of meaning. These include the extension of hands over the gifts at the pre-narrative invocation of the Spirit, the raising up of the elements on saying the words of Jesus, and the bodily action of genuflection or profound bow. None of this is demanded by the text itself, but it injects a theological preunderstanding into the recitation of the text.[76]

Actions within the Canon and communion rites have also been used, as they still are used, to distinguish members of the congregation of the Church between clergy and faithful. When such rites begin to change or to be questioned, it is a sign of new endeavors to allow the union in the body, with its interchange of charisms and ministries, to take precedence over hierarchical orderings. This is clearly an area in which the performative may go outside the prescribed for the sake of living the eucharistic mystery more perfectly, in due time leaving its trace in what is passed on.

In the performative changes which take place in eucharistic celebration down through the ages, as in such changes as they occur today, what is at stake is the oral and bodily nature of tradition. What is passed on is given immediate expression in what is said, in how it is said, and in what is bodily enacted, whether in saying or in wordless

---

[75] See *Ordines Romani* I, IX and XVII, in Michel Andrieu, *Les Ordines Romani du Haut Moyen Age*, vols. 2 and 3 (Louvain, 1960, 1961)

[76] In medieval practice, the significant point of the transfer of prayers from Communion to consecration has already been noted.

ritual. In effect, every celebration is an act of interpretation, as it is an act of appropriating Christ's memory and gift. When new patterns begin to emerge in the living actuality of community actions, these weave their way into tradition, that is to say, into what is passed on to following generations.

## WORD AND SACRAMENT

There is a twofold narrative foundation to the eucharistic prayer. One is the supper narrative, by means of which the sacramental action is mandated and justified as a proclamation and memorial of Christ's saving death. The other is more complex and consists of the various ways in which the Christ story and event are narrated in Christian teaching. From a ritual as well as from a theological standpoint, this raises the question of how the proclamation of the word and the Eucharistic Prayer are related.

From early times, when Christians gathered for the Lord's Supper, they listened to the teaching of the apostles, transmitted by their leaders and charismatically gifted members, gave praise in prayer, and shared the blessed loaf and cup. The much-cited testimony of Justin shows how by his time a ritual routine had been established.[77] The church of a place gathered on Sunday, listened to the law, the prophets, to the apostle and the Gospel, which were then expounded upon by the bishop. They then prayed their common prayer, and performed the eucharistic action. We are also very familiar with lectionary history, and of the ways in which the reading and exposition of Scriptures became an integral part of the Sunday service. With the Roman reforms of Vatican II, and the lectionary revisions taken up by many Christian Churches, there is more attempt to understand the connection between Church, word, and eucharistic sacrament.

The proclamation of the story of Christ in the differentiated readings for such seasons as Christmas, Easter, and Pentecost is the basis for the principle enunciated by Vatican II and in lectionary revision, that while it is the one mystery which is always celebrated, different aspects of this mystery are highlighted in different seasons and feasts. Thus, there is a sense in which it takes the entire year to keep memory, and this is served by due attention to how the word of God, the Eucharistic Prayer, and other proper prayers coalesce.

---

[77] *Apologia* I, 65–7. In *Prex*, 68-71.

Within the ritual enactment itself it is possible to speak of a ritual flow uniting its diverse moments.[78] In the assembly gathered in the Spirit, the word of God which has been confided to the action and interpretation of the believing community is proclaimed in relation to the saving mystery of Christ. The proclamation is done in many forms that serve its embodiment in the mind, heart and action of the Church. The foundation is narrative, but this is completed by other genres, such as prophecy, wisdom, and hymns. The appropriation of the mystery in this form carries over into the Eucharistic Prayer. Its composition historically and ideally encompasses the word as proclaimed in the assembly, from it taking up its story, its images and its metaphors, to transform the memory into blessing. The power inherent to this blessing, whose words and vigour come from the Word through the gift of the Spirit, transforms the bread and wine, so that in and through them the people have communion in the reality and gifts of their Savior.

Some have offered more theological explanations to underpin a sense of unity in the rite. For Louis Bouyer,[79] the key factor is the coming of the word of God in flesh. Already in the Old Testament, in response to the word of God the people proclaimed in praise God's mighty deeds. They did so not only in the Temple, but in synagogue and meal rituals, where they offered the sacrifice of praise through which the world was restored in God's word. In the Christian Eucharist, the word whose sending and presence is proclaimed in the Scriptures through the word of the Church enters into the action of blessing whereby God is praised and thanked, thus transforms the gifts, and is himself present in the gift and in the giving. The sharing of the body and blood of the word made flesh is thus the communion sacrifice of reconciliation with God in Christ, who has come forth from the Father's bosom for our salvation.

Louis-Marie Chauvet[80] more recently related various modes of bodily presence and form that relate to God's word and the mystery of Christ. These comprise the taking body of the word in the tradition formed by the Church's written Scripture and its interpretative transmission,

---

[78] D. Power, *Eucharistic Mystery* 50f.

[79] *Eucharist* 29–135.

[80] L.-M. Chauvet, *Symbole et Sacrement. Une relecture sacramentelle de l'existence chrétienne* (Paris, 1987) 165–322. *Symbol and Sacrament* (Collegeville, 1995).

the body of the flesh and blood offered in gift to the congregation, and the body of the Church of discipleship that lives in the world by the gospel ethic and in virtue of the gift given to it. Related to the universe by its bodily ritual and its cosmic symbols, related to the tradition of the Scriptures by its corporate, body-enfolded ritual, the Church is the living body in which Christ is present through the symbols of the bread and the wine, shared bodily, at the shared table of those who are one body. For him, the Eucharistic Prayer is the central moment in as much as it is the action in which there is a reciprocity between God's giving and the gift of itself on the part of the Church in which the word has taken body. The Eucharist in its bodiliness is the remembrance of the cross, whereon God's self-giving and Christ's self-giving constitute God's own presence to the world.

## OFFERING AND GIFTS

In treating of the Eucharistic Prayer, its sacrificial expressions and understanding have already been discussed. What requires more thought in a theology of celebration is the significance and place of the gifts of the people. How much are these offerings accessory to the sacrament, how much are they inherent to it?

There need be no disagreement about the call on Christians to bring offerings to the Eucharist, both the bread and the wine for the sacrament and goods to serve the needs of the Church and of the poor. It is also commonplace to affirm in line with New Testament teaching that the celebration of the Eucharist is the occasion for them to make an offering of themselves. At issue is whether such offering, especially that of bread and wine, is in any way integral to the sacramental rite and meaning.

That of Irenaeus of Lyons is one of the earliest testimonies which includes the offering of bread and wine in the very nature of the eucharistic sacrifice.[81] Basing his thought on a comparison with the Old Testament order of sacrifices he includes several points: (a) an offering is made of the earthly realities of bread and wine, symbolic first-fruits, in recognition of the Creator; (b) the offering of the first-fruits must include the sacrifice of a christian life, done in the freedom of those redeemed in Christ in the New Covenant; (c) this offering is

---

[81] Irenaeus, *Adversus Haereses* IV.18. In *Irénée de Lyon: Contre les hérésies* IV/2, critical edition by A. Rousseau and L. Doutréleau. *SCh* 100 (Paris, 1965).

done through thanksgiving, in invocation of the name of the Word/Son; (d) the prayer of commemorative Eucharist transforms the bread and wine into the body and blood of Christ, which the faithful receive as gift; (e) this total action is the sacrifice of the New Covenant, which Christ left to the Church at the Last Supper.

In the Latin medieval Church, offering by priest and faithful was much accentuated in liturgy and theology. However, this did not necessarily mean that the Church's offering was given primary place in theology. Thomas Aquinas attended to the sacrament more than to the offering of sacrifice, but he located the sacramental representation of Christ's sacrifice in the consecration of the Church's offering of bread and wine through the action of the priest acting in the person of Christ.[82] He outlined the ritual actions of offering by the faithful, consecration of the gifts, and communion in the consecrated bread and wine. The sacrifice, as something done to the gifts in representation of Christ's passion, is in the consecration, not in the offering.[83] Because of the custom of Mass-offerings which was familiar to him, he devoted some questions to the offering of the Mass as sacrifice for the living and the dead, but he underlined the limited value of such an offering[84] and did not integrate it well into his basic explanation of the Eucharist as memorial and sacrament.

The controversies of the sixteenth century centered around the understanding of the cross as a propitiatory sacrifice and the application of this same notion to the Eucharist, as celebrated by an ordained priest. For both Reformers and Apologists, the sacrifice of thanksgiving and the sacrifice of propitiation were kept quite distinct, and the dominant soteriology referred to the death of Christ as the once-for-all sacrifice of propitiation. In practice, the issue was whether all grace that is imparted through the Eucharist is given through the communion received in faith, or whether by offering in the power of Christ the ordained priest can obtain some grace or benefit for the living and the dead.[85]

[82] *STh* III, Q. 83, art. 1 and art. 4.

[83] *STh* III, Q. 83, art. 4.

[84] III, Q. 79, art. 2, 5 and 7.

[85] While this was answered in the affirmative by the council, theologians were left free to disagree on whether this occurred *ex opere operato*, analogously with the sacraments, or by the power of intercession. See D. Power, *The Sacrifice We Offer*, 158f.

In ecumenical conversations and statements, the issue is colored by this late medieval and tridentine proposition that the Eucharist is propitiatory offering, i.e., salutary to those for whom it is offered, in some disjunction from the Communion table. Though there is a new accent on the sacramental and memorial character of the eucharistic sacrifice, meaning that its nature as sacrifice comes from its representation of Christ's sacrifice, the differences in background still have some effect on celebration.

In relation to the words used in the new Eucharistic Prayers of the Roman rite, it is asked in ecumenical discussion whether it is proper to say that the Church, and Christ through the Church, offers the body and blood of Christ. One Roman Catholic position, adopted in the international Lutheran/Roman Catholic dialogue,[86] is that the Church does indeed offer the body and blood, in communion with Christ himself who is the principal offerer. This, the statement says, is the only worthy gift which it has to offer to God, and is expressive of the Church's own self-offering in dependence on the offering of Christ. The Lutherans on the other hand stated that they prefer to avoid all such language, fearing that it supports all too readily such practices as private Masses and Mass offerings, though they reaffirm Martin Luther's own statement: "that we cast ourselves upon Christ with unwavering faith in his testament," so that our prayer, praise and sacrifice are offered through him.

Problems have also been raised about the phrase that the faithful "enter into Christ's self-offering." If this refers to a response to the gift of Communion (as in the liturgy of the *Book of Common Prayer*), or means that we offer the sacrifice of praise through him, all can agree that this is so. If it means that offering of selves through the gifts of bread and wine is intrinsic to the sacramental action through which the sacrifice of Christ is sacramentally represented, there is no consensus, but some theories are offered.

Hans Schulz[87] and Edward Kilmartin[88] point to the offering of the bread and wine, within the commemorative blessing, as the key moment in the sacramental representation of Christ's sacrifice. The

---

[86] Loc. cit.

[87] H. Schulz, "Patterns of Offering," *SL* 15 (1983) 34–48.

[88] E. Kilmartin, "Sacrificium Laudis: Content and Function of Early Eucharistic Prayers," *ThS* 32 (1971) 233–71.

Church participates in the sacrificial offering of Christ, on the cross and at the Supper, by offering bread and wine in commemoration of this offering, but it is Christ who sanctifies the offering. In this fashion the offering by the faithful achieves nothing of itself, but in an action of communion with creation and of self-offering it presents to God that which the Spirit will sanctify and through which it brings about the sacramental memorial of Christ's sacrifice in an action of total gratuity. They believe that this is more in keeping with the language of early prayers, for example, the Anaphora of Mark, the Roman Canon, and the Anaphoras of Basil and John Chrysostom. They find this understanding supported in the thought of Irenaeus of Lyons, noted above.

Kenneth Stevenson also takes note of the offering of gifts in explaining the tradition of calling the Eucharist a sacrifice.[89] He depicts an action in three moments, which fit into the celebration. These are story, commemorating Christ's action and proclaiming the forgiveness of sins; the gift made to God by the people in proffering the bread and wine, and the response to God's action upon the offering through the pledge of a spiritual sacrifice. The element of sacrifice is totally subordinate to God's initiative in approaching us with the offer of grace in Christ proclaimed in word, and to the divine action that sanctifies the offerings.

### MINISTRIES

The basic principle governing ministry in the Eucharist is enunciated by the Constitution on the Liturgy of Vatican II, when it affirms the character of the liturgy as an act of the Church, sacrament of unity, in which all actively participate, each according to one's order or office in the Church (*SC* 26). The *Ordo Missae* of the Roman Missal applies this principle to the Mass, prescribing that each and all do whatever properly belongs to them in the celebration (*IGMR* III.58). The Church is served by a variety of gifts and ministries, and its unity in diversity should appear in the eucharistic action.

Another principle important to the configuration of participation and ministry in the eucharistic assembly is that of affirming the varied modes of Christ's presence (*SC* 7). Present in the assembly, he is present in the prayer of the congregation, in the proclamation of the Word, in different ministers, in the person of the ordained presider,

---

[89] K. Stevenson, *Eucharistic Offering*, 5–7.

and in the sacramental species. The call of the Spirit to gather in Christ's memory to give worship to the Father, the proclamation and teaching of the Word, the common prayer in its various forms, the sacramental action, together build up the Church as the sacrament of unity. Ministries are inspired and appointed to serve this multiple liturgical action through which in the Spirit Christ remains present and active in the Church as his body.

A third principle is that the celebration of the Eucharist belongs first within the local church, as the primary sacramental action of those who live together day by day in the communion of Christ's Spirit. Hence the local bishop or a presbyter who shares the communion of the local presbyterium with him is the normal presider (*IGMR* III.59).

The action of the assembly as such, in its reality as Christ's people and body, is primary in all theological considerations of celebration. The instruction in the Missal pinpoints the role of the ordained minister in accord with its understanding of the Mass as primarily an offering of the eucharistic sacrifice. In this, the ordained presider acts in the person of Christ, offering the sacrifice through him to the Father, in the Holy Spirit (*IGMR* III.60). However, his ministry in acting in the name of the Church and in calling forth the participation of the whole congregation has to complement this.

In numbering other ministries, the Missal for the most part takes into account those services which were customary in early church tradition, but became obsolete because of the clericalization of the liturgy. These ministries include those of deacon, reader, and psalmist. It also takes note of some ministries more particular to our day, such as that of commentator or that of usher, and that of those who take up the collection (*IGMR* III.68). Beyond this, one may note that over the last three decades, different regional and local churches have developed their own peculiar ministries, according to local custom and cultural form.

It is the explicit intention of the Roman *Ordo* to affirm and appropriate the Church's tradition. Therefore, it is necessary that one recognize the rather provisional nature of its listing and explanation of ministries. The assimilation of tradition is also an active process, involving reflection not only on the central reality of Eucharist, but also on the reasons why certain procedures were at any time adopted. It means considering how the configuration of ministries in any local church may now help insert the liturgical action into the culture and life of the people.

Reflection on tradition in relation to present reality would also serve a more lively and living appropriation of the deaconal order in the eucharistic liturgy, from two different angles. In early church communities, the service of deacons forged the link between the body of Christ as a communion in charity and the body of Christ as a communion in worship. From the New Testament onwards, one sees that communion at the one table had two complementary meanings, that is, communion at the one table of common sharing and concern, and communion at the one table of the Eucharist. The one could not be properly realized without the other. It was the maintenance of this that fell to the charge of deacons. They had a role both in the collecting and administration of common goods, and in liturgy, where they represented and fostered the gathering of the community charity into the table of Christ's charity.

In Eastern Churches, the deacons also developed a strong role in leading the people's participation in the divine liturgy. The *Ordo Missae* looks at their place too much in terms of office and special liturgical charges, not enough in terms of service to community participation. This particular deaconal role, however, may well be made a more living part of eucharistic action by being apportioned among different persons, rather than referred to ordained deacons. In this example, one sees how a proper theological understanding of traditional ministries can help them to emerge in completely different forms in today's churches.

In relation to the past, one may well ask whether the Missal is rather narrow in its interpretation of the relation between ordained presider and congregation, or whether it has not relied on hierarchical principles more heavily than on those of community action and participation, allying this with a particular focus on sacrifice which is not exhaustive of the whole of tradition. While the participation of the congregation has increased with the inclusion of more ministries, there is some tension in both practice and theology between the role of presider and the role of ministers and congregation. That is because the Eucharist can be considered from two different angles. The one is that of the priest, when the action is seen to be primarily his action, in which others share. The other is that of the Church or community, from which angle the Eucharist is seen as the sacrament of the community, and all ministries, including that of presider, are seen in relation to its fullest realization as a participatory action.

The use of semiotics can help us to see what is actually going on. It studies the text of directives and prayer to see how roles are related, and what signification or effect is related to what words or whose action. For example, in the analysis of the Eucharistic Prayer it is useful to see how the prayer's rhythm determines participation and the relation between presider and congregation, as well as the congregation's relation to Christ and Spirit. Semiotics also enables us to examine performance and perceive how bodily action, chant, and congregational response affect the signification of what is being done. This semiotic analysis has to be related to a critical consideration of how theologies of sacrament, priesthood and congregation have been affected by "non-theological" factors, or perspectives on ritual and ministry that come from a source other than the Gospel. Since adaptation and inculturation are always necessary, such factors belong within the theological in a fuller sense, but care is required to ensure that they do not misrepresent the sacrament or the participation of the community as an organic body of believers.

CONCLUSION

To complete a theology of eucharistic celebration, space would need to be given to some consideration of the place in which Eucharist is celebrated, to the music and rhetorical forms used in prayer and proclamation, and to diverse rites such as the penitential and the prayer of the faithful. This is not however possible here, where attention has been given to the primary elements of the action.

In a theology of eucharistic celebration, the aim and purpose is the promotion of the celebration of Christ's pasch and sacramental gift. It is as a sacrament of the Church, Christ's body, that Eucharist has been here considered. It has been developed in the form of an interpretation of and reflection upon the rites and liturgies of Eucharist. It has also been looked at primarily in relation to the local church, or indeed to the immediate community in whatever form or place it gathers. This inevitably includes the consideration of where Gospel, tradition, and culture intersect, as it encourages taking account of the relation of sacramental celebration to ethics and christian behavior.

The future of an effective memorial of Christ, and of an effective participation in his gift, lies in the retrieval of those elements crucial to community celebration, and open and adaptable to the cultural forms in which the sacrament may continue to find its place in local churches, of different cultural concentrations. The perception from the past of the marvelous diversity, within a catholic unity, in the celebration of the mystery fosters such a growth for the future. In the course of history and even today, diverse developments reflect the cultural and historical perspectives of those who gather at any time as Christ's body. These have to be understood in cultural context, but they also need to be critically considered, lest they hamper the action of the Spirit and the integrity of the memorial. Given this relation of Eucharist to Church within culture and history, and the centrality of its celebration to the very existence of the Church, some points emerge by way of synthesis and overall perception of this mystery.

As the memorial of Jesus Christ, the Eucharist is a complex ritual, culminating in the blessing and communion, conceived as one single action. It is through this action that Jesus Christ, sent by the Father for the salvation of the world, continues to give himself and the life of the Spirit, in the sacrament of his body and blood. The memorial which he commanded in giving this sacrament to the Church, is enacted in the power of the Spirit and is the effective representation of Christ's death, by which God's forgiveness and life were given to the world. The eucharistic liturgy in its beginnings focused on the death itself, though referring it to the mystery of the incarnation and to the resurrection. This salvific death was imaged and conceived in different ways, especially as victory over the powers of death, as the pasch of the New Covenant, as sacrifice. In time, at its heart, in the *anamnesis* after the Supper Narrative, the celebration adopted a more comprehensive proclamation of death, resurrection, ascension and sitting at God's right hand, in the expectation of the Lord's return. This affected the way in which the Eucharist is related to Christ's sacrifice. It can either be seen as a remembrance of this sacrifice, an entering into it with thanksgiving and self-offering in the power of the Spirit, or it can be seen as one with the action in which Christ the High-Priest perfects the sacrifice of his death in the exercise of his heavenly priesthood.

Diversity of forms and images, however, remains integral to the diverse ways in which Christ is present in this memorial, in the invocation and power of the Holy Spirit. His passion and saving mysteries are thus present to the history of peoples, giving an eschatological focus to lives lived in the communion of hope, across cultures and churches. In the celebration, word and sacrament converge as complementary components of the one memorial action, in which the pasch of Christ is proclaimed, remembered in prayer, and shared in Communion. As a sacrifice, the Eucharist is primarily a sacrifice of praise in which the sacrifice of Christ is proclaimed and represented. Some offering of gifts, and self-offering of the faithful, properly belongs within the total ritual, but its precise relation to the memorial and sacrament is diversely understood. Whatever be the way of understanding this, the vital reality of eucharistic celebration is that in drawing the faithful to himself, in the power of the Spirit, in thanksgiving proclamation and in sacramental Communion, Jesus Christ draws them into the communion of his life with the Father, in the Spirit.

## Bibliography

Giraudo, C. *Eucaristia per la Chiesa: Prospettive teologiche sull'eucaristia a partire della "lex orandi."* Rome, 1989.

Kilmartin, E. "The Catholic Tradition of Eucharistic Theology: Towards the Third Millennium." *ThS* 55 (1994) 449–54.

Marsili, S. "Teologia della celebrazione dell'eucaristia." *Anàmnesis* 3/2:9–16.

Mazza, E. *The Origins of the Eucharistic Prayer.* Trans. R. Lane. Collegeville, Minn., 1995.

Meyer, H. B. *Eucharistie, Gottesdienst der Kirche.* Part 4. Regensburg, 1989.

Power, D. *The Sacrifice We Offer: The Tridentine Dogma and Its Reinterpretation.* New York, 1987.

_____. *The Eucharistic Mystery: Revitalizing the Tradition.* New York, 1992.

Stevenson, K. *Eucharist and Offering.* New York, 1986.

# Subject Index

The following pages list the chief or more commonly treated subjects that are pertinent to the study of the Eucharist. This index does not contain the names of persons, events, and places recorded in this volume.

*About the editor:*

Anscar Chupungco, O.S.B., is director of the Paul VI Institute of Liturgy in the Philippines and professor of liturgical inculturation at the Pontificio Istituto Liturgico in Rome. The Liturgical Press has also published Father Chupungco's *Liturgical Inculturation: Sacramentals, Popular Religiosity, Catechesis* (1992).